AIR AMERICA

"RIPPING UP ASIA FOR FUN AND PROFIT, WHEN 'WAR TOOK THE PLACE OF TELEVISION'"
Kirkus Reviews

"A rousing, colorful account of Air America and the men (and their women, booze, heartaches, and laughs) from the days of the Flying Tigers to the fall of Saigon."
Library Journal

"An eye-popping, swashbuckling story"
Milwaukee Sentinel

"Bravery and craziness ... The CIA's stark madness is revealed"
Denver Post

"Heroic tales of fearless men in the most hair-raising, heart-thumping conditions imaginable"
Saturday Review

Other Avon Books about the War in Vietnam

Nonfiction

DISPATCHES *by Michael Herr*
M *by John Sack*
THE RAID *by Benjamin F. Schemmer*
THE TEN THOUSAND DAY WAR:
VIETNAM 1945–1975 *by Michael Maclear*

Fiction

AMERICAN BOYS *by Stephen Phillip Smith*
THE LAOTIAN FRAGMENTS *by John Clark Pratt*
WAR YEAR *by Joe Haldeman*

AIR AMERICA

CHRISTOPHER ROBBINS

AVON BOOKS NEW YORK

Originally published in Great Britain under the title *The Invisible Air Force: The True Story of the CIA's Secret Airlines*

AVON BOOKS
A division of
The Hearst Corporation
105 Madison Avenue
New York, New York 10016

Copyright © 1979 by Christopher Robbins
Cover photograph copyright © 1990 by Tri-Star Pictures Inc.
Published by arrangement with the author
Library of Congress Catalog Card Number: 78-9861
ISBN: 0-380-89909-4

First Avon Books Movie Tie-in Printing: August 1990
First Avon Books Printing: October 1985

AVON TRADEMARK REG. U.S. PAT. OFF. AND IN OTHER COUNTRIES, MARCA REGISTRADA, HECHO EN U.S.A.

Printed in the U.S.A.

RA 10 9 8 7 6 5

To the men who flew the planes

CONTENTS

INTRODUCTION

The day before I first heard about Air America I dined in the exotic Oriental Hotel in Bangkok with James Bond. The significance of this encounter with the greatest symbol of the fantasy, cloak-and-dagger world of the super-spy, where the highly improbable is routine and the impossible all part of a day's grind, passed me by at the time. There was nothing clandestine about the dinner where Roger Moore, who was starring in the latest Bond escapade, entertained a group of journalists on the beautiful terrace of the Oriental. An old Asia hand sat down with us and told us very unlikely stories about the real Shanghai Lil. Someone remarked that the night was humid and sticky, perhaps the monsoon was about to break.

Looking back, I find it uncanny how apt this atmosphere was for the real world of intrigue I was about to discover: the scarcely believable activities and super-secret machinations of a spy airline, set against a backdrop of steaming jungles and colorful cities.

The following morning the monsoon did break, and when that happens in the Far East the rain is relentless. I sat trapped in a car as the rain drummed on the roof, waiting for some break to allow me to dash to the entrance of a wooden house situated in an old part of the city where the *klongs* were still waterways and had not been covered with concrete and turned into roads. I was with a couple I had recently met who were taking me to visit an American pilot and the pet gibbons he kept. "This guy flies for Air America," the husband said meaningfully. The information meant nothing to me and it must have showed. "Air America's the spook airline," he continued. "CIA."

He added that the only thing they had in common with the spook pilot was the fact that they too had pet gibbons. At the time I was much more interested in these gibbons than I was in Air America or the CIA, for I had been wandering about the Far East on a story for *The Observer* in London on animal smuggling. It had taken me from the teeming markets of Calcutta to the depths of the jungle in Thailand and the Malaysian peninsula. In Bangkok I was anxious to find out how animals, listed and protected as endangered species and whose export was banned, were being taken out of the country.

The rain showed no sign of letting up, so we decided to make a bolt for the front door. It was only about twenty yards, but by the time we reached shelter we were soaked. The rest of the morning was spent sipping drinks, while steam rose gently from our jackets, and admiring the pilot's two gibbons (Lyndon Johnson and Elizabeth Taylor Rosenfield) who came swinging down from the trees, whooping joyously, to play with the guests on the veranda.

There were several Air America pilots present that morning, and one of the first things that struck me about them was that they were men who liked a drink. Our host turned out to be a genial type, and as someone who seemed to have flown into every corner of the country, he gave me some valuable pointers on the animal-smuggling business. He also made it clear that government export restrictions did not worry him; he was going to fly his gibbons out of the country next to him in the cockpit of his plane and have them shipped from neighboring Laos where no such ban existed.

A little later I was having a drink with an American war correspondent who was taking a few days' leave from the rigors of Saigon. "This Air America is a rather unorthodox airline," I said naively. "The pilots seem to use it to smuggle their pets out on."

The war-hardened, whiskey-soaked noncombatant looked incredulous. He had found it odd to start with that while the war in Vietnam was floundering through its final stages, a reporter in the Far East should be more interested in the passage of parakeets and the fate of monkeys. He put down his drink, leaned toward me, and spoke in a low and measured voice. "Air America have flown opium; they've flown guns and bombs and ammo; they've dropped spies into China and special units into North Vietnam, flying so low their wheels are in the foliage most of the way. They've been involved with every sort of kook and weirdo that a war throws up, goddamn it, and all you're interested in is that they're smuggling pet poodles without the right papers."

My story took me into the jungle of southern Thailand and across the border into Malaysia, where I flew from Penang to Singapore. Leafing through the airline's magazine, I started to read an article on a pretty young hostess. It was a straightforward PR piece about how much she enjoyed being with the airline and serving the passengers and so on, but one paragraph caught my attention. The girl was explaining how she had trained as a secretary once upon a time but had always dreamed of being an air hostess. "Before this I flew with Air America, but that was different, very different. Once I went to work and had to fly on a plane full of dead bodies ... better not say anything about that."

At this point the hostess did not add to her cryptic remark on Air America, and the writer, as singlemindedly interested in the airline's image as I was in animal smuggling, did not press her. My interest in Air America had been aroused but did not go very far. Whatever the airline was up to they were no great shakes in the animal-smuggling business, and when I eventually wrote my article they warranted only a line: "Some animals have been known to have been smuggled out on Air America, openly talked about in Southeast Asia as the CIA airline."

What came to intrigue me about Air America was that while everybody seemed to know it was a CIA airline and that it indulged in some nefarious activities, nobody really knew anything about it at all. Journalists described Air America as being "everywhere" throughout Vietnam and especially Laos and spoke of its pilots as hard-drinking soldiers of fortune who did their work for both pay and adventure. But what did this mysterious airline do, how many planes did it own and what were its limits of operation? Everyone was vague.

And with good reason. Firstly, those hard-drinking soldiers of fortune knew that their jobs were on the line if too much booze led to loose talk in a bar in front of journalists. This was unlikely, even without the threat of dismissal, for almost to a man they were temperamentally antipathetic to reporters, whom they saw as only slightly less venomous than their declared enemies. Secondly, the directors of Air America, both in the field and back at HQ in Washington, were more than happy to meet a straightforward question with a straightforward lie. Thirdly, the paymasters and overlords, the CIA, hardly knew the answers themselves and were not about to say anything to anybody anyway.

Slowly I began to build up my contacts within Air America and was careful to keep in touch and widen my knowledge of ex-AA personnel. My primary interest was in the men who flew the planes. They might be difficult, reluctant to talk to me or downright hostile, but they were not liars. First of all I thought it might make a lengthy but interesting article. Then I saw it as a very long investigative piece, maybe a series, and then . . . my God, what have we here? I had opened a seething can of worms.

The story behind most airlines would be a predictable and somewhat dreary tale. We can imagine that Pan Am, British Airways, and Lufthansa have had their moments, what with teething problems in the early days and the drama and tragedy of air crashes, but in the main it is a dull business mostly concerned with profit and loss. It would come as a shock to find out that Pan Am once supplied air support for an invasion of Red China or that British Airways had been the lifeline for Tibetan horsemen parachuted into the Himalayas to fight a guerrilla war; it would be impossible to accept that Varig jets had bombed Guatemala City or that TWA had supplied a mercenary army of opium farmers 30,000 strong and carried their dope to market. It would be unthinkable that any of the world's major commercial airlines would indulge in illegal overflights of Russia and China, support rebel troops against legally constituted governments, manufacture its own napalm out of Tide and petroleum, or drop forged money over a country like confetti.

But Air America did all of the things mentioned above and much, much more. Perhaps equally staggering is the simple, bald fact that at its zenith Air America was, in terms of the number of planes it either owned or had at its disposal, *the largest airline in the world.*

The history of Air America is an adventure story that could have been picked straight out of a boy's magazine. The company served as a model for Milton Caniff's shady outfit Air

Expendable in the comic strip *Terry and the Pirates*. The real-life story is more extraordinary. Naturally, the airline did not conduct all of its affairs with its name emblazoned across the fuselage and a movie showing in the central section. Sometimes it was called this and sometimes it was called that, and there were many times when it was not called anything at all; the planes at its disposal ranged from 727 jets to small Cessnas and helicopters. But one way or another it had the capability to get the job done. There will be pedants at CIA HQ in Langley, Virginia, and at the Air America head office in Washington who will play with words and pretend that Air America as a company did not do this or that, so I had better explain what I mean when I use the name: Air America is a company incorporated in Delaware, but it is also a generic name used to describe all of the CIA air activities whether under the name of Civil Air Transport, Intermountain, Air Asia or Southern Air Transport. There is a web of dozens of CIA airlines throughout the world which should perhaps go under the title CIA AIR. But that is a logo you will not find anywhere.

The CIA air proprietaries came about as a direct result of the creation of the Agency's Directorate for Plans, or Clandestine Service—dubbed the Department of Dirty Tricks—which pursued programs of covert action. According to its charter these included: "propaganda; economic warfare; preventive direct action, including sabotage, anti-sabotage, demolition and evacuation measures; subversion against hostile states, including assistance to guerrilla and refugee liberation groups; and support of indigenous anti-Communist elements in the threatened countries of the free world." As the CIA developed its paramilitary capability over the years, it created and maintained large commercial proprietary corporations. These CIA proprietaries were business entities, wholly owned by the Agency which either actually did business or appeared to do business as private firms. The biggest and most important of all the proprietaries were the airlines, and Air America grew with the war in Indochina to be the largest operation of them all. It saw the most action and encountered every sort of problem and situation that such a vast but clandestine outfit might be expected to run into. It made significant profits for the CIA, competing directly with privately owned corporations, and was worth hundreds of millions. Its activities were run under the strictest secrecy, made possible because the DDP is exempt even from many of the CIA's own internal review procedures on the grounds of national security. I have concentrated mainly on Air America in this book because it was the largest, its activities were the most wide-ranging, and the period of its growth and the men it attracted to its ranks were the most fascinating.

As an outsider and an individual with limited research and financial resources, it would be impossible to write the definitive story of CIA AIR. That will never be fully revealed. But I have attempted to give the broad picture and to tell a story that has never been told before and thereby give an idea of how the CIA used airplanes.

Even the Agency itself was never quite sure just how big its air arm had become. It proved impossible to figure out exactly how many planes it had under its control, and personnel figures were similarly imprecise. Richard Helms, onetime director of the CIA, asked one of his staff officers in the mid sixties what he thought was a simple question: "How many airplanes does the CIA own?"

An officer with extensive Clandestine Service experience was assigned to make a study of air proprietaries' operations, and after three confusing and frustrating months he put a huge map of the world, dotted with hundreds of colored pins, in a secure Agency room. Then for an hour he talked about the dozens of airlines and the hundreds of planes the Agency owned. The map could only be 90 percent accurate at any given time, the officer explained apologetically, as the airlines were constantly leasing planes to one another, changing engine and tail numbers, and cannibalizing planes for parts. So after a three-month investigation from inside the Agency itself they still had no clear idea of how many planes they owned, although he could say that one of the Agency's holding companies, the Pacific Corporation, which included Air America and Air Asia, alone accounted for more than ten thousand people, almost as large as the entire work force of the parent CIA. The whole of this operation was supervised part time by only a single senior CIA officer who lamented that he did not know "what the hell was going on." Director Helms sat in stunned silence as his staff officer shuffled colored pins and flags across the map of the world in an attempt to explain what proprietaries were operating with what equipment in what countries. A witness described Helms as being "aghast."

This is not to suggest that Air America was badly managed or ineffective. It was a superbly run organization that made large profits, had a good record of safety, and did whatever job that was put before it, living up to its company slogan: ANYTHING, ANYWHERE, ANYTIME—PROFESSIONALLY. Its civilian status allowed it to operate without the bureaucracy and red tape that surrounded the military, cross international borders with a minimum of fuss, and break the rules whenever a mission demanded it. And, above all, it was effective because the men hired to do the flying were among the best and most experienced pilots in the world, who were prepared to risk their lives on a daily basis to fly unarmed and unprotected into places the military, and even the madmen of the Marine Corps, feared to go. Many of the fixed-wing pilots had weathered a number of wars before they joined up—with General Claire Chennault in China, World War II, the Korean War, supplying the French in Indochina—while the helicopter pilots were hand-picked from the thousands trained during the Vietnamese war, and Air America only picked the best.

Once the Vietnam war was over , the CIA's clandestine air force was considerably reduced, but it did not disappear. Many Air America pilots retired to clip coupons in the U.S.A., or went on to work for well-paying, non-CIA outfits in Iran or Alaska, but a few simply changed wars. Several flew in Angola in the mid-seventies, while a few continue to fly a top-secret airlift of American arms to that country—via Zaire—to the rebel guerrillas of Jonas Savimbi in his struggle against the Cuban-backed Marxist government. Other ex-Air America types were recruited to fly Contra re-supply missions into Nicaragua, operating out of El Salvador, Honduras and Costa Rica.

(When the ageing C-123 transport plane—serviced in Miami by Southern Air Transport, once owned by the CIA—was shot down in Nicaragua at the end of 1986, it was revealed that the pilot, William Cooper, the co-pilot, Wallace "Buzz" Sawyer, and the cargo kicker, Eugene Hasenfus, had all been old Air America hands during the CIA's decade-long secret war in Laos during the sixties. Cooper and Sawyer were killed while Hasenfus became the most recent of a line of men involved with CIA air operations to fall into enemy hands: CIA agents John T. Downey and Richard G. Fecteau were shot down in an Agency airplane on an illegal flight over Communist China in November, 1952, and were abandoned to rot in Chinese jails for the next 20 years, then in May, 1958, Allen Pope was shot down on a covert CIA bombing mission to supply Indonesian rebels in Sumatra, where he was jailed for four years until he was released to return to the U.S. and a new job flying for none other than Southern Air Transport.)

Meanwhile, the logistics and training end of the Contra supply mission also involved people with close ties to the CIA's air proprietaries. Retired Air Force general, Richard Secord, named as one of the principal "civilian" suppliers of arms and equipment, had previously served as the officer at Udorn air force base, in Thailand, who used Air America to ferry arms and supplies to the war in Laos. Ed Dearborn, onetime chief pilot of Continental Air Services in Laos, and the head of the CIA's Cuban mercenary air force in the Congo before that, trained pilots for the Contras. It's a small covert world. It is not always easy to differentiate, in this world of "smoke and mirrors," which of these men are under contract to the CIA, or work for "Cut-out" corporations (private front companies at least once removed from the Agency), or are merely "freelancers for democracy"—mercenary soldiers of fortune with a taste for adventure.

A few Air America pilots have crossed the line, and been convicted of flying drugs for criminal consortiums, while a tiny percentage have actually flown under the flags of countries hostile to the U.S. Ed Wilson, the CIA agent who turned terrorist, hired Air America pilots to fly in Libyan dictator Muamar Qaddafi's war with Chad, while in the summer of 1987 Air America veteran Billy Pearson was killed while flying a helicopter gunship for the leftist government of Surinam.

Once the Vietnam war was over the CIA's operational need for covert air support was greatly reduced, and the Agency's air assets re-organized. Numerous disclosures in the press had made many CIA proprietaries, owned outright by the Agency, a liability. These were sold off, while other, new fronts were created.

But the type of man who flew the planes never really

changed. This group of "tin jockeys" has been dubbed flying legionnaires, aerial cowboys, airborne buccaneers, Yankee air pilots, and the CIA's high-fliers, but under any name they formed "the finest bunch of airplane drivers that has ever been got together anywhere." This is a story of that unique breed of men and the extraordinary airline they flew for.

ONE

JOINING THE LEGION

"Everytime there's a war the same damned people always show up," an old Air America hand, veteran of a number of wars, observed. "The funny thing is you never see them in between." To many old aviators who had last seen each other in the Korean or Second World War, Air America seemed to be a select club for aeronautical survivors. Too old by Forces' standards for active service, but too young to spend the rest of their lives fishing, they had answered advertisements in their local papers for an airline in Southeast Asia which needed pilots, and found themselves together with old friends.

Originally, in its early days, Air America quietly approached Air Force pilots to take on its clandestine missions. These men would then disappear from the military in a complex process known as "sheep-dipping" after seeming to go through all the legal and official motions of resigning from the service. The pilot's records would be pulled from the Air Force personnel files and transferred to a special AF intelligence file. Friends and relations would be told a cover story about the resignation and the man would become, to all outward appearances, a civilian. At the same time his ghostly paper existence within the intelligence file would continue to pursue his Air Force career: When his contemporaries were promoted, he would be promoted, and so on. Sheep-dipping became extremely complicated when a pilot was killed or captured. There would be all sorts of pension and insurance problems, which was one of the reasons the CIA found it necessary to create its own insurance proprietary complex.

But as the burgeoning air proprietaries soon became too large to rely on sheep-dipped Air Force pilots alone, they had to recruit personnel like any other airline. Air America reached its peak during the Indochina war and conducted a number of recruitment drives across the country. There were times when the procedure was standard: A potential employee would fill in the appropriate forms and then go for an interview at the company's HQ in Washington, D.C. And then there were times when recruiting was eccentric.

"The hiring process was kind of funny," said Neil Hansen, who was to become an Air America legend. Hansen was flying for the Teamsters' Union as Jimmy Hoffa's aerial chauffeur, and under constant FBI surveillance, when he first heard of Air America. The money seemed good, it was an overseas posting, and he was eager for a change; so he applied in writing. When there was no reply after a couple of weeks he called up the office to be told gruffly that the company was not hiring at that time.

The very next day Hansen had to fly to Chicago. He received an urgent call from his wife telling him that an H. H. Dawson in Washington wanted him to phone collect as soon as possible. It struck Hansen as strange, as this was "Red" Dawson, Air America's boisterous personnel manager, who had spoken to him only on the previous day. But he made the call.

"Are you still interested?" Dawson wanted to know.

"Hell, I called you yesterday," Hansen replied. "Sure I'm still interested."

"When can you leave?"

"I have to give two weeks' notice," Hansen said, a little started by such an abrupt approach.

"So two weeks from tomorrow?"

"Well yeah, I suppose so."

"Good. I've a couple of questions," Dawson said. "Can you fly good?" At this stage Hansen began to wonder if he was the victim of some sort of practical joke but he went along with it anyway. "I was in Washington yesterday and I'm in Chicago today and I flew all the way."

"Yeah okay," Dawson said. "Do you drink a lot?"

"Well I'm sober now and I've got to fly back," Hansen replied, shaking his head in disbelief.

"Okay. We'll send you the tickets and some money."

The conversation was so vague that Hansen felt he should fill in the gaps himself and offered to fly to Washington for a proper interview. "I thought they might like to talk to me or at least see what I looked like. It seemed reasonable. Most employers do want to know what you look like or talk to you anyway."

The Air America personnel manager seemed irritated by the suggestion. It would not be necessary, he said and rang off. Hansen was hired. "I thought, Jesus, I don't know if I really want to work for an outfit like that."

Within weeks he was on his way to Taiwan. His experience, as he had clearly stated in his original application, was bush flying in Canada and in small executive aircraft. He found himself posted to Japan to fly a DC-6, a plane he had never flown in his life, on the "book run," carrying the *Stars and Stripes* newspaper to U.S. Forces stationed in Korea.

It was part of the deal that an Air America pilot had to be prepared to fly anything. If a pilot whose experience was in military transports found himself assigned to a single-engine STOL (Short Take-off and Landing) aircraft and objected, it was pointed out to him bluntly that he had been hired as a professional and was therefore supposed to be able to fly what he was given. And if he could not, he was free to pack his bags and go home.

There were those who did just that. One recruit was out at the airport in Saigon at the end of a working day and watched the station manager, Les Strouse, disposing the airplanes. "What are you moving them around for?" the rookie asked.

He was told that the base was expecting a rocket attack and they did not want all the same type of aircraft destroyed if they took a hit. "That was the last we saw of him," Strouse said. "Had he stayed until morning he would have found out that we did take a hit that night, right in the middle of the ramp."

New arrivals could find their orientation flights impressive. "After a short indoctrination period in Taipei I went up to Saigon where we were told about the hazardous conditions, the lack of navigational facilities, the inadequate weather reporting stations and so on," Art Kenyon, a fixed-wing pilot who was to fly a C-46, recalled. "Then I went through an area orientation program sitting in the right-hand seat as copilot.

"We flew about thirty miles south of Saigon, down in the Delta, where there was a laterite strip of a reddish mud and clay composition. I was asked to make some landings, and on about my third or fourth an Army Caribou cut me out a little bit. I had to extend my downwing leg in order to let the

Caribou land and had just begun to go down when I was hit by small arms fire. A single shot came through the left wing of the airplane, fragmented and then entered the fuselage. I was in a slight bank at the time, and as soon as I heard the impact I put the power to it and started to pull up, raised the landing gear and tried to get some altitude between me and whoever was shooting at me. I turned to my left and said the training was too goddamn realistic. We didn't have to get cut out by another plane *and* shot at to prove that flying in Vietnam was hazardous."

Laos offered the same baptism by fire. "I got fired at on my first trip with a AK-47, a heavy Chinese machine gun," Tom Grady, a helicopter pilot, said. "At ground school you heard all the stories, but the big stuff really shakes you. It took ten years off my life."

An exotic airline hiring mercenary pilots attracted some interest in the press. There were stories of men being offered "$1,000 a week and a box to come home in," and one would-be tough guy who wanted to join, having heard "they have some divisions that get a little rough once in a while," dejectedly told *The New York Times* that he had been rejected because he wore glasses. Reporters wrote about rugged-looking young men with briefcases moving swiftly in and out of Air America's Washington office, remarked on the luxurious wall-to-wall gold-colored carpet, and noted that the men talked in whispers and closed doors behind them. It was all good cloak-and-dagger stuff but no mention was made of the CIA.

The men who were being hired, although told that if they were not prepared to be shot at they might as well stay at home, were certainly given no inkling that the airline was owned lock, stock, and barrel by the CIA. Often men who had gone along for an interview with Air America found themselves hired by Air Asia and were given their tickets by Civil Air Transport. "It was a little confusing, all those names," one pilot said. "My wife was sort of suspicious about it and asked who I *really* worked for. 'Hell, I don't know,' I told her. 'Who cares?'"

Many would fly for Air America for years and only find out about the Agency connection through an article in *Newsweek*, and even today many are unsure exactly how it fitted into the scheme of things. Others, about 15 percent of the pilots, would be assigned to clandestine missions almost immediately. A vocabulary of euphemism and understatement evolved as a result of the men's uncertain status. The CIA became known as "the customer," ammunition became "hard rice," and any covert mission was called "black." Spies dropped behind enemy lines were "infils" when they were taken in, and "exfils" when they were brought out; the troops of the mercenary army were the "friendlies" while the enemy became the "bad guys." Flights under heavy enemy fire were referred to as "sporty," while an experience that took a pilot close to death would be described as "fascinating." It was a way of easing the tension and keeping one's nerve.

In the very early days, up until the end of the Korean War Air America tended to recruit active-duty people from the surplus of pilots created by the war. A man could make two or three times as much as he could in the Forces, so it was attractive to make the move. Later, civilians would be approached through a grapevine of the like-minded. But when the company began to mushroom in the mid sixties it was necessary to advertise and solicit young chopper pilots who had done their tour of duty with the Marines or the military and were already trained and battle hardened. The sort of flying that Air America went in for would turn the average jumbo pilot's hair white in a single flight.

Pilots are well-known to be a breed unto themselves; of those in Air America some were heroes and a few were crooks, but together they formed a truly unique mix. Individualistic and not overfond of authority, with a taste for adventure and cold cash, they somehow combined courage with an edge of craziness that pulled them through the toughest situations. Flying airplanes has been described as hour upon hour of boredom interrupted by moments of sheer terror, and perversely it seemed to be the moments of terror that kept them in the job.

An idea of an AA pilot's character can best be given by describing one or two of the company's more colorful personalities. If any one pilot of Air America deserves the reputation as the airline's living legend it is Art Wilson, known throughout the Orient as "Shower Shoes." Wilson had flown "the hump" over the Himalayas into China with the Flying Tigers in the early forties and was still with AA at the very end on the last day of the Vietnam War when Saigon fell. And he flew through it all in the simple rubber sandals the men called shower shoes.

His particular war horses were the old faithful C-46s and Gooney Bird transport planes and he had amassed a staggering amount of hours in them. It takes years in commercial aviation to clock up a thousand hours, and younger pilots would quiz him in awed tones on his record. "Shower Shoes, how much time have you in that aircraft out there?" one pilot asked him in the operations room in Vientiane.

"Oh, about four thousand hours."

The young pilot looked disappointed. "I would have thought after fifteen years you would have more time in C-47s," he said.

Wilson nodded toward the Gooney Bird on the tarmac. "Four thousand hours in *that* C-47 there." It was said there was a C-46 that he had fifteen thousand hours in and that the old pilot's grand total was thirty thousand hours.

Wilson was born in China and grew up there, speaking the language like a native and able to write more characters than most Chinese. He liked to give the impression of a country hick, but behind his scruffy, somewhat absentminded image was a highly intelligent and well-read man. He was the aeronautical version of the sailor with a girl in every port and knew the Far East like his own backyard. He lived like a native, and among his more disturbing Eastern habits was his taste for "bloots"—unhatched baby chickens which are eaten raw, feathers and all.

In 1966, with six logbooks with twenty-five thousand hours on them to his credit, the company discovered he did not have a pilot's license. He had to return to the States and attend a flying school in Louisiana to get his FAA license to complement the Chinese license he flew with. Never a snappy dresser, Wilson shuffled into the flying school and told them he wanted a commercial license. The young instructor told him it was usual to start on a Cessna and work up.

"I want to get in that thing out there," Shower Shoes said, indicating a DC-3.

"You've got to start on something small," the young instructor said patronizingly.

"Son," Wilson said, dumping his pile of logbooks on the table, "I've probably spent more hours in one of those than you have breathing."

The shower shoes were frowned upon officially, and there were endless attempts made to persuade him to wear other more acceptable and professional footgear. An instructor who visited Vientiane to give the pilots classes on jungle survival techniques was appalled to see Wilson sitting before him, fresh from a flight, with only shower shoes on his feet.

"Now, how long do you think it would take you to walk out of the jungle in *those*?" he asked.

Wilson scratched his head thoughtfully. "Well, let me see ... The last time it took two weeks. Time before that it was around six." On one occasion when Wilson was shot down, he hid the aircraft so well that a rescue team failed to locate him. But Wilson employed his own techniques for survival; bad copilots were made to sit on their hands and were not allowed to touch any instruments throughout the flight. And he never flew without his carefully packed survival kit—a plastic case with a plastic zipper containing a sandwich, a can of beer, and a spare pair of shower shoes.

When the company finally insisted that he wear proper footwear he would hobble across the tarmac in GI boots, then kick them off in the cockpit for the comfort of the beloved shower shoes.

He never flew on a Sunday. When a Chinese scheduler once approached him at the airport and told him his plane was ready, he shook his head. "I don't fly on Sundays, son. They know that up in scheduling." It was an old pilot's superstition but a well-founded one. "I've had too many friends killed on a Sunday," he explained to a colleague.

A pilot of a different generation who extended Wilson's tradition for idiosyncrasy and eccentricity was Neil Hansen. Tall, lean, and laconic, he was the sort of character who can be imagined hitching his horse to a post and kicking open the swing doors of a saloon in some dusty cowboy town. He became known in AA as "Weird Neil" and the nickname seemed to attach itself to him naturally. "He was just weird," a colleague said by way of explanation. "You never knew what he was going to do." Among his experiences with AA was a hectic day when he was shot down once, crash landed once, and then was in a chopper that had to make an emergency landing. He temporarily became a Buddhist monk in a village outside of Vientiane, Laos, where he lived like a native. "Working with the people as a monk, you're the father confessor, the doctor, everything. It was a lot of fun working with them, I really enjoyed it," Hansen said. "Buddhism is an interesting philosophy, and like all religions it's a power philosophy. I was always interested in how they could get a guy to sit down and pour a can of gas over himself and I saw how it was done. Give me your mind and I'll have your ass."

New copilots who flew with him were subjected to unnerving practical jokes. They would climb aboard, eager to make a good impression on the captain, and Hansen would hand over the controls of the airplane and tell them the direction to hold. Then he would slip out a coloring book and a box of colored pencils and begin to crayon.

"Hell, I'm missing a red," he would complain to his kicker (air freight specialist), pro Beetle Bailey. "I'll trade you a green and an orange for a red."

"Uh-huh—I want a green and blue as well," Bailey would say, driving a hard bargain.

The rookie copilot would usually pretend that he found nothing unusual about the captain and his kicker as they continued to color away like kids in a kindergarten. "Hey, Neil, can I do the barn?" Bailey would ask.

"All right, but mind you stay in between the lines now. You spoilt the farmyard scene when I let you do the cow. Blue indeed!"

In bad weather, or under fire, such conversation had an unsettling effect on the uninitiated.

After a long career with AA and a hair-raising stint in Cambodia, Hansen found himself back in Laos after the company had pulled out, flying for the enemy.

"I went back there to fly for the Fairy Prince, who was queer and really dug pilots. He'd buy you drinks and everything, a sweet devil. I was flying this C-46, dropping rice to the Pathet Lao. Just rice. They didn't expect me to drop ammo, which was really quite fair, considering. Everybody else had left the country, but AA had given two C-46s to Royal Air Laos which were rice-drop airplanes. There was another pilot, a Lao, but he couldn't drop rice to save his ass. He dropped it in rivers, in the jungle—it went all over the goddamn place.

"The Russians were there supporting the Pathet Lao as well. I used to think that our military and organizational setups were bad, but theirs was hard to believe. They had this massive bureaucracy and hierarchy for a two-airplane operation." Hansen made himself so useful that when he wanted to leave he found that he was denied an exit visa and had to be smuggled out of the country.

"Weird" Neil Hansen and Art Wilson epitomized the individualistic nature of the men who flew for AA. And yet it was hard to miss a member of the company, for they wore a distinctive uniform. They *looked* like soldiers of fortune. The company provided them with a two-tone gray outfit, a light shirt matched by trousers of a darker shade, and a peaked hat with the AA insignia on it. The men usually abandoned the hat for a baseball cap, and some even wore Stetsons, and all wore the inevitable sunglasses. But most distinctive of all was what became known as AA jewelry. Some wore gold necklaces and rings, but almost without fail they sported a solid gold Rolex on one arm and a solid gold bracelet hand-engraved with their initials, sometimes in diamonds, and the Chinese four seasons design, on the other. One pilot commissioned a goldsmith to do elaborate work on a bracelet, but the craftsman was caught stealing gold from his employer and the job had to be completed in jail. The bracelets were big and gaudy and the biggest weighed half a kilo.

The pilots claimed that the AA bracelets originated as something to barter their lives with if they were ever shot down and captured by the enemy. As the enemy would have cut off their arms to get the gold, it is more likely that the pilots' naive theory was created to allow them to indulge themselves in a little ostentation.

Spend enough time with pilots and their divisions and hierarchies become apparent. The fighter pilot needs a different sort of courage and ability to maneuver his way through a cut-and-thrust dogfight than the bomber pilot who must plough relentlessly through exploding clouds of antiaircraft fire. In Air America those differences manifested themselves between the men who flew the STOL aircraft and landed on uphill strips less than six hundred feet long and the men who flew the C-46s and C-47s and dropped rice and ammo in all weather. There was an even wider division between the fixed-wing people and those who flew the helicopters, which was not just a question of differing temperaments and skills but boiled down to a generation gap.

Most of the older men had spent a lifetime in the services

and had been through very different kinds of wars from the
one the helicopter pilots had fought in the Marine Corps. They
rarely mixed socially and the younger men often saw their
seniors as throwbacks who looked out on the world through
the blinkered and one-directional spectacles that seem to be
handed out to all military men along with their long-service
medals, although tunnel vision in Air America was not always confined to the older generation.

The chopper pilots held, and deserved, a reputation for
being larger-than-life hellraisers, spoiling for action, whereas
the older military types had most of their drinking, whoring,
and brawling days behind them; but not all.

Helicopter pilots were quite simply a different breed of cat.
"They were younger than we were," a fixed-wing pilot explained, "and they had the wildest parties and were the biggest boozers and the real hotshot Charlie aviators. We were
altogether an older and more staid bunch. The rotor heads
were a clique and didn't mix much."

Young men not only had the chance to prolong the adventure of active duty but also had the opportunity of early command. "I was twenty-seven years old when I finished flying
with the Marines," one said, "and I could have got a job with
the scheduled airlines and maybe gone on a waiting list for
twenty years before I had command of my own plane. With
Air America I had command right there and then and I liked
it."

It was said of the "rotor heads" that life beneath the swinging propellers of their machines had scrambled their brains;
also scrambled were the beliefs and illusions of an older generation. Where the older men respected authority, the
younger ones held it in contempt; while the older pilots
swelled to the flutter of the flag, the younger ones tended to
look carefully at whoever might be waving it. And if it was
a young gung-ho CIA case officer with scant regard for their
safety the younger pilots were not beyond taking a swing at
him.

Helicopters had been used in combat in Korea for the first
time, and at the start the people who flew them tended to be
terrible pilots. The aviation world looked down on the helicopter and the man who flew it and the idea took root in
pilots' minds. When the chopper finally came into its own in
Vietnam and became of prime strategic importance, things

were made even worse because of the jealousy and ill-feeling formed between the Air Force and the military's helicopter jocks. This feeling was carried over into Air America, where a chopper pilot was able to fly more hours and make more landings than the fixed-wing people. And as many special projects were paid for by the number of landings, the chopper pilots were committing the cardinal sin of making more money than the senior men.

The young men sensed the resentment and reacted against it. "They didn't like us because fixed-wing pilots lost jobs through helicopters," Ron Zappardino said. "We were all new people who would not accept any of the old ideas. We had flown in a war as recently as six months before, probably some of the toughest flying ever, where enemy contact was made every day. And then along came these fucking old farts who have been flying for thirty years, and haven't seen action since the Second World War, and started to tell us how to fly in combat. They were very protective of their own positions and didn't like our attitude and we didn't like theirs. It created a great division. They had a limited mentality and no vision and thought the war was going on forever. We all knew—get your money and get out, it ain't gonna last."

The younger men tended to see Air America as a place to pick up some quick cash and a chance to get ahead; the older men believed it would be the Indochinese airline when the war was over. The young had seen the war in Vietnam up close and had been confused and hardened by it. "All the time I was in Vietnam I was trying to figure out why we were there and justify myself being there," said Mike Barksdale. "At first I thought I was there for some higher reason, but I didn't really feel that way by the time I got to Air America. By then it was just a business. I wasn't there to save anybody from the Red horde anymore. I stayed on to make a few bucks and enjoy a job I liked doing."

He saw the older pilots as stuck in a rut. "They gave you the impression they didn't have anyplace else to go. And they sure didn't have anywhere else where they could make that much money. I heard a colonel say to some of the guys over there, 'Just make sure you don't become Southeast Asia bums,' and at the time I didn't know what he was talking about. But I figured it out after I was there for a while."

There were few among the chopper pilots who ever contemplated a career in the military, and this too led to a division. "All I've got to say is if somebody is retired military it's two stripes against him," said Wayne Lannin. "To be in the military for twenty years means that you've had to kiss ass not to upset anybody. Now the guys who had *fought* in the Second World War or Korea were the ones you could usually relate to, sit down and talk. But there were a lot who had never been to war but would pull rank because they'd been with the company for years and had seniority."

The proportion of ex-Marine pilots in Air America to Air Force or civilians was surprisingly high. It is significant because there were not that many Marine aviators. "Most of the helicopter pilots were ex-Marines, which figured, because to be a Marine you've got to be fucking mad," Ron Zappardino said. "We were all slightly unbalanced, otherwise what the fuck were we doing in the Marine Corps, where somebody was going to beat you, punch you, shove you and push you, and make you die? You're trying to prove something to yourself. So you're talking about a bunch of unbalanced idiots who loved what they were doing.

"There were no restrictions. I could do things nobody would normally be allowed to do with an airplane. You could physically take the aircraft and push it right to its limit, test your ability as a pilot, go into the worst possible areas of the world and successfully complete a mission. And the country was backing it.

"I wouldn't have flown for the North Vietnamese Army for ten thousand dollars a month. There was a semblance with Air America that what you were doing was right. I was there for my country, the money, and the fun and I didn't give a shit who was right or wrong. Most guys believed they were saving the world. But they wouldn't have done it for a thousand a month—it's a lot easier to save the world for four."

Air America's pilots have been called mercenaries, but there was a great difference between them and the rest of the world's soldiers of fortune or professional adventurers. The true mercenary will bear arms under any flag, and his master is whoever holds the purse strings. Most of Air America believed they were in it for Uncle Sam, struggling against the evils of communism, and would not have been there otherwise. Many of them lost this simplistic ideology as the war dragged on, became disillusioned by the bureaucratic bungling and waste, and became bitter as the death toll of their colleagues grew while little was achieved. But few of them would have stayed as long as they did or taken the same risks if their paymaster had been South Africa, say, or the Angolans.

But the money was good. A pilot could earn up to $5,000 a month if the going was tough enough, and there were tax advantages and travel facilities on top of that. And life was cheap and easy in the Far East, where it was usual for every family to have at least a couple of servants.

The high rates of pay led to jealousy among the services, but the boys in Air America were liable to rub it in rather than apologize. It was necessary for the Air Force to pick their argument at the right time in case they ever needed an Air America chopper to haul them out of a tight spot.

At the height of the war in Laos, when an up-country relay station had been knocked out by enemy action, the only way for radio contact to be maintained was to transmit messages to an airplane circling high above the mountains which would then relay them on. This was dull work but one of the many jobs Air America undertook.

An Air Force captain in trouble called in, trying to get word back to his base that he might have to declare an emergency. He wasn't quite sure, he said, but he wanted them to be ready. It was his misfortune that he happened to pick a Texan and retired F-102 pilot, to tell his troubles to. "Negative on that emergency," the Texan drawled indifferently. "We can't take care of that now, we're busy."

"What do you mean you're busy?" the perplexed Air Force captain demanded. "What the hell are you doing?"

"What do you think?" came the drawn-out, abstracted response. "We're up here counting our money."

They liked the money, but it only explains a part of the motivation. There are a lot of places in the world where an experienced pilot can fly airplanes in less hazardous conditions, and given the ability of many of them, it's clear they could have done as well with an orthodox airline. But for old combat fighters there is no psychic income whatsoever in sitting at the controls of a modern jet.

Art Kenyon, who flew fixed-wing in Vietnam, describes the difference well. One day he was flying an Air Force captain he shared an apartment with in Saigon up to Han Quan when they ran into bad weather. There were no navigational aids in the plane, so Kenyon was flying time and distance and let down below the clouds at around twelve hundred feet. Spotting a river he recognized, he headed for an isolated field, checked it over for obstructive goats, dogs, or parked bicycles, and made his approach.

"Jesus, you're not going to land there?" the Air Force captain exclaimed.

"Just watch."

They went in dragging the plane over trees and housetops, made it onto the rough strip, and came to a halt three quarters of the way down the runway. Kenyon said that his Air Force friend was "absolutely fascinated," a charitable euphemism meaning he was frightened to death.

"I can remember as a very small child my father would hide behind a corner and jump out at and startle me," Kenyon explained. "I was scared but thrilled. And I think that has been a prevailing factor in everything I've done. In the war I used to go out on operations and encounter no flak and no fighters—a milk run. I'd drop my bombs and go back and feel cheated a little bit.

"I often said to my friends that Air America could have had me for a lot less. They could have had me for nothing. I enjoyed the flying, I enjoyed the risk, and I enjoyed the satisfaction of the skill which I had developed. I sure as hell can't complain. It was the most interesting and enjoyable decade of my life."

In an attempt not to attract only those interested in money Air America in Washington did not make the pay sound especially good during the interview. Applicants were told that their base pay would be $650 a month and this put some people off. The real money was earned through overtime and hazard pay. On top of that "black" projects were paid well and in cash, with no records kept. "The money was paid into out joint account in the Bank of Miami," an Air America wife said. "I was expecting something around six hundred and fifty dollars, yet the very first check was for nineteen hundred. When I saw it I was still in the States and didn't know what my husband was up to." I said, "You better get out of that job, you must be doing something wrong.'"

Although it was quite possible to earn five thousand a month, while chopper pilots occasionally picked up checks for

$8,000, the company was not giving the money away. The feeling among the pilots, returning to base with the fuselage of their planes peppered with bullet holes, was they had earned every cent. "Nobody got wealthy on the kind of money we made," Bob Dawson said. "I don't think the salaries of the pilots began to cover the risk involved, and certainly there are dozens of dead over there who confirm that. If they thought they were going to lose their lives they wouldn't have sold them for anywhere near what they got."

The conflict in Southeast Asia may not have been the best of wars, the Air America pilots said, but it was the only war they had. It was the sort of war where a man could leave home in the morning, risk his neck numerous times during the day, and return to the comfort of his house in the evening, enjoy a dry martini with his wife, and be served a good dinner by his servants. The company became a home for old fighter pilots where they could mix with their own kind and feel vital. "Take this war away and what would we have?" one pilot told a reporter at the time. "Most of us would go back to the States and become dirty old men."

There was no equivalent to Air America anywhere else in the world, so for those with combat flying in their blood there was nowhere else to go. "Those guys got together and had a world," Charlotte Wierdt, a pilot's wife said. "Back home people were in their own world and nobody wanted to listen to their war stories. Air America was a place where they could relive their wars, shoot them down again. It was high adventure, and if you didn't like adventure you didn't last long." Her own husband, Leonard, paid the highest price of all for the adventure when, cruising low in Laos in a Pilatus Porter, searching for a colleague who had crashed, his own plane slipped and careered into a tree.

People in aviation say that there is not much fun in flying jets. Avionics has turned pilots into electronic engineers, and the touch of the Red Baron has gone. Air America fliers had the opportunity to fly planes which real pilots had flown back in the days when aviation was aviation. Finally, they were neither mercenaries nor soldiers of fortune, but true romantics. "It was a haven for pilots from all over the world," said Fletcher Prouty, a retired USAF colonel who acted as liaison between the CIA and the Air Force for nine years. "I've met every sort there. The company paid a good salary, kept the guys busy, and were not too restrictive on their extracurricular activities. They had a darned good air force—they could do anything."

Among the older men there was sometimes a desperate side to their involvement with the company, an attempt to make up for past failures and recapture lost youth. Many saw themselves in the mold of Lord Jim, escaping from something at home into the exotic Orient in the hope they would find a more meaningful life and a better self. Some of them were turning their backs on the human disaster of their past lives or merely escaping the terrible prison of a loving wife, two kids, a dog, and a mortgage in small-town America. All of them had once experienced a period of great adventure and then found themselves working as salesmen. Out there in the Orient, with their lives on the line, it was possible to prolong the moment of high adventure. The danger meant that friendships were more truly felt; there was an edge to life and the beer tasted better. There was never a shortage of people eager to join.

There were those who reveled in the disclosures that the company they worked for was owned and run by the CIA. Exactly the right touch of intrigue had been added to the derring-do of their everyday lives. "Some people played the super-spook image of the airline up to the hilt," Les Strouse, onetime assistant manager of the STOL program in Saigon, said. "They would slide around always looking over their shoulder and had just about everything except the slouch hat and the raincoat. And they would usually be the characters who had the run-of-the-mill clearances and weren't involved in the clandestine part of the operation."

"Not too many people worried in Air America whether they were working for the CIA or the Defense Department or whoever," said Mel Cooper, another chopper pilot. "A high percentage had just converted their gung-ho military or Air Force enthusiasm and were still fighting for the U.S. flag, glory and apple pie. And they were the people I had problems with.

"Get right down to it and we were mercenaries; whatever other motivation there was, money was a big part of it and we knew we were making more than the Marines or the Army. Once you decide to do something for money, you should make sure you always do your best to live to spend it. But a lot of the guys acted as if they wanted to give theirs to their wives or heirs.

"About a third of the guys felt like I did. Even when I flew in the Marine Corps there was an awful lot of antimedal sentiment among the younger people. They had seen these young majors get down on their hands and knees after they'd flown a decent mission and been shot at and beg to be written up for heroism. Because of the system, where you needed reports from two or three individuals, they'd solicit. Some of them were unbelievable. They'd write their own reports and say, 'You don't even have to write it up. Just sign this here.' Most of the people who got the hero medals got them because they fucked-up and lived. They had made a poor decision and got shot up. If they had waited five minutes they would have had the air support or the artillery and wouldn't have got shot up at all.

"There was definitely a group of people in Air America who wanted this hero reputation. They wanted to be known for going in under fire, and they were still going after the medals as they had done in the services, but there were no medals and they weren't getting paid any extra to be heroes and wanted to live."

(In the services air medals were awarded on the basis of the number of sorties flown by a pilot, and it is interesting to speculate just how many medals Air America would have accumulated. "We were flying half as much again in hours than a military pilot," Bob Murray said. "I flew with AA for ten years, the equivalent to fifteen years of military service. That would be one hundred and twenty air medals for that period alone. Not counting the DFC.")

Whatever the jealousies and differences between the groups, the fixed-wing pilots developed a great admiration for the cadet branch of the company when they were in trouble. It was the chopper pilots who flew in under any conditions to lift them out of the jungle when they were shot down, and no risk was too great to save a downed airman. "When an Air America bird went down it was official company policy, but also a pilot to pilot policy, that you busted your ass and risked being shot down yourself to pick up the pilot," Mel Cooper said. "We had an extremely good record on that, much better than the Air Force's Jolly Green Giants. They had a good reputation but what we saw them do was very poor in comparison. Every now and again we would be told to stay out of it and let the Jolly Green Giants go in, but their approach was extremely nervous. When they crossed over into Laos, they knew they shouldn't be there technically and that they would be killed if they were taken by the enemy, and they were also unfamiliar with the area. They would fly over a village that we had lived in, partied in, and acted like they were going to get shot down. It made them cautious."

A helicopter pilot could never buy a drink at the bar of their base in Udorn, Thailand, if a fixed-wing man was around, for a great many of them owed their lives to the rotor heads. Whatever the divisions within the company, they were still a tight group and displayed a united front to the outside world, which they tended to grow remote from. "In the end you got tunnel vision," Wayne Lannin said. "Things soon went stale when you were on leave and people seemed artificial. Everybody who didn't do what you did was less than you, and when we were among people who couldn't talk about Vietnam or Laos we thought they were weird."

In a jam any pilot was a fellow aviator, irrespective of the craft they flew, but the young CIA case officers were rarely accepted as colleagues. "I wasn't very impressed by the Agency people," Mike Barksdale said. "They had some people over there who really acted the super spook and this is the way they came across. They made a little more of it than it was and it got a little old after a while. I often wondered about their recruiting program.

"They struck me as a lot of people who didn't fit anyplace else. If they wanted a job done and it meant hanging your neck out to get in there, a lot of them wouldn't hesitate to put your life in jeopardy. We looked at it a little different."

There was a feeling that the CIA men tended to play fast and loose with other men's courage in the interest of their own promotion. "They thought that if they told the older guys the truth, they wouldn't take the chances to carry out a mission," Mel Cooper said. "What they didn't realize was that most of the pilots they considered too old to take chances had been taking a hell of a lot more chances than they had for a long time. They weren't there on one-or-two-year contracts, most of them had been there ten years or more."

Occasionally there were head-on collisions between pilots and case officers. On one mission in Laos tempers became really frayed. "Why don't you admit it's a failure," Cooper shouted. "You're going to get a lot of people killed."

"You don't understand the big picture," was the CIA officer's pompous reply.

"Sure I understand the big picture. You're trying to get up the ladder in the organization and be another William Colby, but you're trying to get me killed so you can get there."

There were times when pilots refused to go on missions, which was their right, although the CIA did not always understand that.

"I lost all respect for the majority of case officers," Cooper continued. "There were a few who were tactful enough to make you feel like they had taken your risk into consideration and who I considered as friends. But sooner or later almost all of them would show their true colors and very few really gave a shit about us."

The CIA displayed remarkably little understanding of the psychology of the men who flew their planes. In a report, the Inspector General of the CIA stated that a "Number of them do like their wine and their women, but on the job they are all business and very much like the average American." This is an interesting, if meaningless, statement. Although it sheds little light on the character of Air America personnel, it does give us a glimpse of the curious mental landscape inhabited by the CIA hierarchy, where the extraordinary can be described as average.

TWO

FLYING TIGERS

The CIA's secret fliers have a colorful heritage directly linked to the legendary Flying Tigers, who flew and fought in China under Claire Lee Chennault. In 1937 Chennault was invited by Madame Chiang Kai-shek, the American-educated wife of the Generalissimo and National Secretary of Aviation for China, to take on the job of training and organizing the Chinese Air Force on a three-month contract at a thousand dollars a month.

To the military establishment Chennault seemed an odd, even a desperate choice. He was a retired U.S. Army Corps captain, forty-seven years old, physically disqualified from flying duty and partially deaf, a common affliction among early aviators who had been subjected to open cockpits and roaring engines. Worst of all, this seemingly washed-up pilot had always been a military rebel and a maverick.

The air force he was to train in China was a mess. The flying school and fighter-assembly plant were in the hands of Italians under Mussolini, and despite the style and dash of his Fascist generals (one, named Saroni, weighed down by a uniform dripping with medals and gold braid, roared through the streets of Nanking in a black Alfa Romeo limousine) they only contributed to the chaos. The flying school graduated anyone lucky enough to survive the course as a full-fledged pilot, regardless of ability. The assembly plant turned out large numbers of Fiat fighters which proved to be firetraps, far greater hazards to those flying them than to those flown against.

The pilots of the international squadron were a collection of bums and drunks from all over the world, much given to bar flying when they sat in low dives bragging about past exploits. Chennault glumly watched them destroy plane after plane in landing practice and scramble about in confusion on air-raid interceptions when they lost planes without a shot being fired by the enemy. He remarked bleakly that bad as the International Squadron was in the air it was worse on the ground, where the pilots inhabited "Dump Street" in Hankow, the domain of drunkards, whores, and opium peddlars.

By 1938 the Japanese controlled most of China, had sealed off the Yangtze and Yellow rivers and the rice bowl of China with them. They also had possession of the major seaports and had taken over 95 percent of China's industry. There was little Chennault could do with his band of flying drunks in their junk aircraft except collect intelligence on Japanese air tactics and store huge quantities of gasoline, bombs and ammunition in the hope of some future offensive. There were no planes to oppose the might of the Imperial Japanese Air Force because they had all been pranged. The Japanese were free to strafe and bomb where they would, and their pilots flew lower and lower and even put on shows of acrobatics in between bursts of machine-gun fire.

It was not until the beginning of 1941 that the U.S. realized the vital importance of keeping China in the war. Chennault saw his chance to form a real air force, using American fighter planes and pilots. He was allotted one hundred P-40s, already rejected by the British as too obsolete for the war in Europe, and had his plan approved to form an American Volunteer Group to fly them. He was allowed to visit various air bases of the Army Air Corps, the Navy, and the Marine Corps to recruit pilots and ground crew.

His sales pitch was effective. The men were told that the American Volunteer Group was to be run on parallel lines to a military organization but with less discipline and more money. Pilots were to be paid $600 dollars a month, $675 for flight leaders and $750 for squadron commanders, and "unofficial" bonuses not in the contract. There was also to be a $500 bonus for every Japanese plane shot down.

And then there was the secrecy, the intrigue, and the cloak-and-dagger ambience, because under the rules of the Geneva Convention U.S. military personnel were not supposed to be fighting in China. "You'll be agents for the Chinese government," prospective pilots were told. "In other words, we don't want to have it known, or at any rate advertised, that you're going over there to fight against the Japanese or, for that matter, that you were in the Forces. In no way must it be known that you're even in China with the official knowledge of the U.S. government." They were assured that releases could be obtained for them from the Forces and that when their contracts expired they could be slotted right back into the Navy or Air Force without losing seniority and that Uncle Sam was smiling upon the whole project. Before long Chennault had his one hundred pilots and an additional one hundred fifty mechanics.

They began to assemble in San Francisco in secret in the summer of 1941 from all over the States. Special passports were arranged by the State Department and the pilots boarded the Dutch liner *Jaegersfontaine* as salesmen, teachers, actors and every other profession, including an undertaker and an inordinate number of missionaries. This proved unfortunate, as there was a group of twenty-five real missionaries on board who were soon convinced the devil had entered their drunken and rowdy colleagues.

The missionaries were not the only ones who saw through the pilots' cover. The Japanese had found out too and announced over the radio that they would sink the *Jaegersfontaine* for carrying a group of mercenary American bandits bound for China to fight the Emperor. Two U.S. Navy warships escorted them from off Hawaii until, after passing from escort to escort, they arrived in Singapore by way of Manila and Java. There they took a Norwegian ship to Rangoon.

At first Chennault might have thought his hundred pilots showed much the same style as the international squadron, for they were a raw gang. In Rangoon they got drunk and ripped the sarongs off the Burmese women in the street and were arrested for wearing their high Texas boots into the pagoda there.

It was Chennault's task to turn these wild Americans into an effective weapon in the air. His tactics were revolutionary and far different from any they had ever been taught in the Army or the Navy. The men were irregulars pitted against larger forces than they could ever master, and Chennault drilled them in the aerial tactics he had advocated to the Army Air Corps but which had never been accepted. His emphasis was on teamwork, the idea being that two planes working together were more effective than three or four breaking away and fighting as individuals. Each morning after breakfast at dawn the pilots took to the air for mock battles. The theory was simple: the lead ship went in for the kill while the wingman protected his tail.

The Chinese began to talk of Chennault's men as tigers, the name stuck and the First American Volunteer Group became known as "The Flying Tigers." A couple of the pilots had seen an RAF squadron of Tomahawks decorated with shark's teeth along the noses of the planes and similarly painted their P-40s. A tongue was added and a single eye of red and white. It was a fitting and symbolic mixture, for the Japanese traditionally feared the shark as a symbol of evil while the Chinese looked upon the saber-tooth tiger of Fukien as their national symbol.

In six months the Tigers were officially credited with the destruction of 299 Japanese aircraft, a conservative figure confirmed by outside sources. Unofficially it was estimated that a possible 300 other Japanese planes had fallen prey to the Tigers, along with 1,500 airmen—pilots, navigators, gunners, and bombardiers.

And yet at any one time Chennault had no more than forty-nine combat planes capable of operation and seventy pilots trained to fly them. The men were thinly spread between three bases and had been taught to defy all the rules and regulations of textbook flying and go against all the percentages and statistics. The Tigers' own casualties added up to eight pilots killed in action, two pilots and one crew chief lost on the ground in bombings, and a further four pilots missing in action. Nine other Flying Tigers were killed in accidents while in training or gunnery practice or while ferrying planes from Africa to China.

Despite this record an Army general pronounced them, "The most undisciplined outfit I've ever seen." And on the ground that is exactly what they seemed to be. They drove their jeeps into the sidewalk shops of Kunming, which was their HQ, and ran over pushcarts and rickshaws, while their idea of a joke was to upturn some Chinese laden down with produce carried in buckets balanced on gin poles.

When America officially entered the fight in China on July 3, 1942 it was decided by the U.S. War Department in Washington that the Flying Tigers should lose their identity as an aerial guerrilla force and be inducted into the U.S. Army Air

Force. Chennault was offered a general's star, and his pilots commissions as captains and majors, to stay on and form a nucleus about which to train the new men who were to be sent over. But it was one thing to convert the Flying Tigers into the U.S. Armed Forces with a stroke of the pen and another to convince its unruly personnel to go with it.

Things were not helped when Col. Clayton Bissell arrived from Washington to arrange for the induction of the Flying Tigers. His speech was an arrogant, military one and the men saw only too clearly that they were not being asked to join, but were being told. It was precisely this official and removed manner, threatening all the inconveniences of regimentation and discipline, that they had joined the Flying Tigers to get away from. Even Chennault could not convince them. The men were tired and battle-weary and not about to sign up. Bissell made the fatal mistake of threatening them: "If you don't sign up you'll be inducted anyway, as privates if need be, as soon as you get off the boat in San Francisco. And I do mean as soon as you get off the boat."

On June 28, 1942 it was announced that Chennault would command the China Air Task Force. Only five of the original Flying Tigers stayed on, but Chennault managed to keep the original spirit alive. The accomplishments of this ill-equipped force, constantly starved of fuel, bombs, spare parts, and replacements and often directly blocked by disapproving Army superiors, have become one of the legends of World War II. Under Chennault the air force in China remained nonconformist and an Army inspector reported that its pilots and mechanics were unshaven, wore muddy shoes and unpresentable uniforms, and lounged about playing poker in between air raids and alerts. It was the sort of official report Chennault was used to, but throughout the war he never told his men to shine their shoes.

The pilots had other things to do. There were no extra crewmen to load bombs and gasoline and they often had to spend hours working with their mechanics and armorers preparing their planes to fight. After going to bed after one o'clock in the morning the crews would often be woken up at three, told to load their bombs and machine guns and take off on the first of perhaps five combat missions that day.

The Nationalist Chinese saw Chennault as a savior, while the war turned him into a figure with an international reputation. Personally cold and forbidding, he was a powerfully built man with a hawk nose, a face crisscrossed with wrinkles, and a chin set in awesome determination. He was known to swallow scorching *chiles pequeños* and *jalapenos* like candy, and had a penchant for Indian wrestling with his men; he never lost. When Winston Churchill first clapped eyes on him at a conference in Washington he remarked, "I'm glad that man is on our side."

After the war Chennault returned briefly to the States intending to retire to his native Louisiana and a quiet life; he soon found that China was in his blood and that a peaceful old age was not. Eight years of war had turned China from a sleeping giant into a crippled one and had left the nation's land, water, and air transport shattered. Chennault returned to China to found an airline in which he undertook to move the desperately needed relief supplies that had been sent out by the United Nations Relief and Rehabilitation Administration—UNRRA—but which were accumulating on docksides and in warehouses along the coast instead of being delivered to the interior. In return for flying supplies into the country the airline was given permission to fly commercial goods out.

Postwar China was hardly the place to start a commercial airline. There was runaway inflation, the Communists were pushing forward across the mainland, and there were a couple of other airlines already operating with the best routes assigned to them. On top of that the American pilots who were to fly it could not speak the language or even pronounce the names of the cities where they wanted to land. But Chennault went ahead and formed CNRRA—the Chinese counterpart of the U.N. relief and rehabilitation organization—Air Transport. And the tongue-twisting title was immediately shortened to CAT.

The birth certificate, or founding document, was signed in the Broadway Mansions on Shanghai's Bund on October 25, 1946, and the main partners were General Chennault and Whitling Willauer, who later became ambassador to several Central American countries. "When I went to work for CAT they didn't even have any airplanes," Stuart E. Dew, one of the original CAT pilots, recalled.

His first job with the airline was to wait on the ground in the Philippines until fifteen Curtiss Commando C-46s and four Douglas C-47s were purchased from war surplus. CAT was in business with around a dozen pilots. Dew flew a C-47 to Shanghai, the first CAT aircraft in China.

The fields they operated out of were mostly dirt strips or abandoned World War II runways. Pilots serviced their own planes, working outdoors through the night in knife-edged winds. There were no hangars.

Their control tower was a parked C-46, and for weather reports they relied on local Chinese meteorologists, who determined wind direction and velocity by means of a revolving wooden rooster on a long pole which they stuck out of the window of the weather hut. Some of the written reports were poetic: "Black night, star bright" or "Visibility invisible on account of darkness."

The company could not afford uniforms, so the pilots wore their leftover Air Force and Marine and Navy garb which they made more comfortable by ripping the sleeves out of the blouses and lopping off their trouser legs at the thigh. Usually, in the steaming heat of the jungle, they flew in nothing but a pair of shorts.

The men were of the same breed as the original Flying Tigers, adventurers and individualists, but from now on they were to fight in a different kind of war. Instead of strafing and bombing and aerial dogfights the men were involved in an endless war of supply, flying unarmed transport planes instead of antiquated fighters and landing repeatedly amid Communist shell bursts as they supplied Nationalist cities under siege. They flew in sacks of rice to feed the troops, raw metals for alloys to keep defense plants in production, cash for failing banks, and medical equipment and serum.

Pilots grew used to carrying anything and everything, some of it very odd. "The strangest cargo was some of the passengers," said Stuart E. Dew. Humans apart, CAT carried hog bristles, silkworms, leopards, bears, and even a basket of assorted cobras. Within eight months the airline was aggregating one million ton miles per month and in less than a year had quadrupled that figure to four million. Initially CAT had been a poorly financed bush operation, then it received a two-million-dollar loan from UNRRA which was repaid in full by the end of CAT's first year in operation. During the first six months of 1948 the airline operated twenty C-46s and two C-47s to account for over 14 million ton miles. "The money wasn't very startling—at base rate it was a regular airline wage," Dew said. "Except we did an awful lot of flying. There was an extra ten dollars for every hour over eighty flown a month and no rules as to how many hours we could fly. I think the legal maximum normally was one thousand hours a year. Well, I remember flying two thousand."

First-class passengers on CAT's routes sat in hard bucket seats and were separated from steerage by hay and cotton bales. Steerage passengers were of the four-legged kind, and when the partitions fell in turbulence cows, goats, and pigs would wander down the plane. The chief pilot claimed he had mastered trimming the ship for the occasions when full-grown cows walked from tail to nose, upsetting the weight and balance adjustments, but never grew accustomed to turning his head to find one calmly chewing the cud in his cockpit. It was all in a day's work and led to a remark released for publication by the airline: "Cattle, sheep, and pigs intermingled with paying human passengers without apparent distress to either."

Also intermingling with livestock and passengers were agents of the newly formed Central Intelligence Agency. The Agency had been created in 1947, and in the summer of 1948 National Security Council Order 10/2 created an Office of Policy and Coordination to conduct "small" and "plausibly deniable" spying, subversion, and secret propaganda activities. The office quickly attached itself to the CIA, where it was officially known as the Plans Division and unofficially as the Department of Dirty Tricks. Over the next two years the Agency took increasing control of the airline, which it looked upon as having perfect cover.

The Nationalist Chinese were losing the war against the Communists and CAT began airlifting goods and ammunition into besieged cities. Pilots soon began to accept the extraordinary as the norm when flying in such conditions. Anything could happen and frequently did.

When Sterling Bemis lost himself in the remote and unchartered Ordos Desert during the conflict, he accepted with a stolid calm that he would probably not get out alive. The Ordos is a lifeless wasteland, where drifting sand would soon bury his plane from sight and there was not a hope of getting out on foot. Off course, his radio out of order, Bemis watched the gas gauge sink to empty until the engines coughed and he bellied the plane on soft sand.

A couple of hundred yards from where he landed was a mud hut and the pilot made for it. Miraculously, inside was a field telephone. It took Bemis a long, painful ten minutes to raise the courage to pick up the receiver and see if it worked. Taking a deep breath and with his heart pounding hard enough to burst through his rib cage, he gave the handle a crank. There was a crackling and then after a moment an operator answered. Bemis, wondering if he was suffering from desert madness, asked to be put through to CAT in Lanchow. He gave his location, and as soon as it was daylight a rescue plane came out for him.

That may sound like a very unlikely anecdote, but it is a true one. The field telephone had been part of an air-warning system that General Chennault had installed in the old Flying Tiger days. It had never been disconnected. Bemis was able to call, collect, from the middle of the desert.

Throughout the war the men made themselves as comfortable as they were able and shared a blue Oriental villa on a cliff overlooking the Yellow Sea, affectionately known as the Opium Den. It was sparsely furnished but boasted an exotic bar known as the Zebra Room because of its garish canary-yellow and royal-blue alternating stripes. They also had their own swimming pool, hacked out of solid rock and filled with stolen Navy drinking water which had turned malignantly stagnant. An odd assortment of Chinese servants washed and cooked, and one, Chung, was designated official ice cream maker. It was his solemn duty to have ice cream ready twenty-four hours a day and he had been supplied with a freezer to that end. When Chung heard a CAT plane returning from a mission he would dash out, leap into a rickshaw, and race to the Opium Den, wildly churning the freezer.

There was also a number of pets: twenty-one adopted stray dogs, a pair of parakeets, and a panda. At one time there was also a troupe of Russian dancing girls in residence who had been won by a pilot in a poker game. And then there were the pilots themselves: Ken Milan, an inveterate borrower of cigarettes and toothpaste, known as "Radar" because he picked up everything; George Davis and Dave Lampard, former RAF pilots and the only British pilots licensed to fly in

Nationalist China, known as King George and the Duke of Windsor; Randall Richardson, who went under the unhappy sobriquet of "Rich" due to his disastrous business affairs. (He had once invested all his savings in a luxurious nightclub in Tokyo, complete with velvet curtains, a jaza orchestra, and two revolving bars. On the opening night he invited five hundred guests for free food and drinks. The guests arrived at seven, and at seven-thirty the club caught fire and burned to the ground. The next day he signed up with CAT.) Largest of all the residents of the Opium Den, both in reputation and in bulk, was Capt. James B. McGovern, known throughout the Far East as "Earthquake McGoon."

McGoon, who had a fierce black beard to go with his fearsome build, had fought through the Second World War with Chennault and had shot down a confirmed six Japanese Zeroes. He was a 300-pound giant who flew in shapeless coveralls which he stuffed full with peanuts before a long mission. When he had eaten four or five hundred of them he would turn over the controls to the copilot, wriggle down on the seat, and doze quietly until the final approach. Landings tended to be tail-high because he was unable to yank the stick past his belly to elevate the nose of the plane.

As a mercenary, his approach to money was lighthearted. He once filled a bushel basket with his month's salary which he proceeded to drink up in a hectic race against inflation, reaching the bottom of the basket just as the financial market collapsed. Sometimes pilots would be paid in Chinese currency and its value would fluctuate and melt away before their eyes, although a few of the shrewder ones turned this to their advantage. Since money values differed ten or twenty times between North and South, as the civil war waxed and waned, anyone with access to an airplane was able to exploit that difference.

As the Red Chinese pushed south, the key city of Weihsien was surrounded and for weeks CAT provided the only contact with the defending troops. It became clear that the city was doomed and Earthquake McGoon flew in Lew Burridge and John Plank to salvage office records and equipment. After dropping them off, he headed back in his Gooney Bird, planning to pick them up the following day. That night the airfield was overrun and the men were trapped.

First of all they hid in the attic of a Presbyterian mission near the airfield for several hours until a sudden downpour of rain gave them the chance to slip through the Communist lines into the city proper where they took refuge in a walled schoolyard. There was no food and even the leaves on the trees in the yard had been devoured by the starving population. The pilots dined on a few boiled peanuts found in their pockets. All through the night they heard the enemy loud speakers blaring their names, demanding that the city should give up the two foreign devils who were responsible for all their miseries.

Through Chinese friends they managed to get word to CAT where they were hidden, but the schoolyard was less than four hundred feet in length, and even if a plane could manage the length it would have to squeeze between high buildings on either side with only eight feet clearance off each wingtip. Any attempt to rescue them was a crazy proposition, but their colleagues did not hesitate.

An L-5 was borrowed from the Marines and flown to Weihsien at daybreak. The pilot took it down safely into the schoolyard, but on takeoff the overloaded plane crashed into the brick wall of a ruined ammunition factory. No one was hurt but the plane was a write-off. In the afternoon another rescue attempt was made in a small plane, but a sudden downdraft dropped it like a stone, shattering the landing gear. There were now four, not two, CAT pilots stranded in the schoolyard. "Enough for bridge," remarked Earthquake McGoon, circling overhead in his C-47.

CAT purloined yet another L-5 from the Marines, and under cover of darkness Bob Rousselot took it into the impossible strip. The plane's lights were shone on the surrounding brick wall to show up the Communist troops as they tried to climb over, making them easy targets for the defenders. And as soon as it was light they tore down the factory wall and repaired the landing gear of the crashed plane with baling wire. The first plane got off, carrying three pilots, passing less than a dozen feet over the heads of Communist riflemen. But Rousselot hit a heap of rubble at the end of the yard and cracked up the second L-5.

The Communist troops moved in on the schoolyard but took cover when they heard the whistling of what they took to be delayed action bombs; McGoon was tossing empty beer bottles at them from his C-47. The original plane returned and the two remaining pilots hurled themselves aboard. The plane was turned around and the engine gunned when there was a shout and a lone figure ran toward them with a canvas sack. It was the postmaster, who had bicycled out to the schoolyard with the last bag of mail.

Earthquake McGoon had solemnly informed his colleagues that whatever the circumstances he would never bail out. "I'd only have to walk," he grumbled. For a massive man he had tiny, delicate feet, and his favorite footgear was a pair of moccasins, unlaced and slit across the toes for added comfort. So when on a routine cargo mission in a C-46, together with a Chinese copilot and radio operator, bad winds forced him off course he did not bail out. For nine hours he flew searching for an alternative field and at midnight radioed that he was running out of gas. He kept flying until he spotted a dry riverbed and bellied the plane onto its gravel bottom, directly in the path of a patrol of Red soldiers.

McGoon and his crew were marched at gunpoint along a steep trail toward a mountain village, but after a couple of hundred yards he sat down and began to massage his feet. The soldiers threatened to shoot him if he did not move. "Go ahead," McGoon said peevishly. "I'd rather be shot than walk any further on these feet of mine."

The Chinese realized that their prize catch was not going to be moved by threats and commandeered a horse from a neighboring farm. McGoon was loaded onto it and the procession moved into a village where, together with his Chinese colleagues, he was slung into jail.

The news of McGoon's capture was a blow to CAT's morale. A gloom hung over the men's favorite hangout, Pop Gingle's in Hong Kong. Gingle's was a home-from-home, a little bit of America: the menu featured Yankee pot roast and corned beef and cabbage; there was a brassrail bar with glass pitchers of cold Stateside beer, a nickel jukebox blasting cowboy ballads; and Pop always had all the latest basketball scores. The place was presided over by Pop himself, a benign, bald Buddha with sagging jowls and a mighty paunch, the only waistline in the Far East that exceeded McGoon's. Pop got into the bar business after thirty years in the Navy when he went out with his shipmates to celebrate his discharge and awoke the following morning to a monstrous hangover, an empty wallet, and a bill of sale for the bar. He never returned to the States but became a father to wandering Yanks.

McGoon was his favorite son. He used to live at Gingle's when in Hong Kong and sat at the bar with his rear end spread over two stools. When he returned to the mainland Pop would affectionately stow a shank of ham or a five-gallon jug of chili in his cockpit to keep McGoon cheerful. When news reached Pop of his capture by the Communists, he drew out his savings, mortgaged the bar, and offered $100,000 in cash to General Chennault. "Use it all if you need to, but get my boy back."

The first concrete news came when the two Chinese crew members escaped through enemy lines. They had been thrown with McGoon into a tiny cell with a single barred window. He managed to pull the bars apart enough to allow the Chinese to slip out, although his own bulk would not have squeezed through the entire window.

McGoon made a terrible prisoner. Feeding him posed a logistical problem for his captors. Jail rations were just not enough, and the guards offered him their own food in an attempt to still his bull-like roaring between meals. His beard grew thick and long and he saved his wine allotment for one long binge on his birthday when he quaffed it all and burst out of his cell like a berserk gorilla and smashed up the prison furniture. Attempts to indoctrinate him misfired. Every night there was a period of political education when his captors attempted to convince him that they were the sincere friends of the oppressed peoples of Asia. "If Communism is so honest," McGoon countered, "how come some bastard stole my razor?" Similarly, he challenged their argument that they were liberators. "Prove it by turning me loose."

And they did. McGoon was taken to the border, given five dollars, and shoved across with a sigh of relief. Nobody recognized the considerably slimmer and bearded McGoon when he pushed his way to the bar at Gingle's and boomed, "Set them up. I've got half a year's thirst." He had been missing for exactly six months.

Throughout this period CAT continued to airlift goods and ammo into besieged cities and landed behind Communist lines to deliver medical supplies and rescue the wounded. Their installations were constantly overrun by Mao's advancing forces; their equipment was sabotaged by defecting ground crews; and a number of pilots were taken prisoner as city after city surrendered or was pounded to rubble.

At Chengchow in northern China, which was completely cut off, cotton was flown in to sustain mills employing twenty thousand people, and when the Nationalist armies were surrounded in Manchuria, an airlift of fifty flights supplied two hundred tons of cargo a day. At Taiyuan, another beleaguered northern Chinese city, CAT provided a lifeline to the army of an old warlord under pressure to surrender. It was possibly the largest and most hazardous airlift in history. Pilots flew round the clock over enemy territory, knowing what a forced landing might mean, as their names were all on the Communist list of war criminals. It was a rare flight that failed to draw enemy fire. As Communist batteries pinpointed airfields, pilots would approach one strip, wait until the mortars zeroed in, and then duck into another. Flak bursts shot off trim tabs, tore holes in the fuselage, and gashed tires. The overloaded planes could carry no extra gas in case of an emergency, and freezing temperatures iced up carburetors, and froze pressure gauges and trim tabs. On drops, when they had to remove cargo doors in order to kick out one hundred bags of rice, cabin temperatures often registered 40° below zero.

As the Red army tightened its grip on the city, airstrip after airstrip came under artillery fire, and as fast as one became untenable another would be built nearer the walls of the city. Fifteen strips were used in all, and while some C-46s flew in heavy military equipment, others circled the city and dropped bags of rice to the starving population. But at most all CAT could do was delay the inevitable collapse.

Thirty regional stations were gobbled up in a year, and as the airline retreated with the fleeing Nationalist forces, CAT's main base was moved five times and each move cost $500,000, as vital repair parts and tools were left behind and maintenance became an increasing problem.

A 328-foot LST—a former U.S. Navy Landing Ship Tank—was salvaged from the muddy bottom of the Yangtze River, loaded with irreplaceable machinery and converted into a floating machine shop and repair base and used as a mobile office. It was named the *S. S. Chung*. In Shanghai it was kept anchored in the Whangpoo River, but as the city was engulfed by the enemy, Chennault gave the order to fly the planes out while he set to sea aboard his floating machine shop. Pilot

Felix Smith, who always carried his third mate's license against an emergency, navigated the craft down the China coast to Canton, where it was tied up in the Pearl River estuary. They were still scraping off the barnacles and caulking its gaping seams when the Communists closed in on Canton. The *S. S. Chung* was loaded up once again and escaped to Hong Kong, one jump ahead of the enemy.

As CAT left the mainland, their planes were mobbed by Chinese swarming the airfields in an attempt to get aboard. "I had to stand at the door with a tie-down stick, which we used for cargo, and hit people over the head," Stuart Dew said. "I had to get the other pilot to go up and start the left engine and run it at high speed and give it full power. Those poor people were sailing up against the tail of the thing. It was something we had to do to get out. We were overloaded and otherwise we couldn't have taken off.

"In the end they even lost control of the troops. We were operating at night and I saw a bunch of guys heading for the airplane and I knew they wanted to get out of there but I was afraid to shut down the engines. And these guys, they just ran straight into the props. They had helmets on and I could hear it as the props chopped into them."

"Men offered fantastic sums in American dollars to get their families out," said William Severt, who was on the last plane to leave Mukden where he was base manager. "I remember one woman with a small child who tried to give us her wedding ring." The C-46 was already loaded with refugees beyond capacity and the crew had to flash a powerful light into the faces of the hysterical crowd, blinding them long enough to haul in the ladder and slam the door. "They tried to drive a truck in front of us to block our takeoff, but the whirling props frightened them. We gunned our engines down the runway, leapfrogging over Chinese who knelt in the path of the plane, still wringing their hands and pleading to be rescued."

Even in Hong Kong the problems of the *S. S. Chung* and CAT were still not over. After a month spent overhauling the hulk from top to bottom, there was a mutiny by Communist sympathizers among the work crew on the eve of departure. They battened down the hatches and locked themselves below deck and there was a skirmish before CAT officials and Hong Kong police gained control of the craft over the mutineers.

They left behind a trail of sabotaged electrical equipment, including the anchor hoist. Resourceful pilots drove a ten-ton truck onto the LST, hitched it to the heavy anchor chain, and ran back and forth across the deck through the night, raising the chain, link by link.

The LST sailed away, but Chennault lost seventy-three planes, which had survived the Communist guns, in a legal wrangle. Great Britain had officially recognized the Red Chinese government, and local courts in Hong Kong ruled that the planes in the airport belonged to the People's Republic. It was to be two years and eight months before a British court reversed the decision, and by that time the planes had been subjected to the humidity of the tropics, salt air, and been stripped of their instruments, their tires, their propellers and, in some cases, their entire engines.

Losing a war is an expensive business and the airline was on the rocks. Pilots had their salaries cut in half and were advised to look for alternative employment. It was at this time that the CIA stepped in and played Lady Bountiful, and CAT became the first link in what was to become a multi-million-dollar commercial empire of diverse and deftly disguised "proprietary" companies—owned by the Agency itself—to help carry out and cover up many of its most clandestine operations.

The CIA first arranged cash advances to CAT in 1949, "ostensibly to deny the assets of this company to the Communist Chinese." It also provided perfect cover and had demonstrated its potential as a paramilitary force. The advances made to the company were eventually credited to the Agency's purchase of the corporation. A lawyer for the airline organized a new company, Civil Air Transport, allowing it to keep its original initials. The company was funded through the American Airdale Corporation.

According to Lawrence R. Houston (former CIA General Counsel involved in establishing the first set of proprietaries), a series of meetings was held in which it was determined that the Agency needed to contract for air transport in some of its operations, particularly those involving arms and ammunition. "And so we entered an arrangement, I think in September of 1949, whereby we would advance them a sum— the figure of seven hundred and fifty thousand dollars sticks in my mind—against which we could draw for actual use of the planes at an agreed rate. And we did draw down, I think, all the flying time and expended the seven hundred and fifty thousand dollars between September and about January, at which time we suspended any further payments or drawdowns. I think the money was exhausted."

Chennault was to fly repeatedly to Washington to ask for financial assistance, and each time the CIA gave him money and increased their stake in the airline. They received an option to purchase the assets of Civil Air Transport, and any unused portion of the advances was to be credited toward the purchase price.

In the summer of 1950 Chennault was back in Washington once again in desperate straits for funds. The Agency decided that its operations in the Far East would have a continuing need for secure airlift and therefore to buy Civil Air Transport outright. It then sought the approval of the Department of State and spoke to the Assistant Secretary of State for the Far East. He pointed out that it was basic U.S. policy not to get the government in competition with the private sector but agreed in the circumstances, as there was no private industry involved in the area at that time. They also accepted the Agency's somewhat implausible logic that by buying the airline they were denying its assets to the Red Chinese. The State Department decided it would go along with the deal on the understanding that the CIA would divest itself of the private enterprise as soon as it was feasible. In fact the Air America complex grew and grew and was used by the CIA, as a solely owned proprietary, for twenty-five years, and even then it was only sold off to appease an embarrassing rash of exposés. But like the man who once owns a car and then wonders how he ever got along without it, the CIA needs airplanes.

Under the new arrangement CAT was reorganized as a Delaware Corporation under a CIA proprietary holding company called the Pacific Corporation and thus became the original link in the CIA air empire. Its new base was in Washington, D.C. for administrative purposes and in Taipei, Taiwan, where both the airline and the defeated troops of the Nationalist Chinese had ended up, together with the Chinese Nationalist leader, Chiang Kai-shek.

Once settled on Taiwan CAT was to prosper. A regular four-engined passenger service was inaugurated to Tokyo,

Bangkok, and Hong Kong, and unscheduled international flights ranged as far as Africa and Europe. Pilots were ordered to abandon their T-shirts and shorts and reluctantly squeezed into crisp blue uniforms, complete with a cap bearing the company emblem. The eager young airline would take on any job that came along, and during a severe drought in Japan, CAT was chartered to carry a group of rainmakers over Osaka in an effort to sow the clouds with silver iodide. A fine sprinkle of rain fell over the countryside as a result, but the skeptical farmers were more inclined to credit nature than CAT for the phenomenon. On the next trip the pilot took the precaution of mixing a little emerald-colored dye with the other chemicals. Startled Japanese were treated to a chlorophyll cloudburst and CAT collected wherever it rained green.

In June 1950 the Korean War broke out and business boomed. CAT was chartered by the United Nations to aid in Operation Booklift, the massive air bridge to the fighting forces in Korea, and in two years the airline flew more than fifteen thousand missions for United States Combat Cargo. But despite a reputation as the world's most shot-at airline, it remained mostly unknown to the majority of Americans; the CIA connection remained a well-kept secret, even though Frederick Downey, one of its agents, was riding aboard a CAT airliner when he was captured on a mission over China.

Even on a purely commercial level, flying for CAT had its moments. Pilots had to be prepared to fly race horses to New Zealand on one flight and carry Moslem pilgrims to Mecca on another. The biggest job the airline ever undertook was the transportation of a young Siamese elephant from Thailand to Japan. The elephant was enticed up a ramp onto the plane by a native mahout with whom she was secretly in love. When the time came for the handler to leave, the elephant became inconsolable and expressed its unhappiness by ripping out the overhead air-duct system with its trunk and stamping one of its feet through the corrugated metal floor.

The mahout was shanghaied protestingly as an elephant-sitter and flown without clothes or visa to Tokyo. The elephant was pacified and swayed contentedly, rocking the plane from side to side. The plane seesawed down the Bangkok runway, its wingtips brushing the ground right and left with each shake of the elephant's head. "The worst part of it was," said the pilot resentfully, "the rest room on a C-46 isn't designed for elephants, and after the trip was over we had to rip the whole airplane apart and replace the rusted control cables."

CAT also provided His Highness, the Sheik Prince of Kuwait, with his first air flight. This was almost a diplomatic impossibility, as the prince's royal advisers informed the pilot on the flight that, due to His Highness's exalted position, no one was ever permitted to sit ahead of him. Faced with the cancellation of the flight the excited Prince magnanimously waived his royal prerogative and settled for a private compartment hung with rare Oriental tapestries just behind the cockpit.

The Kuwait runway had been spread with thick carpets for the occasion, and the plane's tires sank into the priceless silk rugs. The prince was so delighted by the flight that he presented each crew member with a solid gold wristwatch, set with a pair of thumbnail-size rubies and engraved with each crewman's name, and also offered to buy the airline. The CIA demurred.

By 1954 CAT had become the biggest and most profitable flying service in the Far East. *S. S. Chung*, the salvaged LST, had been taken to Taiwan and, together with an auxiliary barge called the Buddha, had been transformed into an enormous machine shop and repair complex. A pair of 120-foot Quonset huts gave added space, while the ships' interiors were subdivided into a maze of compartments and corridors. A thirty-seven-foot air-conditioned parachute drying tower bisected the photo lab, which was slotted neatly between the hydraulic shop and the L-shaped electric shop. A fully equipped machine shop ran the length of the main deck, and stacked above and below it were the paint and fabric shop, woodworking shop, plating shop, print shop, instrument shop, propeller shop, ward rooms and sleeping quarters and mess hall, and a complete dispensary with X-ray machines which doubled in use to check thin aircraft forgings and castings.

"One could walk through that ship absolutely amazed at the beehive-like activity on board," an observer from the USAF recalled. "Hundreds, perhaps thousands, of Chinese worked in that ship on stages, rather than floors or decks, joined by narrow catwalks. Many of those workers worked in small basketlike spaces, barely large enough for a small Chinese. Parts and materials were brought to them and poured into each work space as through a funnel. The worker would finish his special task and then drop the part through a short chute, where it would end up for the next worker to do his part. The whole operation worked on a sort of force-of-gravity basis, with the finished item falling out at the bottom, ready for an alert runner to carry it to the packaging room."

The possibility of a Chinese invasion of Taiwan was taken seriously at that time, and a crew of forty Chinese sailors and marines stood on twenty-four-hour alert, ready to evacuate the unique two-million-dollar repair shop.

One war was to follow another for CAT, and as the Korean War drew to a close, the French were heavily engaged in a losing battle in Indochina. The CIA was involved in activities in both North and South Vietnam at this time and were anxious to assist the French in their struggle against the Vietminh. In an attempt to block their offensives and seal the Laos/Vietnam border, the French established a fortified base in a wide upland valley called Dien Bien Phu, and in November 1953 CAT helped the French air force in airlifting sixteen thousand men into the valley. But by March the following year the Vietminh had the garrison surrounded and cut off. The U.S. government decided not to go directly to the assistance of the beleaguered force but to approve of covert military support. CAT was contracted to fly in supplies and provided with C-119s, flying boxcars, by the USAF for the task.

After a hasty training in flying these planes, CAT pilots took them up to Haiphong in North Vietnam, where they established their base. The CIA made use of these flights up to North Vietnam by loading the planes with secret agents and military equipment to be used in a clandestine network then being organized. It is interesting to note how early the CIA had a foot inside the door of Indochina.

Twenty-four CAT pilots arrived in Haiphong with their suitcases and as many creature comforts as they could carry. The French were surprised to see one pilot wheel a large enameled fridge out of his C-46 and were further dismayed to see the flight coveralls of violently colored shirts and shorts that the men intended to fly their missions in.

During the first nights of the siege of Dien Bien Phu successive waves of Communist troops stormed the French defenders until thousands of their dead were piled so high upon one another that the attackers could not charge over them. The pilots called the besieged city "The Slot," due to its position in a narrow valley between two high ridges blazing with Communist batteries. Enemy fire pinpointed the planes as they approached from either North or South, and if they overshot the drop zone on their first run they had to turn around and try it again.

"I'll tell you, flying over Dien Bien Phu was spooky," Stuart E. Dew said. "You'd go over there and they'd shoot the hell out of you. We all wore armor plating; it was in the days of flak vests, and I would sit on as many books as I could and I'd get as small as I could. Normally, I always felt I could cope with most things that would happen to an airplane but when you're sitting up there like that there's nothing you can do. Those guys would be shooting at you and you'd have to make a drop in a certain position and you'd just have to sit there and take it. And it scared the hell out of me."

An ingenious French sergeant devised a reversed bombsight which spotted the planes through a cross-hatched grid and corrected their aim after the first drop. In the beginning CAT pilots went in low in their lumbering, unarmed C-119s while the French fighter escort would circle above them at 10,000 feet. "The fighters were supposed to go in and shoot up the antiaircraft installations, but they never flew as low as we did to drop. They didn't have their hearts in it," Drew said.

The CAT fliers would often add cigarettes and beer bought from their own money to the supplies they dropped, and when Earthquake McGoon heard that the colonel-in-charge had been given a field promotion he parachuted him a set of new insignia attached to a congratulatory bottle of champagne. On his way to "The Slot" McGoon would sort through his mail and drop unpaid bills behind the enemy lines.

The Flying Boxcars would be rocked by flak on every mission. One pilot took a 37mm shell through the wing of his plane, tearing out a chunk as big as a manhole cover; another had his oxygen bottle punctured by a .50 caliber slug only a few inches from his head and told his colleagues afterward that the whistling noise of the escaping gas scared him more than the bullets. The chief pilot, Paul Holden, became the first casualty when a flak burst chewed his right arm almost in two. He tore a strip off his shirt, held one end in his teeth while copilot Wallace Burford flew the damaged plane back to Haiphong. Earthquake McGoon inspected the flak-ridden cockpit as Burford landed and shook his head. "Somebody must have been carrying a magnet."

A week later after McGoon had completed a drop and was pulling into a climb, machine-gun fire severed his elevator controls. The plane went into a spin, and while McGoon fought with his left rudder to regain control, he remarked calmly over the radio, "I seem to be having a little trouble driving this thing." He bounced the plane back to Haiphong, grumbling, "Now I know how it feels to ride a kangaroo."

As he landed, Burford greeted him with the innocent query, "Anybody borrow my magnet?"

One evening before a mission McGoon had a heart-to-heart talk with a young Chinese boy whose parents had been killed by the Communists and who had been adopted by the CAT pilots, who named him Cueball. Earthquake had cast himself in the unlikely role of overseeing the boy's education. "Don't cut school while I'm gone, Cueball," he told him. "I always used to play hooky when I was your age. I wouldn't study or do what the teacher told me, and look at me now—nothing but a stick jockey pushing a freight plane around the jungle so he can get shot at. You don't want to grow up and be like me."

The following afternoon McGoon was piloting a plane in a routine flight of six C-119s and ironically had drawn Wallace Burford as his copilot. As they walked out to the plane McGoon ribbed his friend, "Now maybe we'll find out which one of us carries that magnet." Also on this flight in another plane was Steve Kusak, who had arranged to go on leave with McGoon. The two men had plans to go down to Saigon and eat at the excellent French restaurant, Croix de Sud, known as the Crock of Suds. The last time they had been in Saigon they had enjoyed a blood-and-thunder movie where a stiff-upper-lip British hero had met peril after peril with the remark, "Piece of cake." McGoon had been much taken with this and had added it to his repertoire.

As they arrived at the drop area, Kusak went in first, then looked back to see his friend's cargo parachutes blossom a little high. At that moment Burford's voice came over the radio: "We've got a direct hit. Where the hell are the fighters?"

Kusak flew up behind McGoon's plane, which was making a slow turn to the left, and saw the damage. The left wing had been hit, splitting off the leading edge, and the engine was throwing oil so hard that it spattered against Kusak's windshield. Then a second shell hit the crippled plane, tearing a hole in the right rear boom. The plane slipped off sharply, almost careering into Kusak as it lurched out of control. The C-119 was rapidly losing altitude and Kusak radioed Haiphong for a rescue helicopter and told McGoon to jump for it.

But the giant with the delicate feet still nourished a deep-rooted prejudice against walking, despite his capture by Communist Chinese. It was simply not his style. "Give me the best heading for Haiphong over low ground," he said over the radio. "I'll keep going as long as I can."

Kusak watched the plane barely skimming over the mountaintops and saw its shadow increase in size as it flew closer and closer to the ground. He asked McGoon if he thought he could make it. "Piece of cake," was the reply.

When the plane was just a few feet from the ground Kusak heard McGoon's voice say calmly, "Looks like this is it, son." The left wingtip dug into the hillside, the plane did a slow deliberate cartwheel and exploded in a sheet of flame. McGoon and Burford had carried a magnet each.

Less than an eighth of a mile ahead around a bend in a river was a small strip where they could have landed. And the following day Dien Bien Phu surrendered.

McGoon's colleagues took the deaths badly. That day CAT had flown eighteen missions and been badly shot up and ended up making drops from ten thousand feet. Those who had volunteered for the job because it offered some extra cash and some "sporty" flying were finally forced by the company to stick with it or lose their jobs.

"McGoon was dead and two other planes were hit hard and the guys just about decided that they weren't going to go anymore," said Stuart E. Dew. "They didn't send us the next day and the following evening they surrendered."

Air America's destiny was already mapped in these early missions. That year there was to be plenty of work for CAT in North Vietnam, ferrying refugees to the South. Pilots would fly ammo and supplies to beleaguered troops in Indochina for the next twenty years, and carry countless refugees and watch city after city fall and countries collapse. And not a few of them would share the same fate as the legendary Earthquake McGoon.

THREE

INSIDE THE COMPANY

The CIA was quick to realize the excellent potential of owning their own airline but it took some time before it owned CAT outright. This initial hesitancy was to cost it dear in terms of organizational control in the early years, but as its airline network grew, the era of the Flying Tigers could be looked back upon as one of innocence and simplicity.

It is worth looking briefly here at the complex corporate structure of AA as a background to its worldwide operations over the past thirty years. It is remarkable that so much remained secret for so long, but even despite the air proprietaries' blown cover and the testimony on their activities given by Lawrence R. Houston, former CIA General Counsel, to Frank Church's Senate Committee on Intelligence activities, AA management remain tight-lipped and secretive. Any enquiry put to them directly, even of the most general nature, continues to be avoided with polite disdain. It is even considered faintly amusing that an outsider should attempt to tell the story when the CIA itself, the owners and overseers, often had only a shaky idea of what was going on.

"It'll take you fifty volumes to write it, you know," Clyde Carter, AA's president at the time of writing, chuckled indulgently. "You'll never track it all down."

The first time that I visited the AA offices on the third floor of 1725 K Street N.W. in Washington, D.C., was in October 1976. Three months previously I had been told that the office was going to close "in a month." There was little activity and it was clear that the few personnel still employed were the remnants. Maybe the office was partly kept open as a dead end, a practical block to further enquiry where the inquisitive could be fobbed off. I was shown into an office where a tall man with a western twang greeted me. I introduced myself and offered my hand. The man smiled, took my hand, but did not give his name. I explained my intention to write a book and asked if I could check through files or cuttings in non-controversial areas. The man explained apologetically that there were no files or cuttings and he really could not help me. "Three months ago I was told this office was going to close down within the month," I said as I was about to leave. "When is it going to close?"

"In a month," the cowboy replied with a broad grin. To my amazement the reply was accompanied by an exaggerated wink.

An encounter during the same period with George Doole, Jr., the man who masterminded the AA complex and ruled over it until his retirement in 1971, was similarly agreeable and unhelpful. After initial surprise that I had discovered his phone number, Mr. Doole agreed to meet me in his personal office at 1730 M Street N.W., Washington, D.C., for a midmorning appointment. The names Botsford and George Arntzen Doole were on the door of the office, and inside it was even quieter than AA. A single secretary seemed bored to distraction and unsure of what to do with herself. Two smaller offices to the rear had tables in them, but not a scrap of paper littered either. There were no filing cabinets or indeed any of the usual paraphernalia found in the offices of the smallest and most moribund businesses. It seemed apparent that neither George Doole nor his associate, Botsford, spent much time there.

Doole turned out to be a portly, bouncy figure in a gray suit and a neat little hat, a wry, friendly character who was the epitome of the perfect clubman. With a good-natured wag of his finger, he forbade me to use my tape recorder or take notes. Although he would like to help me, he said, I might misrepresent him in the way I used his answers. He was always being misquoted. *The Washington Post* sensationalized everything so.

I explained that if I misquoted him it would not be malicious but because I could not tape him or make notes. George chuckled. I asked if he could make any background material available to me. He could not, he said, because I was bound to get it all out of context.

When I countered that if he was to give me a full official

version of AA's activities I would be less likely to get things
out of context, George Doole decided to tell me the "real"
reason he was not prepared to help. He was writing his own
book, helped by a whole committee of researchers, so I was
the competition. His book would be very, very complete, he
assured me, but no neophyte or amateur could possibly tell
the story of AA because it was too complex, too wide-ranging.
He did not deny that it was owned by the CIA. "We've put it
on the record."

George Doole told me that initially he had worked for Pan
Am as a pilot—flying the very first DC-3 down to South
America, where they took over from the Clipper flying
boats—and then went to Harvard Business School. He returned to Pan Am, where he became chief pilot, and then left
the company to set up Air America.

The spook connection is a thing of the past, George Doole
said. He was active in the family business of Arntzen Enterprises, which has interest in a number of air operations from
Iran to Indonesia. He flicked through a thick book of color
photographs of helicopters in snowscapes, helicopters with
cannibal tribesmen posing in front of them, helicopters taking
off from oil rigs. I saw ARIZONA HELICOPTERS emblazoned on
one chopper and thought I saw AIR VENTURES, INC. on another,
but Mr. Doole was turning the pages quickly.

In the elevator he said that he hoped my book would be
more than "bar folklore and hokum." He would be very concerned if I wrote anything incorrect about AA, he said.

The current president of AA at the time of writing, Clyde
Carter, is as evasive as his predecessor. Several phone calls
over a period of two years, when I attempted to make official
contact with AA and the Agency, were singularly unreward-
ing. "I certainly would not discuss the affairs of the company
without the consent of the board of directors—and I'm not
particularly willing to take the project to them.

"Neither I nor anybody else has the authority to give out
the data of this company. AA is a closed corporation and it
doesn't give out public information." A letter I wrote to the
company asking for a contact within the organization or
Agency who could provide me with data "in areas no longer
controversial . . . the official number of employees, profits, the
number of pilots killed in action and so on" was returned to
me. It was accompanied by a dense note from Clyde Carter.

"By way of clarification, during the telephone conversation you refer to, I suggested that if you had specific questions you cared to ask that you might address them to the company; that if they were questions I could and might answer I would consider them, otherwise, if I knew of any other person to whom your questions might be directed I would consider forwarding such questions to them.

"I know of no individual who has the knowledge to respond to your general categories of factual curiosity; therefore I am returning your letter attached."

Threading one's way through the corporate tangle of the AA complex is as fascinating as it is frustrating. An idea of the scale of the CIA's air arm can be grasped as one company connection leads to another. Sometimes an airline would be wholly owned by the CIA, like AA, sometimes it would be partially funded by the Agency, and sometimes it could just be counted on for favors. Airlines partially funded and set up by the CIA were Air Ethiopia, Air Jordan, and Iran Air. An officer of United Business Associates, a related proprietary to Southern Capital—the central corporation in the CIA's insurance complex—explained one of the methods the Agency used to win over foreign governments.

UBA attempted to finance a national airline for Libya when it was still a kingdom. Several million dollars was made available to the company from other CIA proprietaries. "Our interest was to lend money for the purpose of controlling the airline," the officer said. "It was to offset the Communists from moving in. The way we set it up was like this: we had to offer them control over twenty percent of the stock of the corporation and we would lend them the money. Then we would have to put one of their natives alongside every American in a similar position. Talking about kickbacks, that's the name of the trade over there. That's how we covered the men of the cabinet. And if we ever called that note, they would have taken the franchise away."

In the case of Libya the UBA did not win the franchise but there were many other countries where the Agency was more successful. One of the men who was instrumental in working with the CIA to set up Air Iran in the early fifties was Orvis Nelson, an aviation veteran who set up sixteen airlines in his time. (He died in 1976.) Nelson claimed that he was never under the Agency's control and did not go into details about which of the airlines was involved with the CIA. But he knew as well as anybody the intelligence value of an airline.

"If I were sitting in a position where I was curious about what was going on in troubled areas, there are two things I'd be damn well interested in. The first is information. The second is transportation to get in and out, to get any information, and, perhaps, to do some other air activities. You have mobility. You know who and what are going in and out. You know who people's associates are. You are in a position to move your people about."

All of the airlines partially funded by the CIA would have a section of planes available to the Agency at any time.

The CIA also set up proprietaries for special operations. The Double-Chek Corporation, funded in Miami, was used to provide air support to Cuban exile groups and recruited the American pilots who flew the planes for the Bay of Pigs invasion. It also paid pensions to the widows of the four American pilots who lost their lives and warned them to keep quiet about their husbands' former activities. Similarly another Agency proprietary, CARAMAR (Caribbean Marine Aero Corp), hired the Cuban exile-pilots that flew B-26 bombers against Cuba.

The Agency's "operating" companies actually carried out business as private companies while its "non-operating" companies only prepared to do business. The latter varied in complexity according to their tasks and the most elaborate were legally licensed to conduct business with nominee stockholders, directors, and officers overseen by one of the Agency's proprietary management specialists. Air Ventures, Atlantic General Enterprises Inc., Aviation Investors Inc., Consultair Associates, and the King-Hurley Research group were all CIA non-operating proprietaries and among their jobs was the purchase of Helio-Courier planes which they provided cover for.

Certain American airlines have cooperated closely with the CIA. Continental set up a subsidiary in Laos, Continental Air Services, which provided cover for numerous CIA men and did exactly what the CIA asked them. In Panama the Agency had a deal with Pan Am in the mid-fifties which allowed CIA men to rummage through baggage during transit stops. The airline went as far as providing them with mechanics' overalls.

In the Far East AA goes back to 1946 when a "Chinese partnership" formed by Chennault and associates in October of that year were given a one-year CNRRA contract, commencing in January 1947 flying aircraft provided by the U.S. Government. The airline was called CNRRA Air Transport, but the name was changed to Civil Air Transport at the start of 1948 when the contract was not renewed.

Then in 1950 the CIA reorganized its air arm. The Far Eastern activities were grouped under the umbrella of The Pacific Corporation, originally incorporated in Delaware on July 10, 1950, as Airdale Corporation, which changed its name to Pacific on October 7, 1957. (In fact the CIA proprietaries were known euphemistically inside the Agency as "The Delaware Corporations." Delaware was chosen for their incorporation because of its lenient regulation of corporations.) The Pacific Corporation became the holding company of Air America, Inc., Air Asia Co., Ltd., and Civil Air Transport Ltd.

From the very outset there were managerial problems in running the somewhat unwieldy proprietary, which was overseen by the Office of Policy Coordination. "OPC was a curious organization, determined as being attached to the Agency for quarters and rationing, with policy guidance from State (the State Department), which was an impossible situation," Lawrence Houston stated. "Very nice fellows were doing the negotiating [for CAT] with OPC." Unknown to Houston, a deal was made which gave the vendors the right to repurchase at any time within two years.

"I thought this was really inconsistent with our whole position. And during the next two years they negotiated out that repurchase agreement and in its place substituted an agreement to give them a first refusal, if we were to dispose of the airline. That first refusal plagued us for years. They used to make all sorts of extraordinary claims under it, and it was never exercised and eventually it was sort of forgotten when the owners died."

During the early fifties there were two struggles over the air proprietary inside the Agency: where control should lie inside the Agency itself and what policies should apply to the operation of the company.

"The struggle within the Agency ranged all the way from sort of quiet management discussions as to what was good management, to sometimes rather vociferous arguments of who's in charge here," Houston said. "And the operators always said, 'Well, we need to call the shots because it's our operation.' And this is what we were running into all the time, of red-hot operators opposed to what we would consider good management."

In 1954 Houston went out to the Far East, accompanied by a consultant whose specific job was to examine the organization of the airline. The consultant declared it a mess. The airline's management was restructured in a way that made it more responsive to the Operations Directorate.

Civil Air Transport had several DC-4s and began modest operations between Hong Kong, Taipei, and Tokyo and soon acquired DC-6s. As the overt side of the airline's operations grew, the problem of direct competition with private corporations arose for the first time.

Northwest Orient Airlines was then flying to Tokyo, Seoul and Manila, and an executive of the company, who was chairman of the Civil Aeronautics Board in the late 1940s and early 1950s, had noted the CIA's interest in the area. "He became head of Northwest," Houston said, "a very tight manager, a very capable fellow, and he used to complain that we were interfering, we were taking passengers off his airline."

In 1959 he went to the Civil Aeronautics Board for a decision, maintaining that private industry should not be interfered with by government competition. The Agency argued the need for cover and said that they made every effort to restrict carriage to the minimum necessary to maintain it. Although some passengers traveled on CIA aircraft rather than Northwest planes, the impact was minimal and unavoidable, Houston claimed.

One of the members of the CAB turned to the head of Northwest during the hearing and said, "You ought to be glad that you don't have a really good, reliable competitor in there. If you were being competed with by private business, you'd have real headaches. You ought to be real glad it's not worse than it is." The CAB came down on the side of the Agency.

Later, in the mid sixties, a private company was to squeeze the CIA a little tighter. Continental Airlines had essentially the same objection as Northwest that it was questionable for a government-owned business to compete with private companies in seeking government contracts. Continental had been awarded lucrative non-CIA MATS (Military Air Transport System) contracts to fly troops to Vietnam and wanted a larger share of the profitable S.E. Asian business.

The CIA agreed to this on the basis that it could have back-up service if any country in S.E. Asia evicted Air America because of its CIA connections. Continental created a wholly owned, Nevada-registered subsidiary, Continental Air Services, and named old China-hand and CIA veteran Robert Rousselot, who had seventeen years' experience with CAT, as its president. Moreover, in August of the same year Continental paid more than a million in cash for the twenty-two aircraft and 350 employees of Bird Air, which had worked with and had contracts from the CIA for several years. R. L. "Dutch" Brongersma, who had been manager of Bird Air and also had associations with CAT, became the general manager of Continental Air Services.

The company was not to regret its move. AID (Agency for International Development) contracts alone totaled $24,288,000 until the close of business in mid 1972, and Continental president Robert F. Six could happily tell stockholders that the airline's operations in Laos, Thailand, and Vietnam were "very profitable." The CIA's Laotian air transport network was bolstered by Arizona Helicopters and Lao Air Development, companies which also benefited from the rich pickings of AID contracts put their way with the blessing of the Agency.

As the AA complex was essentially the CIA's Far East air operation, Southern Air Transport became the Caribbean and South American clandestine air arm. Although the corporation was technically a separate entity, not involved with AA, it was actually an integral part of the complex from a management perspective. All management decisions for Southern Air Transport were made by the same CIA consultant and advisory team that established AA policy.

As in the case of CAT, the CIA decided to buy an already existing company. SAT had been founded in 1949, and for the next twelve years F. C. "Doc" Moor and Stanley G. Williams tried to make a success of the small Miami-based company. They owned one C-46 and leased two others, and business consisted of flying cargo from Florida to the Caribbean and the Bahamas. The company was losing money, in debt, and had assets of little over $100,000.

This unsatisfactory state of affairs was transformed overnight with a wave of the clandestine wand. The CIA paid $300,000 for the company, Moor and Williams remained officers of the corporation and nominally owned 50 percent of the company. The airline acquired two DC-6s from Air America when the CIA took over on October 1, 1960, and immediately began to fly international MATS contracts to undisclosed destinations. Profits jumped to $75,000 within three months of the CIA takeover, the balance sheet showed assets over $2.5 million, and the company was no longer in debt.

SAT was built up as a contingency against the possibility of future Latin-American interventions, and the Agency did not want to depend on the U.S. Air Force. The official analysis of the intelligence community had concluded that political, economic, and social conditions in Latin America had deteriorated so badly that a long period of instability was at hand. The Agency wanted to be sure that it had the assets for any contingency.

SAT and AA have often overlapped in their activities in Africa, where the CIA's need for air support, especially in the Congo in the sixties, has been brisk. The CIA has had a financial interest in a plethora of companies, of which Pan African Airlines, based in Lagos, Nigeria, is a good example. Although not an outright proprietary, it has done considerable business with the CIA and 80 percent of its revenues comes from a single U.S. government contract for air service to remote outposts in West Africa, and the CIA is a major participant in that contract to the tune of $575,000 a year. (Seven Seas, an airline based in Nairobi, Kenya, has serviced certain of the CIA's needs in East Africa. Dag Hammarskjold, onetime United Nations secretary, was flying on a Seven Seas plane when he met his death in a mysterious and unexplained crash.) Pan African was set up in 1962 in close cooperation with the Agency and is considered to be a covert asset.

It is the largest subsidiary of Africair, the holding company of a Miami man named Thomas R. Green who runs a string of air companies in Florida, Africa, and the Caribbean. Green served on the board of directors of Southern Capital, the CIA insurance proprietary, while Africair's Washington attorney is James Bastian, the longtime attorney for Air America and onetime secretary of Air Asia. The man who owns 15 percent of Africair, Marvin L. Evans, ran Southern Capital for the CIA until his retirement in 1973. There are minor air companies all over the world which share this incestuous relationship with the CIA.

The CIA also leaned heavily on the USAF planes making the "embassy run" all over Africa—and the world—when embassies were flown in supplies. In Africa the CIA code name for this was Project Eagle and it had a huge, limitless potential.

SAT was also needed by the CIA because Air America had run into a technical difficulty. The airline had been deeply involved in a Military Air Transport System contract from the early fifties. MATS contracts kept the proprietary's air fleet in constant use and paid good rates. It was essential for AA to get these contracts if it was to maintain such a large inventory during times of paramilitary and covert inaction.

MATS changed its policy in 1956, requiring that bidders on their contracts be certified. As AA could not become certificated because of a technicality these contracts were switched to SAT; the money from them stayed in the family. But the air proprietaries were becoming increasingly complicated, and the CIA was getting involved in acquiring more and more aircraft which, in the words of Lawrence Houston, were getting "awfully damned expensive." It was felt inside the Agency that certain projects were demanding new and expensive equipment while in fact older aircraft were already available for the job.

It was decided that an amorphous group working on an informal basis should be created to keep abreast of the various air proprietaries. A February 5, 1963, memorandum entitled "Establishment of Executive Committee for Air Proprietary Operations" (dubbed EXCOMAIR) noted that the committee was "to provide general policy guidance for the management of air proprietary projects, and review final recommendations for approval of air proprietary project actions."

EXCOMAIR was an attempt to achieve overall coordination, conduct a thorough inventory of all the equipment that the Agency had in the aviation field, and keep track of who needed what. Lawrence Houston was appointed chairman of the committee, and representatives were appointed from the

Clandestine Services, the Support Directorate, and the Agency's executive suite. The proceedings were so secret that the executive secretary was instructed not to keep minutes or even take notes.

In 1968 EXCOMAIR met to deal with a request from George Doole for several million dollars to modernize SAT. He argued that as every major airline in the world was using jets, Southern needed to follow suit if it was to live its cover. He added that the airline should have the best and most effective equipment available in case the Agency needed to intervene in South America.

The request met with some opposition at the meeting from a CIA officer who quoted an intelligence estimate which had been presented to the President to the effect that open U.S. intervention in the internal affairs of Latin America would damage an already bad American image. A Clandestine Service officer working in paramilitary affairs replied, in effect, that however accurate the intelligence estimate might be, they had a responsibility to be prepared for the worst possible contingency. Doole's request was approved and SAT received its several million dollars for jets.

In addition to flying MATS contracts and covert missions, the airline also fulfilled far-flung commercial charters such as the multimillion-dollar one from AID to deliver relief supplies to Bangladesh. As a full member of CIA Air, SAT was able to benefit from the interchange of equipment, favorable loans, and government contracts and bought, leased, and sold planes within the empire.

Another large Stateside air proprietary was Intermountain Aviation, Inc., which operated from a former U.S. Air Force base in Marana, Arizona, just outside of Tucson. A subsidiary of a Nevada holding company called Pan Aero Investment Corporation, Intermountain was founded in the fall of 1961 as a direct result of the Agency's Bay of Pigs fiasco. Cuba had convinced the Agency that it could not depend on the U.S. Air Force for air cover and needed its own strike force. SAT had been formed to provide a long-haul heavy transport capability, while Intermountain was to provide close-in air support for guerrilla operations.

Intermountain's cover was that it acted as a storage base for U.S. and foreign aircraft, offered a full service and maintenance facility, and also provided a fire-fighting parachutist service for the U.S. Forest Service. In promotional material the company claimed to provide "total air support for remote operations." Intermountain helped train, supply, and deliver "smoke jumpers," who were able to drop into rough country from low altitudes to establish field camps from which remote operations could be carried out—activities which bear a close resemblance to the activity of special services and spy teams. Intermountain also had STOL aircraft, developed a pinpoint parachute-drop system, and repainted and reconfigured aircraft to special requirements.

The company provided a service and maintenance facility for all sizes and kinds of aircraft and had a virtually unlimited capacity for the reconfiguration of air frame, engine, ordnance, avionics, fuel, cargo, and passenger capacity. Marana, with its dry Arizona climate, was a good place to mothball planes in between covert missions, and they would be ferried back to the U.S. by AA pilots. Intermountain was a major operation.

The only area in which it was not equipped was helicopters, and this gap was filled by Arizona Helicopters, a subsidiary of a Delaware corporation called Air Services International which was based seventy-five miles away to the northwest in Scottsdale. Although there was no formal connection between the two companies, Arizona acted as the rotary wing of the fixed-wing Intermountain fleet and advertised "worldwide operations" which included contracts in Laos and Nepal.

Intermountain was used in 1965 as a conduit in the sale of B-26 bombers to Portugal for use in that country's colonial wars in Africa. Officially there was an explicit U.S. Government embargo on weapon exports for use in Angola, Mozambique, or Portuguese Guinea but unofficially the government, at its highest level, had decided to sell twenty B-26s and the CIA proprietary was following orders. Seven B-26s were flown from Arizona to Lisbon by an English pilot, John Richard Hawke, hired by a firm called Aero Associates.

The operations cover was so thin that Soviet and Hungarian representatives at the United Nations attacked the transaction. Accused of violating its own official policy, the United States could do little but deny the charge and look for scapegoats. John Hawke, the English pilot, and Francois de Marin, a Frenchman who had acted as middleman in the deal, were brought to trial in a federal court.

"Yes, I flew B-26 bombers to Portugal for use in their African colonies, and the operation was arranged through the State Department and the CIA," Hawke admitted. Lawrence Houston denied that the Agency had been involved in the transaction. He did admit that the Agency knew of the bomber shipment five days before it began but offered no explanation why it had not acted to stop it. Unconvinced that the two accused had deliberately violated the law, the jury found Hawke and Marin innocent.

Despite this, Intermountain's cover was not blown and it was not until August 1970 that the company's clandestine activities attracted the interest of the press. A small private plane flying at the extremely low altitude of five hundred feet over Tucson's National Golf Course crashed and exploded, killing both men inside. The press found it difficult to get anybody to comment on the incident.

The Federal Aviation Administration sent a special man from Washington, but he would say nothing. The plane, an experimental model of a Beechcraft S-32, had been on special lease to the UNIVAC division of Sperry Rand Corporation, which refused to comment. It had flown out of Intermountain's Marana Air Park, but naturally Intermountain did not want to talk about it. This stimulated interest among the local press, but they grew silent when Washington passed the word that to ask questions about the crash was to threaten the security of the nation.

Local editors asked Mo Udall, U.S. representative from Arizona's Second District, to take the matter up with the White House. In a letter to William E. Timmons, Deputy White House Assistant for House Relations, the congressman said that while he felt most Tucsonians were willing to accept the necessity to keep secret operations secret, they did expect their elected representative to know about them.

A high-level CIA staff officer visited Udall at his office and confirmed that there was classified work being carried out for the Agency at Marana, but denied that such operations were aimed primarily at Latin America. It was just a contact point for outfitting and maintaining aircraft for the CIA generally, the staff officer said. Udall passed on this information to the editors and left them to decide what they should print. They agreed to keep quiet.

* * *

Once the air proprietaries had been established and were running smoothly, they presented the CIA with a problem that was quite unique to the Agency—one of their operations, instead of costing millions, was making enormous amounts of money. What were they to do with the profits?

When I suggested to George Doole that this must have been a difficulty, he answered disparagingly, "Where were you brought up that profit was a difficulty?" Similarly the CIA's Chief of the Cover and Commercial Staff told Frank Church's Committee on Intelligence Activities that proprietaries were merely part of an arsenal of tools the Agency had to have in order to fulfill its job and that their operations were run for specific purposes unrelated to profit: "I am not in the business to make money," he said.

In fact there was a real fear of profits within the CIA because by law they were obliged to return them to the U.S. Treasury, a difficult operation to undertake without attracting attention. The obvious answer was to let the proprietaries reinvest their profits in themselves by buying new equipment and expanding.

During the early years of proprietary airlines the CIA had provided funds and subsidies, and although the companies had been greatly used, they essentially cost money rather than made it. There was even a period when the companies became inactive and the CIA debated whether it was worth the expense to keep them on. In between paramilitary operations there was little for the airlines to do, while they were saddled with expenses such as crews' salaries and the maintenance of grounded aircraft. The National Security Council considered in 1956 whether to continue to subsidize AA and decided to do so on the recommendation of Allen Dulles, then director.

When the proprietaries did begin to show a profit, a policy decision was called for. The CIA General Counsel ruled in 1958 that "income of proprietaries, including profits, need not be considered miscellaneous receipts to be covered into the Treasury but may be used for proper corporate or company purposes." The companies, which began to generate business in tens of millions a year, were allowed by the CIA to use their profits any way they saw fit. They conducted their own financial affairs with a minimum of oversight from CIA HQ.

It was largely the genius of George Doole and his organizational flair that made the proprietaries into prosperous concerns. Although revenues never quite covered the CIA's total capital investment, the huge contracts with AID (altogether AA has received $136 million in publicly recorded AID contracts in Southeast Asia) and the U.S. Air Force and so on made the Far Eastern proprietaries largely self-sufficient throughout the sixties. The booming business made certain high officials within the Agency uncomfortable, but they could not help but recognize the advantages. "There are things here better left undisturbed," the executive director said. "The point is that George Doole and CAT provide the Agency with a great number of services and the Agency doesn't have to pay for them."

One of the major criticisms that proprietaries attracted from those who were aware of their existence and the nature of their operation was that their profits were being used to provide secret funding for covert operations, a "back door" process that avoided inconvenient scrutiny by the Executive and the Congress. The CIA's far-flung commercial empire was able to fend off its own earnings as well as government funds. Proprietary revenues from outside the CIA averaged over $30 million per year (and only the CIA's insurance companies made a profit apart from the airlines) according to the Senate report. This, of course, is money earned independently of Congress and not reflected in the CIA budget, which is secret anyhow. Critics found it sinister that a clandestine service might have an independent income.

However, the Senate Committee, after hearing what the CIA had to say for itself, decided to give it a clean bill of health. In its final report it stated:

"In general, these mechanisms (proprietaries) have operated with a proper concern for legality, propriety, and ethical standards at the headquarters level. The deviations that have occurred were in the field and generally in the area of operations, rather than management personnel. Moreover, the use and past expansion of the proprietaries was a direct result of demands placed upon the Agency by Presidents, Secretaries of State, and the policy mechanisms of Government. This is particularly true of the large air proprietary complex used to support paramilitary operations in Southeast Asia."

In fact the committee was given much the same treatment that George Doole gave me. The Agency chose only to confirm the obvious, while the testimony of Lawrence Houston was vague and rambling. According to sources familiar with the committee's work, the staff conducted virtually no independent investigation, relying almost exclusively on records volunteered by the Agency. "The proprietary section of the report was done in the last month or two, and it was based on whatever the CIA told them," one source said. "The Agency wouldn't let them see, for example, the basic files on the air proprietaries."

The Agency pulled strings in other Government agencies, from the Civil Aviation Board to the Internal Revenue Service in order for AA's cover to remain intact. In the early sixties the company received an exemption from the Contract Renegotiation Board on the grounds that renegotiation personnel might discover the CIA was involved in the company. As a result the Agency was concerned that it was making 40 percent profit on the Air Force maintenance contracts, which may well have been the subject of renegotiation had it not been subject to the exemption. "So the question was what to do about it," Lawrence Houston said. "And finally we made a voluntary payment against part of the profit on that contract to the Air Force."

It was a small sop to the service which the CIA took so much from in the form of bailed aircraft and personnel. It was a continual source of antagonism to the military that the CIA, because of a variety of circumstances and a need for certain skills, "borrowed" a major or colonel from the Navy, the Army, the Marine Corps, or the Air Force. The Agency used these men to great advantage, but they did not pay them. The officer would still draw his salary from whatever force he had temporarily left. This was a constant irritant to the military, who had to justify every line of an open budget and had to pay for men they had no return from, while the CIA, which does not have to justify its budget in the same way, paid out nothing.

But being paid by the CIA was the least of the Air Force's worries when it came to dealing with air proprietaries. "The CIA wouldn't pay the bill most of the time because it wasn't sent to them, it wasn't rendered," Fletcher Prouty said. "Because we didn't care sometimes if they used an airplane and didn't pay us. What we cared about was the whole principle that we could plausibly deny involvement. That was our biggest problem."

Prouty headed an office in the Pentagon known as "Special Plans," which went under the code name "Team B," and dealt with the clandestine air activities of the CIA for which hundreds of military units had been created. The code name for the program that dealt with Air Force-owned aircraft bailed to the CIA (or CIA owned planes flown about with Air Force markings) was Tab-6, which had sub-categories and coded project names for operations in Tibet, Indonesia, Laos, Africa and so on. The USAF kept records on Tab-6 aircraft in a special office in Dayton, Ohio, where a Tab-6—cleared individual, Robert Poe, was in charge. Poe had direct contact with the Pentagon through a Robert Freyvogel. It was extremely problematical to plant something as necessarily flexible and irregular as Tab-6 into a rigid, run-of-the-mill organization like the Air Force which had set procedures and standards.

In the civilian world the CIA had to square away such organizations as the Internal Revenue Service. The air proprietaries had been told from the outset that they would be required to pay appropriate taxes and in the mid fifties AA received notice of an upcoming audit by the IRS. Company officials went to the Agency and said that such an investigation might pose a security problem.

The CIA decided the audit could be used as a check on the company's cover. They went to the commissioner of the IRS and asked for the audit to be conducted by a team on an unwitting basis to see what they could learn. Later those conducting the audit were told they had begun to look into an Agency proprietary and it was discontinued. "We thought it would be a good test of the security arrangements," Lawrence Houston said.

"They put a very bright young fellow on and he went into it. They came up with discrepancies and things that would be settled in the normal tax argument—the corporate—IRS argument—and all of these were worked out eventually." Then the CIA disclosed to the young accountant that the company was owned by them and asked him what he had suspected as he conducted the audit.

"Well, I knew there was something there, and I thought, what a wonderful asset it would be for the Russians to have,

but I came to the conclusion that it was Rockefeller money."
Later on when a conduit company was threatened with an
audit, a former U.S. official said, the IRS would get a call
from the CIA saying, "Get your people off their backs."

AA's security proved to be so tight that even IRS investigators were confused. (Had the bright young fellow continued
the audit, he would have come across an accounting quirk
common to many CIA proprietaries: reports listed exactly the
same figures for all categories under assets and liabilities,
year in and year out.) An army colonel, George Wertenbaten,
was placed inside the Federal Aviation Authority, who in
turn thought he came from the Defense Department.

But behind the paperwork of corporate complexity, inter-
departmental wrangling, and bogus bookkeeping the CIA airlines were very real indeed and went about their myriad
operations, ranging from flying passengers to waging war,
unhindered.

FOUR

SECRET MISSIONS

CAT flourished through the Korean War, owing to its many airlift contracts from the U.S. military for cargo and passenger flights between Korea, Japan, Okinawa, Guam, Manila and many other Pacific ports of call. The busy national airline of Taiwan was flying legitimate business to all the places where the CIA had major operational offices. What was more, the airline even had a good public relations image, and back home in the States the few people who had heard of it thought of it in terms of the heroic exploits of its daredevil pilots. More extraordinary still, it made money. The CIA could hardly believe its luck.

The airline was able to undertake special flights without attracting comment when the CIA had a requirement at its secret bases in Okinawa, the Marianas Islands and elsewhere. It was busy enough to provide cover for a multitude of secret operations. A top-secret memo written by Brig. General Edward Lansdale described the airline's role: "CAR, a CIA proprietary, provides air logistical support under commercial cover to most CIA and other U.S. government agencies' requirements. CAT supports covert and clandestine air operations by providing trained and experienced personnel, procurement of supplies and equipment through overt commercial channels, and the maintenance of a fairly large inventory of transport and other type aircraft under both the Chinat (Chinese Nationalist) and U.S. registry.

"CAT has demonstrated its capability on numerous occasions to meet all types of contingency or long-term covert air requirements in support of U.S. objectives. During the past ten years, it has had some noticeable achievements, including support of the Chinese Nationalist withdrawal from the mainland, air-drop support for the Indonesian operation, the air lifts of refugees from North Vietnam, more than two hundred overflights of Mainland China and Tibet, and extensive air support in Laos."

It is clear that the CIA's air arm was considered a great logistical success in itself although the operations it was involved in were often failures in the long term. The "Indonesian operation" supported the rebels who fought the Sukarno government, while the 200 overflights referred to CIA guerrilla operations and spy drops in China and Tibet. Other operations in which the CIA's air power was essential were in a successful coup in Guatemala and a lifeline to Chinese Nationalist troops driven from China's Yünnan province into Burma. These are not operations normally associated with a commercial airline.

During the fifties the CIA began to use CAT to drop guerrilla teams into China and for overflights. The American CIA agents John T. Downey and Richard G. Fecteau were aboard a CAT plane when it was shot down by the communists in November 1952. It was officially claimed that the men were employees of the "Department of the Army" and the CIA was so determined to maintain this cover that the agents were left in Red Chinese jails for twenty years. Fecteau was released in December 1971, shortly before Richard Nixon's trip to Peking, but Downey was detained until March 1973 when Nixon finally acknowledged publicly at a press conference that Fecteau was a CIA agent.

BURMA

It was in Burma that the CIA undertook its first secret war and, together with logistical air support, attempted to invade Communist China on three occasions.

While many of the defeated Nationalist Chinese troops were evacuated to Taiwan, other remnants of the army crossed the border into Burma. Once there, the CIA began to regroup them in the Shan States in one of the most heavily classified operations ever undertaken by the Agency. It was so secret that top-ranking officials in the State Department were completely unaware of it, so was the U.S. ambassador to Burma, who was put in the humiliating position of constantly denying its existence. Even the CIA's own deputy director for intelligence did not know of it.

There were originally fifteen hundred Kuomintang troops who had entered Burma and then refused to surrender to the Burmese Army. This band made its base fifteen miles from the Thai border, in mountain country and the Burmese Army, with four major rebellions already on its hands, was too weak to shift them.

The CIA intended to mold this stateless army into a border force that would create an impenetrable barrier stretching from Tibet to Thailand. Burmese intelligence officers reported that unmarked C-46s and C-47s were making at least five parachute drops a week to KMT forces in their mountain fastness. A constant, reliable air supply line meant the army could grow and the Burma-China border was scoured for KMT stragglers until before long it was four thousand strong. A base camp was opened on the Chinese border where unmarked C-47s made air drops of supplies and ammo. The KMT's general was also spotted commuting between Taiwan and Burma by way of a landing strip in Thailand.

In April 1951 the first attempt at the reconquest of China's Yünnan province was launched. Two thousand troops of the Yünnan Province Anti-Communist National Salvation Army, accompanied by CIA advisers and supplied by regular air drops from C-47s, crossed the border into China. They moved northward in two columns, but were driven back by the People's Liberation Army in less than a week. Casualties were terrible, including several dead CIA advisers. Another contingent two thousand strong was sent across the border in southern Yünnan and was similarly overwhelmed and driven back into Burma.

Undeterred, the CIA intensified its efforts. An old World War II landing strip was reopened to allow large two- and four-engined aircraft to fly in directly from Taiwan or Bangkok. A CAT airlift brought seven hundred regular KMT soldiers from Taiwan, and Burmese intelligence reported that the C-47s began a regular shuttle service with two flights a week. A Bangkok-based CIA front company, the Sea Supply Corporation, began forwarding enormous quantities of U.S. arms to the base. The KMT were equipped with brand new M-1s, .50 caliber machine guns, bazookas, mortars, and antiaircraft artillery and had enough to spare to recruit eight thousand more troops from the surrounding hill tribes, tripling its force to twelve thousand men.

As this army prepared itself for yet another invasion of China, it used its new muscle to indulge in banditry and take control of the local opium trade. It extended its territory to include Burma's major opium-producing region and monopolized all of Yünnan's illicit opium production. It virtually became a nation state. Revenue collection centers were opened, locals were forced to pay various gate and ferry fees, and customs duties were levied on all commodities brought into territories controlled by the stateless army. Hill-tribe farmers were required to pay an annual opium tax, which was collected in kind. The opium was sent south to Thailand either by mule train or aircraft, and Burmese military sources claimed that much of it was flown out in unmarked C-47s to Thailand or Taiwan.

The broker for opium in Thailand was the notorious General Phao, a virulent anti-Communist and the CIA's man in the country. The general has been variously described as "a superlative crook" by *The New York Times* and "the worst man in the whole history of modern Thailand" by a respected Thai diplomat. The general protected KMT supply shipments, backed their political aims, and guaranteed support for them among the Chinese community in Thailand. In the CIA's eyes this unholy alliance provided a secure rear area for the KMT.

The final invasion of China was launched in August 1952, penetrated sixty miles across the border, and was then driven back. Although they did not expect to overrun Yünnan with a force of twelve thousand men, the CIA were confident that the peasants would rise up against Mao and flock to General Chiang Kai-shek's banner. This they conspicuously did not do.

Having failed in China the KMT turned their attention to Burma itself, and late in 1952 launched a full-scale invasion of the eastern part of the country. After one skirmish Burmese soldiers discovered the bodies of three white men who bore no identification other than some personal letters with Washington and New York addresses. Burma was obliged to send three crack brigades to drive the invaders back.

Throughout this period Burma had officially pleaded with the United States to apply pressure on Taiwan to withdraw the troops. Unofficially the CIA was accused of supporting the troops. The luckless United States ambassador, having demanded assurances from his superiors that this was not the case and been told emphatically that the United States was not involved, passed on the disclaimer. These denials became so ludicrous that the Burmese Chief of Staff of the Army finally told him flatly at a diplomatic gathering, "Mr. Ambassador, I have it cold. If I were you, I'd just keep quiet."

The Burmese government claimed that the Chinese Nationalists were attempting to take over the entire country and charged them before the U.N. with unprovoked aggression. Despite a vote of censure for Taiwan and agreement between a Four Nation Military Commission (Burma, the United States, Taiwan, and Thailand) to complete KMT withdrawal from Burma, the guerrillas refused to go. Only after Burma took the issue to the U.N. once more was there an agreement to withdraw two thousand KMT troops. CAT was to fly them to Taiwan after they had marched to the Thai border.

The withdrawal was a farce. The Burmese delegation was not allowed near the staging area by Thai police commander General Phao, and the first batch of fifty soldiers emerged from the jungle carrying an enormous portrait of Chiang instead of their guns. When the United States put pressure on the KMT to bring out their weapons, Chiang responded by threatening to expose CIA support of the KMT in Burma. Of a total of seven thousand persons flown to Taiwan a high percentage were women, children, and crippled noncombatants.

Most of the 1,925 soldiers eventually evacuated were boys and members of Burmese hill tribes and the weapons they brought out with them were rusting museum pieces. Half of the guerrilla force, and the best of them, remained in Burma. Impatient with their attempts to expel the KMT through diplomacy, the Burmese Air Force bombarded and captured their base and drove its two thousand defenders south to the Thai border. In the next two months CAT flew a further four thousand five hundred KMT troops to Taiwan.

This still left six thousand troops in Burma, and fighting was to continue for seven years. Throughout this time there was evidence of air support to the KMT and U.S. supplied weapons. In the year following the "withdrawal" the Burmese press reported that six hundred KMT troops had been smuggled back into the Shan States from Taiwan. A new commander was appointed, a new HQ set up, and the KMT continued its role as opium baron. When the Burmese army overran one of their camps in May 1959, they discovered three morphine base refineries operating near a usable airstrip.

The KMT continued its activity from its new base near the Mekong until 1960 when Burma made a secret agreement with the Chinese Communists for combined operations against them. Ten thousand KMT troops defended their main base, an elaborate fortifications complex complete with a runway capable of handling the largest transport aircraft. After weeks of heavy fighting five thousand Burmese troops and three full divisions of the People's Liberation Army finally overwhelmed the fortress on January 26, 1961. Inside the base, American arms of recent manufacture and five tons of ammunition bearing distinctive red, white, and blue labels were discovered. The following month a U.S. World War II Liberator bomber was shot down en route from Taiwan with supplies for the guerrillas. A note of protest was sent to the U.N.

The State Department disclaimed all responsibility for the arms and promised appropriate action against Taiwan if investigation showed that its military-aid shipments had been diverted to Burma. Taiwan also refused to accept responsibility. The weapons had been supplied by the "Free China Relief Association," it insisted, and had been flown to the guerrillas in private planes.

CAT began to airlift four thousand two hundred KMT troops back to Taiwan until the government announced the end of the flights and disowned the six thousand who remained. The crack KMT units which had retreated across the Mekong into northwest Laos were to be hired within months by the CIA for a secret war they were to conduct in that country. If their airline had provided effective support throughout the Burmese operation, it was to become indispensable in Laos.

INDONESIA

It had been a dangerous mission and the pilot had carried it out successfully. Allen Lawrence Pope had just completed a bombing and strafing run on the Ambon Island airstrip in the Moluccas, part of Indonesia, in a specially modified B-26 bomber which had been fitted with a nose assembly for eight .50 caliber machine guns. On the face of it Pope was just another of a group of aerial mercenaries flying in support of a rebel insurrection aimed at overthrowing the pro-Communist leader President Sukarno. And, but for misfortune, that is what those few people in the world who paid any interest at all to the incident would have believed: an eccentric American fighting in an obscure war in an unheard-of place.

As Pope banked his plane and prepared for the flight home, he was hit by antiaircraft fire. The right wing burst into flame, the plane spun out of control and plunged toward the sea, and in view of the events over the following months there were to be many people in Washington who fervently wished that Pope had gone down with it. But the pilot managed to jump clear, and he drifted toward a small coral reef where his chute was snagged on a coconut tree. Pope was captured intact except for a broken leg. One of the CIA's most ambitious, and disastrous, projects to date was about to be exposed.

Throughout the rebel uprising in Indonesia the U.S. government had gone out of its way to emphasize its hands-off, neutral policy toward what it stressed it considered to be an internal affair. When the rebels formally appealed for American arms, they were told flatly by John Foster Dulles, "The U.S. views this trouble in Sumatra as an internal matter. We try to be absolutely correct in our international proceedings and attitude towards it. And I would not want to say anything which might be looked upon as a departure from that high standard."

Rebel air attacks on the central government continued to be reported by Jakarta until the premier asserted he had proof of overt foreign assistance to those rebels in the form of planes and automatic weapons. "As a consequence of the actions taken by the U.S. and Taiwan adventurers, there has emerged a strong feeling of indignation amongst the armed forces and people of Indonesia against the United States and Taiwan. And if this is permitted to develop, it will only have a disastrous effect in the relationships between Indonesia and the U.S."

The States were playing with fire which could lead to a

third world war, President Sukarno warned. They had decided to fight the rebels on their own, he continued, but there were thousands of volunteers available if they wanted, a veiled allusion to a secret offer of pilots from Peking.

In the face of these charges the U.S. President himself, Dwight D. Eisenhower, called a press conference and emphatically denied any involvement. "Our policy is one of careful neutrality and proper deportment all the way through so as not to be taking sides where it is none of our business.

"Now, on the other hand, every rebellion that I have ever heard of has its soldiers of fortune. You can start even back to reading your Richard Harding Davis. People were looking out for a good fight and getting into it, sometimes in the hope of pay, and sometimes just for the heck of the thing. That is probably going to happen every time you have a rebellion."

Three weeks after this pronouncement Allen Pope was shot down. The Indonesian government withheld the fact for nine days that an American pilot had been captured. When they did announce it, the American ambassador to Indonesia was naturally quick to explain that he was "a private American citizen involved as a paid soldier of fortune."

The Indonesians had good reason not to take this statement at its face value. In Washington there was a diplomatic scramble to keep Sukarno sweet—and silent. Within five days the State Department approved the sale of badly needed rice for local currency, and an embargo on $100,000 of small arms, aircraft spares, and radio equipment was lifted. It was assumed by the CIA that Pope was "clean" when he was taken, and that he carried no incriminating material.

At a news conference called by the Indonesian Army this optimism was shattered. Documents and ID papers showing that Pope had served both in the U.S. Air Force and as a pilot for CAT were produced, and he was said to have been on a $10,000 contract. Philippine pesos, 28,000 Indonesian rupiahs, and U.S. scrip for use on American military installations were found on him. It was said that there were between three hundred and four hundred Americans, Filipinos, and Nationalist Chinese aiding the rebels, and Pope was accused of bombing a marketplace where a large number of civilians were killed on their way to church.

The CIA was not mentioned by name, but it came as a shock that the Indonesians had so much documentary information. They had official reports that all the men on the mission had gone through a rigorous security inspection before the flight. Crew members were supposed to strip naked and be examined by proper authorities to ensure they had no personal effects or ID upon them. Only then were they supposed to proceed to a room where nothing but the flight clothes they were to wear was available. This procedure was clearly more to the advantage of the CIA than to the pilots, who knew very well that if they were captured and found to be stateless they would have no legal right to appeal to the United States and would almost certainly be shot as spies. The CIA saw this as part of the deal, but most pilots did not. Pope probably had his papers hidden somewhere in his plane, and the fact that he could prove beyond doubt that he was an American on official government business changed his status from that of expendable adventurer to valuable political pawn.

But apart from showing a developed sense of survival, the pilot proved to be tight-lipped. The details of one of the CIA's most ambitious foreign projects remained secret. In fact it was a big operation.

The CIA had originally made contact with an Indonesian attaché in Washington and made it clear that it was prepared to support rebel leaders from one end of the Indonesian island chain to the other. An HQ was established in Singapore where Frank Wisner, the Deputy Director of Plans for the CIA, went personally to head the operation. Training bases were set up in the Philippines, together with airstrips on remote territory. An old World War II airfield on a deserted island in the southwest Pacific was reopened and prepared for bomber and transport operations. Vast stores of arms and equipment were supplied, the U.S. army took part in training the rebels, and the Navy made over-the-beach submarine backup support available. A fleet of fifteen B-26 bombers from the Korean War were supplied by the Air Force which spent a considerable amount of money modifying them and ensuring that the planes were nonattributable and that all airborne equipment was "deniable" (these B-26s served the CIA well and passed back and forth among the Agency's air proprietaries in the course of being used in the Congo rebellion, the Bay of Pigs Invasion, and Vietnam).

Tens of thousands of rebels were armed and equipped from

the air and over the beach, and rebellion broke out in various parts of the island chain. The struggle dragged on, and the CIA threw everything it could muster into the attack. The Indonesian Army was forced to deal with the uprisings one at a time, and while they launched a full-scale counteroffensive on the main island of Sumatra, it seemed that the rebels would be victorious on the other islands. Eventually the rebels proved unable to win decisive victories or enlist the aid of neutrals, and the war turned in favor of the loyalist forces. This failure in Indonesia led to the firing of Frank Wisner and the ignominious breaking up of the whole team which had worked on the program.

The pilot Allen Pope was comfortably interned in a small bungalow in the mountains of central Java, where he received good medical treatment for his broken leg. As an individual, he certainly had all the personality traits of the soldier of fortune. He had dropped out of the University of Florida to bust broncos in Texas and had volunteered for the Korean War, where he flew fifty-five night missions over Communist lines. The end of the war created a vacuum in his life. He returned to Texas, married, and worked for a local airline, but found the life dull after combat. The marriage ended in early divorce, and Pope signed on with CAT and was one of the pilots who braved Communist flak to drop supplies at Dien Bien Phu.

He renewed his contract and after three years was a captain earning $1,000 a month. He lived in a villa outside of Saigon, remarried, and spent his leisure time big-game hunting in the South Vietnamese jungle. But life had become settled again, so when the CIA approached him to fly combat missions in Indonesia he was intrigued.

President Sukarno kept Pope on ice for nineteen months as a hostage to continued American overtures. The pilot was eventually brought to trial before a military court and accused of flying six bombing raids for the rebels and killing twenty-three Indonesians, seventeen of them members of the armed forces. Pope pleaded not guilty and the trial went on for four months.

He admitted to flying one combat mission—the one he had been shot down on—but testified that the others were of a reconnaissance or noncombat nature. He said that he was not on a $10,000 contract, but was paid only $200 a flight (a much more likely arrangement). Pope's diary containing detailed entries of various bombing missions was produced by the prosecution, but the pilot claimed it referred to activities of all the rebel pilots. When asked what his "real motive" was in joining the rebels he stated, "Your Honor, I have been fighting the Communists since I was twenty-two years old—first in Korea and later Dien Bien Phu."

Pope was sentenced to death. An appeal was rejected by the appeals court and he took the case to the military supreme court. It seemed unlikely that the death penalty would be carried out, as it had not been since Indonesia had gained independence eleven years before. Even so, it was not until 1962, when Kennedy was President and relations between the United States and Sukarno had improved, that he was freed. He had been a prisoner for four years.

Pope was let out of prison without prior notice, taken to the U.S. embassy for interrogation, and then put aboard a Military Air Transport Service plane and flown back to the United States. He was kept hidden away for seven weeks before the State Department revealed his release. Back in Miami, his life disintegrated. Within six months his second wife had filed for divorce, charging him with "extreme cruelty" and "habitual indulgence in a violent and ungovernable temper."

The case developed an odd atmosphere of secrecy and intrigue about it. "There's an awful lot of cloak-and-dagger mixed up in this," his wife's Miami lawyer said. "I can understand it, but I don't have to like it." He refused to comment further.

In fact Mrs. Pope had been told by a security agent of the government that any mention of her husband's CIA connection at the divorce hearing would be detrimental to her case. She heeded the warning and left the CIA out of it, but testified that since her husband's return from Indonesia he had insisted upon keeping a loaded .38 caliber pistol by their bedside, despite the danger to their two young boys. She also testified that she had only been given $450 since her husband had left her seven months before. Pope did not contest the divorce, and his wife won the action and custody of the children on grounds of cruelty. There was no financial settlement because Pope was declared outside of the jurisdiction of the court.

He was back within the family embrace of the CIA's air proprietaries, except this time one of the company's initials was different and it was not CAT but SAT—Southern Air Transport—that he was working for. Like CAT, SAT had offices in Taipei, but it had a home base at Miami International Airport. The company's Miami attorney (Alex E. Carlson, the lawyer for the Double-Chek Corporation, which had hired the American pilots who flew at the Bay of Pigs) explained that the company was a small cargo line which "flies chickens from the Virgin Islands." Translated into more direct truth, Southern Air Transport was the CIA's Caribbean and South American air arm which also fulfilled certain contracts in the Far East. Pope had put his belongings into storage (which included ten stuffed birds, four animal heads, one stuffed animal, antelope antlers, and water buffalo horns) and left the country to pursue further his career as a clandestine airman.

TIBET

Back in 1948 the Dalai Lama of Tibet had requested CAT to inaugurate an airmail service to China, where traditionally correspondence was carried the four hundred miles by human runners. Only one airmail trip was actually made by the airline, but it was to have other dealings with the remote, mountainous country with a cargo more lethal than letters.

Tibet is a mysterious country which straddles the Himalayas and the clouds between India in the south and China in the north. It has been cut off from the rest of the world for centuries, a place hardly imaginable for Western man except as a romantic Shangri-la, untouched by modern civilization. The lives of its thinly scattered 1,300,000 population were mostly taken up with spiritual pursuits, and its capital, Lhasa, was a city of Buddhist monks and temples. Its ruler, the Dalai Lama, is considered by his subjects to be a manifestation of the absolute Buddha in human form and is revered as a god.

Then in 1950 Communist China invaded Tibet and, despite fierce opposition and guerrilla fighting, had complete control over the country within a year. Although the Dalai Lama was allowed to remain on the throne, many of his loyal guard, the fearsome Khamba horsemen, fled as refugees and began to filter across the borders of India, Nepal, and northern Thailand.

As sporadic fighting continued throughout the fifties, the CIA decided to recruit specially screened Khambas and train them. They were to be given full air support by CAT, which meant they were to be totally dependent on long-range air transportation for all their food and ammunition. Anthony Poe, a CIA field officer who was to become a legend in the clandestine warfare of the Far East, began to recruit Khamba tribesmen who had escaped into northeastern India. He then escorted them to a secret training base inside the United States.

The idea was to teach the most promising Tibetan warriors guerrilla warfare skills, equip them with up-to-date weapons, and then send them back into Tibet either on foot or by parachute drop. It was important that the base within the States provided similar conditions to those in Tibet, were the *average* altitude is fifteen thousand feet. The Agency decided on Leadville, a town situated in the Rocky Mountains of central Colorado and the highest in the country. Nearby was a site made to order. Only fifteen miles to the north in a secluded valley at nine thousand three hundred feet, surrounded by mountain peaks, was the old Army base of Camp Hale, which had been used to train ski troops in the Second World War. Even more attractive to the Agency was the position of Camp Hale—it was almost as remote as Tibet itself. In 1957, the first Tibetans were flown to the camp, where a vigorous training program was put into operation, the air arm of which was provided by Intermountain Aviation, yet another of the Agency's growing number of proprietaries. As they completed their training, the men were to be flown back to the Far East, both to Taiwan and Chiang Mai in Thailand, the initial staging posts from which they were then to be infiltrated into Tibet or China on long-range sabotage operations. The program mostly used C-130s because they had adequate range and altitude and, better still, a rear door which could be opened in flight to allow troops to jump out. Sometimes the planes would fly in moonlight so clear that the high Himalayas could be seen one hundred miles before they reached them. Operations officials at the Agency directed the crews to fly as low and close to the horizon as they could with safety so that their radar profile would be obscured by ground clutter. The disadvantage was that flying low played havoc with long-range navigational signals from remote sites, so when the crew flew combat teams into remote areas of Tibet or western China, the navigator would have to take star shots to verify the electronic navigator signals he received, which grew dimmer and less reliable as each hour passed.

The Khambas themselves would sit quietly beside the heavy airdrop pallets that lined the center compartment of the plane. Usually they would be accompanied by Agency men who would sit in the forward area of the huge cargo compartment, wiling away the time by playing nickel-and-dime poker and occasionally getting up to pour coffee from the plane's airborne kitchen hot plate.

There was nowhere in Tibet where a plane could safely land and take off, so these operations had the disadvantage of having no pickup capability. This proved to be a weakness on several counts. Primarily the CIA could not retrieve agents, and in many cases it was obvious that pilots would not have enough fuel to return to Chiang Mai. Missions usually took all the range a C-130 had and a little more, which made precise navigation and careful verification of wind conditions essential, as any major shifts in strength and direction could effect the range. Pilots often had to land in India, which technically constituted an emergency landing except that preparations would be made ahead of time. This was awkward because the Indians did not like the arrangement, fearing its discovery would lead to trouble with China, and fussed about it constantly. The Agency enjoyed a better relationship with Pakistan, in the days when Bangladesh was still East Pakistan.

Much of the Tibetan guerrillas' energy was spent on mining the two major roads between Tibet and China, which the CIA hoped would slow down the flow of Chinese men and material moving into the country. Communication lines were cut, there was intermittent sabotage, and occasionally a force of Chinese Communists would be ambushed. Essentially it was a policy of harassment, but the CIA were happy to bolster the Tibetans' impossible dream of ousting the Communists.

A rumor that the Chinese intended to abduct the Dalai Lama created an uprising within the country in 1959. Communist generals in Lhasa had invited the Tibetan leader to attend a play which was to be put on by the Chinese military. The Dalai Lama suspected a plot, and when his followers heard of the invitation they surrounded the palace to protect him and prevent him from going. The Chinese opened fire with mortars.

It was to be a short-lived and ineffective rebellion, and the Dalai Lama had to flee for his life. It is probable that without the expertise of the Colorado-trained Tibetans, and the handful of CIA case officers who accompanied them, the escape would not have been successful.

The Dalai Lama slipped out of his palace disguised as a soldier and, accompanied by a handful of loyal aides and members of his family, made his way through the steep mountain passes into rebel-held territory. As he moved south his party grew, swollen by guerrillas and soldiers loyal to their leader. When he crossed the border into India, where he was granted political asylum, his following had grown to a party of several thousand.

Inside Tibet itself open warfare broke out between the natives and the Chinese army. Infuriated by the Dalai Lama's escape, the Chinese were merciless and thousands of Tibetans lost their lives. CAT transport planes continued to supply the rebels, while Chinese troops moved across the border in Bhutan, Sikkim, and India and there were frequent skirmishes.

The training at Camp Hale intensified. One of the CIA's major preoccupations throughout the years of this program was security. Remote as the camp was, it would not do for any of Leadville's 4,314 residents to come across stray Tibetans. Secrecy was effectively maintained for a long time, but a cover story was necessary to stop local gossip about what went on up at Camp Hale. A story was planted in the *Denver Post* to the effect that the Defense Atomic Support Agency was carrying out a top-secret testing program at the camp, while there were also assurances that this work did not include the setting off of nuclear weapons. The *Post* reported that the exact nature of the program was highly classified and that nobody was saying precisely what was being tested. The camp was administratively attached to Fort Carson in Colorado Springs, the newspaper continued, but that even top officials there did not know what was going on. Thus mystified, the residents were also directly threatened when the Fort Carson public information officer was quoted as saying: "I was told a quick way of being put in jail is even to ask what they are doing. It's so secret."

And secret it stayed for a while and might have remained so except for an unfortunate accident. In the early hours of a hard midwinter morning on December 7, 1961, fifteen Tibetans, accompanied by an armed American troops, boarded an Army bus which had its windows painted black and started on the 129-mile journey to Colorado Springs. Under cover of darkness they were to board a C-124 at Petersen Field, an airfield six miles east of the town serving both as a municipal airport and a USAF base, but coming down, the bus skidded off the treacherous, icy mountain road into the snow. The accident held them up for hours, and when they arrived at the airfield it was daylight.

Employees of the Kensair Corporation, a small aviation company on the airfield which operated a flying school and sold Piper airplanes, were in their hangar having their morning coffee. The hangar was situated next to an area used by the Air Force. Kensair's manager Henry "Hank" Wood had noticed an Air Force C-124 Globemaster parked next to his company's small Piper Colt which was about to be taken out by a twenty-year-old student pilot. As the men sipped their coffee Bill Watts, who ran the flight school, burst into the hangar.

"Hank, we're surrounded," Watts said breathlessly. "There are guys out there with guns. They told us to get back in the hangar, push our airplane back in the building, and lock the door."

Hank Wood scarcely believed what he had heard, put down his coffee, and went outside to see what was going on for himself. A young GI dressed in green battle fatigues with a particularly unpleasant manner told him to halt. Hank Wood lost his temper and shouted, "You get off my property—what in hell is going on here?"

"Get back inside," the GI snarled, pulling a pistol and sticking it in Wood's face. The manager did what he was told, convinced that the young soldier would have no compunction at pulling the trigger. Under orders from the soldiers, who were armed with automatic rifles and machine guns, Kensair employees rolled their Piper Colt back inside the hangar and the door was shut on them.

Trapped inside, Wood called the local sheriff and told him

they were surrounded by armed troops. To the sheriff it sounded as if it could be a hijack attempt, so he rounded up two deputies and raced out to the airfield in a police car.

Halfway across the airfield it was stopped by armed MPs, and an officer politely told the sheriff he could go no further. Agents from the Army's Criminal Investigation Division were also stopped. Employees of the Maytag Aircraft Corporation were detained in a nearby hangar while a telephone repairman about his business up a pole on the field was ordered down by a soldier armed with a pistol.

At this time the Army bus rolled up, and the Kensair employees witnessed what they rightly held to be an extraordinary spectacle. "There was fifteen Orientals got out of the bus and onto the plane. They were wearing some type of uniform—green fatigues, just like the GIs. Each one of these Orientals had a white tag around his neck. As each man got on the Globemaster, someone at the door checked the tag." Mechanic Harold Ravnsborg had his camera in the hangar and took shots out of the window.

About an hour and twenty minutes later the Globemaster took off and the armed guards departed in their jeeps. The stunned employees were left to gossip among themselves and speculate what had happened. *The Colorado Springs Gazette Telegraph* carried a brief story that same afternoon saying that civilians had been held at gunpoint and that Henry Wood had been stuck up by a soldier. The Army refused to comment.

Later the same day a high-ranking Army officer from Fort Carson arrived on the airfield and lined up the Kensair employees in the manager's office. "We had to hold up our hands and swear we wouldn't talk about it for six months," Wood said. "He had a book with him and he read the law to us. He was telling us all the things that could happen to us if we talked about it. The guy threatened us; he said we were under the highest secrecy in the world." The officer told them it was a federal offense even to discuss the incident. Amateur photographer Harold Ravnsborg was so unnerved by the talk that he quietly removed the film from his camera and burned it.

The following day two Denver newspapers ran stories on the mysterious episode at the airport. An Army spokesman issued an official apology: "The Army regrets the poor judgment used in handling this affair and also regrets any repressive measures which may have been taken by Army military policemen." Brig. Gen. Ashton H. Manhart, the commander of Fort Carson, stated: "We were involved in a very sensitive project. It was a matter involving national security."

When the story went over the services, it seemed like a minor incident but a bizarre one. A reporter in the Washington bureau of *The New York Times* thought that civilians held at gunpoint in Colorado Springs, saying they had seen what they thought to be Chinese soldiers, was worth a follow-up call to the Pentagon. Within minutes the Pentagon called back to ask *The Times* to kill the story on the grounds that it would be detrimental to national security. The story might raise the tension between Washington and Peking to a dangerous level. *The Times* accepted the government's argument and agreed to dig no further.

There was great relief at the CIA, whose long anonymity was fast dissolving. In the wake of the U-2 Affair and the disastrous Bay of Pigs invasion of Cuba, the American public were getting to know the Agency on account of its blunders. A further disclosure of the high-risk Tibetan project, which sounded similar to the training of Cubans in Guatemala for the Bay of Pigs Invasion, would have brought trouble and embarrassment down on the heads of the CIA.

It had been clear that the Tibetan operation could only harass the Chinese, although the CIA special operations officers encouraged their Tibetan trainees to believe that they were being prepared for the reconquering of their homeland. Certain CIA operators even believed their own propaganda and came close enough to their men to join them in esoteric Buddhist prayer. According to Victor Marchetti, CIA analyst and coauthor of *The Cult of Intelligence*, this phenomenon of emotional attachment is not rare in the clandestine business and is particularly prevalent in special operations. The officers who engage in special operations often have a deep psychological need to belong and believe. Several who worked directly with the Tibetans felt they had been undone by the bureaucrats in Washington; the Tibetans were certainly betrayed. There were periods when air support was not maintained, especially after the U-2 incident when all CIA planes were ordered not to violate international borders and the Tibetans were left to fend for themselves.

According to Fletcher Prouty, liaison officer between the

USAF and the CIA, there were more than fourteen thousand Tibetans dependent on air support for food, arms, and equipment when he was ordered to ground the planes after the U-2 had been shot down over Russia. The Agency argued that the men would die and their entire population would become ineffective if they were denied air support, but the order stayed. Equipment destined for them was held up at CIA supply points in Okinawa, Taiwan, Thailand, and Laos while many of the Tibetan guerrillas were rounded up and slaughtered.

Although the CIA's Tibetan operation achieved little, there were occasional intelligence windfalls. One came when Tibetan guerrillas ambushed a small Chinese military convoy on a lonely mountain road and several bags of mail containing official governmental and military documents were captured. The mail was returned to CIA operations in India and was duly analyzed in detail by the Agency's China experts in CIA HQ in Langley, Virginia. From this data the CIA was able to assess the Chinese role in Tibet, and it was clear that they were in full control, although they suffered predictable difficulties in their attempts to impose Communist rule on a feudal and religious mountain community. The documents also gave the CIA an insight into the failures of Mao's Great Leap Forward.

To help support the Tibetan operation, the CIA established an air proprietary in the mountain kingdom of Nepal which shares a long frontier with Tibet. An AID contract was awarded to a Delaware corporation called Air Ventures, Inc., between 1963 and 1967, ostensibly to assist a telecommunications project within the country. Ventures flew charters for the Nepalese government while covertly supporting the CIA-trained guerrillas inside Tibet.

The Communist grip continued to tighten on the country. In 1964 Peking ended the rule of the lamas and deposed the Panchen Lama, their own man, and he was publicly beaten and humiliated in Lhasa. Then in 1966 the Red Guards overran Tibet and smashed the temples in an attempt to destroy entirely the culture and religion of the country. The Dalai Lama struggled through the sixties and early seventies presiding over a fragmented exiled community in Dharmsala in India, while an organized guerrilla force of reportedly seven thousand men, financed and supplied by the CIA, continued to harass Chinese troops across the border. In 1967 the Nepal contract was transferred from Air Ventures to Arizona Helicopters; then, in the secret Henry Kissinger–Chou En-lai meeting that set up Nixon's 1972 visit to China, one of the trip's preconditions was that the U.S. terminate its Tibetan guerrilla operation. The Tibetans were duly abandoned.

FIVE

LAOS—THE SECRET WAR

Air America would never have grown into the biggest airline in the world if it had been limited to supporting the CIA's clandestine intelligence missions. These may have been far-flung and demanded an unusual capability, but there was only a certain need for planes and pilots. Air America mushroomed when the CIA began to fight a secret war in Laos at the same time that the Pentagon had committed the U.S. military-industrial complex to the fight in Vietnam. Both wars proved excellent for business.

The CIA maintained a secret mercenary army in Laos for more than a decade, and it relied on Air America for air support. From the very beginning the war in Laos had a crazy, Alice in Wonderland quality when the State Department and the CIA each backed different political leaders to head the Laotian government after the right wing government which had originally been put into power by a CIA-rigged election was removed in a bloodless coup. The government and the Communist opposition factions were led by princes who were half-brothers, and the confusion was compounded when the capital of Vientiane was officially declared neutral territory. This meant that Air America wives rubbed shoulders in the local vegetable market with Communist troops doing their shopping, while newsmen were able to attend government briefings in the morning and cross the street for rebel briefings in the afternoon.

The convenience of this arrangement did not lead to a clear picture of the war. When correspondents complained to the Minister of Information in Vientiane that they were receiving conflicting reports he answered hotly, "If you *will* talk to different officials, naturally you get different answers." A confused press was no bad thing for the CIA, who must have invented the much quoted ambassador who spoke of the affairs of every country in the Far East when he said, "Anyone who thinks he understands the situation here simply does not know the facts."

Laos is a remote and mountainous country where there are few roads and long-range travel is difficult. Journeys are measured by the natives in the number of days they take on foot; an eight-day trek through mountains and jungle was converted into a thirty-minute plane ride. On clear days, which are rare, pilots could admire the country's beautiful scenery. Below them row upon row of sharp-ridged mountains stretched across the landscape, sometimes jutting up like knife blades and sometimes shaped by the elements into fantastic shapes.

This secret war in difficult terrain demanded a particular type of aircraft, and AA acquired a bewildering array of special-purpose planes. The most essential, apart from helicopters, were the short takeoff and landing planes known among the pilots as STOL. These were capable of operating from strips the size of football fields. AA senior pilot George Calhoun said that in certain conditions STOL aircraft could land in seventy-five feet: "If you want to go all out and operate the bird on the ragged edge of nothing."

The Helio-Courier was the first STOL aircraft to be used by the CIA when they bought twelve to fifteen of them for use in Laos in 1957, and the plane immediately became the Agency's favorite workhorse. On the one hand, it was a perfectly conventional small airplane that could fly at 185mph and yet land on an unprepared strip comfortably in 120 feet. It was an aeronautical breakthrough and could fly unusually slowly if needed and land on the roughest of strips. All airstrips in Laos were classified as "Helio" or "Others." The plane could land on any strip that did not have boulders on it and had an enormous range of landing possibilities. Landing is a very fixed procedure for most aircraft, but the Helio-Courier could land while turning, which meant it could use curved or "boomerang" shaped strips on the top of mountain ridges. Its air speed could be as low as 35mph due to its larger than normal propeller geared to run slowly, and in a 15mph headwind it could slow down to 20mph, enabling a man to step off the wheel onto the ground without the pilot landing the plane.

"They had hundreds of Helios, literally hundreds of them," Fletcher Prouty said. "They'd be under U.S. Army insignia, USAF insignia, USAF insignia, foreign insignias as well as AA, so that at any one time very few of them would ever show up. There was a twin-engine Helio that most people would swear doesn't exist. I'm not even sure it's in Jane's."*

Flying such revolutionary aircraft had its own particular problems, and the pilots did not always share their superior's enthusiasm for the craft. "The Helio was a tricky, sneaky little son-of-a-bitch," Bob Dawson said. "You had to be with that thing all of the time or it would get you. It was light in the tail, and you could tip it up on its nose if you braked heavily. The controls of the aircraft for on-the-ground landing and take-off were really eccentric."

Robert Wofford agreed: "The Helio is a tricky airplane, a nasty little bugger. It had some very tricky control features which made it particularly difficult to handle in a cross wind. But it's a tough little airplane and it served us admirably."

It was largely succeeded by the PC-6 Pilatus Porter, designed and built by Swiss engineers for operations in the Alps and on glaciers. This is a high-wing monoplane powered by an enormous turbo-prop engine, and can carry ten passengers at speeds from 40–174mph.

Pilots preferred it. "They are fabulous planes to fly, although you get no speed out of them," Bob Dawson said. "There's nothing tricky or dangerous about the airplane; it's just as honest as it can be. I've never flown in an airplane as safe, reliable, and predictable."

Also in the AA stable were such planes as: The DO-28 Dornier, a German-built twin-engine monoplane used for larger loads and requiring a more conventional landing strip (it was used by the Katangese air force in the Congo as a bomber by the simple expedient of removing its doors and cranking bombs out by winches); the C-123, a high-wing twin engine assault transport powered by two piston engines, has a cargo door that opens at the rear and can carry a 10,000-pound payload. It can clear a fifty-foot obstacle—the standard

*The encyclopedia of the world's aircraft. There is no entry for a twin-engine Helio.

military takeoff criterion, though not AA's—with two thousand feet of takeoff run. Similar to the Dornier was the DeHavilland "Beaver." Also used were the Caribou and the Otter, the old faithful Curtiss C-46 Commando and the Douglas DC-3/C-47 Dakota (Gooney Bird) and a collection of Cessna Bird Dogs. And a large number of helicopters.

One of the things AA pilots could rely on throughout Southeast Asia was superb maintenance. If an engine part looked worn, it was immediately replaced; if a spark plug was burned out, the whole set was replaced. Each helicopter had its own flight mechanic who checked the aircraft twice a day. The company was not concerned with cost but only that their planes were in perfect mechanical condition and could be called on at any time.

Most of an Air America pilot's time was spent taking off and climbing, then descending and landing; the average journey was only twenty minutes long, and pilots flew as many as sixty-eight missions a day. "American breakfast was available at the airport in Vientiane, and afterward you'd go out, preflight your airplane, and then go into operations to find out where you were going," William Leinbach said. "You might be going to Long Tieng, and you'd fly up there and report to the customer. 'Here I am, I've got the airplane, what do you want me to do?' Then you might have to go up to site Lima 5, a forty-minute flight. The kicker would tie down the load and you'd fly over there and they might say they had some wounded for Sam Thong. Then you'd fly a few people back to Long Tieng, where they'd give you some ammunition to drop at Lima 32. You couldn't go there direct because the bad guys had guns over the PDJ [Plain of Jars] so you had to go around. You didn't make mistakes, because if you did you either flew into the side of a mountain or got shot down. People who made mistakes didn't stay very long.

"By this time it might be noon. You'd drop the ammo off with parachutes and then you'd fly back and land. Then they might want you to take some troops over to Lima 14 and bring some back, relieving an outpost. Then we'd take some fuel to site 5, where we had been earlier in the morning, pick up some more wounded for Sam Thong. Then we'd fly back to Long Tieng, pick up some rice, and drop it free fall to some little outpost. Then there would be some people who had to go back to Vientiane. Altogether you'd put in a twelve-hour day and probably average eight to ten hours of flying."

Dozens of crude landing strips were hacked out of the jungle, and mountain ridges were planed off to enable Air America to land. As the Meo mercenaries were mountain people who shunned the lowlands because of flooding and mosquitoes, many of the runways were highly elevated and only three- to six-hundred feet long and rarely straight. There was likely to be a fifteen- to twenty-degree bend somewhere along the average strip, while an up slope gradient of forty-five degrees was quite usual. "Landing up the mountain is the easiest once you have become psychologically adjusted to that kind of thing," Bob Dawson said. "Even without a reverse, brakes or anything else you can stop as you are going against gravity, usually loaded up. You could land much shorter than four hundred feet, but it was nice to be able to allow for approach and judgment clearances to take care of errors in judgment which the wind often created. Six hundred feet was plenty. Plenty."

In a high wind it was possible to make zero landings and takeoffs in a Pilatus Porter as if in a vertical takeoff aircraft. "The big problem was taxiing during high winds. I would take the plane with its broad wings, get it out on the runway, and park it next to the tower. In a thirty-five-knot wind all you had to do was to rev up and you soared like an elevator going up to the level of the people in the tower. Headed into a thirty-five-knot wind with a ground speed of thirty-five-knots, your actual ground speed is zero. It's an amusing thing to play with. It fascinates the tower people."

Laos was the most dangerous posting an Air America pilot could draw, far worse than Vietnam. An airfield in Vietnam would be guarded at its perimeter, which meant a pilot could take his plane in high at twenty-five hundred feet, where he was out of range of most antiaircraft weapons, and then let down and land in safety. In Laos, Communist troops would sit in the jungle at the end of a strip waiting for a plane to land, when they would open up from the very edge of the runway.

Most pilots who had been in World War II, Korea, and Vietnam said that they were shot at more in Laos. And it was in Laos, in a war that was not officially happening, that Air America lost most pilots. "Hardly a day went by that some airplane didn't come back with a hole in it," Bob Dawson said. "Frequently you'd come back and there would be bullet holes in the fuselage and you never knew how you got them, where you got them, when or anything else. I was subjected to greater hazard during my time with Air America than at any time I was in combat in any of the three wars I was in. And I was a fighter pilot.

"There were times in World War II when you went to dive bomb a city and there was great danger from antiaircraft fire for a few minutes, but the hour and a half you spent getting there and the hour and a half getting back, there was relatively little risk. A combat tour then was a short thing, and there were so many people involved that a single individual rarely faced that much danger. Air America, on the other hand, was a sustained, day-in-and-day-out operation that went on year after year. In Laos for six, eight, or ten hours a day for maybe eight years, every landing, every takeoff, every departure and every letdown and every flight was a risk.

"I've gotten exhilaration and excitement out of flying jets in combat when you pitted your abilities with speed and maneuverability against the enemy. Laos was the same game but with different tools. There it was a little ol' slow, unarmed airplane and it's not your guns or your equipment you're using but your wits. And you're fighting against that armed enemy who is going to shoot you, the weather conditions, poor facilities, difficult landing strips and things like that. It's exciting and exhilarating to beat them and I could have done it forever."

Even the helicopter jocks who had flown with the Marines in Vietnam found Air America a tough assignment. "It was very similar to the support I flew for the Marines, except the only difference was that Air America was willing to let us go against much greater odds," Mel Cooper said. "We went places the military wouldn't dream of going many times. The Marine Corps would never have sent us on a mission where we had to fly ninety miles over enemy territory and be fired at by 23mm and 37mm antiaircraft guns. Before they would commit helicopters, they would send the fixed-wing boys in to wipe out enemy gun emplacements the best they could, using mass bombing and everything. Air America would send us out and say, 'The last fix we had on that 37mm was here, so fly four or five miles over there to get out of his range.'

But those things could be easily moved, and their crews knew that if they stayed in the same place they would be bombed, so they would open fire and move on."

The greatest enemy in Laos, and one which claimed more victims than the Communist machine guns, was the weather. The pilots said there were three flying seasons: foggy, windy, and rainy. Five months of intensive rain each year is followed by seven months of indifferent summer marred by winds, thick dust clouds, and the smoke from the farmers' slash-and-burn method of agriculture. In bad weather when a pilot would drop down low into a canyon, he would have to wait for a hole in the clouds, hopeful that he would be able to recognize a certain rock formation or even a particular tree so that he would know where he was and whether to take a right or left turn or take the plane back up. Conditions were further complicated by the altitude and high winds and quirky air currents around the mountain tops which had to be taken into consideration.

"The varying intensity and direction of the wind, gusts, and drafts, the lack of or sudden presence of thermals can affect an aircraft's flight path so radically and so suddenly that when I went into a strip I'd be searching for the smoke of small fires to establish the wind direction," a pilot said. "You had to take your time and play it carefully."

Villagers eager to have Air America land with supplies under any conditions could complicate things further. One pilot observed the wind sock at a village strip hanging straight down, but when he landed found the wind dangerously strong. "We know plane not land when sock flies," an amiable native explained, "so we put rocks in sock."

In bad weather the greatest danger was not being hit by enemy fire but flying into the side of a mountain, known among the men during the rainy season as "rock-filled clouds." Robert Wofford, a fixed-wing pilot, remembered flying back from the Plain of Jars and being trapped in a canyon by weather. "I followed the canyon around, flying underneath the weather, and it was dropping closer and closer all this time. It's a phenomenon of weather that as it gets lower, it changes the whole aspect and appearance of the ground. You think you know where you are when all of a sudden you're not so sure."

Unknown to Wofford, a helicopter was following him, assuming the plane would lead him home. "The weather had blocked off the true gate, which would have taken me into the strip, and I veered off to the left into this false gate which led into a blind canyon. And there we were, both of us milling around a tiny area. I had the flaps cranked down and was going fifty-five mph and going round and round in circles. The chopper picked a flat spot and sat down. I couldn't do that, and I couldn't get out, so I had no choice but to bore on up through the clouds." In a maneuver that was similar to driving a car blindfolded in traffic, knowing there were mountains over and around him, he took the plane up in as tight a circle as possible until he knew he was high enough to be clear.

Sometimes inefficient ground control, combined with bad weather, turned flying into a game of Russian roulette. Jim Parrish remembered trying to land a load of ammunition in the royal capital of Luang Prabang and leaving thick cloud to go into the strip only to find himself in the middle of a squadron of Lao T-28s that were taking off. He banked the plane sharply and climbed back into the clouds. Later he found out there had been no one in the control tower.

The maps provided during the early days in Laos were very inaccurate, based on work done in the nineteenth century by French priests, which meant that pilots had to "eyeball" the flight, watching for landmarks below them to make sure they didn't get lost. In bad weather they had to rely on dead reckoning, a term used when there were no points of reference to bring a plane to its destination and they flew time and distance. Usually, whatever the weather, they undertook the journey and certainly accomplished difficult missions more often than the military would have done under the same conditions. But the Air America pilots were paid by the flight, whereas the military were paid anyway.

This sort of flying, without radar or navigational aids, could be called bush flying—although some pilots said it was more like being in the Congo with Dr. Livingstone—but, whatever the name, it took intuition and real courage.

Runway conditions varied from the passable to the appalling. A pilot could rarely tell from the air whether a strip would be waterlogged or if there were unseen obstacles hidden in the grass. Maintaining surfaces was a constant problem and erosion was so bad that a runway that was usable at the beginning of the week would tear off an aircraft's tail wheel by Friday.

"Sometimes it scared the hell out of you to see some of the places where you had to land and take off," Jim Parrish said. "In the wet some of those runways were so damn slippery you couldn't even keep the plane under control when you were taxiing. That's pretty bad."

Even Wattay Airport in Vientiane, the capital of the country, was little more than a muddy pasture, and when the Mekong burst its banks during the monsoon it was flooded. Air America planes simply taxied through lakes of water five feet deep and carried on. The floods never caused an aircraft to stand down at any time.

Helicopters in Laos faced their own peculiar set of complications. Around the Plain of Jars there were peaks eight thousand feet high and temperatures would reach nearly one hundred degrees, which meant choppers operated on decreased power and lift, so much so that the H-34 had to carry a light fuel load. Making a parachute jump from a chopper in trouble also posed its own problems. "When it's in controlled flight a helicopter makes a great jumping platform," Mel Cooper explained, "but once you are out of control and coming down, you have the rotors to contend with. You can usually clear the main rotors, but then you get caught on the tail rotor. There were very few successful jumps, and the records show that most people went into the blades."

Laos also had a unique man-made season of its own when the villagers set fire to their fields in preparation for the year's poppy planting. The burn-off is one of the most awesome sights in the mountains when whirlwinds of flame shoot hundreds of feet into the sky and a cloud bank of smoke rises two miles above the fields and the whole country becomes enveloped in a blue haze of smog. Visibility is reduced to half a mile and less. "Like flying around inside a milk bottle," one pilot said.

The CIA began operations in 1959 with guerrillas from the Meo Tribes in Laos as part of a regional intelligence-gathering program. Agency personnel were sent to Laos to supervise eight Green Beret teams teaching Meo guerrillas on the Plain of Jars. Then in 1960 the CIA recruited elements of the Nationalist Chinese paramilitary units based in northern Thailand to patrol the China border area. From such small beginnings Laos was to attract the highest spook population per capita in the world.

Even nonspooks soon found themselves involved in the CIA's program of training the secret army. One was Edgar "Pop" Buell, a retired farmer from Indiana who arrived in Laos in 1960 as an agricultural volunteer for International Voluntary Services (IVS), a Bible Belt version of the Peace Corps. On Pop's first flight into the countryside of Laos in a C-47 Gooney Bird, accompanied by seven passengers and seven barrels of gasoline, he tried to make small talk with the young man sitting next to him. "What are you doing here?" he asked innocently.

"I'm a technician for PEO," the man replied.

"What's PEO?" Pop asked.

"Program Evaluation Office," the man said, curt and unhelpful.

"Well, I'm new here and I don't know what that means," Pop blundered on. "What I want to know is what kind of work do you do. Is it government work?"

"Look mister, I don't know you," the man snapped. "I'm a technician for PEO. Let's leave it at that, huh?"

In those days the Indiana farmer was still naive. "God almighty, what are people out here trying to hide?" he exclaimed. He was soon to find out when he became a one-man supply corps for the CIA's secret army and coordinated Air America planes in their drops of rice and supplies on the Plain of Jars.

Air America also provided the air transport for the CIA's recruitment drive as it built up the clandestine army CIA. Operators and Meo officers flew to scattered mountain villages, leapfrogging from peak to peak in helicopters and Helio-Courier aircraft. They offered the villagers guns, rice, and money in exchange for recruits, and organized landing strips to link the village with the CIA HQ.

Nearly nine thousand men were equipped within a year and began operations on the Plain of Jars, where they blew up bridges and supply dumps while snipers shot at neutralist and Pathet Lao troops. CIA control of these operations was considered to be excellent, even though they only had nine case officers and nine Green Berets in the field. A further ninety-nine Thai police commandos worked with the Meo.

Then in May 1961 the Communists and neutralists retaliated in force and assaulted the CIA mountain HQ and began shelling the base camp. After suffering two weeks of intense mortar fire, it was decided to abandon the base. Vang Pao, the army's leader, led his troops to a new HQ and Pop Buell followed close behind, leading nine thousand civilians. While the troops made the transfer without incident, hundreds of civilians, mainly children and elderly, died during the jungle march.

The pattern of the war was already drawn up: the struggle for control of the Plain of Jars, which changed hands almost every year, and the perpetual movement of the Meo soldiers and their families. General Edward G. Lansdale of the CIA wrote a report for foreign-policy officials in the Kennedy administration outlining the problem they were facing: "As Meo villagers are overrun by Communist forces and as men leave food-raising duties to serve as guerrillas, a problem is growing over the care and feeding of noncombat Meos. CIA has given some rice and clothing to relieve this problem. Consideration needs to be given to organized relief, a mission of an ICA ('humanitarian' foreign aid) nature, to the handling of Meo refugees and their rehabilitation."

This critical problem was solved by a combination of Air America supply drops and the stamina and field genius of Pop Buell. He set out on a fifty-eight day trek around the perimeter of the plain to arrange for the delivery of the desperately needed supplies. It was estimated that there were seventy thousand misplaced Meo refugees facing starvation.

At first Pop Buell could only put together a makeshift airlift of rice, blankets, clothing, cooking utensils and seeds. From dawn to dusk for three months he sat in the cargo compartment of a C-47 flown by Dutch Brongersma and Johnny Lee, two old China hands who had been with the Flying Tigers. "How many bullet holes can this old bucket take before it comes apart?" Pop asked Dutch after one mission.

"Just one, Pop, if it's in the right place." Then nonchalantly, he drew twenty-seven circles around the holes in the wings with a red grease pencil. They had been fired upon every day of the airlift.

The Alice in Wonderland nature of the war was such at this time that the various U.S. agencies at work in the country had little idea, if any, what one another was up to. Pop

Buell had no idea that by supporting the refugees he was also contributing to the secret CIA army of Vang Pao. Apart from what he could see from the air on his daily flights over Meo encampments, he had no idea what Vang Pao was doing. His main worry was whether the supplies were falling safely, and he decided to fly into the mountains and find out. The only transportation available was a C-46, which meant he would have to jump, no small undertaking for a frail, sixty-five-year-old who had never worn a parachute in his life.

He was dropped near to Vang Pao's position, intercepted by Meo troops, and led through the jungle to their leader's secret camp, which consisted of a group of U.S. Army huts and hundreds of makeshift shelters. When Pop arrived, a crew of Meo were hacking at the underbush with crude steel knives preparing a rough airstrip. Parked nearby, to Pop's intense annoyance, was an olive-drab American helicopter. In one of the army tents he came across an American Special Forces captain and an American civilian who identified himself as "Uncle Dan," a silliness the CIA went in for.

"What the hell are you doing up here?" Uncle Dan asked.

"I'm gonna ask you the same question," Pop replied. "Goddamnit, I risked my neck to jump out of a goddamned airplane with a parachute into a goddamn jungle which I didn't know was friendly or enemy. Then I walk a whole goddamn day with bushes in my face and leeches on my legs. I get here and see a goddamn chopper just sitting there like somebody's limousine. I'm supposed to be feeding seventy thousand people up here. I think there's at least fifty thousand more starving people wandering around out there who need my help. Now I find you Americans sitting here with transportation and nobody in Vientiane knows a goddamn thing about you."

"That makes us even," said the captain. "We didn't know about you either. We knew somebody was feeding these people, but we never knew who."

"Well, you're looking at him, buddy, and that old routine of each American agency running around up here without telling the other ones what he's doing has got to stop, right now. You're in the Army, and this fellow must be one of them people riding a broomstick around for the CIA. I'm an IVS volunteer, but I represent AID." Buell suggested that they all cooperate for a smoother operation, and from then on his work was carried out hand in glove with the CIA.

Both military intelligence and the CIA attempted to put him on their payrolls, but Pop preferred to stay an IVS volunteer on his $65-a-month salary. "I ain't been a goddamned bit impressed by some of the things your outfit's been trying to do out here," Pop told Uncle Dan. "I'll tell you people what I'm doing, where I'm going, and what's going on there, but I'll expect you to scratch my back a little bit too. When I need a little something extra for my refugees, I reckon you'll have to help me out."

The refugees created by the war relied totally on Air America, whose planes could alter weeks of starvation, when the wounded suffered without medical supplies, in a single drop. Enough food and supplies could be dropped in a morning to supply and feed five thousand people for a month.

The crazy three-way civil war was artificially patched up by the Geneva Agreements of 1962, which stipulated a deadline for the withdrawal of all foreign military elements. Inspectors of the International Control Commission, set up to supervise the neutrality accords and made up of Poles, Canadians, and Indians, checked and counted each military adviser as he left the country. There were 666 of them, and by the deadline the only uniformed Americans or intelligence officers left in Laos were the Army and Air Force attachés and their staffs at the embassy.

The ICC had no way of similarly checking the Communist foreign military out of the country, as they were not permitted to visit Pathet Lao territory. It was estimated that there were ten thousand regular North Vietnamese soldiers in the country, of whom only forty were counted passing through the only checkpoint the Communists permitted the ICC representatives to observe. Behind this phony neutrality which existed only in the world's newspapers and in the minds of diplomats, the war continued.

The problem for the United States was essentially cosmetic: how to seem to keep the Geneva agreements and yet evade them at the same time? Military advisers and CIA personnel moved across the border of Thailand, where they were flown in every day like commuters by Air America, whose entire helicopter operation was based in Udorn. At the same time civilian personnel were not covered by the agreements, which meant that Air America was really about to come into its own and take on every duty that would normally be carried out by the USAF. The U.S. embassy declared that Air America flights were humanitarian while CIA men took AID posts as cover. Pop Buell, with IVS, stayed on too, but his agricultural training had taken a strange turn and a few weeks after the agreement came into effect he was directing Meo guerrillas in dynamiting six bridges and twelve mountain passes along one of the country's main roads.

Pop had discovered a virtually uninhabited mountain bowl called Long Tieng which he made into his mountain refugee headquarters. It was taken over by the CIA and General Vang Pao, and Pop moved nineteen miles away to Sam Thong. The CIA base of Long Tieng became one of the most secret spots on earth and developed into the largest Agency field HQ in the world. It was second in size only to the Agency's urban mission in Saigon and, after Vientiane, was the largest city in Laos. From the air its thousands of aluminum roofs gave it the look of an American urban sprawl, while on the ground it was crammed with sophisticated electronic gear. A macadam airfield was built, the only one in northeastern Laos capable of handling jet aircraft in trouble, and the USAF conducted secret bombing missions into North Vietnam and eventually all over Laos itself. CIA men, posing as assistant military attachés from the embassy in Vientiane and working in the field with Army units, were directed from the base. Journalists called it Spook Heaven.

The year of 1962 was relatively quiet but the following year the CIA went on the offensive throughout northern Laos. Anthony Poe, who had led the Agency's Tibetan Khambas, was in charge of the base at Long Tieng and organized and expanded Meo commando operations into Sam Neau Province, which had been a Pathet Lao stronghold for fifteen years and was famous for the quality of its opium. Hundreds of trained Meo guerrillas were flown by Air America helicopters and Helio-Courier in a lightning advance from mountaintop to mountaintop. As soon as a village was captured and the Pathet Lao defenders eliminated, its inhabitants were put to work building a landing strip, further expanding Air America's communications. Refugee supplies, organized by the indefatigable Pop Buell, would then be flown in together with arms and ammunition. The CIA's strategy throughout this offensive was to concentrate on mountain ridges populated by Meo tribesmen and turn them into fastnesses while leaving the towns and villages in the valleys to the Pathet Lao. The Air America landing strip at Hong Non was only twelve miles from the limestone caverns near Sam Neau City, where the Pathet Lao later housed their national headquarters, a munitions factory and a cadre training school.

Pop Buell's informal refugee relief program, together with the small volunteer AID mission in Vientiane, suddenly became a massive operation backed by a multimillion-dollar commitment from Washington. More Air America planes were chartered, and air transportation alone cost AID more than $8 million per year. The drops were a well-planned and complicated operation. USAID was given a requirement of how many people they would have to feed in a given area and then attempt to supply them on a rota system. The schedule had to be flexible because of bad weather, and a pilot's drop sheet would list three primary targets and a further three or four alternatives. "It gave you a good feeling to go to some little mountain peak and drop twelve thousand pounds of rice almost into their cooking pot," a pilot said.

The entire Air America fleet was committed almost every day and one plane down for scheduled maintenance created a problem which meant that three or four others would have to be changed around to cover for the one out of commission. Air America crisscrossed the country, flying in supplies, mostly over hostile territory where an elaborate system of coded markers was established. Code letters made up of cerise panels laid out on the ground, and in hot areas where hostile troops were active, the code would change day by day. If a camp was overrun and the signal was not changed, the pilots stayed away.

"You were not supposed to go anyplace unless there was a signal out," said Miles Lechtman, who worked for Air America as a kicker for eight years. "One time we had been out on a delivery and the customer asked us to go on a particular flight. I asked what the signal was. He said, 'Never mind about the signal.'" Lechtman, like other Air America personnel, was only too familiar with the CIA's disregard for men's lives if they wanted a job done badly.

"Hold it, you had two airplanes shot up there last week and one of them barely got back," Lechtman objected.

"You mean to tell me you're not going to go without a

signal?" the CIA officer asked contemptuously, attempting to put on pressure.

The plane's captain, who was standing behind his kicker during this exchange, stepped forward. "That's exactly what he's telling you."

The case officer shrugged and turned away. Lechtman later found out that another plane had been sent on the mission. It limped back to base peppered with flak.

The pilot's approach to a drop was a minor art in itself. "We dropped in circles, figures of eight, rectangular patterns—whatever the terrain called for, or the turbulence or the weather," one explained. "The majority of the drops were on hillsides, little cliff tops and mountaintops and we had to pretty much drop in one direction. We wanted the bags falling perpendicular to the terrain so that when the rice went out of the plane it wasn't only going to have the momentum from the aircraft, it was also going to start being affected by the wind."

The drops were made from an altitude of eight to nine hundred feet, which was high enough to allow the double-bagged rice to lose almost all forward motion and low enough to prevent the bags breaking on impact. "If the sacks did break, there would be a mad scramble between the people and the pigs to get out there and pick up that rice," Porter Hough said. "Those pigs were smart. They had learned to listen for the airplanes and knew they meant rice. They would stand there just clear of the drop zone, just like people, then as soon as the plane stopped circling they'd all go running to beat hell."

Most of the pigs had arrived in the same manner as the rice, out of the sky. "We'd drop them on parachutes and you'd hear them going out of the back of the airplane squealing their bloody heads off," Robert Wofford said. "They'd be in crates, and when they'd hit the ground they'd often break and those pigs would go in every direction. One time we shoved a big porker out the back and the chute didn't open and he hit the ground with one hell of a bang. They had pig for dinner that night."

The planes flew low enough to allow the pilot to make his drops with reasonable accuracy. "You varied your aiming point up to fifteen to twenty feet before an average wind, or fifty feet if it was a good strong wind," Wofford said. "As you went into it, the load was back by the door which made you a little tail heavy, and when you dropped the tail went up and the nose went down. You were rising anyway with the sudden loss of weight, especially later on when you were pretty much empty on the last couple of pallets to go out. I always dropped with twenty-five percent flaps to get the tail a little high so that when the rice went out it gave you a safety margin so it wouldn't hit the tail. There were a million minor things that had to be coordinated."

Two kickers, one American and a Thai or Lao, were stationed in the back of the plane with the cargo, which was loaded onto pallets placed on rollers. As the plane reached the drop zone, the pilot rang a bell and a kicker would begin to push a load toward the open door. "One fellow drops back just as the load is at the door and about to leave, and the other fellow just continues right on out the door pushing the load all the way," Wofford said. "And this guy's got a strap tied around his hand which is foreshortened just to the right length so that as he goes out of the door it jerks and pulls him back in. The first time I went up on a drop, I was in the back watching the process and I damn near had a heart attack when I saw that kid run out of the door with that load."

Kickers always wore parachutes in readiness for the times when the strap didn't hold, and there were occasions when they went out the back of the plane with the cargo. "One guy fell out twice," Lechtman said, "but he liked to jump a lot so the company thought that was just a little bit of a coincidence and he was told to leave. The funny thing was he came back as a 'customer' later on."

One of the village chiefs was so fascinated by the rice drops that he asked if he could go up in an Air America plane to see where the rice came from. The chief flew on a drop and peered awestruck into the plane's cockpit and watched the kickers at work. He was so thrilled by the experience that he fell out of the plane. Two weeks later a villager appeared on an Air America strip and announced without resentment, "Thank you for rice. Our chief, he broke his head."

The C-123s and Caribous would land big loads of provisions in Vientiane which would then be taken up country either in a C-46 or C-47, STOL aircraft or helicopters. "I guess I hauled more rice than grows in China in a year," Porter Hough said. "The big free hand-out. It got to be an old joke up there that when the school teachers asked the children where rice came from they would point at the sky."

Sometimes AA included baby food in their drops, an unlikely dietary complement for tough mountain mercenaries. The hill tribes lacked certain vitamins in their diet, which their CIA overlords had attempted to provide with pills until it was discovered they were feeding the vitamin tablets to the pigs. Baby food, like apple sauce, provided the necessary missing ingredients, which the Meo enjoyed, so AA hauled case upon case of the stuff.

Pilatus Porters used for rice drops had been especially converted. The seats were taken out of the back and two drop doors were built into the bottom of the plane and were controlled by the pilot pulling a lever. One kicker would sit next to the pilot and another in the back and the plane would carry enough rice to load each door with six hundred pounds at a time. The normal procedure for a small plane dropping to a position was to go in high while the pilot checked the situation out to see what people on the ground were doing. If they looked like they were under cover or the position was quiet the pilot continued his evaluation until he was sure it was safe to drop, but if people were standing around casually the drop was begun immediately.

Out over the Plain of Jars when the enemy were not shooting and the weather was good, pilots on rice drops could enjoy the beauty of the rolling green grass surrounded by mountains. "I never got tired of flying the Porter over Laos, looking down on the beautiful scenery," Bob Dawson said. "It was a constant panorama of beauty, both peaceful and calming. I remember one beautiful day when there were just a few fleecy clouds in the sky and I was dropping to a little hill not more than one hundred fifty feet high which Vang Pao's troops had just occupied and dug into.

"I went down and looked at the position. The troops, dressed in their olive-green American uniforms, were standing around in their slit trenches and fortified positions. They were standing up on the sandbagged areas looking as if they weren't worried about a thing and I wasn't alarmed at all. This was an exciting thing for them, when a plane made a drop, in an otherwise boring routine subsisting in their fortified hilltop.

"I went down at an angle wanting the bags to hit flat so

they wouldn't scrape along the ground and rip open. The kickers had loaded the door and I made a successful drop onto the bank, reached down to my left and pulled the lever to close the door. Then at a very slow speed with partial flaps at sixty-five knots, I turned the plane to the left.

"Vang Pao had a liaison officer flying with us who doubled as a kicker and he was exchanging communications with the hilltop via a walkie-talkie. While I was doing my business, he was talking to someone on the ground. Then, after we made the drop, he went back to help load and set his radio down on the floor by the copilot's seat.

"You made your orbit depending on the efficiency of your kickers, and the idea was to make it just big enough to get the cycle right, and just as they sit down you roll out on your next run. You want to get it over with as quickly as you can to minimize your exposure.

"We were about to drop again and go through the same routine. The troops were still standing around on the parapet, and I had just shifted hands to pull the lever to open the door when I heard a *rat-a-tat-tat*. It didn't soak in, it sounded like a sewing machine. Then there was a *pap-pap-pap-pap* sound as the bullets came through the floor of the plane and they sounded like firecrackers. Immediately I banked to the right, but I didn't get the drop off, as I had only just shifted hands."

Dawson had gained experience in three wars of how to take evasive action and flipped the plane to the left and then to the right and went into a dive. "Why are you going down, why don't you climb?" the Meo officer shouted.

"At the rate this airplane flies?"

Dawson figured that whoever was shooting at him was at the very base of the hill and wanted to put it between them. He took the plane across the treetops so the gunner was unable to see where they were, and then, as they headed back across the plain, he began to climb. "One of the axioms of flying is that you always trade something for altitude. The higher you are the safer you are."

The Meo liaison officer reached down to pick up his radio, which was still on the floor of the plane by his right foot. There was a bullet hole right through it. "Before that he was all right, but then he got scared," Dawson said. "He was a funny-looking guy anyway, but all the way back his eyes got wider and wider." Dawson called his base and told them he had sustained ground fire from an AK-47.

Safe on land, he looked over the plane and counted thirty-five holes in it, mostly in the tail, with a few scattered through the body. "I figured out there were sixteen projectiles which had hit the airplane, and they had gone in and come out again making a couple of holes each. But apart from that radio not a goddamn one of them hit anything."

There is still some doubt in Dawson's mind who pulled the trigger. "Sometimes I wonder if it wasn't a guy in the position. We had instances when we supposed it was our own people shooting at us. I guess they were just bored."

One such incident involved Ralph "Cotton" Davis, a Pilatus Porter pilot originally from Wyoming. He had overloaded his plane with an army major and thirteen others for a short hop between the CIA base at Long Tieng and another position just five miles over the mountains. In between the two bases was a fortified position on the ridgetop, and it was necessary for Davis to put the Porter into a steep climb immediately after takeoff. A Meo soldier on the ridge watched the plane crawl slowly toward him and in a moment of boredom fired off a shot. The bullet went straight through the pilot's heart and killed him instantly while the plane crashed into the mountain and burned, killing everybody on board. The soldier was executed on the spot by Vang Pao.

The millions of AID dollars that Congress thought it was appropriating for civilian help were mostly being used for support of the secret army, although tens of thousands of refugees were also fed. Deceiving the U.S. Congress was considered a legitimate tactic of the secret war; of course, the enemy knew exactly what was going on, but the CIA was determined that the American public should not share this knowledge. Air America spoke openly of its humanitarian drops of rice, blankets, and medicine but did not mention what the men called "hard" rice drops—ammunition, grenades, bombs, and weapons to the secret army.

Almost all Air America pilots dropped "hard" rice, and there was so much of it to be ferried around that they hardly thought of it as clandestine. But a small percentage among them were given special clearances and earmarked for top-secret operations known as "black" projects. It was a small program, and only four crews were trained, each consisting of a pilot, copilot, flight engineer, navigator, and two load-masters.

"Officially I was on the Air America C-123 program," Jim Parrish said, "but I was also part of a very classified program that even people inside the company didn't know about." Parrish was considered eligible because he had been involved in several classified programs when he was in the Air Force and had one of the highest clearances, top secret and nuclear, that went back many years. "I was never told I was dealing with the CIA, but I always knew."

The pilots were paid in cash. Every couple of months it would be handed to them in an envelope. The rate was $50 for each drop, so that three drops a night would mean an extra $150.

"We would be picked up in Vientiane and taken to Tak Le for eight to ten days, depending on how big the job was, and would then go back to Vientiane and fit right back into the C-123 program. The other guys were supposed to think we had been on leave and ignore the dark rings around our eyes."

Tak Le was a big place but not much different to look at than any other air base unless one studied the layout of the camp. The secret-projects compound was a separate base within the main base, like a keep protected by an outer wall and a moat. There was a high perimeter fence around the inside core which contained a hangar guarded by Americans in civilian clothes, part of the CIA's Detachment 3. When the hangar door was closed, even the Air America crew with their top secret clearances were not supposed to go within one hundred feet of it, but occasionally they could not help but glance inside and see a strange plane with straight wings like a glider sitting there—a U-2 spy plane, later superseded by the SR-71.

"The hush-hush program used USAF C-130s, and although we started out in the mid sixties with four crews, by 1970 we only had one left. One flew into a mountain and several other people lost their lives," Parrish said. Their job was to fly in large supplies of ammunition into forbidden territory under cover of darkness. "We weren't supposed to and we knew we weren't supposed to, which is why we did a lot of it by night."

The Air Force would deliver the planes, which were painted completely differently from their usual official coloring and had screw-on Air Force insignia and Scotch tape markings.

(In fact, the 3M company had the contract to manufacture these kits.) It took about two hours to convert one of these planes so that when it was stripped down it would be non-attributable. The result was what the CIA referred to as a "sanitized" aircraft.

This was a delicate part of the operation, and the Agency and the Air Force took great pains over it. All planes have tail numbers and their engines and instruments are numbered as well, which makes disguise difficult. The CIA would keep a list of the aircraft that had crashed and then create two or three airplanes with the same tail number and two or three with no tail numbers at all. Then, in an exceedingly complex operation using very careful manipulation and scheduling, they would cause aircraft to show up in places two at a time, making them impossible to follow. On top of this Air America had the capacity on Taiwan and at Udorn to actually manufacture their own planes. The idea was to create a plane that did not exist, one that even the manufacturer back in the States would swear had never been made. Instruments and engines were produced with no serial numbers and no decals, which was a problem in itself because an engine is dye-stamped, and even if the numbers are erased the stamp can be seen on the metal.

Nonattributable engines created other problems apart from identification. Engine serial numbers are coded and cataloged so that the men who do the heavy maintenance on them can work from drawings and instructions that are in turn coded to match the engine series involved. When all these markings are removed it needs special crews to work on them, and they in turn have to be given top-secret clearances.

If anything happened to an engine when a plane was far away from its regular base, a message would immediately be sent to the nearest Air Force base commander telling him to fly a maintenance crew to get the engine and to "melt" or destroy it. Instead of working on the plane and revealing the classified nature of its mission, the CIA preferred to destroy a costly engine. Then, before the plane could continue its flight, that engine would have to be replaced by another nonattributable one.

"You've heard of laundered money—that's nothing to laundered aircraft," said Fletcher Prouty, who as USAF liaison officer with the CIA had the unenviable job of keeping track of what the Agency was doing with Air Force planes. "If the Agency needed an Air Force plane I'd give them one, but I'd try and put somebody on it or at least, if it was a totally clandestine mission, have somebody out there who would just fuel the plane. He could note the time the plane took off, the time it came back, and who went on board. In other words I'd run a counter-Agency operation, and I had the best system for monitoring the Agency that ever existed."

Prouty attempted to keep track of planes by having people all over the world collecting their fuel chits. This meant he could find out what each plane was doing, but usually only after the event. "You can't make something as big as Air America invisible, the trouble is you can't follow individual movement. They have the ability to run doubles on you. They can mount three airplanes from three different airports at the same time, only one of which is going to carry out a mission while the others are simply cover. And they would cover for the one actually on the mission by having another one in the air with the same number. Later on you might be able to figure it out, but not while it was being done. It was very clever.

"What we cared about in the USAF was the whole principle of being able to disclaim plausibly that we were involved. Whenever we loaned them an airplane, I wanted to be god-damn sure that it was cleaned out and could not be readily connected to us. Obviously it could be identified as a type of plane the Air Force used, but we had so many programs that Pakistan or somebody else was running that we would be able to disclaim it."

At Tak Le the Air America crews who flew these sort of missions spent their time completely cut off from other personnel on the base. Everything possible was done to make the men's isolation comfortable. "The afternoons that we weren't flying were spent playing volleyball," said Porter Hough, who was part of a "black" C-46 program. "We had a nice air-conditioned room, spring mattresses—which at that time was a decided luxury—but you never got off the base. The food was out of this world and there was such a variety. They always won the U.S. mess kitchen award of the year for the whole of the U.S. services. They had the best cooks. Wonderful strawberry shortcake."

"We could get an assignment and we pretty well knew what

time of the month they were coming in," Jim Parrish said. "We worked in rotation—the first crew in would be the last crew out. They would give us a show time, and that's all, and a C-46 or C-47 would pick us all up in Vientiane. We would take enough civilian clothes for ten days—with no AA markings or anything to tie us in with the company—and then they would fly us down to Tak Le where we would get a night's sleep and start working the next morning.

"The work load varied. I've flown as many as one hundred hours in ten days and as low as thirty hours, depending on the nature of the assignment. We could get a hell of a lot of work accomplished in a C-130 because we had the cream of the Air Force maintenance there—we had backups and an unlimited maintenance capability and parts supply. We could get anything, even if nobody else could get it. We had the best planes and it was great flying."

Sometimes on night drops the sanitized planes flying at two thousand feet would pass over Chinese helicopters or similarly clandestine missions flying below them at five hundred feet also without lights. "One night we flew up from the royal capital of Luang Prabang and were following the old smugglers' rice-and-salt trail which follows the valleys into Dien Bien Phu," Porter Hough said. "It was a moonlit night and you could see pretty good. Suddenly below me I saw five big helicopters and it was so clear that I could see the exhaust and the blue halo left by the static electricity on the blades."

The men themselves chose not to know too much about the goings-on at Tak Le. "I made it a point not to know so that if I ever got shot down and they started to interrogate me there was nothing I could tell them," Hough said. "I used to walk out of briefings, because if the enemy ever got hold of me and stepped on my little pinkie I knew I was going to tell them everything. So I didn't want to know anything. I only asked, 'What time do I take off and how much does it weigh?'"

Jim Parrish shared much the same philosophy. "There were a lot of things that went on at Tak Le. Supply missions into parts of Burma and India; all our U-2 and SR-71 flights were out of Tak Le. It was the hush-hush base of Thailand. Everything went on from there and it had a tremendous communications capacity. You'd see a hell of a lot of stuff going on and you didn't know anything about it and you didn't really want to know."

Among the most hazardous missions were the night drops inside China and along the Ho Chi Minh trail to small spy teams. These teams were never larger than fifteen men and were more often made up of two or three, and only occasionally accompanied by an American CIA case officer. Small teams would often be dropped in by helicopters. "Infils and exfils—dropping in teams and bringing them out—could be hazardous," Tom Grady said. "They would be wearing Pathet Lao or North Vietnamese uniforms, so you really didn't want to be hit with them on board. And you'd never know what to expect. You'd hit an area by surprise and get out before the shooting got too bad.

"It was rough going in to pick them up too. They would stay out for a week or a month or whatever and very often they were late and hadn't given the right signals or they hadn't been heard of for a couple of weeks when all of a sudden they would show up in the pick-up zone. And they're wearing enemy uniforms, so you don't know for sure who they are."

Instances of mistaken identity were inevitable. In one case a group had been out weeks longer than planned and radio contact had been broken. Suddenly troops materialized out of the jungle with the right signal. They talked to the chopper pilot who was designated to pick them up, and although he was a little unhappy about the circumstances and had the option to refuse, the thought of friendlies running around the jungle chased by the enemy made him decide to go in.

The chopper touched down within a hundred meters of the group and was met by machine-gun fire. The mechanic was hit in the chest, but the two pilots managed to jump clear before their craft exploded. An accompanying helicopter flying search-and-rescue failed to see the men clear their machine and thought them dead and headed for home. The pilots dragged their wounded companion into the tall grass and hid until the enemy finally gave up searching for them. They were all eventually picked up by AA colleagues and flown to safety.

Only occasionally could AA pilots follow a team's progress on the ground. Porter Hough remembered dropping two young couples, who were pretending to be married, into the Ho Chi Minh trail armed with nothing but miniature radios.

The following night the team spotted a convoy and arranged it so that one couple blew up the first truck as it passed a certain point and the second team blew up the final truck. This created a bonfire at both ends of the convoy of thirty vehicles, clearly marking it for the USAF night fliers who bombed and strafed it back and forth until every truck was destroyed.

"The next day we were taking some rice in to friendlies towards the Ho Chi Minh trail and had landed and still had the engines running when an army major and lieutenant asked us if they could hitch a ride back with us," Porter Hough said.

"We sure saw something over there," the major said, jerking his head in the direction of the trail.

"Night before last I dropped in a team," Hough said.

"We were looking at the results of that," the major said. He had checked on the damage done by the bombers and had found that every one of the thirty drivers had stayed with their trucks, chained to the steering wheel. The chain was approximately a meter long, allowing them just enough freedom to step outside of the cab, but they could not escape the deadly air attacks the trail was subjected to night and day.

The trail itself was a vast skein of jungle roads carrying North Vietnamese men and supplies southward. The whole panhandle area of nominally neutral Laos had been turned into one vast military supply corridor. The network carried more than one thousand five hundred and fifty miles of seasonable roads and consisted of hundreds of pathways, some wide enough to carry convoys of trucks, and others just narrow mountain tracks only suitable for men on foot. This intricate and well-developed scheme was supplemented by ten waterways.

The trails meandered, followed diversions skirting bomb craters, but always headed southeast. Most were marked with road signs and provided rest stops for drivers. Along the main roads there were concealed truck parks complete with signs encouraging drivers to PARK AND COME IN AND EAT while warning them against loitering.

No driver took a truck the entire distance, but only the twenty odd miles or so between one base area and the next. As a result drivers were so familiar with their own sections of road that they were able to drive along them at night without lights. Ninety percent of all movement on the trail occurred at night while the drivers rested in concealed way stations during the day and their trucks underwent maintenance.

Most of the trails were impossible to spot from the air because of triple-canopy jungle foilage, while in open areas they were artfully camouflaged with bamboo and wood arches laced frequently with fresh-cut foliage. Where rivers were unfordable, portable bridges were built and placed beneath the water's surface or hidden out of sight along the banks by day to be used only at night. A work force of seventy-five thousand was drafted by the North Vietnamese to maintain this fantastic supply route.

More than two thousand gun positions, from .51 caliber machine guns to 100mm radar-controlled antiaircraft guns effective up to thirty thousand feet, were placed along the trail, mostly concentrated around base areas. AA pilots claimed there were surface-to-air SAM missile sites along the trail, but this was denied by the U.S. military.

The CIA used the Nungs, a national minority of Chinese hill people who had fought for the French and then moved south in large numbers after 1954, to observe North Vietnamese and Vietcong supply movements, and occasionally to ambush convoys or carry out sabotage on storage depots. As most of the Nungs were illiterate, the CIA developed a special radio transmitter with a set of buttons corresponding to pictures of a tank, a truck, an artillery piece, or some other military-related object. Thus equipped the Nung spy would merely push the appropriate button as many times as he counted such objects in any convoy going by him. Each push sent a specially coded impulse back to a base camp, which could then keep a running account of supply movements on the trail. At other times the signals would be recorded by observation planes that would relay the information to attack aircraft for immediate bombings on the trail.

The AA "black" fliers had to keep these teams supplied. "We had to go in and locate them and drop on their signal," Robert Wofford said. "It was the most exacting flying I've ever done, because there were no navigational aids whatsoever. You had to plot out everything down to the second on your map and fly from one prominent mountaintop to another.

"At that time we did not have infrared either. Later on they introduced infrared goggles, and although everything looks green through them, you can see perfectly. But we did it the hard way all the time."

As a rule there was no radio contact with the ground teams and the planes would circle an area looking for a prearranged signal made up of flashlights and a strobe. The signal would often be in the form of a letter, say T, and the crew would be told that there would be a strobe on both ends of the T and that the rest of it would be formed by regular flashlights. As soon as a team deep in enemy territory heard a plane droning above them in the night sky, they would light their signal and the drop would be made.

"The night drops to the watchers were always very small," Jim Parrish said. "They were on foot and moving all the time and they would set up a ring of four and five flashlights to tell us where they were, and we would drop enough supplies to keep them going for a few days.

"A lot of the guys wouldn't go on the night drops. You were strung out there on the border way the hell away from everything with absolutely no navigational aids, working yourself down among a bunch of fog-shrouded hills looking for four or five damn flashlights. The C-123B had very little single-engine capability, and hanging down there under these damn hills was pretty bad."

Weapon drops were a different sort of operation. "We supplied the bombs for the T-28s which the Lao tribesmen flew. We took five-hundred-pound and two-hundred-fifty-pound bombs all over, anywhere a T-28 could take off or we could land. Sometimes a T-28 couldn't get off the high-elevation dirt strips with a five hundred-pounder so they slung a two-hundred-and-fifty-pounder on them. On one occasion we ferried a million dollars' worth of bombs during a three-day period to a site in northern Laos known as Lima 108. The very night we came through, the bad guys came and blew them all up." In the early days of the war, before there were sufficient Laos and Meo trained as pilots, T-28 fighter-bombers bearing Royal Lao insignia were flown by AA pilots on regular bombing missions on Pathet Lao and North Vietnamese positions along the Ho Chi Minh trail.

When in February 1970 one of the C-130s crashed, it made the newspapers. The plane had strayed ten miles off course and piled into the highest mountain in Laos, the top of which was shrouded in thick tropical cloud. The plane exploded, killing the entire crew.

A possible explanation for the crash is that the men were simply exhausted. "It was real tiring," Parrish said. "I would come back from the covert work and have to go straight back into the AA program. Officially it was assumed I had ten days off. I was just gone from the system, and nobody knew that I had flown a hundred hours in that time. When the crew flew into that mountain we were already down to two crews, and that left us with one.

"I personally had flown one hundred and eighty-two hours in that month, plus the AA stint. You got so wornout that you could never catch up. You could never feel good. We were flying dead overtired. There were many, many times when I was exhausted. We never had good conditions and it was hairy all the time. I got to the point where I felt like quitting every day. But I'd just keep on going."

Any survivors of a crash would have been treated harshly. The crews wore civilian clothes, carried no papers, and were flying unmarked planes. They would almost certainly have been shot as spies. "Our status would have been SOL," Jim Parrish said. "Shit Out of Luck."

Darkness amplified all the usual operational difficulties. One Caribou was lined up on its target, and the pilot had just increased the power and was pulling up so the cargo would fall out of the back, when the cargo door blew shut. The result was a pilot's nightmare—six pallets of supplies piled up by the back door, creating an unmanageably tail-heavy aircraft. All a pilot can do in such a situation is put the plane into a tight turn, hoping to hold altitude while the kickers work frantically to clear the cargo door. In this case the kickers freed the load, but there were other times when it cost lives.

Some of the risk was taken out of night flying with the introduction of a sophisticated "Impact-chute." An ordinary parachute drops at the relatively slow speed of 16 feet per second and drifts with the slightest breeze. Pilots had to take their planes down to five hundred feet for there to be any real chance of those on the ground recovering the supplies. The "Impact-chute," on the other hand, was held in a wreathed condition throughout its fall, enabling it to reach a speed of seventy-five to ninety feet per second. A device called a foot, usually a brass weight, tied to a two-hundred-foot line and attached to the chute preceded the load. As it hit the ground before the load, it sent an electrical charge back along the line, triggering off a cutting tool on the canopy which severed the wreathing line, allowing the chute to blossom instantly. This took the pressure off pilots by allowing them to drop from fifteen hundred to two thousand feet. Although first used in 1968 they were not always available.

AA crews also serviced Washington's three-billion-dollar failure known as McNamara's Fence. The "fence" was an exceptionally sophisticated electronic network of sensors, linked, via AA planes circling overhead, to a main computer. It was designed to pinpoint enemy-troop movements from North to South Vietnam and into Laos. A dozen Volpars, specially fitted out for electronic surveillance, operated out of Savannakhet and circled border areas all night long. The work was dull but dangerous, and pilots flew at high altitudes in unpressurized cabins, often in thunder showers, for seven or eight hours at a time.

"The people who dreamt up the idea were down in Florida and saw the land being cleared with monstrous machines," Fletcher Prouty said. "Bowater had first used them down in Peru for lumber pulping and they knock a swath through the jungle fifty-to-sixty feet wide. So our people thought, Why can't we do that on the border of Vietnam and stop the border crossings?

"Their problem was they didn't realize it wasn't border crossings we were having trouble with but the sort of guy who cut our hair in the morning and shot us at night. But they sold the concept and figured that when the land was smoothed down like a tennis court they'd plant electronic sensors on it. It sounded really good in Washington.

"It became a place to spend a lot of money. They planted sensors like you plant geraniums and went out there and seeded the damn things. There was some extraordinarily sophisticated equipment, mostly electronic audible sensors and some heat sensors. On paper back home it looked like a good idea. It was a very elaborate system but had no effect on the war at all. The damn things couldn't tell a cow from a human so that they were always getting false alarms, and after a certain number of those you just don't go anymore." The enemy, ever inconsiderate, ended up stealing most of the components.

Another top-secret Agency project involved dropping millions of dollars in forged Pathet Lao currency in an attempt to wreck the economy by flooding it with paper money. Pilots on routine night drops would be asked to return over Communist lines and drop several packages. "It turned out the packages were full of counterfeit money," Robert Wofford said. "We must have dropped two hundred pounds' weight of money, hundreds of million of kip. They were just in paper bags and had these devices the kicker pulled which ignited a small charge and blew the bag apart. The money was packed loosely, and when the bag blew the money would scatter and drift all over the area. I'm sure a few people ate well the next day.

"When we got back to Vientiane, we had to spend two hours cleaning the airplane because some of the bags burst before we could get them out and we had counterfeit money from one end of the airplane to the other."

Apart from CIA plans hatched in Langley, Virginia, individual case officers sometimes nurtured pet schemes of their own. Tony Poe entertained the idea of putting special teams inside Red China to mine a rich seam of gold he had heard about. A native in the mountains across the Chinese border had run across a yellow metal and mined it. He had then smuggled out a piece the size of a football and floated down the Mekong with it. The discovery excited Poe tremendously and he asked the opinion of AA pilot Porter Hough, who had studied geology. The two men went into a room together and Poe began to unwrap his prize.

"Tony, you're going to be disappointed," Hough said immediately.

"But you haven't seen it yet."

"No, but if that was gold it would be so heavy you couldn't carry it. It weighs twice as much as lead, and a cube fourteen inches on the side weighs a ton."

When the parcel was unwrapped, Hough saw that the metal was copper-iron pyrite but had so much copper in it that it looked golden in color. Poe wrapped the metal up again.

"I was afraid it was too good to be true, there was quite a seam up there." He told Hough that he felt that the Agency would have been prepared to put up money to get the work done, as the metal had been found near an unpatrolled section of the border.

Occasionally the zeal of some CIA case officers unnerved their superiors. One employed Laotians to mix homemade napalm at the side of the runway by stirring large packets of Tide into fifty-gallon drums of gasoline to make it congeal. He called this makeshift but deadly brew "hot soup."

"The favorite project of this one particular customer was to clear out Communist infested areas with homemade napalm," Wofford said. "It was very unofficial and we weren't paid any extra for that. It was done on a favor basis. The customer would come over and ask us, 'Do you want to carry some hot soup today?' Some of the guys would and some of them wouldn't."

Hot soup was dropped from two hundred feet, making the plane a sitting target, but it was a very effective weapon. Double thermite grenades were strapped onto the fifty-gallon drums, which were then loaded onto pallets in pairs and pushed out the back of the plane. A static line would pull the pin, and there would be an eight-second delay before the thermite went off and started burning furiously. Thermite burns at an extremely high temperature and takes only seconds to melt through a steel drum. When the drum hit the ground it would explode, and a pallet of two would raze an area thirty feet wide and one hundred and fifty feet long. The Caribou could carry fourteen barrels, a formidable cargo for a commercial freighter.

This unorthodox initiative displayed by the CIA case officer enraged the U.S. ambassador G. McMurtrie Godley when he heard of it. "The customer probably didn't do it more than a dozen times when the ambassador got wind of it," Wofford said. "Laos is a small country, and there are always people nosing around and reporting back. It was no big secret. All the Lao tribesmen who were preparing it had to do was to laugh and joke about it to somebody.

"Anyway, the ambassador put a stop to it right away in 1970. In fact, I was all set to go out and they had spent the whole morning preparing the stuff and loading it onto the airplane when the customer came out and said, 'Take it off—we've just been shut down.'"

Despite the ambassador's ban, other pilots tell stories of carrying hot soup right up until the end of the war. "Near the end I did an operation with homemade napalm down around Pakse," William Leinbach said. "The friendlies were trying to get an attack going and take back some of the area which they had lost. The enemy were entrenched across this road, dug in pretty solid, and the friendlies were on the other side. The Lao Air Force had no napalm to put down and they couldn't get the T-28s to bomb the area, so I put thirteen fifty-gallon drums of hot soup on my aircraft.

"We set up the drums, and the first time I went across they shot at me all the way down and all the way off. I dropped six drums on the first pass and they fell the wrong way. I had thought they wouldn't divulge their position by shooting, but you could see the tracers. I turned and they didn't expect me to go back after they saw me pull off. I got a pretty good run at them and dropped the next seven from about three hundred feet. And it really hit right on top of their position, and we got a couple of secondary explosions because they had arms and supplies there. It did the job because it forced them out of their dug-in position so that the friendlies could mount their attack."

The ambassador also had reason on occasion to censure overzealous AA pilots. A chopper on alert up in the mountains of northern Laos near the Vietnamese border was keeping watch on an incursion of a valley by some North Vietnamese troops led by an old Russian cargo biplane. The pilots were tossing bombs and grenades from it as they went. The chopper pilot and his mechanic watched the strange procession. "We can fly faster than that thing," the mechanic said, and picked up a Chinese AK-47 they had in the back as a war trophy. The chopper pulled alongside the biplane, the mechanic riddled it with bullets, and it went down in flames.

Back in Vientiane there was a fuss and every attempt was made to hush up the incident. The ambassador let it be known that he was very unhappy, as the chopper's action was in direct contravention of the Geneva accords. But before the ambassador could reach the pilots to reprimand them, Vang Pao had greeted them with effusive praise and a bottle of champagne.

It is easy to understand how the embassy sometimes lost control of CIA agents in the field, by studying the individuals who went to make up this very mixed bunch. The most effective tended to be those who were not programmed by Langley but who had a wider experience of the Far East and sometimes hardly knew the States. These were the types who earned the AA pilots' respect.

One of their most effective agents was William Young. He was born in the Burmese Shan States, spoke five of the local languages, and was an expert on the mountain minorities. The grandson of a missionary who had opened a Baptist mission in Burma at the turn of the century and was looked upon by the natives as God, and son of a CIA man who had organized intelligence-gathering forays into southern China during the fifties, William Young was the natural choice for the Agency to play a key role in building up the Meo secret army under Vang Pao. It was Young who organized the building of dozens of AA landing strips.

He was later moved to northwestern Laos to set up a similar secret army but on different lines. Nam Tha Province is the foreign intelligence or colonial administrator's nightmare. A multitude of different ethnic minorities speaking thirty dialects and languages creates a unique problem which Young managed to overcome due to his rapport with the mountain people.

Instead of a native army run by a tribal overlord, such as the Meo and Vang Pao, he set up a pan-tribal army under the command of a joint council composed of leaders from every tribe. This council was supposed to have final authority on all matters, but in fact Young, who controlled the money, made all the decisions.

One of Young's brainchildren was a group he called The Sixteen Musketeers. Together with the musketeers, made up of Shan and Lahu operatives, Young began opening up the province in mid 1962 and organized the building of runways, selected base sites, and established an operational counter-guerrilla infrastructure.

They opened a secret base at Nam Yu which served as CIA HQ for cross-border intelligence forays deep into southern China. Three miles away an IVS volunteer, Joseph Flipse, established a humanitarian showplace at Nan Thouei, complete with a hospital and school, and directed rice drops and refugee relocation from there. Then in 1964 Young became involved in a political dispute with Thai intelligence officers and was called back to Washington, D.C.

A completely different style of leadership was imposed by Anthony Poe, who followed in Young's footsteps both in northeast and northwest Laos. He was the most colorful, not to say the most gaudy agent of them all. A man of many aliases—Poe, Pat Gibbs, Upin—Anthony A. Poshepny was an ex-Marine noncommissioned officer who fought and was wounded on Iwo Jima and remained in Asia after the war. He had recruited the Tibetans for training in Colorado, accompanied them on their return to the Himalayas, and fought with anti-Sihanouk mercenaries along the Cambodian border in South Vietnam before he went to Laos to train the Meo as the nucleus of the CIA's secret army, where his official cover was "Air Operations Officer—Continental Air Services." He was a hard drinker and an authoritarian, and was able to operate on the ground in the remotest parts of Laos for months at a time. Ruthless in battle, he was also inhumanly brave and was wounded a dozen times when he insisted on going into combat with his guerrillas. He once carried a wounded Laotian officer on his back for dozens of miles to safety, despite the fact that he was seriously wounded himself.

"One thing we appreciated with guys like Tony was that he wouldn't ask us to do anything he wouldn't do himself," Don Carlson said. "If a flight was going to be sticky, he'd go along. We all respected him, although I'm not so sure everybody liked him. He got a little obnoxious when he got drunk."

His leadership could also be barbaric. He bullied his men and bribed them with the offer of 500 kip (one dollar) for an enemy ear and 5,000 kip for a severed head when accompanied by a Pathet Lao army cap. The local troops deposited the ears in a big plastic bag hanging on his porch, but he discontinued the practice when he found that they were becoming too greedy for the money and killing people needlessly. He preserved the heads of his most hated enemies with formaldehyde in pickle jars along one side of his bedroom walls.

Poe sent teams of Yau tribesmen (the most important mountain tribe after the Meo) into Red China and learned to speak their language fluently. This led to a romance with a tribal princess, the daughter of one of the Yau leaders, who lived with him for a number of years in the jungle until the American embassy in Vientiane urged them to get married after local politicians began noting publicly that they had spawned several illegitimate children. It is not known what the Princess thought of the pickled heads in the bedroom.

The attitude of this warlord, married to a tribal princess, with his blatant contempt for bureaucratic orders or radio codes, was greatly resented by Ambassador Godley. They did not come any more hawklike than Godley, but he disliked the CIA men who acted as kings in their own kingdoms. Godley had objected to the irregular hot soup drops and had no intention of allowing a man like Poe to operate independently. Godley's chance came when a young American reporter named Michael Morrow blew Poe's cover in a news agency dispatch which appeared in papers all over the States. The article resulted in a complete investigation in which CIA chief Richard Helms read the riot act to Poe for ever letting anyone know about his activities. After that the ambassador had no difficulty persuading the CIA to send Poe to Thailand, where he was to operate out of Udorn. After the exposé Poe developed a fanatical hatred of reporters rivaled only by his anticommunism.

And then there was Edgar "Pop" Buell. Although he supposedly refused a regular CIA position (and salary) he became integral to the secret army as a one-man supply corps. Pop's base at Sam Thong was the place visiting congressmen were shown round, as evidence of the way their money was being spent to help refugees, while the nearby CIA base at Long Tieng remained strictly out of bounds. The enemy broadcast over the radio that anybody who turned in Pop would receive a million kip reward. Extraordinarily, nobody did.

The most complex character of them all was possibly Vang Pao; courageous, corrupt, a formidable and stoic warrior, adept opium dealer and furiously active family man (he collected six wives and twenty-five children). From the very beginning of the secret war in Laos, Vang Pao was the sort of man the CIA needed; a soldier with stamina who was prepared to bite the bullet and take casualties. VP, as the Americans called him, had his first taste of war in 1945 at the age of thirteen when he worked as an interpreter for French commandos who had parachuted into the Plain of Jars to organize anti-Japanese resistance. Later he led a force of 850 hill-tribe commandos in a vain attempt to relieve the French garrison at Dien Bien Phu. He quickly rose to the rank of major in the Laotian army and was made commander of Meo self-defense forces in the Plain of Jars. These volunteer irregulars went unpaid for months at a time because VP pocketed their salaries. When a lieutenant demanded that the men be given their back pay, VP shot him in the leg.

But he was to prove an able leader of the Meo, and the CIA chose to turn a blind eye to his drug-smuggling activities despite a report from the U.S. Bureau of Narcotics in 1971 that he had financed an attempt by Prince Sopsaisana, the Laotian ambassador to France, to smuggle sixty kilos of high-grade Laotian heroin worth $13.5 million on the street into France. The Prince was busted, but the affair was hushed up.

The heroin had been refined in a laboratory in Long Tieng, VP's base for the secret army and CIA HQ in northern Laos. Embarrassed but unperturbed, the CIA took this unfortunate diplomatic hiccough in their stride, compromised by the knowledge that they had helped VP buy the airline which flew the dope from Long Tieng to Vientiane.

In late 1967 the CIA and USAID gave financial assistance to VP to buy two C-47s from Air America and Continental Air Services to create his own private airline, Xieng Kouang Air Transport. Financial control was shared by VP, his brother, his cousin, and his father-in-law, and the company's schedule was restricted to shuttle flights between Long Tieng and Vientiane, supposedly carrying relief supplies and occasional passengers. USAID apparently supported the project in the hope that it would make Long Tieng the commercial center of the northeast and so reinforce VP's political position and, although they were aware that opium would be part of the commercial dealing, decided to go along with it anyway.

They had little choice. Without VP the entire secret army would have collapsed. He was without doubt the most effective military leader in Laos, the opposite of an armchair general. His CIA advisers complained that he spent too much time in the foxholes and not enough time plotting grand strategy, but the troops fought harder when he was around.

He would often persuade reluctant AA chopper pilots to fly supplies out to his patrols six or seven miles in advance of his lines. "I remember once it was getting dark and VP wanted us to supply a patrol with ammunition," Wayne Lannin said. "The pilot on the other ship said, 'We ain't going out there. No way. They were shooting at the Air Force today with 14.5s.'

"VP asked, 'Will you go if I go with you?' He was damn near in tears. He had his folks out there and they were doing a damn good job apparently. You couldn't turn him down. So we went out there and dropped the supplies off, drew a little fire but nothing to speak of, and he went with us. And often when we went out to resupply forward groups he would be there with them in positions he had no business being in.

"VP was exceptional. He did a lot of things people didn't like—he'd summarily execute somebody who didn't do their job. But he kept the whole thing together, and if they hadn't had him it would have fallen apart long before it ever did. He was a dynamo."

The CIA men mentioned became legends in Laos, but there were numerous others who passed through and left their mark. Ted Shackley, who was CIA station chief in Laos, from July 1966 to December 1968, was found unnerving by many agents who worked under him. Exceptionally tall and thin, calm and reserved, he had cold eyes which sent shivers down the backs of certain of his colleagues when he looked at them. He also had an unusually pale floury-white complexion, for he was careful never to go out in the sun.

His successor was Lawrence Devlin, who was station chief from August 1968 to December 1970. Devlin had served with Ambassador Godley in the Congo during the period of heavy CIA involvement there: Once, during a dull patch, he dropped everything for a secret foray aimed at tracking down Ché Guevara, who was rumored to have infiltrated the country with a band of Cuban mercenaries.

Hugh Tovar, Devlin's successor from October 1970 through 1972, was a different type altogether. Intelligent and sophisticated, with none of the personality excesses of his predecessors, he was the epitome of a company man. It was Tovar who had been CIA station chief at the time of the rebel uprising against Sukarno.

Pat Landry, on the other hand, who ran CIA operations out of Udorn, was an ex-Cincinnati police captain. He wandered around the base flicking his boots with a riding crop, and glared through hard, steely-blue eyes.

"When I went out to Laos, I assumed that the CIA was made up primarily of people—right wing, adventuristic, violence-prone, courageous, tough ideologues," Fred Branfman, a free-lance writer who spent four years in Laos from 1967–71, said. "As time went on, however, and I began to ask around, an entirely different picture began to form.

"Shortly after my arrival, for example, Tony Babb, a USAID community-development official, gave me a ride out to a village in southern Laos. Babb had worked with the NSA international affairs section in its CIA-funded heyday and was later to work with the McGovern campaign on his return from Laos. What kind of guys were they [the CIA officials] I asked him. 'Oh, not too different from anyone else,' he responded. What motives did they have? 'You'd be surprised how many of them are in it for the money.'

"The comment was typical. An AA employee, for example, once explained. 'The CIA is just like anything else. There are a number of benefits over here, and while there are some rough things about it, all in all it's an appealing kind of life: the power it gives you, the money you make. I'd say that none of the CIA guys make less than twenty grand a year; they also get AA travel benefits, PX privileges, good vacation time, and time-off programs.'

"Criticism about the kind of job most of the CIA men were doing was constant. The overwhelming consensus was that few were motivated by ideals, that they just put in a day's work. "The CIA is no good. Most of the guys in it are very stupid and lazy. They just don't want to get out there and do the job the way it should be done. That's why we can't win,' was the way one USAID official who had worked with them for years put it.

"It became clear that although the Tony Poes, the Shackleys, the true believers still existed, they were a dying breed. Instead they had been replaced by a new kind of CIA man— a Hugh Tovar, a Vince Shields. There is no mystery where this kind of mentality developed, of course. This new CIA man was little different in personality from a major personality type of twentieth-century America: the technicians and bureaucrats who build our space ships, design our automobiles, run our computers, staff our government agencies."

To the pilots of AA, who definitely belonged to the old school—Branfman's "true believers"—the CIA men were just "customers." It made little difference whether a flight was a

spook mission, a special project, a routine rice drop, or refugee
flight: the danger involved for the pilot was the same.

During the early years of the war, VP was able to secure
gains which his secret army had made in northeast Laos. But
in the beginning of 1968 the tide began to turn when a massive Pathet Lao and North Vietnamese offensive drove VP
from his stronghold. It was to be the beginning of many Meo
migrations which were to turn the hill tribes into nomads
and refugees forever being flown by AA from one burned-out
village to the next. When VP lost San Neua in 1968, AA
evacuated over nine thousand people in less than two weeks.

Over the next three years the Pathet Lao's winter-spring
offensives continued to drive VP back and the number of
refugees expanded accordingly. In 1970 more than one
hundred thousand were relocated, a further fifty thousand
mercenary dependents in 1971.

"I guess AA hauled evey damn Laotian in the world up
country at least twice," Jim Parrish said. "We moved them
from one Communist taken-over village to another. Little
straggly-assed kids—it was pretty pathetic. Their heart
wasn't in it, they didn't care who was winning but they were
running from the bad guys for one reason or another and we'd
haul them from point A to point B and reallocate them somewhere and give them a few pounds of rice and they would try
it again. You got to feel real sorry for the people."

Many of the refugees passed through Pop Buell's HQ at
Sam Thong, AA's most remote and inaccessible up-country
base, the busiest dirt strip airport in the world. Operations
continued from dawn to dusk throughout the year, and on
average the base handled one hundred and twenty-five takeoffs and landings a day, seven days a week all the year round.
It supplied seventy thousand gallons of fuel each month to
aircraft flying in the area and most of its activity was involved
with refugee movement.

The village did not exist until VP founded it in the early
sixties in a narrow, hidden valley high up in the mountains
seventy-seven miles north and slightly east of Vientiane. The
base was surrounded by strange mountain pinnacles that shot
into the sky and were usually shrouded in mist. But even in
such a remote dirt strip, AA facilities ran to a maintenance
hangar, an operations building, transient billets of twenty-

eight beds, hot-water bathing, a laundry, dining room, and recreation lounge.

There was clay in the area, so Pop Buell decided to teach the refugees how to make bricks in order to build more comfortable and permanent shelters. "I took a brick-making machine up there," William Leinbach said, "and we spent half a day getting the damn thing off the aircraft without it getting broken. Two or three months later it was still sitting there and I asked about it. Pop said he had brought the tribal elders over and showed them it and they said, 'Very good, very good—how much are you going to pay us?' They'd got used to handouts."

Much the same fate met another self-help attempt. AA transports would haul large drums of fuel to up-country bases for the helicopters, but it was soon decided that carrying the empties back was too expensive. Stations were provided with machines that cut off the ends of the drums and flattened them out so they could be used as building material. This went on until it was discovered that a local chief was making a small fortune out of selling the metal sheets.

Throughout the period that the Communists had the secret army on the defensive, casualties were high. The numerous refugees created by the enemy offensive frequently exceeded AA's logistical capacity. By 1968 there were nearly six hundred thousand refugees, an appalling statistic in a country with less than three million inhabitants. Many set out on long marches where they lost up to 30 percent of their number. Those unlucky enough to fall into enemy hands were brutally murdered. In one ambush alone four hundred North Vietnamese troops attacked six thousand refugees and slaughtered one thousand three hundred of them in a bloodbath. Most of the dead met their end after being mutilated with hand-wielded knives. Children were dragged from their parents and thrown against rocks, women were raped and disemboweled, and the old were shot in the legs and left to die. Young Meo were forced to murder their own parents when they were too exhausted to continue rather than leave them to the enemy.

The grisly task of transporting the Meo dead back to their villages fell to AA. "We'd have the chopper stacked full of bodies," Tom Grady said. "Some of those guys had been dead for quite a long time, two weeks or more, and they were pretty ripe. It was the first time I ever used tiger balm, which is a kind of perfume they use for everything over there. You rub it in your muscles and on your body and if the Laos felt airsick they'd stick it up their nostrils. With all those leaking body bags on board it helped get me through the trip."

The secret army was decimated. As early as 1968 Pop Buell could report: "A short time ago we rounded up three hundred fresh recruits. Thirty percent were fourteen years old or less, and ten of them were only ten years old. Another thirty percent were fifteen or sixteen. The remaining forty percent were forty-five or over. Where were the ages in between? I'll tell you—they're all dead."

The mercenaries' displaced dependents formed the largest army of all, and most of them were flown from one village to another at least five times. In certain villages the whole population had to be uprooted fifteen or sixteen times.

"Whenever we got a foothold in the Plain of Jars, we hauled most of those people out of there in a C-130," Jim Parrish said. "You'd go in and they would be herded together like cattle with their dogs and sick kids. We'd run them into the plane until they were so squashed together we couldn't close the doors."

AA suffered its own casualties throughout this period, while near escapes were a daily occurrence. Among the most dangerous missions were rescue operations when pilots went in to save colleagues who had been shot down. Billy Adler, a short, tubby chopper pilot, risked his neck on one occasion trying to pick up a downed Thai T-28 pilot who happened to be the nephew of the Prime Minister of Thailand.

The crashed T-28 was located and the Thai pilot had just attached himself to a sling that Adler had dropped to him from the chopper when the Pathet Lao opened fire. They had been waiting patiently in the jungle, carefully watching the T-28, knowing that an AA chopper would be sure to turn up and attempt a rescue. One of the Pathet Lao bullets hit Billy Adler in the heel and the helicopter started to spin.

The chopper crashed to the ground on its side, but Adler was thrown clear. He attempted to crawl back to his craft to pull out his flight attendant when it exploded. The next thing Adler knew he was lying in the grass. His shortness had saved his life, for the explosion scorched his hair and forehead.

He could hear the jabbering of Pathet Lao troops around

him from where he lay. He realized for the first time that his foot hurt and took off his T-shirt and wrapped it around his wounded heel. It was late in the day and he waited for darkness to fall before he painfully crawled further into the jungle.

The Pathet Lao suspected that there was someone hiding in the jungle but were not sure. One wandered out to the log behind which Adler was crouching and sat down for a quiet smoke. The pilot slugged him in the side of the head and crawled off to another spot and hid behind a tree. Another Pathet Lao came out, settled against the tree and fell asleep. Adler knocked him out cold and hauled him into the underbrush and then spent the rest of the night evading the Pathet Lao's comrades. He never moved far from the crash site because he knew that was where AA would look for him.

At dawn AA were already on the alert and spotted the crash site after a couple of hours and saw that the Pathet Lao were still in the vicinity. A Pilatus Porter flew over the area with its door open while the copilot sprayed the area with an Uzi submachine gun and put the Pathet Lao to flight. In the meantime Billy Adler had crawled back to where the grass had been burned round the crashed chopper and was waving what looked like a red flag. An AA chopper picked him up in a sling.

"Where did you get that red flag?" the pilot asked him.

"That's my T-shirt," Adler replied. Later when friendly troops took the territory, AA went back in to retrieve the name plate off the helicopter and salvage what they could. They found that both the Thai pilot and AA flight attendant had been killed. Every Christmas after that Billy Adler received a gift of gold delivered in a large mahogany box from the Prime Minister of Thailand, but he never cared for flying helicopters again.

In between the action AA pilots needed patience, for there was much waiting around to be done. The parking space for the planes at Vientiane by the side of the AA office was surrounded by beautiful trees, but the pilots grumbled that there was nowhere to sit down. This particularly upset Porter Hough, who liked to sit outside on clear, sunny days and read while he waited for his plane to be fixed or a load to be put on board. With all the solemnity of an inconvenienced warrior he prevailed upon Bob Cunningham, the station manager, to put up some concrete benches. "I don't think anybody would use them," Cunningham said, declining to spend the CIA's money on such trivia.

"But they'd sure look nice," Hough said sadly, thinking of the locally made benches that were decorated with attractive ceramic tiles. Hough asked a second time and then a third, but Cunningham refused to loosen the company's purse strings. He made a joke of it with the ground superintendent and the base engineer, "Old Porter wants some benches to sit out there reading on."

Not to be confused by bureaucracy, Porter Hough bought two benches himself at ten dollars apiece and had them put under his favorite tree that was a full five foot in diameter. Cunningham surveyed them skeptically. "So you were really serious about that?"

"Yep, and if you want them moved you'll have to move them yourself. It took four strong men to put them in there, so you'll need four strong men to move them out."

The benches stayed. "They were perfect for the wives and girl friends who came there to the door of the office and would get tired waiting for aircraft that never came in," Porter Hough remembered. "And in the mornings the guys would set their gear on it to keep it off the ground, which would be wet with dew."

The resounding success of the benches even impressed the parsimonious Mr. Cunningham, especially when he discovered they only cost ten dollars each. "We have funds for this, and if you insist on it we'll pay for it," he said, handing Hough two ten-dollar bills. More benches were bought by the company to the great joy of Porter Hough. "Talk about polished benches, those benches were polished," he said, flushed at the memory of his triumph.

The importance that these benches played in the life of their single-minded colleague was not overlooked by the wags of AA. They paid for a large and distinguished sign from Taipei, bearing the legend in white lettering: "Porter Hough Memorial Park." The entire company was invited to its inauguration, and the uninitiated were shocked when they first arrived. "My God, what's happened to Porter?" But Porter was alive and well, good-naturedly puffing at his pipe and enjoying the joke at his expense. The inauguration of the Porter Hough Memorial Park was a highly successful party.

As the war in Laos continued from year to year the Plain of Jars came under heavy attack and changed hands constantly, almost on a seasonal basis. The CIA and AA set up a big base on the plain known as Lima 22. In the one area where pilots were not subjected to the dangers of mountainous terrain they had to face fierce enemy fire. Routine tended to turn into heroics.

AA often had to go in and rescue Air Force forward air controllers who had been shot down. When a pilot directing air strikes over the Plain of Jars was hit, a group of choppers went out to help. One bird went in at an altitude of eight thousand feet to take a look and started to draw heavy artillery fire and elected to stay up high. A companion ship, flown by Ted Cash who had the reputation of being fearless, decided to go down and began to dive. Air Force A-7 jets covered him to begin with but broke off halfway down when they couldn't take the fire anymore. The barrage was layered, with shelling at the top and smaller-caliber at the bottom, and Cash saw the flak go by him as he continued his dive.

Finally he was low enough to hover behind some hillocks and carefully weaved his chopper toward a ravine where the crashed airplane was lying on its side. As he flew out from behind a small hill, he found himself sitting in the middle of two thousand North Vietnamese troops who had been on the march and were resting at the side of the road. There was a moment of stunned inaction as the troops watched an American helicopter fly through their ranks three feet above the ground.

Cash made it to the crashed plane but saw that the pilot was hanging out of the cockpit, dead. At that moment the North Vietnamese suddenly gathered their wits about them and opened up on him. Cash spiraled upward in a blizzard of bullets and artillery fire and headed for home. Back at base AA ground personnel who inspected the chopper found that it had not taken a single hit.

Pilots never knew when trouble was going to come up on them and a milk run could turn into a flight through hell. Frenchie Smith, known as one of the best helicopter pilots who ever flew, had been flying backward and forward between two points out on the Plain of Jars all day without incident. There was some cloud, otherwise the weather was good, and no enemy guns or traffic whatever had been reported.

But Frenchie also had another reputation: he was said to be a magnet. If anybody was going to get shot at, they said, it was Frenchie Smith. On his fourth trip out, together with his Filipino copilot and an embassy "customer," the world erupted in fire beneath him. In a single moment his instrument panel lit up like a Christmas tree—engine, oil, fuel, and fire lights flashed their warnings simultaneously. The chopper was on fire, the engine was shot out, and at an altitude of only one thousand feet there was nowhere to land but straight ahead.

With all the skill he was renowned for, Frenchie Smith executed a perfect no-engine landing and put the ship down without hurting it—right in the middle of a bivouac area of a battalion of North Vietnamese. The men leapt from the aircraft and ran under fire for the cover of a ditch. The enemy's small-arms fire threw up a dust storm around them and within minutes they had opened up with mortars.

One of the first rounds blew the tail off the helicopter, removing the slightest hope of escape. Frenchie Smith had a survival vest on which had a radio and a couple of flares in it and he put out a Mayday call, asking for help, which was picked up by an AA H-34 which was in the area. Then for six minutes which stretched into eternity they ran along the ditch while the enemy fired at them with everything they had. The customer had an automatic weapon and the flight mechanic had a carbine but there was very little ammo, although they managed to return fire a couple of times to let the North Vietnamese know that they were not going to give up without a fight. After a while Frenchie had the impression that the enemy wanted to take them alive.

Meanwhile he kept up radio contact with the H-34, giving the pilot, Mick Pewer, their exact position and telling him they were very low on ammunition. The chopper came in from the north under fire all the way and took seven hits before Frenchie heard the pilot pull the power back and stagger off to the south. "That's it," Frenchie told his companions. "They probably hit his engine oil. We've had it."

The men used up the last of their ammunition returning enemy fire, which raked the top of the ditch and kept them firmly pinned down. A minute went by and Frenchie had secretly given up when he heard the whirl of rotor blades and looking saw the H-34 returning low over the trees from the south. The chopper swept in and landed by the ditch and the flight mechanic jumped out, firing rapidly to keep the enemy's heads down, while the men ran toward the H-34 with the dirt kicking up around their feet. As Frenchie charged forward he turned to look behind him and saw a North Vietnamese officer running after him firing his pistol. As they scrambled on board there was a minute's delay before they took off. Frenchie looked around at the same time as the customer and saw that the kicker was waiting for two more people who were running up. They were North Vietnamese. "Get out of here!" the customer shouted, and as the bird lifted off it took ten rounds but nobody was hurt.

As they headed out the pilot explained that while he had attracted heavy fire on the way in, when he turned south he had not drawn any, so he decided to take the chance and turn around. He took an instrument check, spoke to his flight mechanic, and thought, what the hell, if he didn't get in nobody else would, as there was so little time due to Frenchie's lack of ammo. Back at Udorn, Frenchie Smith bought the pilot a crate of scotch. After his experience out on the Plain of Jars he always flew with boxes and boxes of ammunition. "You can't ever carry enough bullets," he told his colleagues. The incident had taken the fun out of flying for him and he never crossed the Mekong again and finally quit flying for a year to become the representative of the Far East Pilots' Association in Taipei. After that he continued his career with AA as a maintenance test pilot.

But death was as simple as escape was miraculous. One pilot took a single round beneath his helmet. The copilot took the controls as the chopper careered to the left and flew for thirty minutes back to Udorn which was the nearest base able to administer medical treatment. He flew without knowing the pilot's condition, and it was the longest thirty minutes of his life. The man took a month off directly after the incident, but never flew again and was never the same.

"If you have an accident you have to get back in the bird and fly the next day," Ted Helmers said. "Usually if something happens to somebody you can walk away from it or turn your head, but this guy was too close." While the rest of the world remained unaware of the secret war in Laos, the pilots of Air America were close to it every day, year in and year out. And it was a war that was to escalate in the same way as the conflict in Vietnam.

SIX

VIETNAM

Air America's role in Vietnam was as conspicuous as it was secret in Laos. The company was everywhere. But whereas in Laos it was an integral part of the secret war, a clandestine air force designed to back up a clandestine army, in Vietnam most of its work was aboveboard while keeping up with the company motto of ANYTHING, ANYWHERE, ANYTIME.

And, as in Laos, AA grew with the war. As early as 1954 Civil Air Transport was involved in clandestine support missions. Col. Edward Lansdale and his team of CIA men directed two small groups of North Vietnamese who had been recruited as agents, smuggled out of Haiphong, trained in Saigon, and then sent back to North Vietnam. Civil Air Transport smuggled over eight tons of arms and equipment into Haiphong in the regular refugee shipments authorized by the Geneva accords for the eventual use of these teams.

But as late as 1964 there were only ten pilots serving a handful of strips in a leisurely routine. There was no hazard pay for flying then, because there was no danger. Before the big troop build-up AA was limited to USAID contracts and moving advisers and the CIA around. It was a very small operation commercially, with hardly more than an itinerant Dornier, Piper, or Beechcraft making the occasional flight from Tan Son Nhut, Saigon's airport. At the height of the war there were around two hundred and forty pilots in Saigon alone, there were landing strips everywhere, and it was a seven-day-a-week operation.

Life for an AA pilot during these early years was pleasant, if not particularly lucrative. Saigon was unspoiled and relatively clean for an Asian city. Taxis, restaurants, and housing were cheap, and the flying was not exacting. But as the military began its build-up and massive numbers of troops arrived, the brief calm disappeared forever. "It seemed that everybody came to Saigon," Les Strouse (AA's station manager in Saigon) said. "My own opinion was that none of the troops belonged there. They were supposed to be there to fight a war, not to languish in the hotels downtown. Saigon became a place primarily of GIs getting drunk and being obnoxious. This led to the Vietnamese becoming like that, because they were never that way before. And the American GI has always been that way."

AA began to snowball from the end of 1964, doubling its flying hours within ten months, and then redoubling them during the next eight months. Daily aircraft departures doubled within sixteen months, stepping up in frequency by another third in the next three months. The cargo traffic rate was logarithmic. By 1969 AA was using nine different types of aircraft to meet its schedules, eight kinds of single-and fixed-wing planes, plus Bell 204B helicopters. "The success of such an operation is largely a matter of flexibility," the company announced in its journal, the AA log. "Flexibility is the title of AA's story."

This meant that AA was prepared to fly anything, as usual. They carried visiting VIPs, prisoners, and sedated bulls; Green Berets, the supersecret Special Operations Group, CIA payrolls, and operatives attached to the Phoenix program (an Agency plan to coordinate an attack against the Vietcong infrastructure among all Vietnamese and American police, intelligence, and military units. In the first two and a half years of this program 20,587 suspected Vietcong were killed).

The strangest cargo AA ever carried was some of the people. "But when people get on your plane, how can you tell a strange person from an unstrange person?" Art Kenyon said. "We had some funny-looking people over there, but then funny-looking people gravitate to a situation like that. We had some flights when we carried couriers, presumably. CIA, when we weren't permitted to load any other passengers. One guy would get on with a pouch with classified documents in it and he would be armed, as were most of our passengers. They had all sorts of hardware, and although I've never carried a guy with a bazooka, I've carried them with machine guns, M16s, hand grenades and everything else."

"The young CIA officers wore civilian working clothes and had code names so that we didn't know their real names," Don Carlson said. "You always ran into people who wanted to go someplace, but we didn't ask who they were. We never asked any questions. If they wanted to go someplace we'd take them. Anywhere. Then we'd park and wait for them or go into town with them. They were the customer, we did what they wanted."

The case officers often wanted to go into North Vietnam, and AA obligingly took them, as it was completely out of the question for them to use military or Air Force planes. AA used Helios for these missions. Pilots would land in roads and wait while their CIA passengers snooped around. One pilot flying a Volpar was chased out of North Vietnam by Russian Migs. Hopelessly outmatched for speed and maneuverability, he took a chance and dived through cloud into a valley. He was fortunate enough not to hit anything. The gamble paid off and he crossed the border safely.

One of the VIPs flown by Bob Murray in 1965 was Richard Nixon, before he was president. There were three AA pilots designated to fly VIPs then. "I don't know how they chose us," Murray said. "Maybe we didn't bounce as much as the rest of the guys." Nixon was flown in a Beechcraft down to the Delta, where a motorcade took him into town. He was then flown in a helicopter escorted by five gunships to a USAID farm project. "I sweated over the whole trip," Murray said. "If I had a bald tire or something, the press would have said, 'Nixon escapes death in Vietnam.'" Naturally enough, Murray was paid hazard money for flying Nixon.

The CIA also used mercenaries in Vietnam, mostly Montagnards, but on a smaller scale than in Laos, and again it was AA which carried them around. One of the leaders was in exile with his staff in Cambodia and the Agency wanted him brought across the border into Ban Me Thuot to unite the Montagnards there in the fight against the North Vietnamese. "We had to select a strip just across the border from Cambodia in Vietnam," Don Carlson said. "This guy insisted that first people went in and secured the strip and then he would bring his people out. We brought him and his staff to Ban Me Thuot in a Caribou, alternating with an army Chinook. Boy, he had the meanest-looking staff you ever saw in your life. It scared you just to see these guys getting on the airplane."

AA flew USAID contracts moving people and supplies. They would fly to a province and move supplies from the airport into the villages, hauling cement, tin sheets, and roofing material. Things were still relatively quiet, pilots were well informed on the location of bad areas and tried to stay high enough to avoid them. Some personnel drew tougher assignments, such as the jocks who flew the two helicopters based in Da Nang and who worked the northern area and were frequently up by the Demilitarized Zone.

When the Marines were fighting in the protracted struggle at Khe Sanh, AA choppers worked the area for a week at a time. They flew to the surrounding villages in appalling weather and drew much fire, shelling, and rockets. Their principal task in the area was hauling out the badly wounded.

And even in Vietnam, where there was an enormous military transport capability, AA delivered ammunition. Art Kenyon flew a Twin Beech loaded to capacity with hand grenades. The seats were taken out and cases of grenades loaded along each side of the plane, leaving a narrow aisle down the center. Kenyon then took the pilot's seat and more grenades were loaded in the aisle. "There I was in the front with nothing but grenades down to the tail and no way I could get out," Kenyon said. "If at any time someone had leaned over and whispered 'bang' in my ear, I think I would have dropped dead." But Kenyon added that on the whole he preferred to fly grenades to baby chicks. "Grenades don't stink. One agricultural development program involved flying chicks. We'd have tens of thousands of baby chicks on an unpressurized airplane where the wind blows from the tail section towards the cockpit. The smell of ten thousand baby chicks, let me tell you, is almost overpowering."

On one hard-rice mission near Vitanh, a Mekong River delta one hundred miles southeast of Saigon, a C-47 flown by Bill Pruner, together with a Chinese copilot and a Vietnamese kicker, came under heavy fire. The plane was flying at about twelve hundred feet and approaching the landing field when the Vietcong opened up and Pruner was hit three times—in the shoulder, the leg and the arm—and one engine was knocked out. The plane crashed into a small canal.

The Vietcong kept firing at the grounded plane and

wounded the copilot, who managed to put out a Mayday call picked up by another AA freight plane in the area, which in turn called in an AA chopper. Despite heavy sniper fire the helicopter landed near the downed plane and two men jumped from it wearing AA uniforms but turned out to be Vietcong guerrillas. Both men opened fire on the chopper with automatic weapons and hurled hand grenades while other Vietcong moved in from flanking positions. The helicopter had flown into a trap but despite heavy fire at close range managed to lift off and escape unharmed.

A USAF plane tried to land a few minutes later, but was also driven off by intense ground fire. An hour later an AA helicopter did manage to land, and its crew was met by a sight which was to harden the company's pilots for the rest of the war. They found their colleagues dead in the cockpit of their plane, shot in the face at point-blank range, but there were signs that they had been brutally macheted, for there were deep slash marks on their arms and bodies where they had attempted to ward off the blows.

There was no sign of the Vietnamese kicker, but villagers living nearby said that he had been led away by the Vietcong with a rope around his neck and his hands tied behind his back. A report reached AA more than a year later that he had been seen, but his eventual fate was never discovered. As the chopper took off with the bodies of the dead airmen, a USAF fighter strafed the crashed plane to destroy the ammunition it had been carrying.

The pilot Pruner was the victim not only of the enemy but of a change of mind. A few days before the crash, opportunities arose for some of the men to transfer to Bangkok. The pilots tossed coins and Pruner was among the winners. The night before he was about to go he called up the colleague he had won the toss with and told him he had changed his mind and had decided to stay on in Saigon and earn a little extra money. There was no hazard pay in Thailand, he said.

The ill feeling that these brutal deaths caused among the pilots was directed mostly against the company itself. The management had always strictly enforced a ruling that pilots were not allowed to carry guns on their planes at any time. Many pilots tended to hide a hand gun in their flight bags, arguing that it was suicide not to do so, but the company absolutely forbade it and dismissed one captain caught with a gun in his plane.

The pilots angrily blamed the deaths of their colleagues on this rule and argued that if they had been armed they would have been able to hold off the enemy long enough to allow the rescue helicopter to pull them out. AA supervisors began to turn a blind eye to pilots with guns tucked into their belts and eventually revised the ruling. Pilots had the option to sign for a Carbine or Uzi machine gun as long as they checked the weapon back in after each flight.

Another rule AA strictly enforced was its twelve-hour bottle to throttle stipulation—a pilot was not allowed to fly until twelve hours after he had been drinking. It was difficult to enforce, but not many pilots chose to take the insane risk of flying drunk, although most of them flew on occasions with terrible hangovers and rated the experience as one of the worst of the war. One pilot was dismissed when the company discovered that the milk he drank in the cockpit was laced with whiskey.

"It was very dangerous flying drunk," Wayne Lannin said. "It scared the shit out of me. The H-34 had a kind of autopilot, and as soon as you got off the ground you could punch it and the thing goes by itself. I'd doze off for a while and then I'd wake up and look over at my Thai copilot and see that he was completely uncool, just a mass of nerves. After one look at him I wouldn't have any trouble at all staying awake."

Lannin remembered one particularly drunken night when he took home a girl but was so deep into his cups he never laid a hand on her. He woke up the following morning to the horn of the airport bus waiting in the street to take him to work. Lannin was supposed to have been washed, shaved, and in his uniform with a bag packed ready for a six day stint up-country. He told the bus to go on without him, threw on some clothes, and took a taxi out to the airport. The AA office was a further half a mile down the road.

"I started to walk and the road must have been fifty yards wide, but I missed it and went straight into a canal. I pulled myself out of the filthy, stagnant water and realized I was still drunk." Somebody stopped to give him a lift to the ramp, where the chopper already had its blades turning. "I thought, 'Oh shit, only six months on the job and my career in ruins,' and considered going into personnel there and then and

throwing the towel in." But he went out to the ship and
clambered into the copilot's seat next to Ted Cash, who did
not say a word, looked straight ahead, and seemed impervious
to the ripe smell that Lannin exuded. "Klong water was dripping off me, I smelt like a sewer and looked like hell."

"Looks like you could do with some sleep," Cash said
calmly. "Go to sleep and I'll wake you when it's over."

The chopper bounced off pads throughout the day and Lannin slept for twelve hours without waking up once. It was
not until they got back to base and they were shutting down
for the night that Cash spoke to his copilot. "Hey, time to
wake up."

Later Lannin asked what the day had been like. "Ted said
the roughest part was having me there. When the sun hit
me I started to mildew, and there I was up-country for six
days without a change of clothes. I was wringing them out
every night, but it didn't do any good."

By and large, despite the colossal build-up of the military,
Vietnam was a safer, more routine assignment than Laos.
Every evening pilots either phoned into operations to find
out what the schedule was for the following day, or a driver
would deliver it to their quarters. They would never know
until that time whether they had the day off, were on standby
or a firm schedule. They were then told their takeoff time
and the aircraft number and no more, unless they were going
to be away overnight, which was indicated by the word
RON—Remain Overnight. They were never told their destination.

If they were on call, a crew bus came to pick them up an
hour and a half before takeoff, which usually meant rising
at dawn. There was a cafeteria at the airport with a cheerful
dining room and a kitchen that was able to please the palates
of Vietnamese, Filipinos and Americans. After breakfast
there was a briefing when pilots were told about enemy activity, where to expect trouble and what areas to stay out of.
They were also told where the B-52 high-altitude bombers
would be making their strikes so they could stay out of the
way of the rain of bombs.

In the early days scheduling could be irregular, and some
pilots found themselves continually on uncomfortable and
difficult routes, while others seemed to draw only the easy
flights. Certain pilots would be flying as much as sixty hours

for five days, a sure way of setting themselves up for an accident through exhaustion.

Bribery among the schedulers was suspected. One Vietnamese national working in scheduling doubled as a tennis instructor, and the story went around that those who paid enough for tennis instruction were given the choice jobs. Pilots began to complain and the company evened out the scheduling fairly.

AA ran regular schedule passenger runs from one Vietnamese city to another, such as the Da Nang rocket, a C-46 which left Saigon at nine in the morning, flew directly to Da Nang, and turned around and flew back at midday. The pilots usually flew out over the South China Sea and up the coast for safety. In the early days, when navigational aids were extremely limited, it was often necessary to fly well below five hundred feet during the monsoon season. Pilots would follow the beaches north and often used their windscreen wipers to clear the salt spray off their windscreens. One flight up to Da Nang in a monsoon storm killed eight American college professors surveying South Vietnamese high school and college problems when their plane crashed into a rain-veiled mountain.

The morning briefings were only a guide, and safe areas could become enemy infested without warning. Miles Lechtman, a kicker, was in a C-46 flying south from Da Nang over a supposedly safe area when machine-gun fire peppered the plane's tail. "I got a bullet through my flight bag and I had my foot on it and felt it go through. It went through two paperbacks—thank God I was a heavy reader at the time." He keeps the bullet in the bedroom of his Los Angeles home. A pilot was also saved by a paperback when a bullet lodged in it. Aptly, it was Harold Robbins' *The Adventurers*.

Sometimes AA pilots themselves contributed to the hazards of flying into Da Nang. An Associated Press reporter remembered flying in with Rocky Emerson, a flamboyant, rumbustious character who flew his Porter in cowboy boots and had a voice like Popeye the Sailor Man. "It was only a twenty-minute flight, but all the time going into Da Nang, literally one of the busiest air bases in the world with dozens of bombers taking off, Rocky was clutching the joystick, sitting there yelling, 'Get those goddamn airplanes out of the sky for God's sake, here comes Emerson.' And as he went down onto that huge two-mile-long runway, he cursed everybody in the sky. 'Damn Phantom jockeys can't fly for shit.'"

In good weather when they were not under fire pilots were able to admire the view. Seen from the air, Vietnam is a very beautiful country. "Boy, up in the north the beaches are really pretty," one pilot said. "I had a little peninsula all picked out, about twenty acres, that I wanted to buy when we'd won the war."

Vietnam also had its crop of nightmare strips. At Quang Ngai enemy sharpshooters were regularly hidden in the fields at the west end of the runway. Pilots would sit helplessly in their cockpits and watch the tracers zip by them, and many planes were hit. But the worst strip of them all, which could reduce veteran pilots to jelly, was Gia Nghai.

It was a two-thousand-foot-long dirt strip, with a slight hump in the middle, built on a shaved-off mountaintop with a three-hundred-foot vertical drop at either end. Its two-thousand-foot elevation reduced the performance of the planes, and if the wind blew directly down the runway an aircraft would have to cope with a terrific down draft on approach shortly before reaching the end of the runway as it crossed the vertical drop. "I don't think I ever made a landing there where my knees weren't shaking coming down into the final approach," Art Kenyon said. "I would let out a big sigh of relief every time I stopped and found myself still on dirt." One plane did go off the runway when one of its brakes failed, but the pilot managed to stamp on the remaining brake so the aircraft veered to one side instead of the steep drop at the end. The aircraft was a write-off but the crew climbed out unhurt.

Anything could happen in the most routine day in Vietnam. One pilot, having landed in a small strip with woods on either side, was taxiing to a standstill when Vietcong ran out from the trees and began firing. Bullets thudded into the nose of the plane while one whistled right through the cockpit. Methodically the pilot turned the plane around and taxied to the other end of the strip while the Vietcong ran back into the woods. The pilot climbed out of the plane, calmly inspected it for damage, and when after a brief inspection he decided it was still in shape to fly, jumped back into the cockpit and took off.

AA passengers did not always remain as cool under fire, and their nervousness often increased in proportion to the seniority of their rank. Art Kenyon was chauffeuring a VIP back to Can Tho, careful to keep beneath the clouds. "It happened that this cloud base was descending as I approached my destination so in order to stay in contact with the ground I began letting down. And I guess I was down to seven hundred to nine hundred feet when a whole bunch of tracers went by the windshield. We didn't like to have our passengers alarmed at any time, so I pulled the stick back and eased up into the clouds. I looked back casually to see how he was doing and his eyes were as big as eggs."

The VIP was not doing very well. "Were those tracers?" he screamed in an hysterical falsetto. Kenyon's reluctance to lie to senior officers brought a curt, affirmative nod from him. The VIP sat tight for the remainder of the journey, dumb with terror.

The extraordinary mixed bag of warriors and their hangers-on that AA were obliged to carry without question, from war correspondents to the head of the CIA, led to the occasional hijacking. One chopper crew was faced with an irate soldier when they tried to explain it was not within their jurisdiction to carry him. The soldier leveled his M-16 at the pilot and his colleague. "Take me or I'm going to shoot," he said flatly. They took him. (There was an incident in Laos where native soldiers shot a chopper pilot dead when he refused to take them on a short jaunt to a nearby village.)

There were also mysterious crashes which the company tried to hush up. A Beechcraft flying a senior embassy official, widely held to be a CIA man, as its sole passenger crashed on its final approach into Cuchi. There were bullet holes everywhere, but the oddest thing of all was that they were from inside the plane. Company secrecy over the incident was so tight that no one every really knew what happened. AA personnel understood that the passenger had shot the crew and then died himself in the crash. There were conjectures among the men ranging from the charitable view that the customer's automatic weapon had accidentally gone off, killing the pilots, to wilder assertions that a psychotic CIA man had gone berserk.

Choppers flying into hot areas faced the constant hazard of being mobbed by the locals. AA would fly a USAID customer into a village that had been rocketed during the night so he could assess the situation and arrange to bring in medical teams or fly out the wounded. The wounded would be moved by chopper to an airport where they could be flown to a hospital. "There would be so many of them, and because they couldn't all go at the same time they would mob the ship as soon as we landed," Ted Helmers said. "We could only take eight and there would be eighty people wanting to get on. You had to have a strong man at the door to let one in at a time and then close the door so we could get away. Then a lot of them would stand on the skids. It was important to have a pretty big guy along."

There were also more lighthearted hazards. Art Kenyon took off with his copilot in a C-46 from Saigon one morning and once up in the air called back to base, "This is 22 Bravo estimating to land at...."

"Repeat your call sign again," the company operator cut in.

"Twenty-two Bravo."

"I'm looking out of the window here and 22 Bravo is still sitting out there on the ramp," the perplexed operator said. Kenyon looked at the placard on the dashboard in front of him. He had taken the wrong plane.

The next time Kenyon went out with the same copilot he decided to double check everything. "Every time you and I fly together something goes wrong," Kenyon said. "Let's make sure everything is right this time." They checked the airplane number, checked the logbook number, checked the schedule, and jokingly quizzed one another on their names. Satisfied, they settled back into the cockpit and took off. Once in the air Kenyon picked up the logbook and opened it up. Inside there was a placard with a notice writ large in red type. "Not Fit For Passenger Flights Before Test Flight." The two pilots looked at each other and then looked back at the seventeen passengers they were carrying. Kenyon shrugged, put the placard back in the logbook, and kept on going.

Whatever happened to an AA pilot in the air, he could relax in his home back in Saigon almost as if there was no war going on. Then in 1968 the North Vietnamese took the war into the cities themselves with the Tet offensive. Tet, the Vietnamese new year on January 31, was the perfect time to launch such an attack. The Vietnamese celebrated by firing guns into the air and letting off long chains of firecrackers throughout the night, and the richer the people were, the longer their strings of fireworks. It was not uncommon for strings to hang from the top of four-story buildings to the ground, with a big cherry bomb every six inches. When the North Vietnamese opened up just after midnight their gunfire blended in with the festivities. A total of about sixty-seven thousand troops attacked one hundred two towns across South Vietnam and moved into Saigon itself.

Up in Da Nang, Fred Anderson and Howard Klein were celebrating the new year over a few drinks and Klein was taping the festivities. Round about one in the morning Anderson exclaimed, "Goddamn it, Howard, aren't they ever going to quit?" Klein was listening carefully and fiddling with his tape recorder. He looked up at his friend in alarm. "Oh shit, Fred, this is for real."

In Saigon many AA personnel went to bed, dismissing the shooting as all part of the fun. Ted Helmers, who lived only a mile from the airport, had heard the gunfire but slept soundly anyhow and started out as usual the following morning for work. As he went out of his gate he saw that the streets were deserted except for military police, so he decided to go back into the house and listen to the news on the radio. He found out that during the night the Vietcong had established positions all over Saigon. They would occupy houses in twos and threes, a dozen would hole up in a motel, and there was not a street or a building that could claim to be completely safe.

AA pilots were returning from missions to face the most ugly form of warfare. There was intense fighting inside South Vietnamese cities for several months. The trip out to the airport had become more hazardous than flying. Nobody could be sure where the North Vietnamese were from one moment to the next, and even more unsettling was the knowledge that they could pass the enemy in the street and not know it. Children were sent into crowded cinemas with hand grenades, and bombs were carried into cafés.

AA was flying the CIA all over the country as they attempted to assess the situation. At the very beginning of the

Tet offensive a group of pilots on the way to the airport saw bodies on the street and barbed wire across the gate of the Saigon golf club, which was the entrance they used to reach their operations office. They turned around and passed a USAID vehicle, which was ambushed the moment it drove through the barbed wire. The pilots made for a mechanic's house nearby and lay on the floor of the upstairs bedroom for forty-eight hours while Vietcong moved all around them. By the time they returned to their homes, their families had given them up for dead.

When Fred Anderson returned from Da Nang the night after the Tet offensive began, he went downtown to the Embassy Hotel to meet a group of friends, swap stories, and try and find out what had happened. At ten-thirty he decided to call it a day and the party broke up. One hour later a bomb was thrown into the part of the hotel they had been sitting in and blew out the entire front of the building.

One pilot looked out of his apartment window, which had a view of one of the bridges, to see a long line of enemy troops crossing it. Minutes later he heard them moving around in the bottom of his building. The pilot locked his door, stayed holed up in his room, and it was several days before he could move out.

AA personnel who managed to reach their base were unable to leave it. Men who were flying every day slept out at the airport and went for five days at a time without shaving or a change of clothes. Snipers were within comfortable range of the AA ramp, and every approach to a plane or attempt at refuelling was dangerous. "We were out on the ramp with a big Shell tanker full of fuel when we started to take sniper fire," Fred Anderson said. "We hit the deck, then about fifteen minutes later we tried again but got run off the plane. You could hear the bullets hitting the tarmac with a *tick-tick* sound all around. It took forty-five minutes to make it to the traffic terminal, which was only two hundred fifty feet away. The boy who was driving the Shell truck said, 'I've had enough of this. It's full. It's going to explode, I'm leaving.' And he left. We stayed inside the terminal, and despite shooting through the night the truck was still sitting there in the morning in front of the airplane untouched."

In the middle of this mayhem three thousand two hundred pounds of children's clothes, shoes, diapers, safety pins, and vitamin pills arrived in a massive shipment for Fred Anderson. "I used to work in the orphanage two or three times a month, helping out there among the twenty-five hundred kids. I had never had my personal effects sent out, and the company gave us free shipment on twenty-five hundred pounds. I asked if I could ship out some stuff for the kids instead and they said I could go ahead and never charged me a dime for the extra. It arrived right in the middle of the Tet offensive, but we never lost a bit of it."

Throughout the months of the Tet offensive hazardous takeoffs and landings became routine. Capt. C.A. Winston flew into Dalat in the central highlands to evacuate seven people the CIA considered to be in danger. The only landing spot available was a soccer field in the downtown area, where the fighting happened to be the heaviest. Winston landed amid heavy gunfire and picked up the seven evacuees. A few days later the flight was repeated and four CIA men were picked up.

A Helio-Courier received an urgent call to take in some ammo to reinforce friendlies under heavy pressure at Roth Chow. The pilot took off, staying below the clouds, but lost radio contact on the way. He was careful to look out for enemy action as he went in, but things were quiet and he had a smooth landing. There were troops at the side of the runway looking at him but doing little to help him unload. After he had lost his temper a little, they finally gave him a hand and he took off while things were still clear. Halfway home he made radio contact with the base. "Don't go into Roth Chow," the operator barked. "We've just lost it to the enemy." The helping hands who had received the ammo belonged to Vietcong.

It was not unusual for an airstrip to be held by friendly troops at one end and Vietcong at the other. But the pilots still went in. "I took a Caribou with a load of ammo into a short strip, and because of the enemy we couldn't land the way we normally landed," Don Carlson said. "We came in over a church and nearly knocked the goddamn spire off it. They were shooting at us from the other end of the runway, and I turned the plane around and the kicker started throwing everything out the back as fast as he could."

Halfway through this operation a soldier roared up in a jeep. "Give me two minutes and I'll get a truck," he shouted up at them. "Truck, my ass!" Carlson shouted back. "By the time you get a truck we'll be long gone."

Once a Caribou had landed in a remote strip, the enemy were close enough to be alerted and were ready and waiting for the next trip. They would set up mortars within range of the strip and open up the moment the plane touched down. When that happened, the pilot would run the plane off from under the load. The kicker would open the back end of the Caribou, undo the straps securing the pallets, which were on rails, to the side of the plane, and give the pilot the okay. The pilot held the brakes until he had the plane running at full power, then released them so that the plane jumped forward, leaving the cargo behind.

Even when it was reasonably safe to travel to and from Saigon airport, there was a strict six o'clock curfew. Pilots who landed late were supposed to sleep overnight in cots provided by the company. "I came in just before six one night," Don Carlson said, "and I'd been gone for a week, so I thought, to hell with it—I'm going home. I got out of the gate just before six and I had to drive downtown. That meant being out after curfew and it was spooky. It really scared me. Anybody, friends or enemies, were liable to shoot at you. There wasn't a soul in the streets. That was the longest journey on the loudest motorcycle in my life."

AA planes were used regularly to transport prisoners to Con Son, the notorious prison island where hundreds of men were jammed into small cells known as tiger cages. This routine assignment became controversial after the ceasefire agreement when an Associated Press picture taken in the Mekong Delta showed seven North Vietnamese being led aboard a plane with AA markings. One of the prisoners was wounded in the leg, but walked unaided.

U.S. Ambassador Graham A. Martin admitted that the CIA airline had been used to transport prisoners, but denied that it represented a violation of the ceasefire terms. He said an AA plane had been authorized for "humanitarian reasons" after a request for help to transport a wounded prisoner. He said that he did not know that six other prisoners of war would be put on the plane.

With the signing of the ceasefire agreement in February 1973, the nature of the war in Vietnam changed completely. Young diplomats and paunchy middle-aged pilots quietly replaced the professional soldiers who had been in the forefront of the U.S. establishment in South Vietnam for ten years. Defense contracts for AA more than doubled to $41.4 million (against $17.7 million in 1972).

"The contracts reflect substantial U.S. involvement in the Southeast Asia war," Representative Les Aspin, a former Pentagon economic adviser, told the press. "Apparently, unknown to the American public, the CIA has taken up some of the slack created by our military withdrawal."

As the U.S. formally began to withdraw from Indochina, and the war apparatus was phased out, AA was hiring more pilots. With the majority of the U.S. military forces out of the picture, the role of maintaining a significant American influence reverted largely to the CIA and subsequently the services of AA were more in demand.

Perhaps the oddest contract AA ever landed was at this time with the International Supervisory and Control Commission, formed to police the Vietnam ceasefire. The CIA airline found itself ferrying around Communist officers from Poland and Hungary, two member countries of the commission. The decision to engage the airline placed the Communists in a quandary that they resolved in favor of their personal safety. They recognized the fact that AA pilots knew the terrain better than anyone else. Canada provided the formula that facilitated Polish and Hungarian acceptance, and ICCS Air Services was formed as an offshoot of AA. The planes and choppers of ICCS Air Services carried no markings except for yellow stripes, which were supposed to denote their neutrality. They were flown by AA pilots, who soon became contemptuous of the Commission and referred to it as "I Can't Control Shit."

"ICCS was the biggest farce you ever saw," William Leinbach said. "If the North Vietnamese broke a truce or violated the agreement, the Poles and Hungarians would refuse to check it out. It was a boondoggle, with the Poles buying stuff in the PX and shipping it all home. It was a complete waste of time.

"During that time we had two hats. They'd tell you on the schedule whether you'd be ICCS or AA. If you were ICCS

you'd put your ICCS hat and wings on, and if you were AA
you'd put on your AA hat and wings. The yellow stripes on
the plane made you a good target."

One ICCS chopper was shot down by a shoulder-fired, infrared, heat-seeking SA-7 missile. Everybody on board was
killed, including two NVA colonels. A second helicopter attracted ground fire when it landed near the crash. The Canadian members of ICCS on board pushed forward the Pole
shouting, "Don't shoot! This is one of your guys."

Other Communist members of ICCS were more careful.
Fred Anderson flew the Polish ambassador, a Polish general,
and other members of a Commission team into a hot area.
"Make your stay as short as possible here," he warned them.
"We're not in a secure position and have no guards and no
protection."

The Polish general calmly eyed the pilot. "Young man,"
the general said, "have no fear—they know we're here."

Pilots who witnessed the commission in action were disgusted at the undisguised partisanship of the Communist
members. Bob Murray explained: "The Pole would see a body
and say, 'That's *not* a North Vietnamese.' The Canadian
member would say, 'That *is* a North Vietnamese.' The neutral
member would say, 'I don't know what that is.'" When the
Vietcong blew up oil tanks in the Mekong Delta and rocketed
Bien Hoa, the Polish contingent claimed it was the work of
the South Vietnamese attempting to make it look like a Vietcong attack.

As flying in Vietnam grew increasingly hazardous, many
pilots scheduled on ICCS missions were resentful of making
what they considered to be superfluous trips. "Every day there
was a flight from Saigon to Can Tho and back for the ICCS,"
one said. "Thirty percent of the time it was nothing but a
girl friend swap." Ronald Dubinsky said he flew a case of beer
for a commission delegation and took a CIA man and his wife
to an offshore island to collect seashells. "A complete ripoff
on the American taxpayer."

AA was the costliest item on the commission's budget and
ran to $15 million a year. Although the budget was to have
been provided by the four signatories of the Paris agreement—the United States, South Vietnam, North Vietnam,
and the Vietcong's Provisional Revolutionary Government,
many bills were left unpaid and the United States ended up

having to carry most of the burden. Things were so bad by the end of the first year that AA delivered an ultimatum to the commission threatening to cut off all its air services unless $500,000 in back bills were paid. The commission responded that it did not have the money. When the United States stepped in a Canadian commented, "Well, it's cheaper than the war."

SEVEN

AT HOME

Socially, the world of Air America was virtually self-contained and completely different from that of the military. AA personnel lived off the economy of whatever country they were in, renting houses from natives and buying their food from the local markets, whereas the military lived on bases or in instantly created American suburbs. The pilots and their wives dealt with the locals in their everyday lives, both at work and at home, and grew to know the people, speak a little of the language, and understand their ways.

AA's war was peculiar to itself and the CIA connection made casual conversation with outsiders difficult. The pilots tended to stick together as a group, but did not find this a disadvantage—airmen never run out of aeronautical conversation. From whatever city in the Far East they operated out of there were bars and hotels known as AA hangouts. After a day in the war was done and the flying was over, the pilots played together. In the major centers of AA activity there would be a nonstop round of parties, good-natured and malicious gossip, musical beds, and heavy drinking. Firm friendships were struck while marriages creaked under the strain of wives attempting to live ordinary day-to-day lives when their husbands left them each morning to go to war.

Possibly the best life, even if it offered the worst war, was to be had in Vientiane, the capital of Laos. Despite the war it remained a sleepy rural town set on the banks of the Mekong with an atmosphere that was a strange mixture of both the Far East and France. Houses were cheap to rent, the food and restaurants were good, and people were friendly and honest. Those who lived there felt that life went by so slowly and quietly that they became becalmed by it. Time seemed to lose its meaning. Visiting journalists found that they would spend days without filing a story or bothering to contact the people they wanted to see. There was never a sense of urgency, nothing seemed that important. The atmosphere was enveloping.

It was all not quite real. AA wives out in the marketplace would run across Pathet Lao soldiers, the enemy, doing their shopping. In the early sixties, before the Geneva accord was signed, many pilots lived in the town's Constellation Hotel, which also housed a group of Soviet pilots. Every morning the Americans would leave in their C-46s and C-47s to drop supplies to rightist troops while the Russians flew off in Il-lushin transport planes to drop supplies to the Pathet Lao. At night all the pilots sat around drinking Pernod together and swapping war stories. When the accord was signed in 1962, when everyone thought the war was over for good, there were a series of wild Soviet-American parties. Throughout the war, while Vientiane remained neutral territory, Russian transports would fly into the city from Hanoi. "I watched some T-28s loading up with bombs at Wattay while two Russian 144s taxied across the runway," Wayne Lannin said. "The T-28s took off to bomb, the Russian planes took off for Hanoi and we took off to do our thing. It was very strange."

There were occasions when the war took on a slapstick quality. One night a group of brand-new CIA men had too much to drink and on the way home took a wrong turn and ended up bang in the middle of the compound of the Pathet Lao embassy. The Communists kept them overnight. The American embassy consoled itself in the fact that the men had not been in the country long enough to know anything. Possibly the most symbolic structure in Vientiane was the Monument Aux Morts, the Laotians' answer to the Arc de Triomphe. It was erected partly because the Laotians felt they had not built themselves a monument for a long time, partly in the forlorn hope that it would be nice for their victorious army to march through when they won the war, but mostly because the United States had provided a large quantity of cement with the specific purpose of extending the airport runway. It stood in the center of town, a monstrosity, but not without its own mad charm. AA pilots called it "The Vertical

Runway" and after a particularly good evening some of them would attempt to run up it.

Although Vientiane's true character was essentially sleepy and bucolic, millions of dollars of U.S. aid temporarily turned the place into a swinging town offering every sort of diversion and perversion. "The Strip" in Vientiane numbered enough exotic bars and specialist brothels to keep the most jaded Asia hand entertained. The bars were numerous: The White Rose, Monica's, The Lido, Madame Lulu's, the Green Latrine...

The AA watering hole was the Purple Porpoise, a bar decorated in uncertain taste and run by an alcoholic Englishman named Monty Banks, who wore a mustache, liked to play dice for money, and affected an upper-class British accent as uncertain as the bar's decor. Banks was as protective as a mother hen of the AA boys, who sat around telling tall stories and gave away as many drinks as he sold. His clientele included spooks, military attachés, pilots, and diplomats, but God help any journalist who found himself asking for service. Monty liked his patrons to be able to talk their clandestine shop undisturbed and made it clear that the place was off limits to the press. In between large pink gins Monty was able to slur such comments as: "The Americans who are in this town are the best Americans I've yet met. The people who walk into my bar, the Americans collectively, are human beings who love humanity."

The most famous bar in Vientiane was The White Rose, noted above everything else for its outstanding and unusual floor shows. The bar was in a side street off the strip and was incongruously signposted with a western wagon wheel. Inside it was dingy and its clientele sat around in the little booths or on the wicker chairs, drinking or smoking marijuana. The upstairs was a very old-fashioned whorehouse with tiny cubicles furnished with nothing but single beds. The girls performed impromptu striptease at a dollar a dance. It was generally agreed that the girls at The White Rose were a gentle, friendly crew who never pushed to be bought drinks and gave their favors with an amateurish charm. "You want see show, you want see show," they would ask, giggling, and then promptly take off their clothes. The star of The White Rose was a girl named Suzie, famed throughout Southeast Asia for her ability to smoke cigarettes with her vagina. Given an appreciative audience Suzie was said to be able to smoke a whole pack, sometimes satirically. One patron from The White Rose remembered four drunken Americans staggering into the bar with their wives, something that Asia hands considered in poor taste. They urged Suzie to show their wives her act and at first she was reluctant, but then took off her clothes while the drunks plied her with more and more cigarettes. The women became increasingly embarrassed, but the men were drunk enough to find the display fantastic and whooped and hollered while they piled dollar bills upon the table. Other patrons, who were less inebriated, were able to pick up the subtlety in Suzie's performance which the drunks missed: Suzie was blowing the smoke in their faces.

The exception to Vientiane's dimly lit bars was the Rendezvous des Amis, better known after its patron Madame Lulu and appropriately situated opposite a girl's school. Madame Lulu was a broken-down French woman in her fifties with her hair set in an outrageous bouffant, her face thickly camouflaged in makeup, and a theatrical cigarette holder forever in her hand. She was the discarded mistress of a long line of French generals from the days when the city was ruled by France. Since then numerous civil wars and a booming opium business had provided her with a very mixed clientele, to which the secret war had added its own oddball species of journalists, pilots, and spies.

The establishment consisted of a single, garishly lit room scattered with school desks which served as tables, surrounded by wicker chairs, and had a seedy charm. In one corner there was a small bar where Madame Lulu played old French love songs to herself and was wont to tell the story of her life, in great length and in French, to her clientele, who turned up in force as soon as The White Rose shut for the night. The speciality of the house, indeed the only fare offered, was oral sex, and every one of Madame Lulu's girls had been personally coached by the *grande dame* herself. She combined a tawdry elegance with a spirited vulgarity and shook hands with her new customers by reaching for their testicles. There was an unwritten rule among journalists not to write about the place, a kind of courtesy to Madame Lulu, but it was known through Southeast Asia as the establishment where the blow job had been turned into an art form. Its squalid glamour was lost on many of the AA personnel, who referred to it flatly as The Turkey Farm.

The city's most swinging nightclub, The Spot, was run by a criminal partnership consisting of two notorious Corsican gangsters: François Mittard headed one of the most powerful drug syndicates in Indochina until he was arrested for narcotics smuggling in 1960 and sentenced to five years in a Vietnamese prison; his partner, Michael Libert, had served five years in a Thai prison after being arrested for drug smuggling in 1963.

A profitable gambling casino, described by a journalist as an ugly five-story building stinking like an Indonesian urinal, was built in downtown Vientiane by General Phoumi Nosavan, CIA protégé and political leader of the Laotian right wing. The general had plans to build similar enterprises in every Laotian city, but the King refused to allow one in Luang Prabang, the royal capital, and there were other heated objections.

Although alcohol was almost exclusively the drug used by AA, it was legal in Laos to smoke marijuana and opium. Sometimes, in places like The White Rose, the two cultures existed side by side, and there would be a brawling table of drunks in one corner and a group stoned into silence and reverie in another. The local grass was so strong that most people left opium alone, although there were at least forty opium dens operating within the city. One of them accommodating one hundred fifty smokers, run by the same general who owned the casino, had a sign hung over the entrance— DETOXIFICATION CLINIC.

Certain pilots happily abandoned themselves to a roué's life of excess and debauch. The most extreme was "Dirty" George, whose swimming pool and mind was always brimful with naked Lao girls. George even went as far as buying movie equipment and made his own films, and according to the pilots who saw them he managed to hit a new low in hard-core porn. (When "Dirty" George left the company, he kept the Agency on tenterhooks with his indiscreet, booming voice. One pilot, who had not seen him in a while and then ran into him at AA operations in Vientiane, where George had turned up with a scraggly beard looking generally disheveled, expressed surprise at the encounter. "Why, George, where have you been? I thought you quit the company?"

"I did. I quit," George said amiably.

"So what are you doing now?" the pilot asked.

George took a deep breath and yelled at the top of his voice: "I'm working for the CIA." Pencils fell out of hands, heads swung around, and a tense silence fell over the operations room. "Yeah," George continued, apparently oblivious to the effect he had created, "The CIA—I'm a missionary—I'm with the Christian Involvement Alliance.")

In the midst of war and sexual temptation, married couples attempted to live ordinary lives together. Most pilots made it a rule not to talk about either at home: near escapes and brushes with death were company business and went untold and so did their experiences at Madame Lulu's. Wives passed their time as if there was no war going on. There were interstation basketball matches and the Vientiane Dollies, known as the VDs, would fly down to Udorn to play the wives of the chopper pilots. It gave ground personnel great pleasure to announce these flights over the airport PA system: "The VD flight will leave Vientiane . . ."

Attempting to avoid the war by not talking about it was easy enough, but its reality burst through when a pilot lost his life. "When people were killed it brought it home to you and you went through a period of deep depression," one wife said. "Otherwise you just accepted it. They loved it, you see."

The pilots eased the strain of flying by playing hard. It was as if they had made the decision: Eat, drink, and be merry, for tomorrow we die. "Booze saved the day over there," one pilot stated bluntly. "A social drinker with AA would be classified as a total alcoholic anywhere else in the world." Party drunks were happily tolerated, but the obnoxious and the belligerent were shunned. The commissary, which at one time or another ran out of almost everything, was careful never to run low on drink. Good American bourbon was a dollar and a quarter a bottle, vodka a dollar and ten cents—the result was that everybody had well-stocked bars and drank too much.

"Many times we would party and go out on the town, knowing full well we were on schedule the next day," Robert Wofford said. "But if it was a party you had been looking forward to, you'd go with the idea of just having a couple of drinks and getting home early. It never worked out that way. You'd sit there and drink as much as you ever did and your wife would usually end up dragging you home with the help of somebody else." But for some there was a darker side to the partying, a desperation in the drinking. "Some pilots could drink all night and still fly the next day," Jim Parrish said. "I don't think they were having a good time. A lot of them had broken families back in the States and they were unhappy whether they knew it or not. A lot of them were over here to get away from problems at home. Others took their problems with them."

Heavy drinking by some of the AA wives was more difficult to hide behind a wall of comradely bonhomie. There were many reasons for a wife to take refuge in the bottle: the strain of their men being exposed to danger every day, too much empty time—created by servants—to fill, and the ever-present threat of pretty young native girls who sold themselves for ten dollars. Male egos smashed up more marriages than the war. "You could have all the women you wanted," a chopper pilot explained. "You walked in, threw down twenty dollars and took what you wanted. You can't overestimate how important that was to a lot of these people. Even some of the young ones who couldn't pull it off back in the States—they'd spend six nights in a bar to pick up one honey and the honey would tell them to get lost. Over there they pulled out ten bucks and they were there—'My boy friend, you number one—I love you.' The honeys would jump on them to pull the ten-dollar bills from their pockets. A lot of them needed that. Plus they could change it in a minute, get rid of one and take on another."

It was assumed by the men that their wives were unaware of this. "There was a lot that you saw that you would outwardly condone but inwardly you would shake your head," one wife said. "There were so many darling Asian girls like dolls, and the women knew. It was hard for a wife to accept. That they did it was one thing, but the fact that we were supposed to be so stupid as not to catch on was to feel so put down that it was embittering. You can put on a real good act, but it always hurts. There were some tragic stories in human relations."

Pilots would take girl friends posing as their wives on leave with them, only for their real wives to find the tickets later. Worse, some wives had the destroying experience of finding other girls' douche bags in the bathroom. As most of the pilots were ultraconservative in their attitudes toward their wives, who were not encouraged to develop lives of their own, many of them felt perpetually homesick so far away from home. 'And you'd discover—Gee, I'm doing my good camp fire, Girl Scout business and he's doing his Girl Scout business too."

It became a commonplace for middle-aged pilots to ditch their wives permanently and marry the girls they met out East. AA cynics referred to this maneuver as "the wife trick." It worked at both extremes of the compass, and many pilots who married Vietnamese girls left them behind when the war was over to take up with an American girl. "You know—when you leave the house you're not married anymore," one wife said bitterly.

In the circumstances, it was very important that pilots should not be caught in compromising positions, however innocent, with their colleagues' wives. One chopper pilot, a quiet, easygoing fellow who kept well out of trouble, dropped in on a friend's wife while her husband was away up-country and found her with another temporary AA widow. They had a few drinks together, the pilot complained of tiredness, went up to the bathroom, and passed out. The wives had a problem. They could not leave him there overnight, but on the other hand if he had his trousers around his ankles, they could hardly haul a half-naked airman into a bedroom to sleep it off. They tried yelling and banging on the door, and when that had no effect they opened the door a little, pushed a broom handle through it, and pounded on the floor. There was no movement. Peering in, their worst fears were confirmed: the pilot had passed out on the lavatory seat and his trousers *were* around his ankles. They waited half an hour, but at midnight decided some action had to be taken, although by this time they were edging dangerously near the pilot's state themselves. Their plan, hatched over half-a-dozen dry martinis, was to wrap the seated airman in a sheet for modesty's sake and then haul him out of the bathroom and into the kitchen for some black coffee. They both climbed under the sheet, so they would not witness the man's naked nether half, and went into the bathroom. Still under the sheet, one of the wives took hold of the pilot's arm and shook him. It did the trick. He stirred and then opened his eyes—to be confronted with a monstrous double ghost. In a moment he was on his feet, screaming in terror, convinced that he was in the final stages of delirium tremens, when he heard the women's uncontrollable laughter from under the sheet. Gripped by hysterics, the three of them sank to the floor.

The odd hours and scheduling put pressure on the best of marriages (not to mention individuals' alarming idiosyncrasies: one pilot who had his toe shot off had it cremated and the ashes put in an urn in his home, to his wife's constant and vocal displeasure). It seemed that couples spent either too little or too much time together: husbands spent six days away up-country or six days at home. "It was a tough place to keep a marriage together," Ted Helmers said. "Marriages were spoiled and there was swapping when the men were up-country, often because the wives encouraged it. A couple of them were done in the open and it didn't do anybody any good. But in my case living out there under those conditions brought me closer to my wife."

Many wives grew to feel alienated and were unable to bridge the cultural gap between living in the States and the Far East, shunning the local restaurants and native food. Other wives would stop off at any noodle stand for a snack. It took imagination to keep boredom at bay. "I used to go to a lot of cremation parties," one wife said. "They were great. They don't mourn death but celebrate it. A person might have died a year before, but they had to wait that long to save enough money to have a party. There was always plenty of *lau-lau* and beer."

Heavy drinking and matrimonial bitterness often became an ugly mix . One pilot, who was known to have a problem-wife, arrived home unexpectedly early one day to find her out. He poured himself a drink, sat down to wait, and then poured himself a couple more. A friend dropped by the house and he had a couple with him and by five o'clock in the afternoon he was dangerously drunk. He went out into the street and found a bar where five chopper pilots were having a quiet drink. He walked through the front door brandishing a .45.

"Anybody seen my wife?" he shouted.

"Not since yesterday," one pilot answered.

"You sure?" the drunken husband snarled.

"Yeah," the pilot said, sensing danger. "Come in and have a drink."

"I don't want a drink, I've been drinking all afternoon," the husband said and raised his .45. "See that flowerpot up there in the stairwell?"

"We see it—come in and have a drink."

Halfway up the stairs was a large flowerpot with a plant in it. The husband leveled the .45 and pulled the trigger. Nothing happened. The pilots at the bar relaxed a little on the assumption that the revolver was full of blanks. The husband waved the gun unsteadily, pulled himself up, and fired another shot. The flowerpot disintegrated. "Five assholes and five sets of elbows disappeared over the bar in an instant," one of the pilots said. "Everybody hit the dirt."

This time the pilot who spoke to the husband did it from behind the bar. "Aw, for God's sake—put the gun away and come and have a drink." Temporarily satisfied with the damage he had inflicted on the flowerpot, the husband allowed himself to be coaxed into joining his colleagues. They climbed back over the bar and continued drinking. By the time the husband left them he was beyond anger or any other emotion.

It only took one or two trigger-happy pilots to convince the town's population that the AA cowboys were best handled at arm's length. They were particularly cautious of the younger chopper pilots who stayed overnight in The Apollo (a hotel boasting an elevator, which in a country that only had two, was a real distinction). One pilot staying at the hotel had been out on the town drinking and returned in the early hours of the morning with a girl he had picked up. In the lobby of the hotel she changed her mind about staying the night and said that she wanted to leave.

"Oh, no," the pilot told her. "You're coming up to my room and if you don't I'm liable to shoot you." He continued to walk along the corridor to the elevator, but the girl went back to the front door. The pilot drew out a .25 caliber handgun and fired three shots into the ceiling. The girl turned around and without a word accompanied him to his room.

Meanwhile the hotel manager had called the police. They arrived in force, and as the incident involved an American, the colonel-in-charge accompanied them. The hotel manager excitedly explained that an AA pilot had fired shots into the ceiling while police collected up the casings. A sergeant asked whether his men should wake up all AA pilots staying in the hotel and bring them down to the lobby. It was a serious offense, as it was completely illegal for Americans to carry personal firearms in Laos. The colonel inspected the empty .25 caliber casings. "Let those pilots sleep," he announced. "None of them carry guns this small."

Certain of the AA wives were held in similar awe. The wife of a fixed-wing pilot, a Texas girl with a personality as strong as her accent, was on a motorcycle in Vientiane when a cyclelow, a motorized trishaw, ran her off the road. She picked herself up, dusted herself down, and took off at full speed in pursuit. When she caught up with the luckless driver, she ran him off the road into the sidewalk where she beat him over the head with her purse. After a couple of minutes beneath the rain of blows and abuse he ran off down the street, leaving the trishaw on its side where it was. A local policeman was foolish enough to cross over to her, flick out his notebook, and start to write out a ticket. Meanwhile he muttered in broken English that it was not nice for women to attack cyclelow drivers. The enraged Texan took hold of the policeman's notebook, wrenched it from his hands, tore it in two, and threw it on the ground. The policeman looked into the woman's eyes and quiety slipped away.

Most of the embassy personnel lived on a specially built American compound six kilometers outside of Vientiane, known as KM6, as American as a suburb of Kansas City with kids in baseball hats zipping along the sidewalks on roller skates. AA families, on the other hand, lived in the town itself and became a part of its life. And sometimes victims of it.

It was a paradox of life in Laos that the locals, whose devout Buddhism made them gentle and peaceful, could also provide professional murderers who would kill a man for as little as $25. And in personal matters, involving something such as loss of face or love, they could be coldly cruel. One of the ugliest demonstrations of this involved a beautiful Laotian girl, the country's only movie star, called Chai Fa, which means princess in Thai. Although a native of Laos and a scion of a powerful local gangster family, she had moved south to Bangkok to pursue a career in the movies, for which her delicate beauty and slender figure made her ideally suited.

In Bangkok she met an AA pilot who was supposed to have kidnapped her, taken her back to Laos, and married her. The girl exploited her great beauty with other men until eventually the pilot could stand no more and divorced her. He smuggled the one child they had together out of the country and into the States. When he returned to Laos, he faced the enmity of her family and lived a touch-and-go existence for a number of months.

Some time later Chai Fa married another American pilot, an older man called George Kirkman, and settled down to live with him. Kirkman was a paunchy, unattractive character, known as "Lonesome George." He was not overpopular among his colleagues, who decided among themselves that the only possible motive behind the marriage was financial.

It was only a matter of time before Lonesome George's glamorous young wife took a lover. The two of them, assisted by her brother, formed a plan to murder the middle-aged pilot which would give Chai Fa the man's money and leave her free to marry her lover. She began to mix small amounts of poison into the pilot's food, which made him sick for weeks but failed to kill him. Impatient for his death, the three of them met at the house one night and attacked him. At first they tried to strangle him and then began to stab him repeatedly. Then in an act that was as gratuitous as it was grotesque, they wired the dying man's testicles.

Chai Fa was put on trial and found guilty. She had served a total of six months in prison when a high-ranking official in the police decided that her treachery was overridden by her beauty.

Most serious crime in the city was the province of the Corsican gangsters who had pioneered opium smuggling and flown in out of the country on their charter airlines until they were forced out of business in 1965. This left a large unemployed criminal element.

After months of drinking and carousing up and down the bars of Vientiane's "strip," five down-and-out gangsters decided to branch out into fresh criminal pastures. Led by a Corsican named Le Rouzic, who had reportedly owned a piece of a small charter airline, and his mechanic, Housset, the five men planned and executed the boldest crime in the history of modern Laos—The Great Unarmored Car Robbery. A total of $420,000 cash and $260,000 in checks was loaded into an automobile by two clerks from the Banque de l'Indochine and driven to Wattay airport, where it was to be loaded aboard a Royal Air Lao flight for Bangkok. When the car arrived, a jeep pulled up alongside and three of the Corsicans jumped out. The men used handfuls of pepper, not guns, to pull off the heist and snatched the cash while the clerks sneezed and rubbed their eyes.

Unfortunately for the bank robbers, their free-lance enterprise was frowned upon by Corsicans higher up the criminal hierarchy. To avoid a general police crackdown on their activities in the country, the bosses informed on them. In less than twenty-four hours the police had recovered almost all the money and had arrested Le Rouzic, his mistress, and three of the gang. Thai police, acting on information supplied by their Laotian colleagues, arrested Housset in Bangkok, where they found $3,940 hidden in his socks.

AA personnel kept abreast of the news somewhat haphazardly by reading the hysterically funny *Vientiane Times*, a broadsheet written in English by Lao reporters. The unsuspecting Laotians blithely accepted the most outrageous advertisements: "Cash reward to the value of one half million kips which will lead to the termination (offer of information) of employment ____ ____, AA, Vientiane. A consortium of Vientiane residents feel it is the only way to remove his evil, conspiring alcoholid (sic) wife from Vientiane and save his career. Please contact box 379, Vientiane, Laos."

Close relations with the locals entailed a number of hidden dangers, and the best intentions could be misunderstood. Outside of Vientiane there was a hill tribe settlement of Thai Dan—Black Thais—and Barbara Ritter, who was the wife of a fixed-wing pilot, employed two of them as servants. They were loyal and honest and the relationship between employees and employer became close, so when one said her sister's baby was dying it was natural that Barbara should try to help. When she arrived at the settlement, she found the baby burning with fever and totally dehydrated. The mother was very young and upset and had no milk. Preparations were already being made for the cremation—ashes were being rubbed into the baby's skin and the head man of the village had entered the house to wait with the family for its death. It seemed the most natural thing in the world to Barbara Ritter that she should do everything possible to save the baby's life.

The head man refused to let her drive the baby to the hospital. "No medicine," he ordered unequivocally. Barbara drove back into town to buy a feeding bottle, phenobarbital, and baby aspirin to reduce the fever. The head man allowed her to spoon water into the baby's mouth and feed it a little phenobarbital. Its eyes flickered open and the mother's face lit up with hope.

But it was clear that the baby needed professional care. Barbara Ritter left the settlement and drove to see AA's Taiwanese doctor. "You've got to come," she pleaded, almost in tears. "There's a baby dying which needs help."

"I can't go," the doctor said bluntly. "I can't touch a Thai baby."

"You're a doctor—You've got to go," Barbara retorted. "I gave him some phenobarbital and baby aspirin and spooned some water into him. I can't do anything more for him."

"All you can do now is to pray that the baby doesn't die," the doctor said. "If it does you're going to be in jail."

The baby did live, but Barbara's good Samaritan act could have backfired. "They were not really grateful," she said. "They expect and accept that they will lose a number of babies before they are a year old."

It seemed that the longer AA people stayed in Laos, or in the Far East in general, the greater the cultural gap and the feeling of alienation became—the cliché, the Eastern paradox of the two cultures never meeting. The old hands began to see the mixture of great gentleness and cold-blooded cruelty as hypocrisy and discovered that beneath the smiling deference was a total contempt. "You began to understand after a time how little the people liked us," one pilot said. "It wasn't just the war but something more fundamental. We were foreigners. We had fair skin, round eyes, and we were bigger than they were, and that was three good reasons for them to hate our guts."

There was a feeling too among the pilots that the embassy had a hypocritical approach to AA and preferred to ignore its existence. "We didn't get much help out there," Jim Parrish said. "In fact we got more cooperation from the British embassy than we did our own. They didn't want to be associated with us or have anything to do with us. They didn't even want to recognize the fact that we were Americans. They had to do certain things, give us ID cards and cash our checks, but they didn't really want to do a damn thing for us. They had a hands-off policy as far as AA pilots were concerned." And as a result AA became more and more a world of its own.

* * *

In Udorn, where the entire AA helicopter operation was based, the world was a small one. The whole town was created around the USAF base there and was overrun with military, and although the AA base was comfortable, and complete with a pool, there was little atmosphere. A third of the population of Thai women were said to be prostitutes.

Pilots leaving for Udorn from the States could be forgiven the notion that they were on a church outing rather than about to fly secret missions for the CIA. The instructions slipped to them in Washington were strictly nonclassified. The pilot-agents were supplied with a bus schedule between Udorn's CIA compound, schools, and banks and told all about the supermarket, swimming pool, free movies, the "Club Rendezvous" (which doubled as a chapel on Sundays), and bingo on Tuesday and Saturday nights. "A bowling alley in Udorn has league bowling," the CIA added confidentially.

Hush-hush information was also supplied to wives. "Water should be boiled three or five minutes prior to drinking, but it is safe for cooking and washing dishes if it is brought to the boiling point." The CIA was careful to add that they should bring "plenty of sheets and pillow cases and chinaware, tableware, and kitchen utensils." Other top-secret information provided was that "Thai mattresses are extremely hard and bumpy" and that "shopping is generally done by the servants due to the early hours (6:00 A.M.) one must shop to ensure getting fresh products." Threatened with such domesticity, it is not surprising that the chopper pilots turned out to be a wild crew.

One of the first things a pilot new to the Far East had to cope with was bribery as a daily part of his life. "The first time I went to the police, because I had my motorcycle stolen, they jerked me around for half a day," Mike Barksdale said. "I couldn't figure out what was wrong. I was a new guy and didn't know the name of the game. An AA interpreter finally came down and told me it would be a good idea to offer a reward of fifty dollars to the guy who found it. I was glad to do so because he told me if I didn't the police would have to keep my motorcycle as evidence—indefinitely."

(AA occasionally exacted revenge on the police, as the following item in the company newspaper, the *Air America Log*, demonstrates: "AA soccer team at Udorn won the local cham-

pionship by playing hard at all times and displaying superb
ball control; they downed the border police patrol by a score
of two to nothing.")

The chopper pilots worked hard at their reputation as hell
raisers. "It seemed sometimes that that was exactly what we
were doing," Tom Grady said. "You'd get downtown and there
might be a lot of young Air Force guys in the bar and you'd
just have to show them." One of AA's favorites was the Wol-
verine, where children wandered around with trays of flow-
ers. It was known for pilots to buy the whole tray and then
eat them, stems and all. Another well-used bar was the Rama,
which a group of pilots partly owned in a hopeless attempt
to recoup some of the money they spent on drink. At the bar
at the base there were nine types of imported American beer,
every kind of American liquor, and Beaujolais in twelve-
ounce cans.

When the drink was really flowing, a group might link
arms for a song-and-dance act, the first line of which went
something like, "We are the boys in the gray berets, we are
the boys with the CIA."

Despite its supermarket and bowling alley, Udorn had the
atmosphere of a pioneer town and again it was the wives who
were stuck with the worst of it. "It was like being out on the
frontier of the wild west and aged you very quickly," Wayne
Lannin said. "It was tough on the wives. At the AA compound
the news would come from up-country that a plane had been
shot down and would filter out to the pool where all the wives
were. Everybody would sit on tenterhooks while they waited
to find out who was down and what the deal was. I've been
sitting out there a couple of times when that happened and
it really gave you an eerie feeling. I'd much rather be out
there doing something than just sitting around. It was hard
on the wives because in a situation like that it was all they
could do—sit and wait."

Bangkok was a much better posting in Thailand and several fixed-wing pilots lived there. Some men, posted to Saigon,
preferred to have their families live in the safety of Bangkok
and visit them as often as possible. The greatest danger of
the town was the likelihood of having to play host to the flood
of AA pilots who passed through on R & R hell-bent on having
a good time. And again the city had its AA watering holes—

The Red Deer, Napoleon Café, and Derby King on Patpong Road, the Amarin and Asia Hotels.

It was one city where AA was not an entity unto itself and the outside world intruded. There were foreigners living in Bangkok who were deeply opposed to the war in Vietnam and let any American they came across know it. One obnoxious British barfly, who was always dressed in a white desert jacket and shorts, would confront Americans on any possible occasion. Drunkenness generated moral outrage. "Why are you bloody Yanks dropping napalm on my little friends over here?" he would shout, glaring furiously. "You bloody murdering bastards."

Walter Rosenfield, a resident of the city, was always running into him but attempted to avoid a confrontation by walking away. After numerous awkward encounters, he took the trouble to clip an article from a newspaper in preparation for the next time the Brit started his tirade, which occurred in the bar of The Oriental Hotel. Rosenfield took the cutting out of his pocket, grabbed the barfly by the throat, and jabbed it in his face. "Read that!" The article stated that it was the British, in fact, who had invented napalm at the end of the Second World War. While the barfly read the article, Rosenfield poured a glass of beer over his head. Unperturbed, he continued to read and then, without any reference to the information in the cutting and dripping beer, left the bar with the words: "You're certainly not a gentleman."

Bangkok's AA population resigned themselves, after a brief honeymoon period with the city, to being regularly burgled. The robberies were often carried out by disgruntled servants, and while the immediate reaction of most AA pilots was to pick up a weapon and give chase, their status as foreigners put them in a difficult position. One American who knocked out a burglar with a Coca-Cola bottle found the boy to be a recently fired servant. He had been dismissed because of his drinking and, true to form, was breaking into his ex-master's scotch supply in the kitchen. The American had split the boy's head open and quickly drove him to the hospital to have it sewn up at his own expense. The police, however, were not prepared to let the matter rest there. The American protested that he did not want to press charges. The police told him he did not understand—he had drawn blood, charges were to be preferred against *him*. He was put in jail, where he stayed for five days until a Thai friend could arrange bail.

One evening, at the Bangkok home of Barbara Ritter, the children played ball in the garden before the cook called dinner. "Don't put on all the lights tonight," Barbara told the cook. "Let's just have the candles lit around the table." It was a beautiful evening and they were to dine in the garden. The charming domestic scene was watched intently by a burglar sitting patiently in a mango tree in the corner of the garden. He wore nothing but a loincloth wrapped around his waist and carried a long knife. He waited for the family to settle around the table and darkness to fall.

There was Thai food for dinner that night, but it was a little spoiled by the cloud of mosquitoes attracted by the candlelight. Barbara asked her fifteen-year-old daughter, Vicky, to go up to her bedroom and fetch the Flit gun. "It's right inside the door. Just run up and grab it."

Vicky went into the house and up the stairs, and as she opened her mother's bedroom door and reached in for the Flit gun a hand grabbed her. The burglar pulled her into the room, put his knife against her throat, and warned her by putting a finger to his mouth not to make any noise. The girl was so terrified that she could only nod dumbly. The burglar had entered the bedroom by climbing up a post at the side of the house and jumping onto the upstairs balcony. It was only a few days before Christmas and he had collected up all the presents to carry off. Barbara Ritter had bought jewelry for everyone that year. The burglar shook his knife and put his finger to his lips once more and the girl watched as he climbed over the balcony to make his getaway.

Petrified, Vicky took some time to leave the bedroom. Halfway down the stairs she began to scream. The burglar had climbed free, but seemed to have stabbed himself with his own knife as he jumped down from the balcony. His flight from the compound was marked by a trail of blood and abandoned Christmas presents. Once over the fence he had jumped into one of the city's klongs, but it was clear where he had climbed out again because of a telltale pool of blood in a dirt road.

"I'm so pleased you sent me up," Barbara's daughter told her mother. "I was so scared I couldn't open my mouth. You would have screamed your head off and he would have killed

you." The burglar was never caught and escaped to rob an
other day.

Life in Saigon, of course, was very different. It was no
corrupt locals, robbers, and a culture gap that made domestic
life difficult, but the war itself. The idyllic days before the
military build-up when AA pilots enjoyed a cheap and easy
life soon disappeared forever. "The GIs came in and drove
the prices sky high," Neil Hansen said. "Rentals went from
thirty dollars a month to four hundred. There was very poor
liaison between the Vietnamese immigration and the U.S
embassy and just to get an exit visa was a struggle. There
were very few places where you could go out for an evening
and enjoy yourself. The restaurants and bars were either full
of a bunch of drunk GIs or there was always the half-assed
scare of somebody throwing a grenade into the place. You
didn't go to the movies for the same reason. There just wasn'
much recreation."

There were the usual seedy bars. "None of the AA hangout
in Saigon are the sort of places I'd like to mention," Fred
Anderson said. "There was one that was very, very dark and
it took time for your eyes to adjust to the light. The first tim
I went there I could just about make out seminude bodie
moving around. When my eyes finally did adjust the firs
thing I made out was a naked girl in a booth, sitting on the
bald head of an AA pilot. Enough said."

The war took the place of television. Bob Murray, who wa
shot at thirteen times and shot down twice, took his eight
year-old son all over Vietnam in his plane. "He's been to al
the forward bases and seen all the troops and collected al
kinds of souvenirs from them—a compass off a North Viet
namese officer, helmets, flak vests, ammo belts. We'd land i
forward airstrips where they were expecting nothing but Vi
etnamese and there was this eight-year-old American ki
climbing out of the plane. He's got eighty hours of comba
time in Vietnam."

But the war was not confined to forward strips; it wa
everywhere. "You'd sit up in the apartment and you'd watch
the river and you'd see somebody drop some flares and you'
hear somebody shooting," Murray said. "You were just sittin
there watching the war go on."

And yet, despite this, life was reasonably comfortable. Th

climate was ideal, most families had two cars and were members of the Cercle Sportif, the local equivalent to a country club. Vegetables in the market were good, the fruit outstanding, and if the beef and chickens were tough, they were tasty. Most pilots were reluctant to let their wives go shopping in the central market, as grenades were regularly rolled into it.

Prices went up as the war went on, but the local currency was constantly devalued so it was possible to maintain a high standard of living. "I hired a maid in December 1965 and paid her thirty-five hundred piasters a month," Art Kenyon said. "She stayed with me for six years, and over that period of time I raised her salary from thirty-five hundred to about twenty thousand, but was actually paying her less in American dollars than the day I hired her."

The company attempted to bring the very different worlds of AA together through a house journal called the *Air America Log*, which they started bringing out in the late sixties, produced in Taipei, Taiwan. In its first issue Hugh L. Grundy, AA's overall manager in the Far East, explained the paper's role: "AA is a big airline—its employees now number six thousand. They live in some eight different countries which reach halfway round the world. This new *Air America Log* is designed to be a bridge to span the gap between our people in Thailand, South Korea, Laos, and the Philippines, Vietnam, Okinawa, and Japan and the United States. The log will serve as a means of communication between us all, from north to south, east to west, motor station to front office."

The *Air America Log* was a small, glossy broadsheet full of technical data about the airline, its growing capability and constantly improved facilities. It also carried appropriate Snoopy cartoons and news tidbits. "Three AA traffic agents and a captain made up a singing team to appear on a weekly Okinawa TV contest program. Prizes were a TV set for first, radio for second. The competition was between AA Incorporated and the Kaame-Kotsu Taxi Company of Okinawa. AA lost by two points." To anyone who has ever heard AA personnel sing, drunk or sober, the result would come as no surprise.

The company also used the magazine to boost morale with a series of slogans that appeared at the bottom of its pages. "A plane is no better than its maintenance," "No communication—No airline," "Name the challenge—we can meet it,"

"Professionalism throughout," "You cannot fly without supply," "Find a way you can, not a reason you cannot," "Safety is no accident."

An exasperated, avuncular note occasionally crept in when the company felt the pilots needed a talking to: "Cut out petty differences of opinion and all that jazz. We've just gotta upgrade our personal performance right along with the equipment. Everytime a customer hollers for an airlift, we've gotta be able to respond. We simply must stop grounding planes by such stupid stunts as pranging wingtips."

The salaries paid to pilots created AA's own brand of *nouveau riche*. The ostentatious gold bracelets grew bigger and bigger. "A lot of them weren't educated that well and all of a sudden they're getting more money than they've ever had before," Mike Barksdale explained. "They just didn't know what to do with it. You'd see poker games with ten-and twenty-thousand-dollar pots."

Leave became a time of outrageous overspending. "You'd have six days R & R and you'd have three thousand dollars in cash in your pocket and an air ticket—breakfast in Bangkok, lunch in Bombay, and dinner in Athens," Ron Zappardino said. "You didn't give a shit about the money because you could just go back and make another five thousand. Why should we care? I've bought many dinners for twenty-five people at five hundred dollars—we would flip for it.

"Fill the bath with champagne, live like a millionaire. Guys would hire bartenders for their hotel rooms and end up in bed with three hookers. It was unbelievable. Wild. You just didn't care."

Hong Kong was a favorite stopping-off place where pilots would make for the American Steak House and enjoy a big Stateside salad which the restaurant had flown in from San Francisco fresh every day. Hotel receptionists became used to AA pilots arguing furiously over a twenty-five-hundred dollar, six-day bill.

"I insist! I'm paying!"

"No, no—you paid for dinner."

A rumor that enjoyed brief popularity among the USAF in Vietnam, to the effect that Russian pilots flying for the North Vietnamese enjoyed leave in Hong Kong, was directly attributable to an AA prankster. The pilot was an ex-Air Force captain who flew a Caribou and had a gift for imitating accents. Sitting in the bar of the President Hotel in Hong Kong one evening, he was joined by a couple of F-4 jocks from Vietnam. They were talking loosely about things the AA pilot felt were classified and the three men struck up a conversation.

"What you doing here?" one pilot asked.

"I'm here on a few days R & R." The reply came in a thick Russian accent and two Air Force pilots exchanged glances.

"Yeah? Who you with?"

"The People's Forty-third Fighter Squadron."

"What do you fly?" one asked uneasily.

"MIG-29."

There was a moment's silence before the pilot asked the final question in a subdued tone. "Where are you stationed?"

"Hanoi."

The pilots nodded, then shook their heads. One nudged the other. They drank their drinks and left. And later back in Vietnam they told their colleagues, with their hands on their hearts, of the Russian pilot they met on R & R in Hong Kong.

Not all of the money earned by AA pilots was blown on orgiastic weekends. Most of it was irretrievably lost on appalling business ventures which proved beyond doubt that the best pilots can be the very worst businessmen. This reputation goes right back to the Flying Tiger days. Examples might include Randall Richardson, ironically nicknamed "Rich" because of his disastrous business affairs, including investing everything he had in a Tokyo nightclub which burned down half an hour after it was opened. Another pilot heard that rubies were dirt cheap in Thailand and that gullible natives would swap them for any kind of trinket. He put out the word that he was in the market and was duly approached by a Thai with a fistful of sparkling red gems. After much haggling the Thai agreed to hand them over for a pair of sunglasses, the pilot's wristwatch, and a fountain pen. The pilot returned to his plane, congratulating himself on his cunning, and sat down before the controls. It was then that he noticed that all the red glass had been removed from the warning lights on his instrument panel.

The AA pilots had heard these stories and were not to be outdone. Pilots invested their money in brokerage houses that did not exist, a mercury mine in Canada where the ticker tape quoted $.14 a share but the decimal point had been moved and the real price was $1.40 a share, a ranch in Brazil that was jungle. One pilot worked out a surefire scheme to beat the stock market and lost $250,000 of everybody's money; undeterred he went to England with a system he had devised to beat the dog tracks and lost the little he had left.

"There was all kinds of foolishness and folly," Jim Parrish said. "Pilots are notoriously the worst businessmen in the world." There were bars that went bankrupt and massage parlors that opened and closed so quickly nobody knew of their existence. And with pilots averaging $45,000 a year—half of which was tax free—it was a paradise for the confidence trickster.

"There was one guy who played a lot of cards, and if he owed you twenty cents he would track you down and send over the money by courier," Ron Zappardino said. "He decided to quit AA, and as he owned ten apartment units in Toledo he started borrowing a couple of thousand off everybody to invest in them. Our attitude was if a guy wants a couple of thousand, give him a couple of thousand. That was the way we lived. In the last week he was there he started to play poker with abandon and was losing eight, ten thousand at a crack and then trying to win it back. He was seventy thousand down and had borrowed another twenty thousand dollars when all of a sudden he leaves. The guys were pretty sore and swore they'd get his ass. Then word comes back six months later that he committed suicide. Most of the guys believed it, but a couple went looking for him in Toledo and found he was alive and well—and owned another ten units."

People tried to run businesses in Hong Kong, Singapore and Japan and usually failed. Officially, AA personnel were not supposed to run businesses at all. "If they did it too openly we put it to them that they'd have to get rid of the business or we'd have to get rid of them," Les Strouse said. "Mostly we turned a blind eye to it, as nearly all the businesses had foreign fronts and it would have been impossible to prove one of our guys was involved. We had one fellow who ran a boarding house in Saigon who was to our advantage. If we didn't have a hotel room for a new pilot, we would use him. Theoretically we were subsidizing him, but his rates were cheap and he served meals and it was to the advantage of the pilots we sent there." It would have saved most pilots a lot of money if the company had strictly enforced its rule. Almost everything they touched turned to dust. If they invested in the stock market, it was bound to take a tumble. "I used to put my money in the U.S. stock market and it caught me flat-footed because we were so far away," Mel Cooper said. "I had two years' savings in stock that went from twenty-seven to five in three weeks. There were people in AA who would double or triple their money in an investment and then go and lose it all. It was not unusual for them to do that three or four times in a ten-year period." They even managed to lose money in alcohol. "I invested in scotch and I've still got five thousand gallons of it sitting over there in Scotland in a warehouse and it's worth less today than when I bought it," Bob Murray said.

The best business venture for most of them was to stay away from business. "The smartest were the ones who saved a hundred grand, put it in a bank, and went home and got a job," Ron Zappardino said. "One old boy came out from Alabama, spent three years saving a hundred thousand, and then went back to Alabama."

And then there was a different breed altogether, the pilots who left Southeast Asia as millionaires—the AA underworld. One of the advantages of flying with a secret airline is that its very nature makes crime simple. Borders were crossed with the minimum of red tape, customs were avoided, and it was the simplest thing in the world to smuggle. Gold, white gold (heroin), opium, and human beings were the commodities dealt in by the few unscrupulous pilots who left the war rich. But their stories are told in another part of the book.

EIGHT

LAOS—OPEN WAR

The war in Laos continued to remain an untold story. Dwarfed by the action in neighboring Vietnam, which at its height was covered by a press corps of seven hundred correspondents, the CIA managed to keep happenings in Laos their own private game. Its coverage by the world's press was sketchy in the extreme, the barest outline, and often misleading. Reporters scratched up what they could in Vientiane, while a handful of the more enterprising went on AA rice (soft only) drops. The airline's role, while often mentioned, remained perpetually out of focus.

In 1962 *The New York Times* wrote innocently of its being "a private company under charter to the United States government." In 1964 the paper was describing the company "as an enterprise that is shadowy and vague even by Laotian standards" and went on to say that it was suspected that the airline was not merely hired by the government but *was* the government operating under a commercial cover. It reported an anecdote of several AA pilots drinking in the bar of Vientiane's Constellation Hotel together with a member of their ground crew, a young Ivy League graduate fluent in several languages. The drink flowed and the pilots began to bait him.

"The trouble with you intelligence types is that you want reports on everything—what we heard, what we saw. You have to remember we're supposed to be flying planes," one said.

"The last intelligence man was worse," another pilot put in. "Do you remember all those forms he had printed?" The young man was said to have "flushed and changed the subject."

Two years later, in 1966, the paper had still not properly

172

nailed the airline to the CIA, but stated coyly that it "has been called the Central Intelligence Agency's private air subsidiary."

The *Times* asked: "What is Air America doing in Laos? Probably no one person in or out of the United States could name all that it is doing. One big mission is supplying and supporting the so-called aid projects that spatter the map of Laos like a bad case of chicken pox. . . .

"There are projects that seem to require radio transmitters, occasional bundles of guns, and possibly bags of gold. The mission? It is said that this develops islands of 'friendlies,' or little groups of the local populace who supposedly can be counted on to fight back against the Communists. 'Friendlies' are encouraged and created with presumably judicious supplies of guns, ammunition, and funds. They are supposed to set up informer networks and keep an eye on goings-on in the back country.

"There's plenty going on in the back country."

AA sat tight and said nothing. They did not have to worry about their pilots, who knew the penalty for loose talk and had a natural distaste for reporters anyway. When in 1970 the *Times* asked George Doole, Jr., then president of the Pacific Corporation and chief executive officer of AA and Air Asia, whether his airline had any connection with the CIA it was told: "If 'someone out there' is behind all this we don't know about it." In the same year *Newsweek* ran a short, snappy piece on the airline, noting that most of its services connected with the military involvement in Southeast Asia went unpublicized: "Recently, however, AA came into the spotlight when it flew several hundred Thai troops into Laos to help the CIA-sponsored 'secret army' of Gen Vang Pao defend the outpost of Long Tieng from Communist attack.

"Although in practical terms it is an operating arm of the CIA, AA is owned by a private aviation investment concern called Pacific Corporation. It's managing director and chief executive, a large, affable man named George Doole, Jr., laughs heartily when questioned about dealings with intelligence organizations—but hedges his answer. 'I don't know all of our customers' private business and relations. . . . So help me, that's a fact.' " Large, affable George knew better than that, of course. At the time he had been working for the

CIA for seventeen years, and for most of those years had held a CIA "supergrade" position.

James Cunningham, Jr., AA's Vientiane manager, was suitably vague when questioned by the magazine about operations behind the Pathet Lao lines only miles from the North Vietnam border. "We operate on a you-call, we-haul basis," he said. "We don't go into details."

But the press wanted details. They also wanted photographs, and *Newsweek* sent John Robatan to see what material he could produce out of Laos. "I got go nothing out of Laos," he told me. "All the time I was there I didn't get anything."

His experience in the country is interesting inasmuch as it was similar to that of numerous journalists who attempted to get close to the war. On the surface it seemed that they were offered every assistance, while in fact they were politely led up the garden path. At the same time a watchful eye was kept on them.

"I took a flight up to Luang Prabang," Robatan said, "and it seemed that at almost the last minute before the plane took off a pretty young Lao girl jumped into the plane and sat down next to me. And she spoke English."

It was a bumpy flight, and one particularly violent jolt of the plane threw the girl into Robatan's lap, where she seemed happy to stay for a significantly long time. She remained effusively friendly for the rest of the trip. The girl had trained as a nurse in Houston, Texas, for six months, where she had learned to speak English. Her boy friend was an American in the military in Saigon. But she did not like American Blacks, she said, and was ashamed of the darkness of her own skin and never went out in the sun.

Robatan was invited by her to a New Year's outing on a little island in the Mekong. "It was a happy time. Everybody went out there and built castles out of sand. The Crown Prince was there, drunk out of his mind. It's a tradition for the women to tear the shirts off men—like an ancient fertility rite."

They continued to meet. Robatan discovered that the girl's brother was a major in the Royal Lao Air Force and had been actively obstructive in preventing him flying on a T-28 mission. It became obvious that the girl was pumping him for information. "Tell me what you know about Laos?" she insisted time and time again.

"I don't know anything about Laos."

"But surely if a magazine like *Newsweek* sent you to Laos you must know something—what did they tell you?" she retorted.

"They didn't tell me anything, I came here cold," Robatan insisted. It was the truth.

"She was always pumping me. If she wasn't planted, it was an awfully strange coincidence. She seemed to know my movements and turn up at my hotel. And she had no romantic interest in me."

For transport he had to rely on Air America. "I was told that AA would give me the transportation to wherever I wanted to go. I went to see them, and it was a hell of a process but they did give me transportation. They told me they could send me over the Ho Chi Minh trail or I could go to the front lines. I chose to go to the front. There was no action at all—there were prostitutes running around living with the men. But the whole thing was arranged and had to be arranged through Air America. This happened all the time, you'd go to an area and it would turn out that AA had set up the whole thing.

"The pilots didn't want any journalists around them. If you tried to be friendly with them, you would be totally rejected. They stayed a very close, tight-knit group." The animosity of the pilots was something that any pressman visiting Laos could not fail to notice. "They were very hostile to the press," Richard Pyle of AP said. "A lot of times their reason was that they were antagonized by what they thought was false, misleading, or unnecessary reporting of the war. They didn't like the press because they didn't think the press were doing anything to help things along. They thought we were a bunch of hippies and so on and were over there to cause trouble and undermine the cause. A lot of them felt that any information that was made public was not helpful to their own survival."

"When you asked them what they actually did, you would be told that they were transporting refugees, cargo, and food," Robatan said. "They did do that, but everybody felt that the cargo included an awful lot of arms. They were going out to the Plain of Jars all the time, but nobody was allowed to get close to that place. Everybody assumed there was a war going on somewhere. You did see casualties, and you could get around to a degree but there were definitely places you could not get into."

Mike Putzel, an Associated Press reporter who covered the Vietnamese war for three years, admitted to drawing a blank in Laos. "It was almost impossible to cover the war there. There were silly stories like the Pathet Lao knocking over Attopeu, a provincial capital. Everybody fled into the hills, and a howitzer battery changed hands four times without casualties. The soldiers just kept abandoning it until it was eventually captured by a tiger. That kind of thing led you to believe there was no war going on really. It was a circus. And then the endless war for the Plain of Jars, which none of us ever saw, but every year it would change hands."

The company, meanwhile, affected a pose of great openness. "'Go out and photograph anything you want—we're not doing anything covert here.' That was their line," Robatan said. "But what could you do? You went out into their warehouses and there were tons of boxes and cartons and crates. Big deal. You couldn't start ripping open boxes to see what was inside."

Air America, like the Lao girl on the plane, seemed much more interested in Robatan than he was in them. "One night in the White Rose there was a group of AA, and a friend of mine went up and took a photograph of them. He walked up to them, took the picture—and ran. Sometime later I was up in Luang Prabang and there was an open air place with a thatched roof where you could buy a snack or a beer and there were these three AA guys. And, man, two of them were hostile as hell toward me! They kept asking me, menacingly: 'Where's your tall friend?'

"But the third guy was very very nice and eventually he and I went to a bar together. It became pretty clear he was trying to get something out of me. He wanted to know what I was getting in Laos. He wasn't interested in picking up any girls. It got to be like a briefing. He wasn't trying to find out what I knew about Air America, but wanted to know what I wanted in Laos. I told him that the Laos war was such a closed goddamn thing you just couldn't get to it."

"I didn't understand the war in Laos then and I still don't. The whole thing was ridiculous. There were these three half-brothers, one was in charge of the government, one was in charge of the Pathet Lao, and the other was the King who was politically neutral. Crazy."

It became apparent to Robatan just how sensitive AA were to adverse publicity when the *Newsweek* piece on the company appeared. He was sitting quietly in the magazine's Saigon office, doing a crossword puzzle during the lunch hour, when a young American burst in. "He was demanding to know where he could sign up for Air America and wanted to know who wrote the story. I kept telling him I had no idea, I was just a photographer. He was so adamant, so hostile, so furious I really thought he was going to beat me up. He wasn't just a stray American in Saigon, he wanted information for some reason. He didn't want to join AA at all—he was someone from the CIA who wanted to know who wrote the story."

It almost seemed as if the AA pilots felt they were fighting a private war and wanted to be allowed to carry on doing so with the minimum publicity. The relentless winter-spring offensives of the Pathet Lao and North Vietnamese year after year drove Vang Pao's Meo further and further back. Their 1970 offensive resulted in a flight south of more than one hundred thousand Meo who were relocated in a crescent-shaped forty-mile-wide strip of territory between Long Tieng and the Vientiane Plain. Then an attack on Long Tieng during the 1971 dry season forced the CIA to evacuate a further fifty thousand dependents from the valley. By mid 1971 USAID estimated that almost one hundred fifty thousand hill-tribe refugees, of which 60 percent were Meo, had been resettled in the Ban Son area.

This was a desperate situation for the hill tribesmen. A third of their entire number, used to small villages surrounded by miles of fertile, uninhabited mountains, were packed into a dead end perched above the sweltering Vientiane plain. Forced down from the mountains they became stricken with malaria and diseases they had never contracted before. They had also become totally dependent on AA's rice drops.

The workload upon the pilots, especially in helicopters, was tremendous. They were filmed by NBC, the one and only documentary to show AA in action, at the climax of the battle for Long Tieng. "Only the performance of the charter planes enabled the army to turn almost certain defeat into at least a temporary standoff," the narrator said. "Only helicopters could land to pluck out the seriously wounded. North Vietnamese artillery was shelling the airstrip, enemy snipers were firing up at the planes, enemy machine guns up on the hills were firing down on the planes. But the friendlies were out of water and ammunition, so the planes went in anyway. They shared the narrow airspace with fighter bombers trying to blast the enemy off the ridge line. To the charter pilots it was just another mission."

A pilot told the viewers: "It goes in spurts. Last February when we didn't have so much antiaircraft we had twenty-seven airplanes hit in one month. This December when the flak was more intense we had twenty-four airplanes hit. However, the hits can be more serious because you're dealing with a larger-caliber weapon.

"That is part of the challenge, that is why we are here. It's not a death wish by any stretch of the imagination. It's a little competition with the other side. I try to survive by using my talents against their talents and usually it wins."

As the war dragged on and the friendlies lost more and more ground, pilots faced tougher and tougher odds. One pilot outraced his North Vietnamese pursuers for two miles in the jungle when his Porter was destroyed on the ground by enemy mortar fire. Jim Russell had been assigned to fly a customer, known as Swamp Rat, and five of his mysterious associates, to a location coded as Site 113. "It was a classified operation and I didn't know any of the passengers," Russell said. "All I can say is that I was the only American in the plane." After some passengers disembarked and others got aboard at an airstrip about 125 miles north of Vientiane, he was ordered to look for a landing site near Ban Tha Si, about one hundred miles northeast of the capital.

"Swamp Rat told me they were looking for a place to load refugees, and I should have known right then that it was going to be bad. I talked to people on the ground and they said everything was secure so I landed." He taxied to one end of the tiny strip and turned the plane around. Swamp Rat climbed out while Russell stayed in the plane.

"There I'm sitting, filling out the log and the prop is unwinding—and I knew it was a trap. As soon as the prop stopped, the first round hit. It blew holes in the airplane. They were waiting for us."

Russell scrambled out of the plane, and another mortar shell landed between him and Swamp Rat. The explosion knocked them both down and Russell cut his arm as he fell. "They put a hundred rounds down there before you could blink." He thought of crawling into a hole and waiting for the arrival of a rescue helicopter, but then saw troops coming down off the mountain, and there were so many of them they looked like an army of ants.

"Who's that, Swamp Rat?" Russell asked.

"The enemy."

They began to run toward the jungle and the troops fired after them. Two of Swamp Rat's team hung back and tried to hold them off with their M16s before plunging into the jungle themselves. For the next hour and a half they raced around in bamboo and foliage while the North Vietnamese went in after them. "They were real close. I could hear them thrashing around in the bush out there looking for me. I was still laboring under the illusion that when it was all over I was going to get back to my machine and fly out of there. This was what aviators do—they don't walk, they fly."

It took a while, but that is exactly what he did when an AA rescue helicopter reached the scene and hoisted Russell out of a small jungle clearing. A second helicopter rescued Swamp Rat and his companions. Russell was fifty at the time of the incident, had been with AA seven years, and won the Silver Star and two Distinguished Flying Crosses piloting B-24 Liberators in World War II, was wounded once, and had sunk a Japanese ship off the coast of Borneo.

"But I never had to run around on the ground trying to save my life before." Two days after losing his plane and nearly losing his life, Jim Russell was flying again.

One of the tasks of the fixed-wing pilots as the secret army retreated from the Plain of Jars was to pinpoint stragglers. If they had radio contact, they would be guided to a pickup spot where choppers could go in and lift them out. Robert Wofford flew a Porter on such a mission, together with a group of Lao and Meo officers who were acting as interpreters.

They came across a small group of stragglers on the top of a rocky outcrop who were waving at them wildly. As they failed to make radio contact, one of the interpreters asked Wofford to fly over them low so he could drop a message containing instructions on where to go and how to get picked up. Wofford circled, dropped the flaps, and slowed down to fifty mph to enable the interpreter to accurately drop the message which he had wrapped around an ammo clip.

The plane lined up on the stragglers, slowed right down, and flew directly toward the group. A hundred yards away Wofford could see clearly that there were five of them. Suddenly they stopped waving, dropped their flags, and reached down to pick up AK-47s. "We were eye to eye, I was coming in on their level, and they just blasted away and emptied their clips. I couldn't do anything, I was already committed. They started firing when I was a hundred yards away, and they were still firing at me when I went ten feet over their heads."

Wofford flew right over them and began to climb and headed for Long Tieng to check for damage. There was only one bullet hole in the plane, which had gone straight through a strut eight feet from Wofford's head. "It was a bloody miracle that they missed. Pure blind luck."

The mechanics at the base said they could fix the plane temporarily so he could fly back to Vientiane. While he was waiting for the repair, a jeep roared up driven by a young Meo officer with a smiling general sitting next to him. "Captain Wofford," the young officer cried, extending his hand, "my general wants you to have this ring."

He handed the pilot a woven silver Meo ring with a turquoise embedded in it. Wofford was touched. "Jeez, that's real nice," he said, accepting the gift. It was a little uncomfortable on his finger, and as Wofford never wore jewelry anyway, he took the ring off once the general had driven away and put it in his pocket.

"The next day I was up-country and the customer there lived with the natives, spoke excellent Meo, and understood their ways and customs. I showed him the ring. He laughed and thought it was funnier than hell. It turned out that their custom is that if somebody has exceptional luck they give them a gift, hoping the luck will transfer. Strangely enough, even though I thought it was funny and I'm not superstitious, I lost the ring that day. And I've never been able to find it since."

But lucky escapes were increasingly matched by fatalities, and the company grew alarmed at the number of men and machines it was losing. The accident and death rate rose dramatically as the military situation continued to deteriorate. In April the AA management sent out a memorandum to all their pilots:

It is with deep personal regret that I confirm the tragic loss of another AA pilot yesterday. The past few months have produced an appalling toll in lives and serious injuries. In light of these events I ask that each Flight Crewmember and each Supervisor reappraise all the factors which make flying in our operation a particularly unforgiving profession. We are called upon to perform under possibly the most difficult environmental conditions in the world, considering the combination of remote, mountainous terrain, absence of modern navigation/communications and air traffic control facilities, active presence of hostile armed forces, absence of adequate means of reporting and forecasting the varied seasonal weather and winds, and marginal airfields and landing zones, to name a few examples. Additionally it must be recognized that performance of support functions such as Maintenance, Traffic, Flight Watch, etc., must be accomplished under equally trying, although different, circumstances. These activities, operating under pressure, have very real problem areas of their own for which crew members must be on constant alert.

The key element which most often determines between success or failure of each flight is the judgment of the individual crew members. Your evaluation of the total situation, including the condition of the aircraft and its equipment, your personal physical and mental state, and the relative urgency of the mission in addition to the factors cited above, culminates in a decision as to whether or not the mission should be attempted under the circumstances. That responsibility is of utmost import, even though such decisions must be made many times each day and thousand of times in a lifetime of flying. The price for only one erroneous assessment of these ingredients all too often is fatal.

It is incumbent on each member of the flying division to exercise alertness, to recognize when support, environmental, and personal factors have combined to produce a risky or hazardous situation requiring the maximum performance by the aircraft of its crew, to exercise sufficient

self-discipline and maturity to refuse missions which require such maximum performance except under life or
death circumstances, and to understand that continued acceptance of high risk operations, except under unusual circumstances, can only lead to further accidents and human
tragedy, and, in the long run, failure to meet customer
requirements. The recent accidents should make it indel-
ibly clear in your mind, as it has mine, that violation of
these concepts does have such results.

It seemed to the pilots that management was suggesting
that accidents were the pilots' fault, some error of judgment
or sheer bravado, rather than increasingly dangerous and
impossible battle with the enemy. A Pilatus Porter pilot
pasted his own memorandum on the company notice board:

The PC-6 is my chariot; therefore shall I want. He maketh
me to come down in green pastures: He leadeth me beside
hostile quarters. He restoreth my circulation, he leadeth
me in the paths of righteousness. Yea, though I fly o'er No-
man's land where mine enemies would compass me about,
I fear much evil, for thou are with me, thy pumps and thy
shafts discomfort me. Thou prepareth a crash for me in the
presence of mine enemies, thy Airsearch anointeth my
screen with oil, my luck runneth out, surely to goodness
thou shalt not follow me all the days of my life, lest I dwell
in the house of the looney forever.

But as the year wore on and the fatality list grew, the pilots'
ability to shrug things off with a nonchalant quip began to
disappear. They began to resent the management's attitude
to them strongly and many handed in their resignations.
Family men especially began to feel that the pay was no
longer ample compensation for the risks they were being
asked to take.
"It's not a question of money, it's a question of safety," one
resigning pilot said at the time. "We're all willing to take a
risk. We do it every day. But if there's a fifty-fifty chance I'm
going to be killed, I'm not going out."
A chief source of irritation was that the CIA had stopped
informing the men honestly about the relative dangers they
were likely to encounter on any particular mission. They felt

that the management always sided with the CIA, urging pilots to "do this one for the customer."

Pilots knew only too well that there was a surplus of fliers and that they were expendable. There were hundreds of chopper pilots available in the United States who, despite being trained by the military and with a tour of combat duty in Vietnam behind them, were unable to find work. AA had a long waiting list of them anxious to get back out to the war because of the money.

Although pilots were allowed to refuse assignments, and all of them did from time to time, the "customer" began to describe high-hazard missions as milk runs. Special missions, which relied on volunteers, attracted fewer and fewer takers. As a result the CIA and AA management began to assign hazardous, special missions on a routine basis.

When people did refuse missions, the CIA agents tended to get emotional about it. Their attitude was that if a pilot turned down an assignment, they did not want him to fly for them anymore. And if a pilot could not fly for the CIA, he was of very little use to Air America. The company never took away the pilots' rights to refuse a mission considered too hazardous, but if they continued to refuse, there were ways of putting pressure on them or easing them out.

Christmas Day 1971 started early in George Ritter's household in Vientiane because he was scheduled to fly throughout the holiday period. The family got up at four-thirty a.m. and opened their presents together. The AA pickup bus called at five and George kissed his wife, Barbara, good-bye.

There were three C-123s working over the Christmas period. They shuttled down from Vientiane to Udorn to pick up their loads and then made their drops. Barbara was disappointed not having her husband at home on Christmas Day, but as an ex-service wife had grown to accept the inconveniences of his hours philosophically. She spent the day with her children, who were excited by their presents, and was delighted that there was no TV to blunt the occasion for them. The Lao servants were excited too by the "American" Christmas, a festival they did not celebrate themselves, and were in raptures over the presents Barbara had bought for them. "Oh, mummy!" the maid's little girl said brightly, "I want to be a Christian on Christmas."

George had a brief stopover at Vientiane airport on the twenty-sixth and his wife went out to have a cup of coffee with him. That night he stayed over in Udorn and then took off the following morning at seven-thirty on a mission. Officially he was on a normal resupply mission, with a destination at Xieng airstrip, and the flight path included a change of course at Sayaboury and Hong Ha. His copilot for the day was Roy Townley, and there were two kickers, Ed Weissenback, an American, and Khamphanh, a Lao. Winds were strong from the southwest and AA at Udorn picked up a radar fix on the plane in midflight, east and north of Sayaboury. Then the plane disappeared.

"I think everyone in town knew what had happened except me," Barbara Ritter said. "The assistant vice-president of AA came by the house, a young fellow I had never seen before. It was just after one o'clock and I knew he hadn't come by to chit-chat out of the clear blue sky. He said he had something very serious to tell me—George's plane was overdue. He didn't use the word 'missing.'

"I knew that pilots who got off course sometimes landed in Burma, so I wasn't too upset that day. I was sure he'd turn up. He always did. Years before in Tripoli in the fifties he was flying an Air Force plane that lost an engine and he was supposed to have crashed in the sea. He was loaded up with cargo and took off over the water and should have gone straight into the drink. But he brought the plane in, barely skimming the tops of buildings. In Laos it was not unusual for him occasionally to have to land in a different place to the one scheduled. I just thought that the old pilot would come flying or limping in somehow."

It was not until the third day that she began seriously to worry. The AA pilots had launched a massive search operation, and flying half a mile apart from one another, they covered the entire area that the plane could possibly have gone down in. The hours they spent on the search were in addition to their regular missions. A Volpar flying a high-level search pattern received one 57mm hit in the right wing, but returned safely to Udorn without casualties.

At night they would return with their eyes red and extended and call on Barbara Ritter and apologize for their failure. The men arranged for the Vientiane newspaper to print a leaflet with a description of the plane, a photograph of the men and a safe-conduct pass, while the company offered two kilos of gold for positive proof of a crash, a piece of the plane or any information that would effectively establish what had happened. These were dropped in their thousands over the area and copies were reprinted in local papers and read over the radio.

On the fifth day of the search Jim Rhynne was flying over a section he was convinced that Ritter might have gone down in. He had studied the direction of the wind and was very anxious to get some pamphlets into a particular area. He thought himself safely above the danger zone and was pushing bundles of pamphlets out of the back of his plane when it was hit by antiaircraft fire. Although it landed safely, Rhynne was badly wounded and lost a leg.

Directly afterward, the search operation was called off. George Doole, onetime president of AA, told me that Rhynne should have been disciplined for taking a plane over an area the company would have expressly forbidden him to go near. "But you can't discipline a man who's had his leg shot off."

AA's reaction to the Ritter crash was extreme. There was something of a management panic when it was discovered that the plane had simply disappeared. The offer of two kilos of gold as a reward was a fortune to the locals—and the disapproval of Rhynne's flight path suggested that the company feared that they might be badly compromised over the affair.

Rhynne had a theory about the crash which most of his colleagues agreed with. The Chinese were building a road in Laos—in the guise of humanitarian aid—which cut through the country and virtually reached the Thai border. It was heavily fortified with sophisticated antiaircraft weapons, and according to an official U.S. estimate at the time, there were fourteen thousand Chinese in the area. The road was strictly off limits to AA pilots, who were ordered not to go anywhere near it. Jim Rhynne told the wives of the missing men that the C-123 had possibly been off course and strayed over the road. The weather had been particularly bad on the morning of the crash and there had been high winds. The Chinese also used false homing beacons on the same frequency as AA's radio in an attempt to lure them into the antiaircraft network. A reconnaissance team that had flown over the road at two thousand feet to take pictures reported four to five hundred rounds of exploding 37mm in the air around them and estimated that there were as many as 300 guns firing at them at one time.

Another theory suggested that Ritter might have been forced down by MIGs or had gunned the engine and landed in China. AA had very good reason to be disturbed by either eventuality. George Ritter's so-called normal resupply mission was in fact a hard-rice drop. His plane was carrying a full load of ammo and white phosphorous. The embassy in Vientiane thought it important enough to send a secret telegram to the Secretary of State in Washington, D.C., the White House, U.S. embassies in Bangkok and Saigon, and the U.S. consul in Hong Kong: INTENSIVE AIR SEARCH FOR C-123 MISSING OVER NORTHWESTERN LAOS SINCE MORNING 27TH DEC 71 HAS BEEN TERMINATED WITH CRASH SITE UNLOCATED AND CAUSE UNKNOWN. VILLAGER AND GROUND TEAM REPORTS AS WELL AS OTHER INTELLIGENCE LEADS HAVE AND WILL CONTINUE TO BE EXPLORED. The telegram listed the crew members and said that their next of kin had been informed. AIR AMERICA, IF QUERIED, WILL RELEASE SUBSTANCE OF ABOVE. GP-2 GOLLEY.

Original press reports out of Laos, reproduced in *The Washington Post* two days after the crash, reported that there were four Americans, a Chinese, and a Lao on board the plane when it crashed. Later, presumably after an embassy flap, AA only spoke of losing three crew members. Nobody picked up on the discrepancy, but it is likely that the two other Americans and the Chinese were CIA case officers.

Nixon's trip to Peking was already planned, and there was a feeling that if the Chinese had an American civilian airliner loaded with ammo in their possession, it could have the same effect that the U-2 incident had on the summit talks. "It seemed to me that they were keeping as much under tabs as they could so it wouldn't disturb any of the diplomacy that was going on," Barbara Ritter said.

She began to develop nagging doubts about the company and the State Department and felt that they knew something that she did not. AA never admitted that the cargo was hard rice and refused to disclose the name of the agent who was supposed to receive it. On a visit to a senior member of AA management in Vientiane she lost her temper in her grief "If you know something and you're not telling me, then some day . . ." Barbara Ritter broke down. The AA officer looked out the window. "He was a nice person, but that was the end of the conversation. It made me feel very unhappy and upset."

Two weeks after the crash the thousands of leaflets that AA had scattered over the area produced some effect. A villager, who had trotted through the jungle for two days, presented himself at an AA station and said that he had information on the crash. He had seen a big bird with fire coming out of the wing, he said, and knew where it had landed.

The CIA was quick to interrogate the villager. An AA pilot who waited for the interrogators to fly them back to Vientiane was disturbed at their methods. He told Barbara Ritter that he thought the Lao was telling the truth but the CIA had bullied him and tried to trip him up. The villager was made to sit on a chair and had a bright light shone into his eyes and was treated like a criminal instead of a man bringing in information.

"The Laos are very gentle people, uneducated, and we all look alike to them," Barbara Ritter said. "The pilot was not a very gentle person himself, but it had upset him. He said he didn't like what went on up there and that he felt sorry for the little hill tribesman who came in. The CIA had roughed him up."

But the authorities seemed convinced that there was no substance in the story. In a secret report to the Department of Defense it was stated: "The story given by the Lao was utterly without foundation, and the Lao has been identified over a period of time as a notorious fabricator. What happened to aircraft 6293 and the crew remains a complete mystery."

In August 1972 the CIA learned through a casual source that Siang Kaew, a member of the Pathet Lao, wanted to defect to the Royal Lao Government, but was afraid of being killed or severely punished. To ensure his personal safety he wanted to defect to the Americans. He claimed to have information on the missing C-123 and subsequent capture of *three* Americans and one Lao. Siang Kaew claimed to be the prison camp commander where the three American airmen, together with four additional Americans and several high-ranking Thai and Lao officers, were being kept.

Siang Kaew was debriefed by a Lao informer, Lo Van Gian, who was contacted by Maj. John B. Wilson, Assistant Army

attaché at the U.S. embassy in Vientiane. Wilson produced
a confidential report on what he felt to be "questionable"
information.

Siang Kaew said that he saw the plane crash. It seemed to
him to have run out of gas and was attempting to make a
landing at Muong Sai airfield. However, it landed in the
middle of a stream nearby, and only the tail section could be
seen sticking out of the water but the Pathet Lao noticed its
tail number—293. Three Americans and a Lao kicker called
Khamphanh were captured. The pilot had a broken arm, the
copilot was suffering from a knee injury. The American kicker
had a injury over the left eye, and Khamphanh had lost a
tooth.

Siang Kaew said he escorted the men to a prison camp.
One of the Americans had a small-caliber pistol which he
gave to one of the guards to sell and buy food for them. There
was some confusion whether the men had been kept in the
camp or moved to Tuyen Quang in North Vietnam.

The camp itself was inside a cave which had a waterfall
running over its entrance. There were two cells inside, one
housing the Americans and the other the high-ranking Thais
and Laos. Outside of the cave there were areas for growing
vegetables, including a pumpkin patch, and there were reportedly fifty enemy personnel within a kilometer of the
camp. The Americans cut firewood, grew vegetables, and
bathed in the stream once a week.

When this information reached AA pilots on the grapevine
a group of the men volunteered to stage a guerrilla raid on
the prison camp. But the idea had to be cleared through the
embassy where it was turned down.

When interrogated, Siang Kaew proved to be unintelligent
and contradictory. He could not pick out photographs of the
crew members, was hesitant over questions and thoroughly
unconvincing, according to Major Wilson's report. He concluded that the entire story had been fabricated to obtain the
AA reward and said that he considered the incident terminated. Short shrift was also given to the theory that the men
were being held prisoner in China.

The crash has remained a mystery ever since. One possible
explanation, in view of the fact that the plane was carrying
ammo, is that it exploded in midair after a direct hit, and
this would explain why no wreckage was ever spotted.

Apart from the personal tragedy of losing their husbands, the wives have had practical problems due to the men's missing-in-action status. It has meant they have not been able to transfer mutual funds, stock, or collect on life insurance policies and have become victims of a technicality. "They paid all of the insurance to the pilots who became 'missing' from the day after George's crash," Barbara Ritter said. "But they have not settled with the crew of plane 293. I feel I've been treated shabbily."

Her children took the loss of their father badly. The eldest son, Philip, suddenly grew old, and lost his carefree young spirit. "He grew very serious. And angry. With the government and the war. He still felt that AA were doing a good job and that his father was happy in it, but that with the whole bungled mess of the war he would never know what really happened to his father. He went back to Laos in August 1974 to find out things, go up-country and ask questions. He was depressed for about six months when he came back, lost a lot of weight, and didn't do well at school."

Karen Weissenback had the unhappy joy of giving birth to her husband's baby two months after the disappearance of plane 293.

One of the costliest missions AA ever took on, in terms of wear and tear in men and machines, was the Saravane operation. Saravane was a town to the west of the Ho Chi Minh trail, close to where it split into three main routes. It was also the closest town to the friendlies' position near the trail sixty miles away. The intention of the Saravane operation, which began in the middle of October 1972, was to drop in three thousand five hundred top-notch Lao troops.

On the very first day a helicopter was shot down, killing a CIA man and two Laotian aides. A Lao general who was on board survived, but the chopper that picked him up took several hits and the copilot was seriously wounded. Air Force doctors, who were not surgeons, had to perform a botched emergency operation to save his life. The word went around AA that the Saravane Operation was a dangerous mission to draw. There began to be friction between pilots and CIA case officers. At one briefing over a projected mission to Saravane a pilot objected to the plan. "No, we aren't going to do it," he said.

The case officer, who was a close friend of the killed CIA

man, was too upset to be diplomatic. "Oh, yes, you are—just as I've got it planned here," he snapped.

"No we're not," the pilot persisted, "because you're going to end up getting some more people killed just like your friend got killed."

The young case officer lost his temper. "You AA pilots are getting paid enough to die anyway," he said. There was a scuffle as the pilot went in swinging, and the case officer lost two front teeth.

"I kept hearing people say, 'That's pretty hairy flying down there, you know,' but was not scheduled to go there at that time," Mel Cooper said. "I got my first taste of Saravane the week before Thanksgiving and it was shaky. We'd normally fly ammo and goods out there, kick it off and pick up wounded, sometimes twice a day. The main equipment drops were made by fixed-wing people. But I didn't like flying eighty miles over territory when you had no idea who controlled it."

The full complement of three thousand five hundred men was never landed because enemy fire was so intense, but around two thousand troops dug in. "We started to carry out some more troops in December, about ten at a time," Mel Cooper said. "There would be five helicopters, one empty for SAR. On the first day that we moved troops I was tail-end Charlie, and artillery, mortar, and rockets started coming in. I used to know what it was by the amount of dust and dirt it threw up.

"We were just touching down, and our people weren't all off when a mortar shell landed less than fifty yards away; then another hit less than twenty-five yards away. And every time after that when I was on the ground I saw artillery of some sort going off. Sometimes it was as far away as a mile, but on other occasions it was close enough and big enough for the dirt to cover the helicopter."

A Caribou flying support limped back to base with half a dozen .50 caliber hits, and the pilots trooped out onto the runway to look at the bullet holes. The chopper pilots knew where the guns were lined up and would fly S turns around them to stay out of range. The fixed-wing aircraft flew straight over them, relying on altitude to keep out of trouble.

On Thanksgiving Day a Caribou making supply drops attracted the attention of a chopper pilot flying close by. "Hey, that's how the other Caribou picked up those six rounds the other day, doing just the same thing you're doing, and he was even higher than you are," the pilot said over the radio. "You better change your path or get higher."

"Yeah, yeah," the reply came back, "you helicopter jockeys are always saying this."

The Caribou continued to make its drop, kicking out about a third of its load on each run. On the last pass the Caribou flew low to impress the helicopter pilots. Suddenly the pilot began to scream over the radio, "I've lost control—hydraulics going—no flight control!" The plane plummeted to earth, killing its crew.

Mel Cooper carried on flying to Saravane for two more weeks. "I was flying with Joe, a guy I hated to fly with. He was a great guy on the ground, but he didn't use good headwork in the air as far as I was concerned. Once he got in the air he forgot about everything but the mission. On the ground he could talk a very safe flight but he never flew a safe flight." Cooper took a five-day break for R & R in Hong Kong and then returned for another six days. Each day the situation was a little worse, and by the end of it Cooper had had enough. He told operations that he was not going back into Saravane.

"I'll resign if you send me back down there."

"Okay, take it easy," the scheduler replied. He said that he would send the pilot to Ban Houei Sai for his next stint, a comparative milk run. Cooper relaxed for the first time in a month.

At five the next morning he was woken up and told there was going to be a change of schedule. He was to go to Pakse—the Saravane run. Cooper refused and scratched out a letter of resignation to the assistant chief pilot there and then. "I'm not going down there anymore. I'm hating myself for doing it. It's just not worth the money. And I'm definitely not doing this for glory or country or anybody else at this point. It's not worth it."

"We tried not to schedule you, but the other guy's sick," the assistant chief pilot said.

"Sure—he's sick with a yellow stripe down his back."

"Look, we absolutely don't have anybody else and we have to go. You've gotta go for us."

The assistant chief pilot pleaded with Cooper to accept the assignment until he weakened and said he would—for the very last time. "Not only had I been talked out of resigning, but when I got down there I found out I've got to fly with Joe again for five days. I was really cursing myself and pretty hard to live with, calling people a few names."

It was the week before Christmas and it proved to be a bad one, for the Air Force had launched an all-out bombing attack on Hanoi. Normally there would have been Navy, Marine, or Air Force jets loaded with bombs in the area which AA could call upon when they were in trouble, but with the attack on Hanoi everything was in Vietnam and the choppers had no high cover. And the enemy knew it.

"They became much more gutsy. We were getting shot at with 37mm every so often, but what was common was being shot at with 12.7 .50-caliber. But the thing that really scared me was the artillery on the ground. I knew that they would saturate the area. Every time you went in you'd change your landing spot because they would pinpoint and saturate it. They weren't accurate, because of the wind and temperature changes, so they couldn't just hit you exactly. It was like playing Russian roulette—the game was that you put yourself in their area and they tried to see if they could put one on top of you. It was driving me batty."

Whenever Cooper became scared and upset with himself, he kept a diary as therapy. "Do I really hate myself so much that for a few thousand dollars I'm willing to stand out there and let people shoot artillery at me? I'm too intelligent to be doing this," he asked himself in one entry.

"We had Johns who loved to get shot at," Cooper explained. "It must have built up their adrenaline, and for some of them it was like having sex. There is something exhilarating about going out and getting shot at and surviving. Some people got to feel they were invincible. One guy, Dave Kendall, got to feel very much that way, and after surviving many shoot-ups he wiped himself out when he hit a fuel truck head-on driving on a rain slick road from Louisiana to Kentucky. But I didn't feel at all invincible."

The CIA was also running another operation on a road that led out of the Ho Chi Minh trail to Saravane and were using helicopters and fixed-wing aircraft to supply the troops they had out there. They had clusters of two hundred troops on three small hills about a quarter of a mile apart from one another which formed a triangle. At night the enemy would probe the positions' perimeter, but it was generally considered that the area inside the triangle was safe in daylight.

Cooper had gone out to the area to pick up some wounded and then headed for what was considered to be the most secure area, right in the middle of the triangle. The chopper was flying low when a wave of tracer bullets arced toward it. "It was another one of those heart stoppers," Cooper said. "All of a sudden, right in front of us and coming right at us was .50 cal. tracers." They were so low that they ducked behind a tree where they could no longer see the tracers, but heard the unmistakable slow pump of the guns.

They flew back into Pakse with the wounded and spread the word that there were .50 cals. around. They were able to pinpoint on the map to within fifty yards where they had been shot at, and a case officer sent a Lao colonel out with troops to sweep the area. It was Cooper's last day of tour, and he was relieved that it was all over, picked up his gear at the hostel, and went into flight operations to ask about airplanes heading back to Udorn. He wandered in just as they were getting ready to send out a C-123 to make a daylight drop on the triangle.

It was the end of the briefing, but Cooper was in time to hear the case officer, Tall Man, sum up. "Well, you probably heard reports from the helicopter pilots that they were fired at by 12.7 this morning. That's bullshit. They weren't fired at by 12.7, because my colonel swept there and there's no 12.7 emplacement or anything else in there. Possibly somebody fired an AK at them."

Cooper listened to this with a slow burning fury. "The guy's about twenty-five, and adviser to a battalion of regiment-sized force, and his military background and experience was zero. A college-educated, trained liar of the CIA. They had given him a course in counter-guerrilla warfare, but other than that he had no experience fighting as a platoon leader, a platoon sergeant or in any combat anywhere. And here he was advising a regimental commander. He was the guy the commander had to talk to to get supplies and everything, so the military paid attention to what he said and would do what this guy told them. It was scary. You'd think if they really wanted to win the war, they'd get better people. He was sitting there and I was listening, and there had already been two aircraft lost out in Saravane, so people were getting a little nervous to say the least, but they were still doing it."

The captain receiving the briefing was Neil Hansen, and Cooper waited for the case officer to finish. "Don't listen to that asshole," Cooper said finally. "I know a 12.7—I've been shot at by them often enough and I've heard the difference. It was not an AK—definitely 12.7. I saw the tracers at a cyclical rate too slow for an AK. I don't care what they say they swept. I don't think they even walked out there."

"If my colonel says he sent people out there, he sent people out there," Tall Man snapped.

"I just heard you say don't pay any attention to the helicopter pilots, mister, and I happen to be one and I know what I saw."

"Well," Neil Hansen drawled, "I'll go—but my crew are all going to be wearing parachutes." It was common to carry parachutes in an aircraft, but unheard of for the crew to wear them throughout a flight. The crew felt Hansen was overreacting and fought him over it, but he insisted.

The reports of .50 cal. antiaircraft worried him less than most other people. "I've seen an awful lot of guys where the idea of somebody shooting at them in anger absolutely ruined their mind," he said. "It never really bothered me a hell of a lot. I don't know why, maybe I'm a little bit dingy. You take your odds, figure the best way to go in and out of a place— sure they can hit you, but I always felt there was more danger in crossing the street in Bangkok."

Hansen accepted the mission and flew out in the C-123 together with his copilot, who among other things had a Ph.D. in etymology. During the drop they were badly hit—.50 cal. from a 12.7.

Cooper heard their "May Day" call come over the air as he tried to sleep crouched in the belly of a helicopter on its way to Udorn.

Hansen battled to keep control of the plane and managed to turn it around with great difficulty and head back toward Pakse. Helicopters were converging on a spot where he had been advised there were no enemy troops and it would be safe to bail out. On the first pass over he told his copilot to get ready to jump and prepared to leave the cockpit himself. Just then the copilot returned, saying he had forgotten his radio. "Goddamnit, I told you to bail out."

By this time the plane had overflown its mark, so Hansen turned it around again, with full power on one wing only, and lined up for another run. He was just ready to climb out of the cockpit himself when the copilot appeared. He had forgotten his camera. Hansen took a wild swing at him, the copilot decided to forget about the camera, but once again the plane had overshot the mark. Hansen turned the plane and began to climb. The kickers decided they didn't want to wait any longer and jumped. The copilot peered out anxiously after them to make sure that their parachutes opened and was helped on his way with a gentle shove. Hansen followed him out.

Two AA choppers went in to pick them up. The one that took Hansen and his copilot caught its tail rotor blade in the trees as it took off. It limped along for two miles over hostile territory, but the blade was vibrating so badly that the pilot was forced to make a crash landing. Another AA chopper came in to pick them up and headed back toward Pakse. "Hell almighty!" the pilot said halfway.

"What's up? somebody asked.

"You're not going to believe this, we're out of gas!"

This time there was quite a crowd to be taken into Pakse—the crews of the crashed C-123 and the two rescue choppers. Hansen had made three crash landings in a single day.

On Cooper's first day out again an Air Force C-119 gunship was shot down after dark. He was in the sort of mood to be difficult at the nightly meetings with the CIA case officer who planned the operations.

"Why don't you admit it's a failure and get out of there? You're going to get a lot of people killed."

"You don't understand the big picture," the officer told him—a stock CIA reply to anybody anywhere, with the possible exception of God.

Cooper was not very popular at the nightly CIA briefings. "They lied to us terribly over the Saravane operation and they lied to the Air Force. They felt that if they told us the truth we wouldn't go. These guys were a little bit irritating. They were young for the most part, and they had the feeling that older guys weren't going to take the chances they were, so they couldn't tell them the truth. What these little assholes didn't realize was that most of the people they considered too old to take chances had been taking a hell of a lot more chances for years than they had. It wasn't a one- or two-year contract, most of them had been doing it for ten years.

"We finally got most of them convinced, although it took knocking those teeth out of one guy, that we were stupid enough to go even if we knew the truth. And that our chance of survival—and theirs, because they often went with us—was a hell of a lot better if we knew everything they knew. Then we could plan some sort of escape. But at the point we had them convinced it was almost over."

At first it was decided, in the case of the C-119 gunship which had been shot down, that the rescue operation should be left to the Air Force's Jolly Green Giants. It took them seven hours to attempt a pickup, whereas AA could have made it straight away, and only two survivors out of a crew of twelve were picked up. The next morning at dawn AA were asked to go to the crash site in a combined operation with the Lao Air Force. The plan was for four Lao H-34s, with ten men in each including a team leader with a radio, to fly to the crash site together with five AA choppers and set up a guarded perimeter to enable the Air Force to conduct an investigation. A Lao general was in charge of the operation, and his chief of staff briefed them in English.

Mel Cooper was still flying with Joe, who as the senior AA pilot on the operation spoke on behalf of the company. "I'm not going to fly the mission with the Lao pilots heading it," he said bluntly. The chief of staff's back straightened at the remark, and when he translated it the general turned red. The general muttered under his breath. "What do you suggest?" the chief of staff translated.

"We'll fly just like you say, but the team leader and the first group go into our birds and you follow us in," Joe said. "I'll pick the point where you can land, and you can all work off me."

The general conferred with his chief of staff. "Fine, we'll do it that way," he said eventually. Cooper was surprised that the general had not fought harder for his plan, and it struck him as odd that the Lao should accept such loss of face without an argument.

At the base the troops were ready and waiting and the AA choppers lined up in front of them. But nobody with a radio or with any apparent rank boarded Joe's chopper. Cooper looked out of the window and saw a captain and a radio operator board the first of the Lao helicopters. Cooper nudged his companion. "Hey, Joe, do you know why they agreed with you so easily?"

"No, why?"

"Because they didn't agree with you at all—they're doing it their way anyway." And as Cooper spoke, the Laotian helicopters started to crank up. Joe jumped out of his seat and started to go over to the general to sort things out when the Lao choppers took off.

"Goddamnit." The pilot cranked up and took off in pursuit in an attempt to overtake them.

"Hey, Joe—they got the radio people, they got the team leaders. Let's just go back to their plan, huh?" Cooper argued.

"They're doing this because they don't want to lose face," Joe said angrily. "I've been over here in the Orient long enough to know how they work, and I'm not going to lose face to those little assholes either. I'm going to land first."

"But why, goddamnit, why? The enemy's probably there by now, why do you want to go down and be the first one to be shot at? Tell me that?"

Joe said nothing.

"If you insist on going in first, I'm going to have to write you up. I flew with you last week, and there were a couple of missions then that I didn't want to go on and you badgered me into them. And my feeling is that I was right and you were wrong but we survived them somehow. But now you're going too goddamn far. For pride you're willing to wipe us out. Dead people have no pride. If somebody is going to get wiped out, let it be them if they want to go in first. I'm not particular."

"No, we're going in first," Joe insisted.

"There was only one place for the choppers to land, and the four Lao birds and the five AA choppers raced toward it. A Cessna bird-dog which had been patrolling the area since first light reported that no enemy had been sighted. 'Go in—we're sure it's no problem.'"

The landing area, beside a rice paddy with tall trees at the side of it, was the size of a football field. In the race to land, the choppers had broken formation and became muddled, flying almost on top of one another. Joe landed first, but the next birds following him were Lao. The remaining AA choppers broke off to wait until the first team had off-loaded their troops. As soon as Joe touched down, there was the distinctive sound of AK fire coming from the direction of the treeline.

"Joe, we better get out of here," Cooper shouted. As the copilot, it was his responsibility under heavy fire to warn the people above not to come in. "Let's get out of here, let's get out of here," Cooper screamed into the radio. "We're taking fire, we're taking fire. Don't land, don't land."

The Laos were not on the same radio frequency, spoke no English, and continued to land, while the AA choppers in the air could not pick up the signal either because of the tall trees. The gunfire was so loud that Cooper knew the enemy had to be close and he leaned forward to look toward the treeline to see if he could spot them. The Filipino crew chief shouted that they were taking hits on the left side and Cooper turned around. Four soldiers had come out of the trees and were standing no more than seventy-five feet from them, blasting away. A bullet ripped the rucksack off the back of one of their troops as he jumped clear and the chopper took three hits.

Most of the enemy fire was directed at the other choppers and on the one directly behind them. Seven of the troops jumping off were killed, while the chopper itself took twenty-seven hits. A further thirty troops were on the ground, with no radio communications and no officer to lead them. They were running around wildly in every direction. Another hazard the men had to face after the choppers lifted off was their own Lao Air Force T-28s which were sent in to bomb the treeline. The lack of radio contact with the men on the ground meant that the bombs were practically dropped on top of them. Later in the day three hundred troops were flown into the area to deal with the enemy. There had been six of them.

Meanwhile, that same afternoon Cooper and Joe made a drop with full T-28 cover to a spy team near the Ho Chi Minh trail. They took out food, a new radio, and two fresh men and picked up one who had fallen sick. Back in the air, flying over no-man's land, the T-28s suddenly broke away and left them. "They were on our frequency, jabbering at a hundred miles a minute, but we couldn't understand what they were saying. It wasn't very encouraging. Then the people on the ground called in to say they had forgotten to put the old radio on the chopper and also that they had some documents and captured AK-47s they wanted to put on board."

By this time they had already climbed to fifteen hundred

feet. "Goddamnit," Joe said, then spoke into the radio. "Okay, I'll come down and pick them up."

"Hey, Joe," Cooper interrupted, "you already got me shot up this morning. Why do you want to go back down in there?"

"Those documents might be important."

"Bullshit."

The SAR chopper with them came through over the radio. "My Thai copilot says the reason those guys were jabbering away there in the T-28s and left in a hurry was that they got fired at by 37mm."

"Well, Joe, that's that," Cooper said. "I guess you're not going in now."

"Sure. We're going to go down."

"Joe, I already told you I'm going to write you up for the shit this morning, but this is really . . ."

"Go ahead and write me up."

Cooper was so angry he began to fight for the stick. There was a dangerous jostle while the chopper weaved about crazily. "I've got it," Cooper shouted.

"Oh no, you haven't," Joe said, getting control once more.

"If you don't want me to bust you right in the mouth, you'll let me fly it," Cooper shouted.

"He starts down and I'm sitting wondering what the hell I'm doing there and I was on the verge of committing armed mutiny."

Joe suddenly had a change of heart. "Forget about us coming back down and picking up that stuff," he said into the radio. "Bury those documents and we'll pick them up another day. There's too much static over the air, we don't have our air cover anymore, and we're low on fuel." Then Joe handed the bird over to Cooper. "Okay, you fly it home."

Cooper flew the forty minutes back to base in silence with his stomach in a knot. "I was thinking that when I got on the ground I was going to bust him right in the mouth. It had gone too far."

They still had the sick man on board and took him to hospital, where Joe calmed his copilot down. "Mel, I'm glad you argued with me, because if I had more copilots who argued with me I'd probably get in less trouble. Once I get in the air I get headstrong and don't want to turn back for anything. But I don't want to die, and I've come close to it several times."

The day's experience had done little to settle Cooper's fears and the letter of resignation was drawn up once again. On December 23, two bird-dog Forward Air Control people were shot down and killed and Cooper was on the chopper sent out to pick up the bodies. While he was out at the site of the crash, two more had their engines short out and crash landed. Cooper's helicopter picked them up. "Things were getting extremely difficult because of the lack of jet coverage. The enemy came up with two or three emplacements of 23M, which is a very effective gun the Egyptians used against the Israelis. They set four 23M guns, which have a total firing capability of four thousand rounds a minute, on a track vehicle. They probably had them before this time, but they never really used them because they knew it would attract a strike. But with the heavy stuff up in Vietnam they had a ball. The army nicknamed the 23M "Golden Hose" because it fired so rapidly—with tracers every so many rounds—that it looked as if a solid stream of water were coming out of a hose. Whenever they started tracking somebody, it was just like taking a water hose with a whipping motion."

That night back in Udorn, Cooper got drunk with the survivors. The following day he submitted his resignation to the chief pilot. Then the two men played handball together and talked things over with a beer.

"Look, you know the North Vietnamese are really hurting because they've been bombed to hell with the B-52s," the chief pilot said. "It has to quieten down. They're spent. It's going to be all over soon. Why leave now?"

After a long talk Cooper sighed. "Yeah, I guess you're right." And he withdrew his resignation yet again.

Cooper was back in Saravane during the first week of January when the enemy finally chased them out. He was in the last helicopter to land there. This time he was with a pilot named Elmer who, like Joe, was oblivious to danger. "There could be bullets flying around and he wouldn't see them and there would be no flinching. He knew he was perfectly safe, no matter what was raining down around him. The enemy had gotten little 85mm artillery pieces by this time, which were extremely accurate and long-range for their size. They had gotten so goddamn good that when you landed you better not be sitting there very long."

As they went into Saravane, stretcher teams ran toward them carrying wounded to be evacuated. The moment they touched down the overpressure of an explosion hit them. Dust came filtering into the cockpit. Outside the wounded had been blown off their stretchers and lay beneath the rotor blades. The bearers had abandoned them and were trying to get into the chopper.

"Goddamn, don't let these guys on," Elmer said and lifted the machine off the ground.

The enemy was trying to track them with artillery and the chopper was rocked by another explosion. They were flying low over the trees as round upon round exploded in their wake. The gunners were trying to put a shell on top of them, and despite a series of ninety-degree turns the chopper could not lose them. Even Elmer was alarmed. The trip back to Pakse took an hour and a half, during which time Saravane received a thousand rounds of incoming, and AA operations had given the helicopter up as lost.

AA told the CIA they were not going to go back in, and shortly afterward the operations officer gave word to the troops to fight their way back to friendly lines, an eighty-mile battle through hostile territory. "I was so goddamn happy when I found out they had been given permission to desert the area," Cooper said. "Christ, that made me feel good. And the fact that I heard the peace treaty was going to be signed in Vietnam and that things were going to quieten down. Everything looked good."

He was sent up to Ban Houe Sai when the Pakse operation closed down, and it should have been easy, relaxed flying. Then overnight it became the only hot spot in the whole country. The place was overrun by the enemy, and a mass evacuation of the Meo began. "So I went for another week under the mental pressure of hating myself. But all the nonsense of the bullets and the artillery was off my back because I've finally done it—I've submitted the letter of resignation. I had my tickets home in my pocket and four days to go. I was going down to New Zealand with a friend and we were going to take six months getting back to the U.S.

"I had it all planned. Then I sat down and thought about it. Everything was quieting down to a picnic, nobody was shooting at us anymore. There had been a ten percent pay rise and I was getting ready to make captain, which would give me another eight hundred dollars a month. And I thought—I'm doing it to myself again. I've lived through the shitty part and now it's easy I'm leaving. The story of my life. I wondered if they'd let me withdraw my letter."

They did, but Cooper's dream of easy flying never materialized. He was transferred from Laos to Vietnam, where he stayed until the final collapse and also flew hair-raising missions into Cambodia. The Peace Accord in Laos was signed in January 1973 and went into effect from the beginning of February.

It was immediately apparent to the pilots that the peace agreement was phony. Although AA's operations were considerably wound down and many aviators were posted to Vietnam, there was still considerable activity in the country. "When that ceasefire went into effect, we put up our flags and the enemy put up theirs and we could see where we were going," Mike Barksdale said. "And I took a look and thought, Oh Jesus, is that where they really are? They're all over the place." The government began to put pressure on AA to leave, but the company was in no hurry to go, although it had begun to make cuts once the peace agreement had been signed. AA dismissed forty-two of about one hundred pilots and began to move planes to other countries and sell others. A dozen C-123 military transports were turned over to the Laotian Air Force and a total of 350 strips were abandoned.

"Some of our old pilots, who would never quit as long as they felt they were needed, felt that now is a good time to get out, to grow vegetables or relax or something," James Cunningham, AA's station manager at Vientiane, told *The New York Times*. He assured the paper that by September 30, 1973, the last AA pilots would have left the country and that by the end of October there would be fewer than fifteen Americans working for the company in Vientiane. Although the Porters were flown south to Thailand in October, AA was to stay on.

The year 1973 proved to be a hard one on personnel. There were eight fatal crashes and nearly fifty fatalities. Pilots who had grown used to the feeling of unreality about the war in Laos took it for granted that they would be shot at during a ceasefire and even took the presence of Chinese transports in Luang Prabang in their stride. "One time they asked me in perfect English, 'Could that AA chopper move over and give us a little more room?'" Mike Barksdale said.

It was also a year when the company faced chronic internal problems with personnel, and it dealt with them harshly in a militaristic manner. FEPA, the pilots' union, responded to the drastic pruning of their members by threatening a strike. They insisted that the company should keep on enough pilots to fulfill the med-evac (medical evacuation) missions within the country. The night before the strike was due to begin the company ordered everybody to stay in their homes. Every pilot was issued with an ultimatum: turn up for work the following morning at seven o'clock or face the consequences. Pilots in Udorn and Saigon were threatened with house arrest and deportation, while those in Vientiane faced actual jailing. Such strong-arm tactics broke the strike, but led to a rash of resignations from pilots who felt profoundly disturbed that they could be treated in such a manner after their years of service.

"One of the things the union was demanding was that all pilots should be paid the same," Mel Cooper said. "The Chinese and Filipino pilots got paid half of what we did. The Thais got a quarter. It was kind of sickening, because three or four of the Thais had worked for AA ever since 1963. But the company wouldn't go for it."

AA similarly resisted claims from the kickers a month later and responded to an attempted strike by firing them all. "The pilots' pay had gone up since 1966 by 60 percent," Miles Lechtman, a kicker, said, "but our pay had only been raised by 3 percent. In 1973 the kickers decided to get sick together and announce that we were organized. We all got fired."

Four days later the company rehired all of the Americans, except for a few recalcitrant types, and half the indigenous kickers. "We were recognized by the pilots' organization, but they didn't help us out. They could have helped us enormously by refusing to fly with unqualified people. As far as hazard money went, we got exactly half of what the pilots and copilots got, although we were in the same airplanes.

"And although we Americans didn't think that we were getting paid enough, the Laos and the Thais were really getting hurt. They were getting 85 percent less. It was sickening, because they were so competent and some of us were not as motivated as they were. They took pride in their work. They were stout people, stupendous to work with, always had a smile on their face even though in some instances they were working with people who weren't fit to polish their boots. What they were getting paid in proportion to what they were putting on the line was just ridiculous.

"What the company did to us was completely illegal, not only under the national labor regulations but under the terms of the federal contracts they had. A couple of people took up their dismissal with senators and congressmen back in the States and they started out with good intentions. But when they found out what was involved [the CIA] they wouldn't touch it with a ten foot pole."

The first AA pilot to be shot down during this "peace" was Howard Boyles, who was flying a Caribou. Boyles had been with AA since 1965 and had been involved in a highly classified program, flying Thai paratroopers up to the border of Burma. When in 1967 the Thais took the operation over themselves, he was transferred with his plane to Saigon for a year and then returned to Laos where he flew many of the dangerous night-drop missions to spy teams in the mountains. He was shot down on a milk run, ferrying household goods to USAID families in Savannakhet.

AA were aware there were missiles in the area and had rerouted the planes, but the missiles were portable and the enemy had moved them. One hit an engine and set it on fire. Boyles feathered the engine while one of the kickers stuck his head out of the door to see what damage had been done and was scorched by flames. He then held his head in his hands and jumped. Another kicker, who had joined the plane at the last minute and had not drawn a parachute, followed him in terror and fell to his death.

The first man landed safely and then spent hours hiding in the jungle from the Pathet Lao and North Vietnamese troops in the area. He made it to the Mekong river and talked a fisherman into rowing him across. On his return he told AA that he had not seen any other parachutes blossom, but added that he was in such pain because of his burns and so shaken up that he could not be sure of anything. Management assumed that the pilot and copilot went down with the plane.

It was six weeks before they managed to go into the crash site. The cockpit was buried deep into the ground and acetylene torches had to be used to cut into the plane. Inside the cockpit the seats were found to be intact, but the seat belts were undone and it was empty.

Originally there were reports from nearby villages that the men had been captured and taken away, but those were later denied. "When anything like this happened, you believed what they told you the first day before they can be briefed," the pilot's wife Mary said. "There was an agent on the ground who spoke to the villagers, and he relayed the information to a small plane, which passed it onto a large plane, which sent it back to HQ. The villager said that he saw two Caucasians in gray being led away by the Pathet Lao. But it was Pathet Lao territory and villagers were told not to say anything or they and their whole families would be shot."

Mary Boyles, like Barbara Ritter before her, has had to endure the awful uncertainty of not knowing whether her husband is dead or alive. And she has also had to face the day-to-day difficulties that her husband's MIA status has imposed.

She is not bitter toward AA, which she believes acted fairly. "These men were paid the salary they were paid because they were taking risks. They didn't have to do it. They took risks every day, and I remember Howard coming back once in the Caribou and there were thirty-eight bullet holes in it. Howard could have quit anytime he wanted to. He knew what he was doing. They were paid to live with danger and they accepted this. And we accepted the possibility of death. It's worse not knowing—you can eventually accept death. What really angers us is that the 'missing' have been written off."

Mary Boyles was later told that six ounces of human ash had been handed over, supposedly the remains of the men who had been executed and cremated six hundred yards from the crash site. "But there is nothing easier in Laos than to get hold of human remains," she insisted. "And any Lao will tell you that an American pilot was too great a prize to be killed."

Mary Boyles flew to Thailand to discuss the matter with a Japanese anthropologist in charge of the case. She asked him if he was prepared to swear in court that the remains were her husband's and he said that he was not. "Then for the next year and a half I was pestered by Graves' Registration, who were trying to change Howard's status to 'killed in action.' Somebody started calling me all the time to accept the findings and declare Howard dead. He was terrible. It was really wearing." Eventually she complained to AA in Washington and heard no more. The family still cling to the faint hope that Howard Boyles was captured.

An embarrassing incident four months after the peace agreement did not help the American airlines' argument that they were restricting their flights to purely civilian work. Emmet Kay, a Hawaiian pilot flying with Continental Air Services, was shot down in a Pilatus Porter and taken prisoner, together with six passengers, in northwestern Laos near the Pathet Lao HQ of Sam Nua. "We were flying around under the impression that the war had ended, and to my amazement I found myself getting in trouble and being captured," Kay said. "In fact, the war was going on as if they had never discussed peace." The company denied categorically that he was on a covert mission, and even today other pilots say that he was hopelessly lost and low on fuel. But Kay has another story.

"That day I was on a recon-and-observation mission and was about seven miles from my destination when I saw this abandoned village. I circled it, didn't see anything, so I made another pass at it real low and slow and that's when we got hit by small-arms fire. We took hits through both wings, through the cockpit, and in the turboprop engine. It just came apart."

Kay was on the side of a hill at the time, made a 180-degree turn and positioned the aircraft uphill to crash land among trees. The wings folded on impact, saving their lives. They were surrounded by Lao and Chinese troops who were stationed in the "abandoned" village.

"I told them the truth—that we were spies. They knew exactly what we were doing, there was nothing to deny. I told them we were spying, on a recon mission. The other six said they were doctors."

Kay was trussed up. His wrists and arms were tied and a rope was put around his neck. He complained that there was no blood in his arms, but the troops ignored him. "I expected to be executed. I knew the job and I always had it in the back of my head that if I was caught I would be killed. Of course I was afraid, but I expected to die."

One of the Laos in Kay's group spoke fluent English and acted as interpreter. Their captors wanted them to kneel and bow down and ask to be allowed to survive. The alternative was for them to have their heads blown off. "I told them I only bowed to God, not to a man. And I wouldn't and I got away with it. I gained their respect from the beginning."

They spent the remainder of the first day under the trees, and at night the Pathet Lao moved them into the village. Kay said that he was treated fairly, and no doubt the Pathet Lao were pleased to have an American prisoner they could make political capital out of. It was evident that they considered him a prize when they allocated two guards to watch over him while his colleagues only had four between them. "The Laotians were so afraid that they did everything they were told. They were like children, begging, crying. They kept insisting they were doctors and that the Americans were bad and that I was bad. They turned on me completely."

The following morning they were told they were going on a fifty-mile forced march over rugged terrain and that it had to be completed within two days. They were forced along a river, and instead of being allowed to march along the bank, they had to scramble over rocks. From six in the morning until seven at night they were pushed forward and things were made as difficult as possible. "It was punishment. Just harassment. Whatever they did, I went along with the guy and figured maybe they'll kill me tomorrow."

After three days they arrived at a village. Kay calculated that they had marched in a circle and that the journey would have taken a matter of minutes in a jeep. As a Hawaiian he was a novelty and his captors were not quite sure what to make of him—his stock is a mix of German-English-Tahitian-Hawaiian. He was as friendly as he was allowed to be, but careful to stand up for himself in small ways. Seven times they threatened to shoot him. "I'm not a fanatic for religion, but at that time I put complete faith in God. I said, 'So be it.'"

The officers at the village were Chinese, and Kay was fascinated to learn they had the use of an extensive field-telephone system. The phones were attached to trees and he learned that the officers were speaking to Pathet Lao HQ about them. He was separated from the Laotians and marched through the jungle for six days.

On the way they had to take cover from two USAF air strikes—Kay assumed the planes to be F-4s out of Udorn and had the experience of being on the receiving end of American bombing and machine-gunning. Eventually they arrived at what his captors described as a "correction camp."

The camp consisted of a vast cave on two levels, containing 288 Laotian prisoners, including six women. At one end of the cave, where the cooking was done, there were grass huts and the whole place was thick with smoke. "Because I was American they would take me out at six in the morning and then again in the evening." He was kept in the cave for a total of twenty-eight days before being transferred to Hanoi by jeep, a journey that took three days.

"We had some dinner, which included beer. It was pretty good. I was really amazed that they could be so nice. We all became very good friends and we ended up playing Ping-Pong, volleyball, soccer and swimming together. I ended up knowing the Cubans, the Cambodians, the Chinese, the Vietnamese—I knew them all.

"You can call it collaboration, but I had nothing to collaborate. I did what I had to do and I talked to everybody. I think that I gained their respect."

Kay was given a tour of Hanoi, shown Russian tanks, and subjected to some simplistic propaganda. Some of it stuck. "They respect us as Americans. They say the basic American is good, and they have the highest regard for Americans as people. They condemned Nixon and his administration."

Kay was receptive enough to this line for his captors to tell him that they were thinking of releasing him one day to "spread peace throughout the world." In the meantime he was taken back to Laos. He was kept in a cave in a valley in solitary confinement for nine months and guarded by thirty-six troops. "I was about three hundred feet underground. It was dripping water and damp and musty. There were mosquitoes, flies; mongeese, bats, and snakes would come in. I usually weigh one hundred and seventy pounds, but I went right down to one hundred and twenty-six. My eyes got a little mixed up because of darkness and they still are weak. And I still have this dysentery I got there, which is something everybody gets—it's something I have to live with. And I have stomach trouble.

"I was able to make it because I had made up my mind I

didn't want to go insane. I told myself I had to live through it. I don't think anybody can be trained to survive under those conditions. You can be trained to survive in the jungle, but as a captive it's up to each individual. I give this to my father—my belief in the flag and my belief in God, my love for aviation and my patriotism, I survived."

He would argue with his guards about America and defend religion. They asked him if he wanted to learn about communism, and when he agreed they gave him books and he took a complete course. "I think to this day they thought I was convinced by some of the ideas. And I did agree with some of them...but it gets involved."

His interest paid off and they gave him better conditions. He was allowed to live side by side with the troops' seven officers. "I ate with them, I bunked with them, and one was an ex-flier and we got along great. I taught school—English, basic mathematics. I told them about Hawaii and America.

"They kept saying that one of these days you'll be going home. And, of course, they said it all depended on Mr. Nixon. When he resigned, they were very happy. I knew about it because they let me listen to the radio every night at nine o'clock—the Voice of America out of Bangkok. I heard about Agnew going out and Nixon going out and they yelled at me—'See! See how bad your country is?' When Ford became President, they were very happy."

During their talks Kay discovered the guards liked to play volleyball but had no net. "If you let me write to the President, I'll get whatever you want," he joked. The guards solemnly brought him paper and pencil. He sent a letter to Continental in Vientiane and received a reply two weeks later. An excited messenger walked thirteen miles to deliver an enormous bag to Kay. Inside it was volleyball and every other kind of game—cards, checkers, Ping-Pong. And cartons of cigarettes.

Kay was allowed to work and carried water for the village and tended a vegetable garden. He was also allowed to write to his wife once a month and received a letter from his son and daughter and some Christmas cards from Hawaii. To a man who had spent nine months in a cave in solitary confinement, these small privileges took an enormous significance. "It was fabulous, just fabulous," Kay said.

Five and a half months after he received the volleyball, he was released. A British embassy airplane, flown by a Canadian called Major Preston, flew him south to Vientiane. They followed almost the same route that Kay had taken sixteen-and-a-half months earlier and flew over site Lima 54, where he had taken off on the last fateful day of his freedom. In Vientiane there was a formal exchange of prisoners between the Pathet Lao and the U.S. ambassador. As they landed at the airport, Kay was moved to see an enormous banner hanging from the terminal, bearing the words "ALOHA EMMET."

Kay dismayed the authorities with his outspokenness to the press. "I couldn't help but make some strong statements, like the fact that we needed China and that Formosa should be given back to China." He was asked discreetly to shut up. "I told them I was still loyal and would lay down my life for my country, but I couldn't help but speak out." He was given full base pay and POW pay for the time he was in captivity and found that Continental had been good to his family. "I have no complaints about that," Kay said. "But they also offered me a lifetime job which never materialized, and a lot of promises were made about me to the State Department but they reneged on them."

By the time Kay was released on September 18, 1974, AA was a shadow of its former self in Laos. The new coalition government had asked the company to abide by a June 4 deadline for the departure of all foreign military units and it had largely complied. It had also announced early in June its intended cessation of flights in Thailand and the sale of its maintenance operation there to a local company.

The company had been criticized by Thai students who had urged their premier to investigate it for alleged "illegal practices" and the nonpayment of $2 million in taxes to the Thai government. AA responded by signing over its airplane maintenance contracts to a Thai corporation, Thai Airways Aircraft Maintenance Company Ltd., known generally as Thai Am. The company would not benefit from the special privileges and immunities that AA enjoyed, which included exemption from Thai taxes and immigration and customs inspections.

No announcement was made about what was to happen to AA planes in Thailand or how the termination of its contract in the country fitted into its general pattern of activities in Asia. In fact the men and machines were needed for other, more desperate theaters of war as the final collapse of the U.S. military in Indochina drew near.

NINE

OPIUM

The most controversial and murky area of AA's entire operation, and the one that seems to have lodged in the popular imagination, concerns the cash crop of the Meo—opium. People who know nothing about the airline connect the two: "Air America? Isn't that the spook airline that flew dope?" Correspondents who felt the CIA and its airline were doing a good job in Laos tacitly agreed that all the evidence pointed to the fact that AA flew the Meo's dope to market, while its critics went on to claim that the CIA had made a direct connection with the Mafia to sell top-grade heroin and swell the war coffers with illegal and invisible gold.

There is no hard evidence to support the extreme argument, and it would be unlikely if there were, but AA was certainly used to carry opium. Many pilots rigorously deny this, others shrug. "I must have carried everything over the years. This and that, a lot of boxes. We didn't look in the boxes." Flexibility was the name of the game, management said, anything, anywhere, anytime. They had customers who had requirements. If the customer wanted twenty boxes moved from A to B, they moved them. You call, we haul—we don't go into details. A box is a box, and if it contains grenades, baby food, or black, gooey opium, that was the customer's business. AA was pragmatic. They flew killers, but they flew doctors too. Hell, they even had a contract to fly agents from the Bureau of Narcotics and Dangerous Drugs [later renamed, the Drug Enforcement Administration].

Opium was an integral part of the secret war and the CIA's involvement in it. Part of the battleground was in the Golden Triangle—comprising the rugged Shan hills of northeastern Burma, the mountain ridges of northern Thailand, and the

Meo highlands of northern Laos—the world's largest source of opium, morphine, and heroin. The arbitrary borders between Burma, China, Laos, and Thailand have absolutely no meaning for the hill tribes who have been moving back and forth across the frontiers for centuries in search of new mountains and virgin forests. Opium was a fact of economic existence, as vital as rice, and in Laos it was legal to grow it, transport, and smoke it.

When the Americans decided to fight a secret war in the country, they inherited the historical legacy of the French Colonialists who preceded them, an integral part of which was opium. Almost as soon as France had annexed Saigon, in 1882, the colonial rulers saw opium as a way to put the new colony on a self-sustaining, paying basis. The various regional opium franchises were brought under the umbrella of a French-administered Opium Monopoly. This was so successful that it was soon able to claim the dubious achievement of increasing opium consumption in Vietnam by 50 percent, reducing the price to the point that the drug became available to consumers previously unable to afford it. Consumption climbed to the point that opium had to be imported from as far afield as Turkey and Iran.

When the Second World War disrupted international trade, the French encouraged the various hill tribesmen in their empire, especially the Meo of Laos, to increase opium production. They had learned valuable lessons in earlier dealings with the Meo when mismanagement of opium farmers, and the harsh treatment meted out to those who traded their crop outside of the Monopoly, had led to violent insurrection. The French changed their tactics from suppression to simply outbidding their rivals.

The end of the war in 1946 brought about the abolition of the Opium Monopoly. The post-war government in France viewed the results of their predecessor's "success" with dismay—more than 100,000 addicts in Vietnam alone, on top of which powerful propaganda had been provided to Ho Chi Minh and the Communists, who cited the Opium Monopoly as the worst example of colonialist exploitation [although, in reality, the Vietminh themselves were financing the arms of a whole division each year through the sale of Meo opium].

As the French civil authorities moved to abolish the trade and worked toward the eventual elimination of addiction, the slack was taken up by French intelligence and paramilitary officers who took the business over in secret. The civil administration's loss in revenue was to be the military's gain.

The First Indochina War [1946–1954] was extremely unpopular back in France where the National Assembly had reduced expenditure to a level that scarcely paid for the regular military. There was no money to pay for the arms and support of the guerrilla units which had been formed out of the mountain tribesmen—the most effective of whom were Vang Pao and the Meo. Opium seemed to be the answer. French Intelligence instigated "Operation X," a clandestine plan to continue the traffic in narcotics, and this paid for the guerrillas, who by the end of the war numbered 40,000, with 350 French officers.

"The money from the opium financed the *maquis* in Laos," said Major Roger Trinquier, the French counterinsurgency expert responsible for training the guerrillas. "It was flown from the Plain of Jars to Cap St. Jacques in Vietnam in a DC-3 and sold. The money was put into an account and used to feed and arm the guerrillas. Naturally, when we were doing it we weren't talking about it. We weren't even talking to the French authorities in Hanoi about it, let alone Paris." However, operation was sanctioned by General Raoul Salan, of the French Expeditionary Corps, and the head of the Deuxième Bureau [military intelligence] in Vietnam.

When American CIA officer, General Edward Lansdale, discovered that the French military had brought up the 1953 opium harvest and was actively involved in the narcotics traffic, he complained to Washington and suggested an investigation. The response, according to Lansdale, was less than enthusiastic: "Don't you have anything else to do? We don't want you to open up this keg of worms since it will be a major embarrassment to a friendly government. So drop your investigation."

At the same time, just across the border in Burma, the CIA was running a covert operation which involved another drug-financed army. In 1950 the Agency had begun to regroup remnants of the defeated Chinese Kuomintang army [KMT] in the Burmese Shan States, where they rapidly became the area's opium barons. After being abandoned officially by both the United States and Taiwan, they dug themselves into the heart of the opium area, where they developed their own defense lines, airstrips, and helicopter landing pads.

Almost all the KMT opium was sent south to Thailand either by mule train or aircraft, and Burmese military sources claimed that much of it was flown in unmarked C-47s.

With the departure of the French from Indochina, after their defeat in 1954, a temporary vacuum was created in the opium business that was promptly filled by the Laotian military high command in conjunction with a tough bunch of Corsican gangsters who ran a number of charter airlines known collectively as "Air Opium." Its pilots were a colorful crew: Gerard Labenski, who managed the Snow Leopard Inn on the Plain of Jars, a hotel which doubled as a warehouse for outgoing opium shipments: René "Babal" Enjabal, a former French air force officer whose airline was popularly known as the Babal Air Force.

The early years for these smugglers were not easy. South Vietnam's President Diem had closed Saigon's opium dens in 1955 and was intent on eradicating the drug traffic, which forced "Air Opium" to devise an elaborate set of routes, transfers, and drop zones. The amount of narcotics they could ship was limited and so were their profits.

It took the most powerful member of Saigon's Corsican underworld, Bonaventure "Rock" Francisci, to change the face of the business. As the owner of Air Lao Commerciale Francisci had a silent partner—Ngo Dinh Nhu, President Diem's chief adviser. Nhu reopened the opium dens, only three years after the President had closed them, to finance his secret police. Francisci was also in league with the all powerful Guerini brothers of Marseilles, the unchallenged masters of the French underworld and lords of a criminal empire that stretched across the globe. Air Laos Commerciale was a late starter, but did not have to take the same elaborate precautions as its competitors. With Nhu's collaboration Francisci's aircraft were able to fly without inconvenience to drop zones north of Saigon on daily flights from Vientiane's Wattay airport. They would pick up anything from three hundred to six hundred kilos of raw opium from dirt strips in northern Laos and deliver it to drop points in South Vietnam, Cambodia, and the Gulf of Siam.

Competitors suffered mysterious accidents and sudden arrests, and were eliminated by plastic explosives and the South Vietnamese police. The Babal Air Force became the first vic-

tim on November 19, 1959, when one of its twin-engine
Beechcraft carrying 293 kilos of opium landed in the Central
Highlands of Vietnam and was promptly impounded by the
police. Without his plane Enjabal had no alternative but to
fly for Francisci.

Gerard Labenski, one of Air Opium's earliest pioneers and
known as one of the best pilots in Laos, was treated even
more harshly. After an attempt to eliminate him by blowing
up his Cessna 195 failed, Francisci used his contacts with the
South Vietnamese government to have Labenski arrested. In
August 1960 the police descended on his entire seven-man
syndicate when he landed north of Saigon with 220 kilos of
raw opium on board. He was given five years in jail.

The opium business boomed, Francisci prospered; and by
1962 he had a fleet of three new twin-engine Beechcraft making hundreds of deliveries a month. Tall, handsome, and with
natural charm, this gangster was able to regale the Vientiane
press corps with boastful stories of his airline's air drops to
surrounded troops and his services to famous diplomats. He
dodged direct questions about dope by saying, "I only rent
the planes. I don't know what missions they're used for."

This casual evasiveness might have been enough had not
René Enjabal fallen asleep at the controls of his plane while
on an opium run for Francisci. Enjabal had taken off from
Wattay and flown south to Savannakhet, where he had picked
up twenty-nine watertight tin crates, each packed with
twenty kilos of raw opium and wrapped in a life belt. He had
then dropped the six hundred kilos to a fishing boat in mid-
ocean and begun the return flight to Vientiane. At the meager
rate of fifteen dollars an hour, and forced to fly for his enemy,
Enjabal seemed to feel the mission was not worth his full
attention and fell asleep. He drifted across the border into
Thailand, where he was forced down by two Thai T-28 fighters. Worried that he might be taken as a spy and unhampered
by any burning loyalty to his employer, he confessed to being
an opium smuggler. The understanding Thais made him
serve a six-week jail sentence and then allowed him to return
to Vientiane. But the incident meant that Air Laos Commerciale, and its activities in the opium business, came under
the glare of international publicity, which included a story
in *Life* magazine. The airline's legitimate business suffered,
but opium smuggling continued unharmed.

Then in 1965 General Ouane Rattikone, warlord of northwestern Laos and big-time opium merchant, displayed an antipathy to free enterprise similar to that of the gangster Francisci. Laotian airports were classified as military terminals, and permission to land and take off required an order from the Royal Laotian Army. Opium runs were usually classified as *requisitions militaires*—military charters—and approved by the Laotian high command. General Ouane removed the competition by no longer granting the Corsicans access to Laotian airports.

As the Americans were drawn deeper and deeper into the Indochina conflict, they became embroiled in the complex world of the Laotian narcotics business. Unlike the Deuxième Bureau of the French, who had controlled and prospered from the drug business, the CIA were relegated to the sidelines where they were obliged to turn a blind eye to their client generals' energetic trading. Although critics charge that the CIA simply followed in the Deuxième Bureau's footsteps, there is more evidence to suggest that the U.S. was embarrassed by the opium legacy, which was a political and propaganda burden. Unlike their French counterparts, the CIA did not lack funds for their war in Laos, and the U.S. embassy in Vientiane went to considerable lengths to control and curtail the trade.

At first, in the midst of a war that was not going well, the various CIA men and American Special Forces types took what was perhaps an excessively pragmatic approach to the problem. In the southern panhandle of Laos, Air Commando Jack Drummond found that the Lao pilots were using their T-28 fighters to ferry opium around. "They were all over the place doing this," Drummond said, "and I thought it was a very inefficient use of airplanes." Drummond took aside the squad-Fon Commander. "I'll make a deal with you—I'll get you a C-47, I'll maintain it, put gas in it and never ask you a question if you'll leave the T-28s alone."

A C-47 was procured out of the USAID program in Thailand and the commander flew every night, but kept his part of the bargain by leaving the T-28s free for combat operations. "It was a good deal for him—although I made him promise that everybody got a cut of the profits, from the pilots to the ground crews. Everybody had a motor cycle in six months and the families of the enlisted guys had enough to eat for the first time." [Greed later destroyed the squadron commander, however, when he was arrested in Saigon with the C-47 loaded full of gold and dope.]

As the U.S. Embassy in Vientiane became increasingly aware of the problem, the ambassador, William Sullivan, sought ways to curtail it. Air Commando colonel, Howard Hartley, arrived in Laos to look into the problem. "After two months of looking at every aspect of the operation of the Lao armed forces, it was abundantly clear that the Air Force was the vehicle for the smuggling, primarily using C-47s and helicopters," Hartley said. "You would go out to the airfield at first light in the morning and notice that several airplanes were missing that you'd seen at sundown the night before. Where were they? Nobody knew. They were gone. Some general had taken one somewhere.

"I thought it futile to approach the problem from the naive view of asking the commanders not to do this. I didn't even pretend to be able to stop it but thought the only way to help, short of taking all their airplanes away and crewing them with Americans, was to put in some sort of Air Traffic Control System so at least we knew where the aircraft were."

Hartley introduced an elaborate system, convincing Laotian Air Force commanders that air assets would be used more effectively. Although the system made it more difficult for field commanders to obtain aircraft for unscheduled activity, and more people knew where most of the airplanes were most of the time, the drug trade continued as before. "I'm afraid as a scheme to control the smuggling it just didn't work," Hartley said.

An example of the peculiar nature of the conflict in Laos was the "Opium War" of 1967. While the CIA pitted its clandestine army of opium farmers against communism, a three-pronged battle for the control of opium shipments from Burma was slugged out between Shan opium warlords, the KMT [National Chinese army units] and General Ouane Ratti-kone. The general had contacted Chinese and Shan opium brokers in the tri-border area and placed a particularly large order with a fast-rising young Shan warlord named Chan Shee-fu. As a result he assembled one of the largest shipments of opium on record—sixteen tons—and when the caravan set out across the Shan highlands for its destination near Ban Houei Sai two hundred miles away, its three hundred pack horses and five hundred armed guards marched in single file in a column that extended over a mile along the narrow mountain trails.

This monumental caravan led to a bloody confrontation when the KMT based in northern Thailand decided to send more than a thousand soldiers into Burma to head it off. The Chinese were worried that the young Shan warlord might usurp their fifteen-year domination of the opium business and looked on the mammoth shipment as a threat. The war was a bitter struggle for Burma's opium exports—five hundred tons annually, a third of the world's total illicit supply.

General Ouane had designated his refinery at Ban Khwan, a small Laotian lumber town on the Mekong River, as the delivery point. The caravan moved through monsoon downpours under constant surveillance by the KMT's intelligence network. An attempt by the KMT expeditionary force to destroy it failed when the Shan's rearguard counterattacked and drove them off. The troops reached the lumber town and dug in for the fight around the general's mill.

Ten days later the KMT expeditionary force caught up and fought a brief skirmish with the Shans just outside the village. The same day both sides were told to get out of the country by General Ouane. The KMT scornfully demanded $250,000 to do so while the Shan warlord radioed his men from Burma, ordering them to stay put. After several days of indecisive fighting several hundred KMT reinforcements arrived and a concerted attack was made on the Shan barricades. Both sides were well armed and it was an intense fire fight. At its height a squadron of six Lao T-28s flew low up the Mekong River and dropped 500-pound bombs indiscriminately on both sides. General Ouane had entered the lists. The T-28s continued to bomb and strafe the KMT and Shans for two days at a rate of four or five squadron sorties daily. Meanwhile the crack Second Paratroop Battalion had been airlifted to Ban Houei Sai; two marine launches were sent to patrol the Mekong near the lumber town and two regular Laotian infantry battalions cut off the only remaining escape route. The general was displaying the sort of tactical brilliance one might expect from somebody who had recently been awarded the nation's highest state decoration—The Order of a Million Elephants on Golden Pedestal with White Parasol (First Class).

The Shans, battered by the continued bombing, piled into the boats tied up along the Mekong's banks and retreated back into Burma, leaving behind eighty-two dead, fifteen mules, and most of the opium. The battle cost the young Shan warlord $500,000 worth of raw opium, thousands of dollars in arms and equipment, and his future as opium boss. The KMT, who had no boats, fled north along the Mekong until their retreat was cut off by the Laotian infantry and they were surrounded. They agreed to pay General Ouane an indemnity of $7,500 for the right to return to Thailand and their 700 troops were allowed to cross the Mekong, leaving behind seventy dead, twenty-four machine guns, and a number of dead mules. Thai police attempts to disarm the troops were brushed aside by the KMT, who boarded eighteen chartered buses and drove off with three hundred carbines, seventy machine guns, and two recoilless rifles.

General Ouane was the victor with a $500,000 cache of opium he no longer needed to pay for. He shared the spoils of war with the men of the Second Paratroop Battalion, and each man received enough money to build a simple house on the outskirts of Vientiane. The General won the right to tax Burmese opium entering Laos, a prerogative formerly enjoyed by the KMT, while the Chinese continued to control the Shan States opium trade.

In Northeast Laos, where the war was fought by the Meo, the CIA were obliged to help Vang Pao move his people's cash crop of opium to market. With the Corsican gangsters no longer flying out of the Plain of Jars, Air America was the only means of transportation available. The airline began flying opium from mountain villages north and east of the PDJ to Long Tieng in 1965 and continued to do so until late 1971.

The CIA had tried to distance itself from the actual transportation of the collected opium from Long Tieng to Vientiane, when in 1967 it gave financial assistance to Vang Pao to buy two C-47s from Air America and Continental Air Services, enabling the general to create his own private airline, Xieng Khouang Air Transport. Financial control was shared by VP, his brother, his cousin, and his father-in-law, and the company's schedule was restricted to shuttle flights between Long Tieng and Vientiane, supposedly carrying relief supplies and occasional passengers. All of the Americans in the know understood the cargo sometimes included opium, but recognized that if the Meo were unable to sell their annual crop they faced economic ruin. And without VP's Meo, the war in Laos would be lost overnight.

In 1969 the opium business took a sinister turn when master chemists brought in from Hong Kong provided Laotian refineries with the ability to produce high-grade heroin— between 90 and 99 percent pure. Much of this lucrative new product was destined to end up in the arms of American GIs in Vietnam. When this new development became known to the U.S. Embassy there was considerable alarm, but new initiatives aimed at curbing the trade would prove as futile as earlier efforts.

Alfred W. McCoy, a painstaking and thorough investigative journalist, visited a typical group of opium-producing villages in August 1971 while working on his book *The Politics of Heroin in Southeast Asia*. He chose the Long Pot district in northeastern Laos, which contained seven Meo and five Lao Theung villages. Located forty miles due west of the Plain of Jars, the district was close enough to Long Tieng to be a part of General Vang Pao's domain, but far enough away from the heavy fighting to have survived.

McCoy interviewed the highest-ranking local official, District Officer Ger Su Yang in Long Pot village itself, a Meo community of forty-seven wooden, dirt-floored houses and some three hundred residents. The village's high altitude made it ideal for poppy cultivation, and despite all the damage done by over ten years of constant warfare, opium production had not declined.

The district officer told McCoy that most of the households in the village produced about fifteen kilos of opium apiece each year. Rice production had declined drastically, however, due to dwindling labor resources as the men were killed in the war. The village had chosen to concentrate on cash-crop opium farming, as they were guaranteed an adequate food supply by AA's regular rice drops, a good price for their opium and a reliable market by Vang Pao.

Traditionally, Long Pot had sold its opium to Chinese caravans from the Plain of Jars that passed through the area several times during every harvest season. Then the caravans disappeared after the 1964–65 harvest when heavy fighting broke out on the plain's western perimeter. They were re-

placed by Meo army caravans from Long Tieng. Commanded
by lieutenants and captains in Vang Pao's army, the caravans
usually consisted of a half-dozen mounted Meo soldiers and
a string of shaggy mountain ponies loaded with trade goods.
At one time the Meo would accept nothing but silver or commodities. However, for the long years of the secret war AA
made commodities so readily available that most opium farmers had grown to prefer Laotian government currency.

Vang Pao's soldiers paid almost $60 a kilo, topping their
competitors' offers of $40 or $50, and enabling them to buy
up all the available opium in the district after only a few
days of trading. The alliance with Vang Pao and the CIA
brought prosperity to the village. It began in 1961 when Meo
officers arrived offering money and arms if it joined with
Vang Pao and threatening reprisals if it remained neutral.
Long Pot became one of Vang Pao's most loyal villages. Pop
Buell devoted a good deal of his personal attention to winning
the area over, and USAID even built a school in the village.
In exchange for sending less than twenty soldiers to Long
Tieng, most of whom were killed in action, Long Pot received
regular rice drops, money, and an excellent price for its opium. Then during the 1969–70 harvest, the procedure
changed. "Meo officers with three or four stripes [captain or
major] came from Long Tieng to buy our opium," Ger Su Yang
said. "They came in American helicopters, perhaps two or
three men at one time. The helicopter leaves them here for
a few days and they walk to villages...then come back here
and radio Long Tieng to send another helicopter for them.
They take the opium back to Long Tieng." The pilots, the
district officer said, were always Americans, but it was the
Meo officers who stayed behind to buy up the opium.

But in 1970 the war arrived at Long Pot. The secret army
was at a low ebb; Long Tieng was under attack; and Vang
Pao ordered his villages to send every available man, even
the fifteen-year-olds. Long Pot raised sixty recruits. A training camp was built on a nearby hill, and the district officer,
assisted by Meo officers from Long Tieng, supervised the
training. It consisted mainly of running up and down the
hillside. AA helicopters began arriving late in the year and
flew the young men off to battle.

Rumors of heavy casualties drifted back to the village and
the elders regretted sending off so many of their young. When

Long Tieng demanded more recruits in January 1971, the village refused. It was warned that unless recruits were forthcoming AA's rice drops would stop. "So they stopped dropping rice to us," the district officer said.

When the annual Pathet Lao-North Vietnamese offensive began in January 1971, strong Pathet Lao patrols appeared in the Long Pot region for the first time in many years. The Americans ordered the area's residents to move south, and many did so, terrified that the air-war bombing to the east would move to their villages. Ger Su Yang, on the other hand, used all his considerable prestige to stem the tide of refugees and retain enough population to preserve some semblance of local autonomy. Rather than move south when faced with the dual threat of American air attacks and gradual starvation, most of the villagers abandoned their houses in January and hid in the nearby forest until March.

Miraculously, opium production was kept up. Even though the village spent the 1970–71 harvest season hiding in the forest, most families somehow managed to attain their normal ouput of fifteen kilos. Heavy fighting at Long Tieng delayed the arrival of AA helicopters by several months, but in May 1971 they finally began landing at Long Pot, carrying Meo army traders who paid the expected $60 per kilo.

But as the war mounted in intensity through 1971 and early 1972, Long Pot's opium harvest was drastically reduced and eventually destroyed. Finally, on January 4, 1972, fighter aircraft attacked the district. Long Pot village was destroyed by napalm.

Many AA pilots privately resented enriching the local generals by flying their dope and were well aware that a great deal of it was ending up just across the border. "We knew that we hauled a lot of dope, although we didn't do it intentionally," Jim Parrish said. "Some of the native kickers were involved in it in a small way, but then there were high officials and generals involved in it too. Some damned Lao general would be the customer who had called up a plane and you had to carry what he wanted you to carry."

The military commander up in Ban Houei Sai made a statement to a group of helicopter pilots as he drank scotch with them: "Last year the opium crop here made me four million dollars." This was not merely self-aggrandizement. In its 1971 analysis of the narcotics traffic in the Golden Triangle the CIA reported that the largest of the region's seven heroin factories, located just north of Ban Houei Sai, "is believed capable of processing some one hundred kilos of raw opium per day." Or 3.6 tons of heroin a year! Considering that American addicts only consume ten tons of heroin annually, this was an enormous and significant output.

The U.S. Embassy was no longer inclined to tolerate its ally's increasingly damaging smuggling activities, the scale of which was highlighted when a high-ranking Laotian diplomate was caught smuggling heroin into France.

The diplomat was no less a figure than Prince Sopsaisana, a member of the royal house of Xieng Khouang. In an audience with the King at the Royal Palace of Luang Prabang on April 8, 1971, Sopsai, as he was popularly known, received his credentials as the Laotian ambassador designate to France. Two weeks later he arrived at Orly Airport in Paris to a warm reception in the VIP lounge.

Surrounded by flunkies, and awaited by the embassy Mercedes, the Prince insisted on waiting for his luggage like an ordinary tourist. When it arrived, he angrily pointed out that one of the many cases was missing. There were red faces among the French, who promised to have it delivered to the embassy just as soon as it was found.

Although not stuck for his overnight things, the Prince had good reason to bemoan the loss of the suitcase. It contained sixty kilos of high-grade Laotian heroin. The French had been tipped off by an unidentified source in Vientiane, which explained the unusual procedure of going through an ambassador's luggage, and the result was the biggest heroin seizure in French history.

The suitcase was quietly impounded until the government decided what action to take. The Prince, meanwhile, made angry phone calls to the airport. A week later an official arrived at the embassy with the case in question, pleased to inform the ambassador that they had found it at last. The Prince flatly denied that it was his.

The French decided to hush the affair up, but refused to accept Sopsai's diplomatic credentials. The Prince protested his innocence, but was finally recalled to Vientiane after two months. Back home the incident caused hardly a ripple. The U.S. embassy chose not to pursue the matter, and within a few weeks the incident was forgotten. The raw opium had only cost $30,000, although its eventual value on the city streets of the United States would have been around $13.5 million.

In earlier years the U.S. Embassy had been reluctant to allow agents from the Bureau of Narcotics into the country, arguing that Laos had no drug laws of its own to enforce. Clearly, an outside agency not involved in the demands of the war, would have written reports which would have been extremely damaging to the Laotian military. It was thought that the pragmatic approach of the Air Commandos was more appropriate.

But the start of large-scale heroin production in 1969, plus the publication of a number of stories suggesting CIA and Air America involvement in drug smuggling, prodded the U.S. Embassy into action. It dispatched a lengthy cable suggesting a crackdown. At the same time the embassy was at pains to point out to the remote bureaucrats of Washington the political complications of any such move. "As the Meo's only source of hard currency was opium you had an extremely complicated economic, social and agricultural problem to solve," the ambassador at this time, G. McMurtrie Godley, explained. "Not to mention the Shan involvement in the business. In the early days opium was undoubtedly transported by Air America, but that was looked into and cracked down on. We also knew that the chief of the Lao Army had been mixed up in the opium business, and I personally thought he still was. The idea was to make it more difficult for him."

The Prime Minister, Prince Souvanna Phouma, wholeheartedly supported the American initiative, while Vang Pao—in the words of the ambassador—"took a very pragmatic view." This was only to be expected. The general himself never touched the stuff, and pointed out that soldiers who smoked opium were no good in combat (although one guerrilla unit was known to be so fond of the drug that it was dubbed the "Dream Battalion"). On the other hand, VP declared that he was not going to deny the old and the terminally ill their traditional and only solace (even Pop Buell used to cure frequent bouts of virulent dysentery with liberal amounts of opium mixed in a glass of whiskey). And then there was the financial aspect...

"The problem in Laos was to get a substitute cash crop and we did what we could through AID," Godley said. The ambassador claims that VP went along with the new American initiative, but there are other reports that the general was extremely angry, and felt cheated, when U.S. planes sprayed poppy fields without his knowledge.

"I can assure you from 1970 on everything conceivable was done to eradicate the traffic," Ambassador Godley said. Further pressure was exerted in mid-1971 when President Richard Nixon issued his declaration of war on the international heroin trade. A new opium law went into effect in Laos in November 1971 and U.S. narcotics agents opened an office in Vientiane for the first time.

"Air America was told by the CIA, 'Damn it, clean things up!'" Ambassador Godley said. Measures were introduced that at least eliminated the small smugglers. Early in 1972 Air America established a Security Inspection Service, which had five inspection units in Laos, consisting of an American chief and three or four indigenous personnel. Under the new procedure the baggage of the pilot and all passengers, and any cargo, was inspected in the presence of an American official. The existence of the system did deter some smuggling, but the big boys of the Lao military remained immune.

The public outcry back in the States prompted the CIA to investigate itself, a tactic in keeping with the Alice-in-Wonderland quality of the war in Laos. To anyone at all familiar with the secret war, this "investigation" has a quite mad quality, but the final report in 1976 of Senator Frank Church's committee investigating intelligence activities states: "As allegations of drug trafficking by AA personnel grew in the spring and summer of 1972, the CIA launched a full-scale inquiry. The Inspector General interviewed a score of officers at CIA headquarters who had served in Asia and were familiar with the problems related to drug trafficking. After this initial step, the Office of the Inspector General dispatched investigators to the field. From August 24 to September 10, 1972, this group travelled the Far East in search of the facts. They first visited Hong Kong, then eleven Agency facilities in Southeast Asia. During this period they interviewed more than 100 representatives of the CIA, the Department of State, the Agency for International Development, the Bureau of Narcotics and Dangerous Drugs, the U.S. Customs Service, the Army, Air America, and a cooperating air transport company." The "cooperating air transport company" was Continental Air Services.

All these scores of agents interviewed culminated in a report from the Inspector General in September 1972 concluding that: "...no evidence that the Agency, or any senior *officer of the Agency*, has ever sanctioned or supported drug trafficking *as a matter of policy* (emphasis added). Also, we found not the slightest suspicion, much less evidence, that any Agency officer, staff or contact, has ever been involved with the drug business. With respect to Air America, we found that it has always forbidden, as a matter of policy, the transportation of contraband goods aboard its aircraft. We believe that its Security Inspection Service, which is used by the cooperating air transport company as well, is now serving as an added deterrent to drug traffickers.

"The one area of our activities in Southeast Asia that gives us some concern has to do with the agents and local officials with whom we are in contact who have been or may be still involved in one way or another in the drug business. We are not referring here to those agents who are run as penetrations of the narcotics industry for collection of intelligence on the industry but, rather, to those with whom we are in touch in our other operations. What to do about these people is a particularly troublesome problem, in view of its implications for some of our operations, particularly in Laos."

After explaining the historical perspective of dope in Laos—"Opium was as much a part of the agricultural infrastructure of this area as was rice"—the Inspector General takes the problem down to grass roots. Meo troops caught smoking the stuff were kicked out of camps, he said, and AA had a rule that opium was not to be carried, and if it was violated, the opium and its owner was put off at the nearest airstrip.

This seems to have satisfied the Senate Committee. It intoned solemnly, "Persistent questions have been raised whether Agency policy has included using proprietaries to engage in illegal activities or to make profits which could be used to fund operations. Most notably, these charges included allegations that the CIA used air proprietaries to engage in drug trafficking. The committee investigated this area to determine whether there is any evidence to substantiate these charges. On the basis of its examination, the Committee has concluded that the CIA air proprietaries did not participate in illicit drug trafficking."

The sudden flurry of interest in tracking down dope dealers that erupted in 1972 kept certain AA pilots very busy. Ever adaptable, the airline now made money by flying anti-drug agents around the country. Bob Dawson, who flew a Pilatus Porter out of Chiang Mai and patrolled the Thai and Burmese borders of the Golden Triangle, had to carry agents from the Thai Border Patrol (subsidized and organized by American forces), the CIA, and DEA in a search for Shan opium caravans and refineries.

"Most of my time there was spent on drug enforcement, and so was most of the CIA agents' in my area. In fact, the CIA had many more agents than the DEA working in drug enforcement. There were a lot of raids carried out by the DEA and we would go in with dogs. We started with aerial reconnaissance, searching for caravans or refineries. You'd look for white, powdery residue on the ground, a source of water, a supply of firewood, and two or three small sheds or a warehouse building.

"We found several and we would raid them and destroy them. Once we captured kilos of the stuff but the Thai police wouldn't let us destroy it—they said it had to go to Bangkok as "evidence,'" Dawson said with heavy irony. "It always created a great political hassle—but that was getting beyond my ken into things I really didn't know about."

The DEA even had native agents traveling with the Shan opium caravans. "We'd take off three times a day—once early in the morning once in the afternoon, and then at night," Don Carlson, who flew a Helio-Courier, said. "There would be somebody with a radio in the back of the plane and he'd talk to this fellow on the ground. He was a Thai and it took an awful lot of guts for him to ride along with those bandits, because if they'd found out about him he was dead. He'd have to sneak away from the caravan each time to make radio contact. We tracked the caravan across the Burmese border and all the way down into Thailand and decided they were heading for this particular town. As they got close, the Thai Border Patrol put a big group of people in there with airplanes and choppers and raided the caravan."

This sudden vigilance confused some of the old Meo who had grown used to taking a kilo into town on AA. "We had all sorts of shakedown procedures, including dogs," Porter Hough said. "You never saw anybody as conscientious at keeping the opium out of Vientiane as AA. I've seen kickers go down the line of natives as the engines started up and throw certain sacks full of grass out on the runway." Hough looked wistful. "The stems made wonderful seasoning."

Pilots even started looking in the boxes they carried. Robert Wofford had been flying up in Ban Houei Sai for several days and was preparing to return to Vientiane when a Lao Air Force officer and his aide drove up to his plane in a jeep. They were manifested for the flight and began to load a group of heavy boxes onto the plane. The Thai "customer" who Wofford had been working for took the pilot to one side. "I think they have opium," he said simply.

"I'll go and check," Wofford said. He asked the officer what was in the boxes and was told that it was Thai cooking rice. Wafford accepted the explanation at the time, partly because the Thai was wearing a gun, and the boxes were loaded. An hour out of Vientiane he called AA's operations manager over the radio.

"Oscar Max, I think I've got a load of opium aboard."

"Come on in. We'll notify the authorities."

Wofford had just touched down when the tower told him to switch back to company frequency.

"Are you on the ground yet?" the operations manager asked. Wofford said he was. "Get back in the air immediately."

Wofford switched back to the tower and asked for clearance and was instantly given it. Incoming traffic was diverted to allow the plane to turn around directly and takeoff. Once in the air, the pilot contacted operations.

"We don't know how long this is going to take," he was told, "but we're getting quite a reception committee together here and we want you just to circle around." The plane circled for forty-five minutes while agents and police were gathered. "Okay, come on in."

Wofford landed once again and taxied up to the terminal where the plane was boarded by Lao police. They began to search through the cargo, pried open the boxes, and found more than two hundred pounds of raw opium. But the Lao officer had not broken any law, as it was illegal neither to use nor to transport opium, but the police confiscated the cache on the grounds that he had declared his merchandise incorrectly. "I'm sure the opium wound up on the market someplace," Wofford said.

"A lot of dope was carried without our knowledge. We carried an enormous number of refugees and equipment, and it looked like they were taking all their household belongings along with them. They could easily hide dope in there. We're wrongly accused of taking the Meo's cash crop to market. I worked up in the Tri border area for countless hours and I knew the customer intimately—used to get drunker than a skunk with him and watch movies—and I would have to say that we did not actively participate in the transportation of drugs. Definitely not."

Countless conversations with AA pilots made it clear to me that on the occasions that AA was used to fly dope, the aviators were kept in the dark. As a group, the pilots were actively opposed to the use of drugs other than alcohol, and only a few of the younger chopper pilots smoked grass. "But as far as anything was organized about bringing the poppies out, they never told us," Mike Barksdale, a chopper pilot, said.

The Inspector General returned the compliment by giving the AA pilots a clean bill of health in his report. "Given the strict anticontraband regulations under which these two airlines have been operating for years, it is highly unlikely that any pilot would knowingly have permitted narcotics or any other contraband aboard his aircraft." Although the investigators noted, "if it is a truism to say that they're in the business for the money," they concluded that the pilots were deeply committed to their job and that the subject of drugs was as much an anathema to them as it was "to any decent, respectable citizen in the United States." One pilot was quoted in the report as saying: "You get me a contract to defoliate the poppy fields in Burma and I'll take off right now and destroy them. I have a friend whose son is hooked on drugs, and I too have teenage children. It scares the hell out of me as much as it does you and the rest of the people in the States."

The fact that the pilots averaged $45,000 a year, half of which was tax free, comforted the Inspector General. "Although the temptation for big money offered by drugs cannot be dismissed out of hand, it helps to know that the pilots are making good money."

It was, of course, a splendid irrelevance for the CIA to go to such lengths to clear AA pilots of smuggling charges. The problem in Laos was not individuals making a little on the side, but the massive drug operations of CIA-supported generals.

There were individuals among the AA pilots and ground personnel, and in the CIA, who dabbled in the trade. As far back as 1963 a CAT pilot was convicted of smuggling heroin into Japan, but managed to get out of the country. Any pilot prepared to fly white gold—heroin—into Taiwan or Hong Kong could make $15,000 a trip. One pilot discovered by the company to be smuggling dope had been making trips for eighteen months. Native kickers, mechanics, and baggage handlers had easy access to airplanes and ample opportunity to conceal packages of narcotics in the airframes.

With AA taking stringent measures against opium smugglers, the only way of moving the dope around was the Royal Lao Air Force. The Security Inspection Service had instructions to keep away, but on one occasion their dogs acted up when they went near a Lao Air Force plane. Guards discovered fifty pounds of raw opium on board, confiscated it, and found themselves in trouble. A complaint was made by senior Lao officials that the opium was a legally consigned transfer to a pharmaceutical company in Vientiane that happened to be owned by a group of Lao generals together with some Frenchmen. Although it was general knowledge that considerably more opium went into the pharmaceutical company than was legally made into morphine, there was a fuss and the security guards were fired for their vigilance.

CIA agents who branched out on their own into the opium-smuggling business were protected by the Agency. Puttaporn Khramkhruan was a Thai national who worked for the CIA in northern Thailand, Burma, and Laos in antidrug intelligence work. He was arrested in 1973 while attending Syracuse University after an investigation into the seizure of fifty-nine pounds of opium allegedly smuggled into the United States from Thailand. Khramkhruan implicated Bruce Hoeft, a Peace Corps employee stationed in Thailand.

The CIA went to great lengths to prevent the case getting to court, and eventually the U.S. attorney's office in Chicago was forced to drop it. When asked why, the deputy assistant attorney general, John C. Kenney, said there had been a series of meetings between Justice Department officials and John Greaney, the CIA's associate general counsel. "Mr. Greaney explained that if Puttaporn Khramkhruan were actually to stand trial as a defendant, the situation could prove embarrassing because of Mr. Khramkhruan's involvement with CIA activities in Thailand, Burma and elsewhere."

Then if charges had just been dropped against the Thai, he might have been called as a witness in Hoeft's trial and the same circumstances would have existed for that case, Kenney said. It was felt by the CIA that the Thai's defense would have revealed information about intelligence sources and the methods and identities of CIA employees and agents. The CIA attorney stated to the federal prosecution that "under no circumstances would the CIA turn over to them or to the district court judge...any of Mr. Khramkhruan's reports made to his superiors in Thailand or in the United States." At that point the Justice Department decided to abandon its efforts to pursue the case rather than try to force CIA disclosure by seeking White House intervention.

This led Senator Charles Percy to say, "Apparently CIA agents are untouchable—however serious their crime or however much harm is done to society. Last year (1974) we learned the very hard lesson that the President of the United States himself is not above the law. Yet apparently CIA agents are untouchable. I wonder if the nation as a whole will or should accept the proposition that some people are immune from prosecution—in this case prosecution for a sizable drug-smuggling operation—simply because they are also involved in sensitive intelligence work, or for any other reason."

Former CIA Director William Colby told an inquiring congressional committee: "It was quite easy to see that his [Khramkhruan's] activity for us would be revealed in the course of the trial. We requested the Justice Department not to try him for this reason. They agreed."

Just what would have been revealed by the trial is open to speculation. The trial might have given the outside world a glimpse of the CIA's complex use of proprietaries. Khramkhruan's supposed antidrug intelligence work went under the cover of a handicraft business set up for him by Joseph Z. Taylor & Associates, a CIA proprietary whose corporate secretary once worked for United Business Associates.

Although AID Director John Hannah had announced in 1970 that the Agency provided no cover to the CIA anywhere in the world outside of Laos, the CIA's Taylor & Associates was then in the midst of a seven-year, million-dollar effort to train Thailand's border police, under the cover of an AID contract. And on July 25, 1974, when Joseph Taylor was appointed as the State Department's Assistant Inspector General of Foreign Assistance, President Nixon stated: "Mr Taylor was a member of the CIA from 1966 to 1974."

It is perhaps the perfect symbol of Air America's and the CIA's Jekyll-and-Hyde attitude to narcotics in Laos, throughout its long involvement there, that an antidrug agent should be *smuggling* opium into the United States.

TEN

CAMBODIA

Every country in Indochina had its own special aerial requirement, and AA had to mold itself to the situation. Cambodia, a country that has not always enjoyed extensive air links, became swamped with airlines overnight after the U.S. invasion in April 1970. The nature of the fighting created a tremendous logistical need for air supply. At first the Cambodian government controlled or maintained garrisons in the majority of the major towns, and most of the fighting was an attempt to keep open the highways leading to the cities. The shaky situation on the roads meant that the cities were only reliably accessible by air and spawned a host of small, privately owned airlines. At first there were half a dozen of them, as enterprising bush pilots flew in a couple of C-47s and ran semiregular commercial flights between cities. Then, as the situation deteriorated, road after road was cut off by the enemy, and the Mekong River was blockaded, more and more airlines sprang up, born out of bribery and corruption and operating on a chaotic, competitive basis. Anybody could apply for an airline license, although it took money. A hefty lump sum was needed for the minister himself, and liberal amounts had to be spread among numerous government officials. Eventually there were more than forty airlines in the free-for-all.

It was a place where people who knew nothing about the air-transport business could employ terrible pilots on truly terrible planes and make good money. Even the unflappable Neil Hansen, who had experienced more than his share of aeronautical nastiness in Laos, felt that flying in Cambodia trumped it all. Hansen had left AA to go ranching in New Zealand and was in the middle of changing wives—"I've had several"—when he lost all his savings. "So I went back to Southeast Asia looking for work and got involved with Jim Ziegler in Singapore and his Mickey Mouse operation TRI-9." Ziegler had bought several Convairs which had been pickled when jets came into service and had been unused for eight years. "The Convair is a good airplane. These had only been flown for a couple of years, but when a plane has been sitting that long, the engine seals dry up and the hydraulic system gets all screwed up and you have a lot of interesting problems," Hansen said. "You get fifty hours on the engine and you've got a good engine, but most of them would come apart on you. That was the bad part."

As an employee of TRI-9, Hansen went up to Cambodia, where Ziegler was leasing a Convair to another company. "The Cambodian outfit was a real wierd setup. Anybody who wanted to apply for an airline certificate could get one from the government. The military didn't have the transport capability and needed airlifts. Chinese shippers controlled the produce market, and they couldn't use the roads for their trucks anymore, so they needed airlines too. All of these Chinese went down to the government office and put in for airline certificates.

"The only thing was they didn't know one end of an airplane from another, so they had to get Americans or trained Taiwan Chinese to organize everything. But they still never really learned the difference between a truck and an airplane, and they thought that as long as they filled them up with gas, they would go—which is not true. There are a few other considerations, like weight displacement, for a start.

"Most of the airlines bought old junk airplanes and were always trying to go the cheapest route possible—and the airplane would break down. As far as crew was concerned, there was no one involved to set up contracts or guarantee hours—you just turned up at the airport and you flew. You'd get out there and maybe you climbed into this guy's DC-3 over here or maybe get into that DC-4 over there. Nobody asked for your license or anything. 'You want to fly it? Can you fly it? Okay—go.' They busted a lot of planes up that way."

Airline operators had the problems of a scarcity of gasoline, no spare parts, and operational chaos to contend with as well as enemy fire. The military allotted a gasoline ration to air-

planes flying rice or troops, and operators would claim they
burned more gas on each flight than they actually did and
then fly commercially on the excess. This was a necessity, as
the military never paid their bills. Officially, the U.S. em
bassy allowed 500 riels, per kilo of goods carried plus a gas
oline allowance to cover the trip, and paid this to the military
who never passed it on. Jim Ziegler of TRI-9 had invested a
tremendous amount of money in military flights and peti
tioned Henry Kissinger and President Ford about not being
paid, with no result. On top of this it was impossible to main
tain any aircraft properly, for spare parts were virtually
unobtainable, and those that were fetched grossly inflated
prices and were totally unreliable. A tire for a Convair, which
would normally cost $300, fetched $1,200 in Cambodia. Most
of them were poor retreads which blew in the wheel well and
tore up the fuel lines. Carburetors which had long finished
their lives were polished up and sold as new. All of this was
capped for Ziegler when he lost two aircraft to enemy rockets
on the ramp of Pochentong Airport in Phnom Penh, and he
finally pulled out of the country.

Hansen stayed on and flew a C-46 for a Chinese who had
rented the plane to an airlines called "Work Together." "All
of the Chinese believed they had the greatest airplanes in
the world, but they don't believe in doing any work on them,"
Hansen said. "In fact, the worst part of flying in Cambodia
was that you were flying junk airplanes, real junk. I got in
this C-46 and, Jesus, it was a basket case. They didn't have
any aluminum or anything, so they had it patched up with
old beer cans so it looked like a patch work quilt. I went
through four new carburetors and none of them worked. One
of the blades on one of the props was loose, and when you
took off, the instrument panel would shake so bad you
couldn't read the instruments. They had the old electric props
on the C-46s that have not been allowed in the States since
the Second World War, and the magnetos were worn so thin
and were so out of time that I couldn't get any power out of
the thing. I'd take off out of Kompong Som, which was a long
strip, and only get up to eighty mph—and the plane's takeoff
safety speed is ninety-two knots. And I'd drop the quarter
flaps at the end of the runway and go staggering out there
over the ocean by the islands, and I'd be sitting there rattling

and shaking, and by the time I climbed a couple of hundred feet, I'd be doing ninety mph.

"I wasn't too difficult a target, but most of their gunners I ran across were too anxious and started firing before you were in range. And they'd use tracers, whereas if they'd used ball ammunition and were pretty sharp, they could have waited and got me. Then I got the rear spar shot out going down and it wasn't worth flying anymore. It was just too dangerous. Everything finally got so bad in the C-46 that I parked it and said—'Forget it!'"

The pilots not only had to fly junk aircraft, but had to overload them to make decent money. Normally a pilot would be paid twenty-five to thirty dollars an hour to fly the legal gross, say five thousand kilos of rice, but the shipper made more if he could send more. Any pilot who was prepared to exceed the legal weight was paid between four hundred to five hundred riels extra. "You took as much overload as you thought you could handle without killing yourself," Hansen explained. "You were reducing the capability of the aircraft to fly on one engine, which was only critical on takeoff and flying low. It meant another minute in the takeoff phase of the operation where if an engine quit, you weren't going to make it. The strips were so short that there was a chance you weren't going to make it anyhow. Four or five hundred kilos more wasn't going to make any difference to how dead you'd be." By taking such risks a pilot could earn $3,00 to $3,500 a month.

With so many airlines competing against each other, it helped to have the tacit support and goodwill of the CIA. Business really began to boom for the private airlines with the cutoff of all U.S. combat activities in Cambodia on August 14, 1973, when a congressional limit was imposed, allowing only two hundred U.S. personnel to be in the country at any one time in support of the war effort. In other words, U.S. private enterprise, helped by the CIA, was to replace the USAF.

But the nifty footwork executed by the authorities around legal obstacles changed nothing for the pilots. AA had stopped paying combat pay to their men after the Paris peace agreement had been signed, arguing that its operations had become purely commercial. This meant that pilots' salaries, without

the lucrative hazard money, were slashed from $45,000 t
$28,000.

The men began to express their bitterness and resentmen
to the press, a true sign of disenchantment, and said tha
whatever other people wanted to call the airlift, they wer
flying high hazard paramilitary missions without extra pa
and with little chance of being rescued if they went down.

The military withdrawal made their work even more risky
not safer. Without USAF search-and-rescue operations, th
pilots knew they had little chance of being picked up an
heard rumors that the Cambodian insurgents never took pris
oners, but executed them. "When you're halfway betwee
Sihanoukville and Phnom Penh and you get fluctuating oi
pressure, that rumor really plays hell with your mind," on
pilot said.

The new reluctance to fly into danger was not just create
by the lack of hazard pay but also by an ill-defined feeling c
disillusionment among the pilots about the war. America ha
entered a strong period of ambivalence in Indochina when i
had withdrawn most of its troops but not its military aid an
had seemed to shift its goals without abandoning its interest:
AA pilots found themselves among the last Americans to fac
combat, and in the absence of high pay or clear U.S. polic
some of them began to doubt why they were doing it.

Unwelcome publicity was given to this dilemma when Ron
ald L. Dubinsky threatened legal action against AA after h
was fired by the company for refusing to fly missions int
Cambodia. Dubinsky replied that his contract did not call fo
him to fly on paramilitary operations.

Dubinsky had flown in Southeast Asia for more than
decade, firstly with the Marine Corps in Vietnam and the
for six years with AA in Laos. "I didn't want to get into th
old game again," he said, explaining his refusal to fly int
Cambodia. "I'm opposed to it. My whole attitude has just gon
to superdove. I have a feeling from what I've seen in Lao
that it starts this way. I just don't want to see us get starte
again by doing this paramilitary stuff. I'm tired of the whol
thing. I'm just through. As far as I'm concerned, we signe
a peace agreement and the war is over. We shouldn't be fight
ing anymore."

Most of the thirty-five helicopter pilots based in Saigo
described flying hazardous missions into Cambodia, ferryin

American military officers—often armed with grenades and rifles—into combat areas, transporting weapons and ammunition for the Cambodian army, evacuating the wounded, and carrying high-ranking Cambodian officers and troops into besieged cities. Almost every morning AA routinely sent one or two choppers from Saigon to Phnom Penh which would return before nightfall after working for the U.S. embassy there. The military men carried by AA, according to the embassy, were merely observers gathering information on the fighting although an American officer had been witnessed giving tactical advice to a Cambodian unit in battle. Pilots frequently flew officers into besieged and embattled areas.

"I've carried American advisers with hand grenades, with ammo belts and the whole works—they looked like Pancho Villa," one pilot said. "You land, they jump out, and you take off." He added that under the direction of a U.S. Army major, he had transported three dismantled 106mm recoilless rifles to the surrounded city of Kampot. Other pilots said they had been ordered to take dismantled 75mm howitzers from one place to another and to transport ammunition and medical supplies in continual airlifts to cities under fierce attack.

The disenchantment of the AA pilots and their sudden willingness to talk to the press—although they asked to remain anonymous for fear of losing their jobs—were given coverage right across the States. This was awkward, for the new approach to the war in Cambodia, from overt military intrusion to covert support, was redolent of the early days of the war in Laos, and the military thought they could use the same tactics. AA had become too visible, and its pilots too vocal, to handle the operation, and the government turned to another airline—Bird Air. This was an old friend, which had been given CIA contracts in Laos, knew the game, and could be resurrected to fulfill a contract in Cambodia. Continental Air Services and Air America would continue to do what they could, although their spook connection had been too widely broadcast. Bird Air was a shadowier and less easily identifiable entity.

Four months before the contract was officially approved, and while the Air Force was still running the airlift, Bird Air began flying supplies in unmarked C-130 cargo planes, supplied by the Air Force, out of U Taphao air base in Thailand. William H. Bird, the company's president and chief executive, said that the company had found out about the possible contract in advance and so was in a position to round up the specialist crews before any other contractor, although he did not say how the company learned of it.

This led to open speculation about the company's relationship with the military and the CIA and charges from critics that the civilian crews were being improperly used to evade restrictions on U.S. military aid for Cambodia. Bird Air had been chartered by USAID, known to be CIA cover in Laos, in the early sixties, and its twenty-two planes were later sold to Continental Air Services, which ferried supplies to the CIA-financed Meo tribesmen.

More confusion arose from the fact that in addition to the William H. Bird of Bird Air there was also in Bangkok a Willis H. Bird, who was a former U.S. civilian air intelligence agent who was indicted in 1962 on charges of seeking to defraud the U.S. Government on construction contracts in Laos and who did not return to the United States to stand trial.

William Bird repeatedly denied that he or his company have any connection with the CIA. "They are a hell of a nice bunch of guys from the ones I have met, but I am just a contractor," he said. He insisted that his company only held a negotiated contract with the Air Force. "It in no way could be called a CIA operation." The original contract of $1.7 million called for Bird Air to furnish five six-men crews from September 1974 to June 1975. The Air Force was to supply the five C-130 cargo planes, all fuel, maintenance, and even physical examinations and refresher physiological training.

Moreover, the contract specified that all employees of the contractor were to be considered civilians and in no way acting as representatives of the U.S. Government. The contractor was not to issue any news releases about events, unless cleared with the Air Force, and was responsible in the cases of all damages and deaths.

An original contract was signed July 11, 1974, with an Air Force master sergeant, Warren H. Shoulois, signing for the U.S. Government. The contract was then officially approved by Col. R.B. Lovingfoss, director of procurement, on January 28, 1975, by which time Bird Air had been flying the Air Force planes for four months. The contract was extended $1.9 million to $2.6 million in February to take in seven more crews and fly thirty planeloads of supplies—about seven thousand five hundred tons—a day.

The crew members hired were all ex-Air Force men. "There aren't many civilians in the world who know how to fly these planes," Bird said, adding that none of them were currently in the military, although some of his crew had left the Air Force in Korea and elsewhere within a few months of being hired. They were paid an average of $3,000 a month while the airline picked up $900 on a round trip between U Taphao and Phnom Penh. "I am only making twelve percent on this one," he told *The Washington Post* at the time.

"I am rather proud of what we are doing. I think we have a commitment, and I am proud the U.S. is doing the airlift and helping to supply the people of Cambodia. I am a contractor and I finish the contract, good or bad. I am not a military man...I am a poor old contractor who just works his tail to the bone."

Continental Air Services continued to go into Cambodia under its own name to fulfill a U.S. government contract to fly between Bangkok and Phnom Penh three times a week.

AA had a contract with the U.S. Government to provide a "logistics management assistance team" to advise the Cambodian Air Force on how to service its planes. When the contract ran out on December 31, 1974, an apparently newly formed company LMAT Inc. (Logistics Management Assistance Team) took over under the presidency of Gary Bisson of Washington, D.C. But the old AA director of the program, E.I. Griffis, became the new director of LMAT Inc. on the first of the year, while the new company kept the same office at the U.S. embassy, c/o Military Equipment Delivery Team.

"It doesn't matter to me what they call it," Jim Schultz, a twelve-year veteran of AA transferred into a new employee of LMAT Inc., said, "As long as the checks come through just the same, I don't care who signs them."

For a time in Cambodia it almost seemed that flights in and out would be milk runs, but all that changed overnight. Les Strouse of AA was scheduled to replace a pilot going on home leave and flew up to Cambodia to check out the area he would be working in. "My predecessor had it all very quiet," Strouse said. "He'd fly up to Phnom Penh, land, park the plane, and go downtown shopping. The day I went over with him, they put a rocket in the parking area. It was the first incoming he had seen since he had been there.

"He checked me out on a few of the strips and then we went back to Bangkok and he went on home leave. We took incoming at Phnom Penh every day that I went there after that for four months."

The flights started out as three days a week, worked up to a daily routine, until toward the end AA pilots were making two trips a day. "I'd get up at The Imperial in Bangkok at five o'clock in the morning and go to the airport for a seven o'clock takeoff," Strouse said. "Then I'd fly for an hour and a half to Phnom Penh and drop off the cargo, which was mostly refugee supplies from the World Health Organization or whoever, and as it wasn't safe to sit in Phnom Penh, we'd fly into some strip out in the country someplace, park, and sit there all day. Or we'd fly around the country, stopping at different strips and hauling people, and then go back in the evening, pick up a load for Bangkok, and fly home. I'd get back to the hotel about seven at night."

Toward the very end, in the few months before the country fell, missions into Cambodia were as hazardous as anything ever flown in Laos. "We had some real sporty flights into Phnom Penh taking in rice," Art Kenyon of AA said. "We took in supplies as the country went down the tubes. Things got hotter and hotter as time went on and we lost territory. For a while we were able to take in stuff in the C-130s, which was then taken out to the hamlets, but then one field would close, and then another, and the circle just kept getting smaller and smaller.

"The Communists got well within sight of the airfield at Phnom Penh and would sit out in the boondocks and watch for one of the C-130s, the big jets, to come in, and we used to hate to be on the ground when one of those came in because they fired rockets and everything they had at it."

There would be as many as thirty to forty planes concentrated on a ramp that was very small, and mechanics who had to go out to work on them were often killed or wounded. The only air-raid shelters on the airfield were makeshift ones made by cutting the sides out of large metal mail containers, which were then dug into the ground while cardboard was put on top of the dirt as a floor.

"I was standing in one of those one time when I heard a rocket coming in and hit the ground," Art Kenyon said. "I had on a GI helmet, and when you're in a bomb area, you never fasten the chin strap. I landed on the cardboard at about the same time that the blast hit right in front of the operations building and that helmet skidded six feet from off the top of my head."

Les Strouse described similar experiences out on the tarmac of Phnom Penh airport. "I spent many tense minutes lying on the ramp. The Communists were two or three miles from the airport—although they claimed to be eight miles away—and were firing 122mm rockets by remote control. They'd put them in position at night and would set them off with a time-delayed detonator. Toward the end they had some of our artillery pieces which they had captured, but they wouldn't fire too many rounds before they moved, so their accuracy was not that great.

"When they fired a rocket and somebody out on the field heard it, they'd call in and a siren would be set off. That gave us a two-to-five-second warning before the impact. About every fifteen minutes they'd blow that siren when they heard one come overhead and everybody would lay down on the floor and wait for it to hit. There were quite a few times when you were just getting off the airplane and it was too late to run for a bunker, so you just flopped on the ground and hoped that it hit someplace else. I got stung by a piece of shrapnel laying on the ramp one day, under the armpit but it didn't break the skin—it was just like a bumblebee. In the end it got to be that you were almost immune to the incoming.

"My whole crew was Thai, and I was the only American, and we all had our Buddhas—a whole chain of them. They wouldn't fly anyplace without wearing them, and they knew I had one and made sure every morning when I got on the airplane that I had mine with me."

Flying conditions were such around Phnom Penh that Jews carried crucifixes, and Christians carried Buddhas, and sometimes it paid off. Pilots were flying Convairs fully loaded at 110 knots into strips that simply were not long enough and relied on the reverse power thrust of the propellers to brake them. On one particularly badly maintained Convair the only way to throw the props into reverse was for the flight mechanic to sit in the back in the middle of the aisle, between the radio racks, and when the pilot gave the signal, the mechanic crossed two wires. It worked, but needed prayer.

The trouble with going into Pochentong airport was that pilots always had to fly through artillery, whether it was enemy incoming or friendly outgoing. A Convair that came in to land on one occasion took an 82mm mortar round right through the copilot's window of the cockpit. The copilot was bending over, looking at a chart at the time; the round passed through the cockpit and went out through the overhead and blew up over the cabin, killing twenty people in the rear of the plane. The copilot and his captain were unhurt except for small cuts on their faces caused by the flying glass.

Intelligence on the enemy's whereabouts was provided by the Phnom Penh Pig Pilots Association: pilots sat around in the restaurant in the early morning, incoming permitting, and told each other what strips were out of gas and where they had been shot at the previous day. And if it was scanty intelligence, it was all that they had, although some pilots swore it was more reliable than that provided by the CIA. (The Association was given its name because most pilots had flown pigs around the country and considered any such mission particularly hazardous. Pigs' urine is high in ammonia content and tends to eat the metal bellies out of airplanes that carry them.)

At least the men who flew for AA and Continental and the USAF aircraft baled to Bird Air knew that whatever fire they had to fly through, their machines were properly maintained. Everybody else took twice the risk flying junk airplanes. There was no shortage of work for any pilot crazy enough to want to fly, and the demand on the country's instant airlines increased when the Chinese pilots of Air Cambodia flew off in their DC-4s to Singapore and did not return. "They didn't tell anybody, they just took off one morning and went to Singapore," Neil Hansen said. "There was a lot of panic; it was a real mess and there was a terrific demand for pilots. Some of the Americans were getting scared of the thing and were leaving, and so were some of the Chinese. It made it quite lucrative for those of us who stayed there—there were just all kinds of airplanes to fly."

Jobs were plentiful and for the asking. Hansen, who had abandoned the disintegrating C-46 of "Work Together" and therefore his job, joined Anghor Wat airline, which ran a Convair and a DC-4, the very next day. He was made captain of the DC-4. "I'd never flown one in my life, but if you wanted to fly one, it was up to you. I got hold of a book and read it overnight, jumped in the plane the next day, and went. The only bad part was that in a heavy plane you really need a copilot, and the copilots we had were *bad*. They had bought their licenses someplace, because it was very lucrative. For a Chinaman, a Filipino or a Thai to be making dollar twenty-five an hour was really big money. Not knowing how to fly had nothing to do with it. You got paid."

Not only was Hansen flying a plane he had no experience with at all, with a copilot who was useless, but he had a bad case of hepatitis as well. "I was just yellow as hell. It didn't make much difference to the flying—you had to make money. I was so goddamn weak I'd go to the top of the cockpit ladder and stand there for a while to get my breath back. I'd sit down and fasten the seat belt as fast as I could, because if I didn't, I came out of the seat when I pulled on the stick." A thin, lean man by nature, Hansen lost twenty-five pounds in the course of the disease.

"We were operating out of Kompong Som two weeks before everything went down the tubes, and my Chinese copilot wanted to go up to Phnom Penh to see his wife," Hansen said. "In a case like that you just hopped on a bird and went; all the crews switched around all the time and gave everybody rides. The only trouble was that my copilot jumped on a 130, went to Bangkok, and never came back.

"So I was without a copilot. I found this dingy Filipino propeller mechanic who had a license, but his biggest problem was that he was too scared to fly. But he'd rent his license out. You were supposed to have a copilot by Cambodian law, but you didn't *really* need one, so if you wanted to fly you could rent his license for twenty-five dollars a day and put his name on the flight plan. I finally talked him into flying with me, but he was so nervous I couldn't believe it and absolutely useless. He couldn't figure out how to pull the landing gear up and down and the rest of that. A real dingy bastard. I didn't know it, but he was still renting his license out all the time he was flying with me. And then I found out he had gotten killed.

"There was an old pilot who was an alcoholic and used to be with Continental and hadn't flown for a year and a half. He hung around and hung around until eventually somebody hired him to go fly a DC-3. I don't think he'd ever flown one before and he lost an engine on takeoff and crashed the plane. He had rented my copilot's license and had his name on the flight plan. The Cambodians really believed he was dead and that was a mess for a while and I started to get a little hassle because I'm flying with a dead man.

"But we weren't flying out of Phnom Penh very often, and when we did I just put down anybody else's name, that I could think of. On the other flights I could still use his name because they didn't know he was dead. So we just kept on operating.

"I had a pretty good deal working down there. I was getting fuel off the military and everybody else and managing to burgle quite a bit. I was operating mostly commercial flights and earning a lot on overload. I was paid in riels, which were hard to convert to U.S. green, and the only thing you could do was take them down to a jewelry shop and buy a gold necklace. But I ended up with a suitcase full of riels, which turned out to be absolutely worthless. So much goddamn paper."

"At the very end, pilots flying on the ammo and rice shuttles into Phnom Penh were wearing flak vests, parachutes, and hard hats," Bob Murray said. "The last time I went into Phnom Penh, I made four landings there in one day." Murray, who was shot up thirteen times during his years with AA and went down once when a bullet took the prop out of his Beechcraft, remembers flying MEDTAC (Military Equipment Team, Cambodia) people into Phnom Penh as the most grueling experience of his career. "On the first landing a rocket landed about a thousand feet down the runway just off to the left. We were just getting out of the plane on the ramp on the second landing when they popped in a 122mm rocket. The third time, on the final approach, they popped a rocket just behind the tail of the aircraft and blew a hole in the right wing. On that same day they blew a hole in the tire of a C-130 sitting on the ramp and also damaged a DC-8. I felt it was beginning to be a bit of a sporty course and they weren't paying well enough for that."

One pilot who grew neurotic under constant fire decided he could take no more. Instead of leaving on an evacuation flight, he loaded his Convair with live pigs and fish and thirty passengers who wanted to go to Kompong Som. He landed them at Dom Muang airport in Bangkok after a journey on which he had filed no flight plan and made no contact with the control tower. The Thais confiscated the pilot's passport, threw him in jail, impounded the plane, and deported the Cambodians.

Airlines with government contracts knew almost to the day when the country was going to fall. Collapse was inevitable within a couple of days of shutting off the rice and ammo shuttles. Les Strouse flew the last U.S. embassy passenger flight out of the country for AA. "We had sixty-six seats on the plane and took twenty-three people out, so anybody who was left wasn't there because there weren't any seats out. We were scheduled for two flights that day, but as so few people showed up for the flight in the morning we didn't go back in the afternoon." Les Strouse shook his head sadly. "Some people would be late for their funeral."

Native refugees were not offered the same comfortable facilities to escape the wrath of the Khmer Rouge. AA moved many Cambodian refugees who arrived in Vung Tau, a port just outside of Saigon. "We picked them up and moved them to an agricultural area in the middle highlands of Vietnam and to a fishing area," Art Kenyon said. "They were bewildered, submissive, docile. We took farmers to the fishing village and fishermen to the farming area.

"These people were carrying all of their worldly possessions, which were important to them. On one of those trips I got out of the airplane to stretch my legs and I noted some fluid dripping from the fuselage. If a pilot ever sees liquid dripping, he puts his finger in it and smells it. It might be a leaking pee tube, but at least he knows what's coming out of the bottom of his airplane. I smelt gasoline, which seemed impossible because it was coming out of the wrong part of the plane. I checked and it *was* gas.

"In the meantime the cargo handlers had opened the aft cargo compartment and gone through everything and lifted out a huge wicker basket, a little bigger than three feet in diameter, with a wicker cover. I lifted the cover off, and there were two uncovered pails which had once been filled with gasoline. This particular refugee had loaded two pails of gas onto my airplane, which would have exploded at any time, and it had spilled out in the turbulence.

"Two pails of gas was real wealth. People came on carrying their pots and pans and dogs. I've had people start a fire on the plane, throw a bunch of sticks on the floor and try and cook food. The thing that lingers in my memory is firewood. Here were people running away from their homes never to return, and they are hugging their prize possession, the only thing they own, to their chests—a bunch of sticks. Then you knew that they didn't have much else."

Neil Hansen, who lacked the embassy connections of his colleagues, missed the fall of Cambodia. Not because he had left the country, but because nobody told him it had fallen. "I was still operating when I ran across a friend in Battambang who told me that the choppers had gone into Phnom Penh and taken everybody out," Hansen said. "I had always thought that if it got real tight, I'd just take the airplane up to Phnom Penh, park it, and get on a 130 and go. I just hadn't realized how tight it had got."

Hansen decided to leave the country the following day by flying up to Phnom Penh, picking the best plane he could find, and flying it south to Bangkok. There were no more evacuation flights.

At the airport it was necessary to act as if he was taking a plane out on a commercial flight. A plane was loaded, and Hansen taxied it out onto the runway together with his "dead" Filipino copilot. Out on the runway Hansen flicked the magnetos on and off. "He was so dumb he didn't realize I was turning the mags off and thought the engine was no good," Hansen said.

He taxied the plane back in and told the copilot to offload it. Then Hansen told him to collect the kicker and his fifteen-year-old girl friend and go into town, pack up their stuff, and bring it back out to the airport. "We're going to Bangkok." His crew took off in a taxi while Hansen stood by the plane, talking to the Chinese skipper.

"We're just going to test hop it awhile," Hansen told him.

"Where you going test hop?" the Chinese asked.

"Just around here."

"You sure you not go Bangkok?"

"I just might," Hansen told him. "You got your family there?"

The Chinese said that they were in the city, and Hansen told him that if he wanted to go along, he would wait while he collected his family. As he told the story, Hansen the adventurer, who was always glib when he spoke of danger and death, broke down. His eyes filled with tears for a moment

and he bit his lip. "But he wouldn't do it. It was a shame."
He snapped himself out of the mood and continued his story.

"Anyway, my guys came back out to the field about eleven
and I loaded them on board. Then I noticed that all the noodle
stands around the airport—which were always in operation
however heavy the enemy fire—well, they had shut down. I
was expecting a convoy of little guys down the road any minute. And then I saw the military pull out. I thought, 'Fuck,
time to go!'"

He took off and headed toward Bangkok without a flight
plan, expecting the Thai military to intercept him at any
moment. He stayed low so that he wouldn't be picked up on
radar and spoke to a Lufthansa captain en route to Hong
Kong. The captain filed for him and Hansen was given clearance to land in Bangkok.

"I landed right there in Dom Muang and was just about
out of gas and didn't have any money to buy any more. I
taxied up and parked about three airplanes down from the
Convair, which had been flown out of Phnom Penh with the
pigs and fish. Here I am, unscheduled, no diplomatic clearance, and I expected to go through a lot of hassle with customs.
I thought that if I had to spend the night in a Thai jail, that
it wouldn't kill me. I'd been in there before. I knew the Thais
pretty well—they're good people, and if you talk to them nice
you've got no problem.

"I sat there in the plane for a while. It was hot, so I dropped
the door. That didn't seem to create a stir—no troops or police
or anything." He spotted the Convair and walked up to have
a look at it. The Thais had impounded the airplane and sealed
it up. "All the pigs had died and it was dripping juice out of
the bottom. It smelled like a gut wagon, and the only thing
they salvaged from that plane were the engines." An Australian nearby, seeing another plane with Cambodian markings, walked over to Hansen.

"Jeez, mate, what have they got in that crate—dead bodies?"

But the inquisitive Australian apart, no one seemed interested in either Hansen, his crew, or his plane. They walked
into the arrival lounge dressed in their uniforms of white
shirts and blue pants and were immediately waved through
the health check. They arrived at passport control, where
Hansen was about to explain why none of them carried pass-

ports, when they were waved through once more. Hansen went to see the chief of immigration.

"I've just come in from Phnom Penh," he announced.

"Yes sir."

"Yeah, well, here I am," Hansen said. The Thai showed no interest.

"Don't you want to ask us any questions? Impound the airplane? I don't know..."

"Did you sign the crew lists?" the Thai official asked.

Hansen said that he had not, so the official handed him a sheet of paper. "I just signed it," Hansen said. "You don't need a passport as a crew member. I had to guarantee that I would take the others out of the country when the plane left and I thought, Sure, if I can get enough money for gas." Hansen had left the suitcase full of worthless paper riels behind and carried only twenty-two dollars on him.

"I filed a flight plan to go on up to Laos because I had friends there, a wife, and hoped that I could get the airplane recertified because it was originally registered in Laos. And I could get my license forged easily there and everything else and be quasi-legal."

He went into Bangkok and checked into the Suriwong Hotel, an unlicensed brothel known as the AA Hilton, where the downstairs rooms were let on an hourly basis and had curtains for doors. "It was five dollars for all night, but the rooms were clean and I didn't mind the mirrors on the wall."

The AA jewelry was hocked and Hansen began making arrangements to fly in Laos. News came from Cambodia that the owners of the airline had been captured by the Khmer Rouge and were presumed dead. As captain of the aircraft and the only representative of the airline, it meant by international law that he was the legal owner. Hansen had inherited an airline.

ELEVEN

VIETNAM—LAST DAYS

As city after city fell to the enemy in Vietnam, AA's pilots' principal function was flying evacuation flights and it was heart-rending work. Even in Laos, where refugees were moved around the country in the tens of thousands, there had been nothing like this. Panic and anarchy swept before the enemy, and the planes and helicopters of AA were mobbed as Vietnamese, who often faced certain death if they were captured, attempted to escape. In some cities South Vietnamese troops ran amok, firing upon civilians and AA aircraft.

The evacuation of the cities took on a pattern: "sensitive" people, those who had worked with the U.S. military, CIA, and intelligence agencies, USAID or whatever, were issued with special tickets allowing them a passage out. AA would fly in, and at first things would go smoothly. On the first day the evacuation would be reasonably orderly, but by the second the disorganization would show. There would be more people milling around the airstrip than could be handled; fighting would break out, and the ticket system would collapse so that often "sensitive" people would be abandoned while other "low risk" individuals escaped. By the third day there would be chaos.

"The evacuations were pretty frightening," Art Kenyon said. "The crowd would be in a panic, completely uncontrolled. We would pull away the stairs and close the doors of our C-46 and people would hoist one another up onto the wings and beat on the windows trying to get in.

"Once, we had pulled into the parking ramp and had only shut down one engine, because it takes time to start up and we didn't want to waste any. There was always the possibility that your batteries might be dead, and if you had one engine going, you had a generator going too, so you could always get the other engine started. We had turned the left engine off while the passengers were loading because the wind blast tended to blow people down and the doors shut.

"There were around nine people hanging onto the wing and a group milling around the left-hand prop. You can modify the C-46 engine start by turning the prop a little bit at a time. That's what I did. I stuck my head out of the window and watched. I turned the prop a foot or two so that if it hit somebody it wasn't going to hurt them. They can see it move and feel it. Then I turned it three feet, then six feet, and pretty soon they got out of the way and I could start the engine. And we just had to blow those people off the wing."

Pilots would wait until their planes were as full and as heavy as it was possible to get them and yet still fly. A C-46 was equipped to carry 51 people, but a pilot came out of Pleiku carrying 142 fully armed combat troops and it took 90 miles to climb to 1,000 feet. The maximum gross weight for a C-46 is 48,000 pounds, and the pilot estimated after the flight that his bird weighed around 57,000 pounds, C-47s, which usually carried a maximum of 30, took on as many as 80 people. Bird Air flew a DC-6 on an evacuation flight and reported 340 people on it.

"I never will forget the sight of the highway going out of Pleiku," Fred Anderson said. "It was just a solid mass of human bodies walking and carrying what they had. And you just knew there would be thousands dying on the way."

It was a time when nerves were taut. As refugees mobbed the planes, shots would be fired in the air, and frustrated friendly troops could be as deadly as the enemy. "Every bit of hostile fire we had from the fall of Pleiku down to the very end was from our allies, the South Vietnamese," Wayne Lannin said. "A lot of it was out of frustration. People get excited; they want out and don't think. It was sheer anarchy; man reduced to his lowest level."

The evacuation of Da Nang was the worst. "It didn't fall—it came apart," Lannin said. "The North Vietnamese had taken Hue, but it was a seven-hour road march to Da Nang even with no resistance. So the North Vietnamese were nowhere near Da Nang—the city fell on its own accord. The soldiers went berserk. They were running down the streets machine-gunning civilians. They were ripping the jewelry off bodies and raping girls. Half the city was on fire.

"There was a small stretch of beach where the army had brought landing barges to it to evacuate civilians. The soldiers were driving tanks, two-and-half-ton trucks and anything they had, right into the surf, stripping off their uniforms and throwing their rifles on the beach. The whole beach was nothing but an army surplus of vehicles and equipment. The troops mobbed the landing barges and would shoot civilians to get on board. They even hijacked two or three merchant marine ships to get out on."

The U.S. consulate in the city had prepared a number of contingency plans for a possible evacuation, the most extreme of which was a helo-lift out of the main airfield under U.S. Marine protection—an eventuality which was considered improbable. "Sensitive" personnel in the city included fifty Americans attached to the consulate—half of whom were CIA officers—and a thousand local employees. But with these people's families and friends, the number of Vietnamese evacuees to be accommodated swelled to ten thousand. The principal plan was for a low-key, phased pullout by air and sea, stretching over a week or so.

It did not work like that. When the North Vietnamese began to bombard the city with rockets on the morning of March 25, there was immediate panic. In the previous ten days more than half a million refugees had converged on the city from all directions. The original CIA evacuation plan was rendered impractical because of a scarcity of aircraft. The city's CIA base chief had requested additional AA planes to help fly out American dependents, only to be told that there were none to spare.

Tickets were issued to Vietnamese for the regular AA run—known as the "Freedom Train"—although it was obvious there would not be enough space. The USAF turned down a request for more choppers on the grounds that the entire fleet was committed to "Eagle Pull," the prospective evacuation of Phnom Penh. However, the airlift began smoothly enough. AA C-47s and World Airways 727s shuttled in and out throughout the first day without much trouble. As each plane came, hundreds of Vietnamese ran across the tarmac to meet it, carrying their most precious possessions and accompanied by their animals and children.

Pilots who attempted to impose some order on the evacu-

ation were soon overwhelmed. "I had seen what happened in
Pleiku, so when we first started moving people out of Da
Nang, I got out of the airplane looking real fierce and lined
people up in a single file," Art Kenyon said. "Some kid ran
out of line and moved up five or six spaces and I grabbed him
and took him back to the end of the line. 'You stand right
there and I'll count you and tell you when to get onto the
airplane.' I was being as firm as I could and I had some control.
But that's with one hundred people—when you got five thousand people out there, there was just nothing you could do."

People were panicking because they thought that every
plane out was the last one. No system had been devised to
tell them that the quicker they let one leave the quicker it
could return. The crowds were so desperate that there was
often a real danger they would tear an airplane up in their
frenzy. The evacuation flights affected some pilots more profoundly than high-hazard missions into combat areas. One,
who had flown for years with AA, was so shaken up by the
sight of refugees beating their hands bloody on the plane's
windows that he quit. Mothers who saw that the planes were
taking off and didn't have time to climb over the heads of the
crowd would throw their babies through the doors.

As the swell of refugees made operations from the main
airport an impossibility, AA choppers began ferrying passengers over to a smaller airstrip near Marble Mountain to
pick up outbound flights there. Panicking evacuees seized the
control tower of the main air terminal. "We were shifting
around all the time because if you stayed in one spot you'd
have five thousand Vietnamese on you in two seconds," said
Lannin, who flew a chopper about the city. "We were picking
our people up and dropping them off at fixed-wing strips and
then a C-47 would take them off. We didn't have the range.
The Vietnamese soon caught on to that, so we'd land short,
shift around."

An attempt was made to resume the airlift from the main
terminal. The first World Airways 727 to land was mobbed
by five thousand Vietnamese. Mace was fired into the crowd
by American security guards, with little effect, and the ram-
paging mob trampled women and children underfoot. The
pilot immediately throttled his engines for takeoff as Vietnamese clung to the plane's wheels.

AA flights were shifted back to Marble Mountain, this time

permanently. Two AA choppers flew into the main terminal to pick up consulate employees and their families trapped among the ten thousand Vietnamese there. The sight of the two choppers, and their offer of potential freedom, incited the crowd to more rioting.

Another two AA choppers ferried evacuees continuously from the city's ICCS pad to the Marble Mountain strip throughout the morning of March 28. By midday both were running low on gas. They flew down to a Marine base south of the city to refuel, and a group of national police there asked one of the pilots for a ride out. When he refused and went to take off without them, the police opened fire. The chopper took four hits and the kicker was wounded in the chest.

As AA controllers continued to shift their pickup operations from one part of the landing strip to another, one group of "sensitive" Vietnamese were overlooked. They were discovered later in the day by the U.S. consul general, who immediately radioed for another AA flight. But in order to ensure a safe landing for the C-47, he had to make a deal with some ARVN troops who had set up an artillery battery just off the tarmac: a number of officers and men could go out on the flight if they held their fire while the plane landed.

Ninety-three people jammed themselves onto that last AA flight out of Da Nang, and more than half of them were Vietnamese troopers. As the plane went to take off, hundreds of other soldiers charged it, grabbing onto its wings and fuselage. The consul general ran along by the side of the plane and attempted to beat them off with his fists. He was knocked to the ground, beaten and kicked, and finally left for dead.

There was to be one last evacuation flight into Da Nang the following morning more terrible than the rest. Ed Daly, the colorful and controversial president of World Airways, ordered two of his 727s to fly into the city. He had failed to get permission from the U.S. embassy in Saigon for the flight, but went ahead nevertheless and flew with the first plane.

As soon as the plane touched down it was mobbed, and within ten minutes it was jammed with 270 people. If Daly had hoped to fly out women and children on the flight, he was to be bitterly disappointed. Every one of his passengers, except for two women and a child, were soldiers from one of the Vietnamese army's toughest units, the Hac Bao (Black

Panthers). They strongarmed their way onto the plane, and one kicked an old woman in the face in order to get aboard.

As the plane went to take off, another soldier, who had been unable to make the flight, ran alongside and lobbed a hand grenade toward the wing. The explosion jammed the flaps open and the undercarriage in full extension. People clung to the wings and the undercarriage, only to fall to their deaths later, while others were crushed under the wheels. Four soldiers rode to Saigon in the wheel wells, but one died on the journey.

A British television crew, which had made the mistake of disembarking when the plane landed, were overrun and unable to climb back aboard. The cameraman threw his camera with its film onto the plane as its doors closed. Later an AA chopper went in and rescued them. The second backup 727 had stayed in the air.

In the midst of all this misery an Air Force plane carrying three hundred orphans out of Saigon for adoption in the States crashed less than a mile from Tan Son Nhut airport. The cargo door had blown off after takeoff, and the control cables had jammed, so the captain was unable to bank the airplane except by changes of power. Fifty adults and children in the lower cabin died from lack of oxygen on the immediate decompression, while others were sucked out of the open hatchway. The pilot tried to make it back to the runway, but could not move to the left to line up with it, kept losing altitude, and finally accepted that he was going to crash. He pulled the power and prepared to hit the ground and narrowly missed a canal which would probably have killed everybody aboard. As the airplane came in contact with the ground, it shed several parts, including the engine pod and wheels, bounced over the canal, and came down on the other side in a marshy rice paddy at a much slower speed. The plane shed its wings and slid to a halt, as water rushed in, drowning many. The nose section broke off and turned over, killing the copilot, while the rear section stayed remarkably intact so that the emergency doors could still be opened.

At the time of the crash AA had a helicopter in the air nearby which flew directly to the scene. Another chopper was immediately cranked up to follow, and Art Kenyon, who was officially off-duty but had gone out to the airport to pick up his mail, volunteered to act as copilot. When Kenyon tried to tell me about the crash, he broke down and left the room. Later on he tried to speak about it again but was unable to hide his emotion. He wept openly as he spoke.

"By the time I got there, the people inside the airplane had opened the emergency hatches and one guy was standing there holding a baby out of the window. The helicopters couldn't actually land in the swamp; they could only set their runners and skids down into the marsh, but they had to continue to pull pitch to keep enough lift to prevent sinking. So it wasn't just like walking under a helicopter with its rotor blades idling; you were standing under a helicopter with the full blast of air coming at you. I jumped out and sank up to my knees in this marsh and began to try and make my way toward the airplane, toward the crash.

"A fellow with a little blood on his face, I think he was sergeant, handed me two kids. I took one in each arm and tried to get back to the helicopter, but lost my footing and went into the mud up to my armpits and was stuck. Finally somebody came and took one of the babies and I was able to climb up.

"But the thing about that which disturbed me and still haunts me..." Kenyon began haltingly, stopped, and then continued with an effort of will, abandoning any last attempt at composure. "A little girl, of four years old, had both her legs cut off, and the blood was running out of her little vagina and the rest of her was jammed up into the plumbing of the fuselage, and you'd look up there and see that little baby's bottom sticking out of the wall...terrible."

They tried to move an American from the plane, who was in civilian clothes and covered in blood. At every attempt the man would scream out in pain. Somebody put a pillow under his head to stop it sinking into the swamp. They also went to move the dead body of a nurse who had flown out with the orphans. Amid the din of the helicopters, the men had to shout at one another.

"What the hell are you doing?"

"This nurse—she's dead."

"Never mind her, there's a whole bunch of live ones. Let's get the live ones out."

Out of a total of 300 orphans only 120 were rescued, although the ones who were alive were relatively uninjured. "There was one whole section of the airplane which broke off, and the ones in there were the ones who survived," Kenyon explained. "A few of them had little cuts on their faces, a bloody mouth or a bloody nose or something, but I didn't see any serious injuries."

Strangely, none of the children cried, not even the babies. "Funny. The babies were quiet," Kenyon said. "None of them whimpered or anything. No noises, nothing at all. It was ghostly."

The children were flown back to Tan Son Nhut, where a CIA secretary who was there later described the scene. "As the children were carried off the choppers and piled into the ambulances, you couldn't tell if they were alive or dead. Nearly every one of them was covered from head to toe with mud, and only after the ambulance began unloading...were we able to sort out the casualties. The nurses would simply pass the children under the shower, saying, 'This one's alive; this one's dead.'

"After a while several other Americans and I began stuffing the uninjured children into jeeps and cars to take them back to the orphanages. Some were still so frightened they couldn't even cry. They were just like limp little rags in our arms.

"None of the babies had name tags, simply wristbands 'New York,' 'New Jersey' and so on, the addresses of their new foster homes. So one of the big problems we faced was simply figuring out who the survivors were. I ended up spending the rest of the afternoon checking wristbands against name lists—and drawing up death notices to send to foster parents in the States."

At the end only Saigon was left. It was clear that it had to go the same way as every city in South Vietnam, but Ambassador Graham Anderson Martin was slow to order an evacuation. Many of the AA pilots who stayed on felt that he knew something they did not. They assumed that the South Vietnamese army would finally make a stand and there was a feeling of false optimism among them but the ambassador knew nothing, and there was no stand.

"The Communists had backed the South Vietnamese troops against the wall—there was no further they could run after Saigon," Art Kenyon said. "I thought the ground forces would turn and fight—I thought they had to knowing they couldn't run any further. I also felt the Communists wanted Saigon in one piece. They didn't want to destroy it to get it. My opinion, and I was as much in error as a lot of intelligent people, was that a coalition would be formed, and I wasn't in any particular hurry to leave. Then in the last couple of weeks I realized it wasn't going to work the way I had anticipated."

This optimism was shared by the ambassador himself who, ignoring reports of collapse and despair, hoped for a political solution right up until the end and delayed the evacuation in the fear that it would create panic. Option IV, the mass helicopter airlift, was considered an unlikely last-ditch resort.

Lulled by the prevailing mood of false security at the top, many AA pilots lost everything they had. "I had contracted with a moving company to pick up one thousand pounds of my high-value stuff, but it never got out," Art Kenyon said. He also lost a large, well-furnished house, a fruit farm, two cars, and a motorcycle—amounting to a total value of $104,000. Hs received $12,000 in compensation from AA and a further $9,000 through income tax. The remainder was the price Kenyon paid in hard cash for staying on. (President Thieu was more fortunate: he had shipped out most of his personal fortune and household effects to Taiwan and Canada early in the month.)

The AA operations chief had briefed the thirty-four pilots still in Saigon on the rooftop evacuation plan incorporated in Option IV. Marine officers had drawn up a plan for bus convoys and small AA choppers to collect passengers at specially designated points around town on "E day" and shuttle them to waiting freighters at Newport docks and aircraft at Tan Son Nhut. The rooftops of thirteen embassy buildings had their chimneys and TV antennae torn out to enable them to be used as emergency pads. Permission to paint large H's to the exact dimensions of helicopter skids on each of the pads to facilitate landings was refused by the ambassador on the grounds that it would startle Vietnamese maids and washerwomen when they went onto the roofs to hang out laundry. Skid lines were marked in dots instead. The operations chief offered to release any AA pilot who thought the plan too hazardous. Only three of them took him up on his offer.

Tension inside the city built up day by day. AA captain Fred Fine began to keep a diary from the middle of April, and its day-to-day entries give a graphic account of the uncertainty, rumor, and increasing danger of life within the city. "15 April: 10:30 p.m. Tremendous explosion. Our apartment building moved. Ammo dump at Bien Hoa. Lots of secondary explosions. Heard today that the evacuation fleet lying off Vung Tau left station and went back to the Philippines to replenish supplies. That will leave all Americans uncovered for 7–10 days." The entries for the next four days report the North Vietnamese army advancing everywhere and massing divisions in the north, west, and southwest of the city, the fall of Phnom, Penh and the allocation of emergency-evacuation aircraft assignments.

On the morning of April 16 a young CIA paramilitary officer operating under the alias of Lew James was captured by the North Vietnamese when they overran the coastal town of Phan Rang. At first it was thought in Saigon that James had either escaped or been killed, as his capture was not announced over Liberation Radio. When news of his disappearance reached his colleagues, AA took to the air for the next two days in planes and helicopters in a hazardous search-and-rescue attempt. AA planes scouring the shoreline buzzed North Vietnamese troops on the march on the coastal highways, and when a Volpar swooped too low over a column of troops, several AK-27 rounds ripped through the wing. The pilot was forced to make an emergency landing on a beach several miles away, where the crew and CIA officer aboard were later picked up by an AA Huey. There were no casualties but the search was called off.

Lew James was beaten by his captors and eventually taken to Hanoi. There he was identified as a CIA man and put through an intensive interrogation. He was not freed until more than six months after the fall of South Vietnam.

Curiously, the first major "black" airlift undertaken in complete secrecy at this time by AA was not for the embassy's vulnerable local employees but for those of Saigon's American news organizations. This was clearly an attempt in public relations by the ambassador to curry favor with the press corps and keep them quiet about his continual refusal to face the issue of a mass evacuation. AA secretly flew out 600 Vietnamese over the next few days and not a word about the operation leaked out to the public. The press "shuttle" turned out to be one of the embassy's most successful evacuation operations.

There was also a secret AA run into Thailand with the

families of the CIA-trained technicians who worked for the Vietnamese Ministry of Defense, when 143 passengers, mostly women and children, were flown out. It seemed that more low-risk personnel were leaving on "black" flights than politically sensitive Vietnamese. There were one or two flights every day from April 20 onward although most of the passengers were made up of friends and relatives of officers of the Defense Attaché's Office who were impatient to leave the country.

Meanwhile AA's day-to-day routine continued to take its toll as testified by the entries in Capt. Fred Fine's diary:

"April 21: Jim Voyles shot down in a Volpar today vicinity Phan Rang. Put out a 'Mayday.' I called for helicopters ... 2500, 2000, 1500, 1000 ft ... but he made it to Vung Tau OK. Went swimming on perfect beach. C-130 and seven Jolly Greens passed over Con Son island at 10:30 this morning heading North East. Inspiring sight and very good for morale. Indicated 7th Fleet in the area."

After dark on April 21 AA C-46s and C-47s began to ferry the staffs of the CIA propaganda radio station to Phu Quoc Island off the Delta. The ultra secret radio station was known inside the CIA as "House 7" because its studios were housed in a decrepit building at No. 7 Hong Tap Tu Street. Altogether there were 144 Vietnamese employees who had to be airlifted, together with their families, and after four days AA had moved one thousand people to the island where they were later taken to Guam by ship. Although one of the Station's most effective evacuation efforts, it was the work of a single CIA officer who had to override much bureaucratic opposition. His enthusiasm might have been fired by the two sexy radio announcers who broadcast as "Mother Vietnam."

"April 23: Situation very tense. Something imminent," Fred Fine wrote in his diary. Under the circumstances it is surprising that AA pilots bothered to stay on at all. It is true that many of them did not expect the fall of the city to be as rapid as it eventually turned out to be, but there was also a feeling of wanting to see the thing through, of going with it to the end. The whole AA operation in Southeast Asia had closed down: Vientiane, Udorn, even Tachikawa in Japan. Now Saigon was encircled by twelve North Vietnamese divisions and the pilots knew it.

"The hardest part of living in Saigon in the last days was

that we knew it was coming apart," Wayne Lannin said. "You wanted to leave and get the hell out of there: you knew it was only a matter of time, and you had all the possibilities of getting killed. But your personal pride prevented you leaving."

It had not prevented the U.S. military pulling out, and only the Marine helicopters and USAF planes remained for the final evacuation. It was to be a little better organized than the others because AA pilots had set up numbered and lettered heli-pads throughout the city, mostly on rooftops, where personnel could be picked up when the time came. They could then be carried to Marine and Air Force landing spots where bigger aircraft could be utilized.

In one week the exchange rate for the piaster dropped from P1200/$1 to P4500/$1. The real old-timers in AA, who had been through it all before when China collapsed, were changing their dollars into piasters and going downtown to buy gold and jewelry. Business went on as usual.

Bar girls had a hard time of it. The withdrawal of U.S. troops had left an abundance of prostitutes and almost a total lack of customers. One AA pilot worked out that on the black-market exchange rate the most beautiful girl would cost $.66 for a short time or $1.11 for all night. "For ten dollars a man could kill himself and die happy."

AA Pilots were particularly popular inasmuch as they represented an escape route from the country. "All day people would come to the door, total strangers, asking to be got out," a pilot said. Just before the seven-thirty curfew one night two bar girls arrived on his doorstep asking to be taken out of Saigon. They wanted the pilot to sign a document sponsoring them, but he explained that he was unable to do so. Instead he offered them a drink, and the girls sat around talking until it was long past curfew. "Well, ladies, I've already explained that I can't help you in my profession," the pilot said, "but as you can't get home, you might as well help me in yours." The three of them went upstairs, had a bath together, and then climbed into bed.

Other transactions between Americans and Vietnamese trying to get out of the country were less lighthearted. A number of Americans had discovered ways to get Vietnamese onto 141s used in the evacuation, and there were a couple of AA people who made a large amount of money through such arrangements. Rich Vietnamese were willing to spend their life savings in order to get out of the country.

"I had two families come to me and ask if I could help them out, as I was working with some evacuation people at the time," Art Kenyon said. "I thought at least I might check into it. I said, 'How many are you?' and he misunderstood 'many' for 'money.' 'We each have a thousand dollars,' he said. I was disturbed that they would think that I would take money for something like that.

"There were many wealthy Vietnamese who were willing and could afford to pay large sums to get out—there were eight or nine in each of my two families. If I had known then that Americans were taking bribes for putting people on the airplane, I would have taken friends and put them on for nothing. I have perhaps an overblown sense of honor when it comes to things like that, but I had scruples and wasn't going to do it even for nothing. I figured it was someone else's decision. I'm sure that there were a lot of people who did get out of Vietnam who were unworthy of the effort."

Other pilots were less ethical. "Some AA pilots were signing out thirty, forty, or fifty people and doing it strictly for the money," Mel Cooper said. "It meant signing affidavits of support saying you would be responsible for their economic welfare in the States and that they would never go on welfare. The pilots who did it for the money worked on the theory that they would never be made accountable for it. It was unenforceable to begin with, I suppose, but the copies of these affidavits were kept at the embassy and never got out of Vietnam.

"The wife of the assistant to the Vietnamese ambassador to Laos lived in the same apartment building that I did. She offered me four thousand dollars to sign herself out and her kids. I don't know why, but I didn't do it."

The final collapse of the city was only days away. Fred Fine continued to make entries in his diary. "23 April: Pres. Thieu resigned. 1:30 p.m. Red alert for two hours, attack expected. Steve's restaurant asked to house entire 40 man ICCS delegation. ICCS CIC said attack coming in next hour. He should know! Nothing happened. 9:30 Reed Chase came to apartment and said he's heard that Gen. Giap (Geo. Washington of N. Vietnam) assassinated and that Chicom troops are now in N.V. If so, the best of best possible news. Not much fun sleeping in town—if one can sleep. Better to be at the airport but no beds available...Wall to wall ships off Vung Tau. Four big carriers plus support ships. 7th Fleet.

"24 April: NV Army was to attack at 6:00 this morning but didn't. That's nice. Now hear it was pro-Chinese NV Gen. Truong Chinh who was shot and not Gen. Giap. US making helipads at airport. Moving many structures, bulldozing buildings, surfacing dirt areas, cutting trees and telephone poles, etc. PX items at half price or less. No more U.S. Beer for sale, quelle tragedy! Same for liquor and wine.

"26 April: Hear lots of bombing SW of town. Have for several days now. Many hundreds of SVN refugees around main gate at airport this morning. Has been that way for past week. Complete news blackout on SVN and US run Saigon FM 99.9 for last six days. Some getting a bit irritable lately. In addition to not knowing whether or not we are going to get out of SVN safely, there's a constant threat of SA-7 'Strella' missiles when flying and many new, unplotted AA positions. Reds now have 57 mm firecon radar position 290 degrees, 8 miles from airport. That's just great! Probably others around Saigon now. Most of us have been living out of an airline handbag for weeks now. All other possessions sent away, given away, or in one suitcase at airport. Atrocities at Phnom Penh." Public beheadings. Gives us something more to think about.

"27 April: Tension building. Lots of rumors. Thoughts of Tan Son Nhut going up and us being unable to fly out. 200 police strung together at Tan Me Thuot and shot."

Daily life took on the disjointed aspect of a dream when hardly a moment seemed to be connected to reality. Wayne Lannin had gone for dinner with an Air Force friend on the night of April 27. The friend explained that he had spent the day preparing those Air Force planes that were to be flown out and destroying others that were to be left behind. "I came home along the main highway that connected Bien Hoa and Saigon and I was fairly high, which wasn't a bad state to be in those days. About midway was the Newport commissary, where we all went out and got out little American goodies. The bad guys were on the side of the river, and Vietnamese gunships were making runs over the top of the commissary to shoot at them. The Vietnamese had a line going like a bunch of ants and they were busy looting the place. It was a very weird sensation.

"Then inside Saigon itself the normal drive home from Tan Son Nhut would take me ten minutes. That night it took me over an hour. Mostly it was military traffic, but there were also the cyclos piled high with loot—I remember seeing one go by loaded with an American refrigerator. People were passing each other, and you knew they had no idea where they were going. Armed soldiers were walking up and down the streets in twos and threes, but there seemed to be no cohesive units. Everything was a premonition of disaster."

Three rockets hit Saigon on April 27, the first in three and a half years to land in the city. Four more hit just after midnight. The Communists attacked northern Saigon at Newport, bombed Tan Son Nhut airport, and began shelling the air base as a signal for the final attack.

On April 28 the airport came under a heavy air attack. "Eighteen hundred hours: A flight of five A-37 [captured South Vietnamese] jet aircraft equipped with MK81 ordnance attacked a flight line area of Tan Son Nhut," the official after-action account by the DAO stated. "A total of six bombs hit the Vietnamese air-force parking area, destroying numerous aircraft (at least three AC-119s and several C-41s). The last two bombs hit between the base operations center and the control tower. No U.S. Air Force aircraft were damaged."

Fred Fine recorded: "28 April. 6:20 p.m. Had Reed Chase's car. Left airline bag at the apartment and took car back to airport. Got 100 yards short of gate when I heard six explosions. 500 pound bombs. Three NV pilots in VNAF A37s from the North. Three Americans in car ahead literally fell out onto the pavement with panicky looks and crawled around to their rear door and pulled out flak jackets. Drove up beside them to ask what was the problem. Unintelligible answer. Asked again and one shouted, 'Small arms fire.' I didn't hear any. Nor did Captain John Fenburg who was with me. ARVN guard rushed up and told us to beat it. Superfluous instructions, I'd say. Drove across grass, down a one-way street the wrong way, and headed for town. Both of us seriously doubted small arms report as it was very doubtful NV Army could be in that section of town. Halfway in town tremendous traffic jam. Lots of inbound cars doing 180s and heading back to airport, which indicated 1) A traffic snarl, or 2) Some terrorist activity. Just prior to reaching heavy traffic heard multiple explosions and saw hundreds of antiaircraft bursts around two A-37s. They missed the planes. Not wishing to get stuck in a jam or encounter terrorists, did a 180 and drove back to 259, a USAID billet housing about 40 AA pilots and supervisory personnel. It's a 7 storey building located about one kilometer from the airport. Went up on the roof and noted many fires and much black smoke at airport. 24 hour curfew immediately imposed so was stuck at 259. Real bright to leave airline bag at 87 Nguyen Rinh Chieu with passport, checkbook, money and other valuables. Found a bed with Capt. Fred Stikkel and another helicopter pilot. Met General Duong Trong Phuong. 7:30 p.m. Tremendous explosion 10–15 miles North East. Probably Long Binh dump. Helluva explosion! Our 112 unit apartment moved. On roof could see many large secondary explosions on this clear night. All AA personnel remained at point where caught at. Some ops personnel and pilots at airport. Telephoned Capt. Art Wilson at 87 Nguyen Rinh Chieu and asked him to get my airline bag. He said 'Don't worry, Freddi Boo. (He's an irreverent type.) I'll get your bag without fail.' In bed about midnight."

It was almost impossible to know what was happening and AA pilots relied on the BBC overseas service for some idea of what was going on in the city they were trapped in. "If you listened to the Armed Forces Radio, you'd never even know there was a war going on in Vietnam, because the news would be about the weather, an election, or an automobile accident," Art Kenyon said. "The BBC, on the other hand, was giving us the straight facts. Some of the stuff we heard on the BBC we knew was true because we had personally seen it, and the rest of it we presumed was true because of the veracity of the first part." Kenyon had preferred the comfort of his own home to that of the USAID building but had changed his mind on a whim on the night of 28th and was sharing a three-bedroom apartment, which was completely furnished but which had just been abandoned, with another AA pilot. They had a couple of drinks together and listened to the BBC overseas service before going to bed. "I can't remember the news except that it was all grim," Kenyon said.

The whole town was awakened at four the following morning to the roar of numerous explosions. Wayne Lannin shouted to his roommate Izzie Freedman: "Izzie, it's incoming again."

"No no—it's only thunder," Freedman replied sleepily. Lannin went up onto the roof and saw explosions over by the airport. "The first thing I thought was, 'Oh man, they've hit the helicopters, we can't get out of here—this is it,'" Lannin said. "You take stock of yourself right then and I was as scared as I've been in my life. You always felt with a helicopter you had a way out. You didn't know about the other people, but you had a machine to get out in. Take that machine away and I was lost."

Art Kenyon was awakened by his roommate beating on his door shouting, "Come on up on the roof."

Kenyon went up onto the roof of the USAID building and looked toward the airport to see it aflame. "It looked like the horizon was on fire," Kenyon said. "There were rockets coming in, endless explosions, and we could see the tails of the AA C-46s sitting up in the glow of the firelight of the burning C-130s which were parked on the old North-South runway. A Vietnamese Air Force C-119, with one of those Gatling guns, was circling just north of the airport, and if you've ever seen one of those things go off at night you know how startling it can be. It just looks like a sheet of fire going down to the ground, with all those tracers, but only one out of every five or six bullets is a tracer. It looks like the airplane is tied to the ground by a sheet of fire. Anyway, we watched the war and I had a beer in my hand. I went down to the apartment to get another drink, and by the time I came back the C-119 had been shot down. They hit it with one of the Surface to Air missiles."

The AA pilots gathered together on the roof, as if at a cocktail party, and together they watched the war for the rest of the morning.

Somebody set up a table and opened some wine. Friends who had worked for the embassy or the Agency and had already been flown out had gratefully bequeathed their liquor to the pilots. Before long the table groaned beneath the weight of magnums of Courvoisier and Jack Daniels. A liquid Last Supper.

"After a point it didn't seem so bad," Lannin said. "I went back downstairs and tried to sleep, but it was difficult with all that artillery going off."

Most of them opted to stay up on the roof. Kenyon had a CB radio and was in touch with the company operations at the airport from time to time. An exhausted flight controller was having problems getting the fleet into the air. Only two AA pilots had been on duty at the terminal when the shelling began and the situation there was chaotic. Jettisoned fuel tanks, live bombs, and other equipment were littered about the runway, while crippled Vietnamese aircraft were weaving all over the tarmac. One F-5 jet had been abandoned on the taxiway just in front of the loading ramp with its engine running. The pilots on the roof of the USAID building were told to sit tight until choppers could be organized to fly out and pick them up.

It was not until after eight-thirty that operations started to pick them up off the roof. The original plan evacuation plan was for the AA helicopters to operate in tandem with the bus convoys to move evacuees from the downtown area to the flight line at Tan Son Nhut. The delay in assembling pilots meant that only a few of the choppers were airborne as the first of the bus convoys started out on their pickup routes. On top of everything else the AA ramp was hit by several rockets, and a group of armed Vietnamese paratroopers hijacked four of the company's choppers, leaving only eighteen to draw on.

Fred Fine, AA's own latter-day Samuel Pepys of the fall of Vietnam, was also on the USAID roof. Wakened at 4:00 A.M. like the others, by multiple heavy explosions, he recorded the night's vigil in his diary: "... saw Tan Son Nhut under heavy artillery attack by 130mm cannon, 122mm rocket, and mortar fire. Many aircraft burning. At that point we all figured that maybe we'd hafta walk and swim out to the 7th Fleet. Intense fire continued to 8:30 before letting up somewhat. AA ramp area took one hit, badly damaging 2 helicopters with minor damage to 3 more. No fixed wing hit. Ops reluctant to launch helicopters for fear of drawing fire. A head in sand (or someplace else) attitude. Without the helicopter pilots at our apartment we couldn't operate. After attack started, many VNAF planes took off. C-130s, C47s, C119 gunstrips, F5s, etc. Thought they were going to pound the Reds, but no such luck as they screamed out of the area bound for U-Tapao, Thailand. Great support! The powers-that-be finally decided that they would launch a helicopter, and the first one off came to 259 about 8:30 A.M. and picked 10 pilots off the roof and back to the airport. Came right back again and picked up six more. On third trip at 8:45, eight fixed wing jocks including myself were taken off to the airport.

"Much activity there plus some incoming artillery in the immediate area every minute or so. Many ground personnel in Ops. Some pretty shook up. Certain amount of hesitation about launching fixed wing planes. But every explosion outside further convinced me that we had worn out our welcome in and around Saigon (Masterpiece of understatement!). About 9:30 we launched C-47s #559 and #084. Then every ten minutes or so another fixed wing took off. I finally got the green light at 10:45. Checked a/c over very briefly and was about to get aboard when Art Wilson drove up and handed me my flight bag. Extremely glad to see that. Started engines and taxied over by our hangar and boarded 24 passengers very quickly. Watched out cockpit window and as the last one got on saw many refugees climbing high cement wall behind my plane. Forgot to mention that during the morning some VNAF pilots stole four of our helicopters. Also, we were all armed and some Ops personnel had to stand off some armed VNAF pilots who tried to board several of our aircraft. Fortunately, no shooting took place. Capt. Ed Adams was about to board his C-46, an ARVN tried to force his way aboard. Ed stopped him and the guy started to swing an M16 around to point at him. The soldier got about halfway around when Ed knocked him on his ass (busting his hand in the process) and disarmed him. That ended that.

"We taxied out and, as we rounded our hangar where we could see taxiways and ramps, a scene of utter chaos confronted us. Bombed out and burned out planes and helicopters, others still burning, debris everywhere. Christ what a sight! Saw that a C-130 was burning right next to the taxiway on one side and a CH-53 on the other. Rather than taxi between the two, which would have forced us close abeam the burning C-130 which was going to blow up any moment, I went thru the civilian ramp past the gutted terminal picking my way around scattered baggage, wrecked autos, bicycles, shell holes, you name it, and rejoined the taxiway further on. Next, at the east-west north-south taxiway intersection, we found it partially blocked by a completely burned out C-130. There was just barely enough room to get by the tail of this hulk. We swung out onto the runway which, by the grace of God, wasn't damaged and took off without further ado. With the Reds all around town, we gained altitude over the city before heading for open sea about 25 miles away to the southeast. As it was surely all enemy territory, we didn't relax until we were well off shore. Then we took stock of our situation.

"We knew we only had 500 gallons of gas so we couldn't make it to our originally planned destination of Brunei, some 700 miles southeast. Also, we could not go to a small air strip 125 miles south of Saigon where we had some emergency gas stashed. So our only option was to head for Thailand. This, in spite of knowing beforehand the Thais didn't want any Saigon planes there. The Thais couldn't care less about refugees; their main concern was and is not offending the Reds. They have now very conveniently forgotten 25 years of U.S. assistance. When I left the ramp at Saigon there were two C-46s and one Volpar heading for 'friendly' territory in Thailand along with four C-47s. The bombing attack the night of the 28th stopped all refuelling so we were short of fuel in most planes. Only C-47 #083 had full tanks. He headed for Brunei."

Fine headed for the USAF base at U-Tapao. "With our short supply of fuel a real plus for us was that the weather was beautiful all the way. We, in our C-47, flew down the coast of Vietnam a ways then, because of the fuel situation, took a deep breath and at 8500 ft headed across the enemy held delta to the ocean on the other side, a distance of 80 miles. Made that leg uneventfully, proceeded along about 15 miles off the south coast of Cambodia, then up the Cambodian west coast and on into Thailand and U-Tapao. Didn't figure any Cambodian fighters would bother us in international waters and saw none.

"Landed at U-Tapao and received a warm welcome from the USAF. The first man I saw at the foot of the ladder was a sergeant and the first thing he said was that he had seen me and my co-pilot many times in Udorn in 1968 and why the hell didn't we stop sticking our necks out and retire. Good to see a friendly face. The next thing I saw was about half the Vietnamese Air Force. There were 70 odd VNAF planes parked around the south end of the airport. I counted a full squadron (25) of F-5 fighters, six C-130s, four C7 As, nine C-47s, ten Douglas ADs, four C-119 transports, and two C-119 gunships plus a scattering of other types. Had mixed emotions upon seeing the F-5s and ADs parked there."

The C-47 #083 that Fine reported as being the only plane with full tanks and which had headed for Brunei was taken out by Art Kenyon. It was not an uneventful journey. Kenyon had been taken by chopper from the roof of the USAID building into the airport, clutching what he referred to as his "runaway kit"—an M2 machine gun, an attaché case, and a small, long prepacked suitcase containing money and a change of clothing. He was subjected to two hours of pandemonium at the airport, where Vietnamese were trying to break in and the enemy was firing into the air in sheer panic.

Eventually Kenyon was given the signal and told to get out as soon as he could. He went to collect his flight kit, emergency radio, and after putting his personal belongings aboard the plane went back to operations. He had just stepped out of the door of the office and taken five or six steps toward his aircraft, which was parked directly opposite 250 feet away, when he heard a rocket coming in. He hit the ramp and it exploded some distance away; then he picked himself up and started running toward the C-47 and heard another rocket homing in. It exploded 400 feet away, directly behind the hangar he was running from. Another rocket came in before he reached the aircraft but landed further away. "The second time when I hit the tarmac I was running and landed in a great big oil slick. I was just covered in oil from head to foot."

They loaded their passengers, made up of AA ground personnel, and then had difficulty starting the right engine. "This airplane had been in outdoor storage for three years," Kenyon explained. "It hadn't been used. They had taken the engines off it and pickled the fuselage. Then in that final month or so, recognizing the need for additional aircraft, they had hung a couple of engines on it and put it up for a test flight, which it had failed. They put it up again and it failed again. The third time I tested it myself and said I'd pass it if they fixed the hydraulic system, which was getting excessive pressure and was chattering."

The right-hand engine was finally coaxed into life and at 11:10 they taxied out past the burning and exploding C-130s. "We had planned to take off to the east, which was the direction favored by the wind, but the taxiway intersected the runway fairly close to the end," Kenyon said. "It was filled

with debris, and unexplainably there was a civilian Volks-
wagen lying on its side with the upper door open. A flak jacket
covered in blood lay beside it and not far from it there was
a motorcycle lying on its side. We just didn't have room to
get between the Volks and the motorcycle so we elected to
take off a little bit downwind. And as soon as we got airborne,
the hydraulic system started chattering and the pressure
went too high."

Brunei had been decided on as the destination because it
was the closest and most direct point. Two and a half hours
out over the South China Sea the hydraulic system blew up.
"There was a big pop and the line ruptured to the hydraulic
reservoir, which is behind the copilot's seat," Kenyon said.
"Because the pressure had been so high, the hydraulic fluid
was extremely hot, which meant there was a possible fire
hazard. The entire cockpit was filled with a very fine hydraulic mist; it was almost like one of those First World War
movies you see with the oil squirting in the pilot's face. We
had oil all over the instrument panel and all over our faces.
There was oil all over my sunglasses and of course I couldn't
wipe it off with my hand. We had a couple of Filipino mechanics on board and they stripped off their undershirts and
tied them around the broken hydraulic line. It didn't stop the
fluid coming out, but it did stop it from spraying all over the
place."

The hydraulic system on a C-47 is of vital importance. It
is needed to raise and lower the landing gear and the flaps
and operate the auto pilot and the brakes. "The auto pilot is
only a nicety—you can do without that," Kenyon said, "but
it's embarrassing to do without brakes, and even worse if you
can't get the wheels down. Also in the C-47 there is a hydraulic pump in each engine, and the hydraulic fluid is the
only thing that lubricates them. Without lubrication they get
hotter and hotter, and one of two things can happen: they
either get so hot that they seize, in which case a little shaft
breaks and you've got no problem, or they get hot enough to
start a fire. So if you've got two hot hydraulic pumps, you can
have two really good fires, one in each engine, and those are
the only engines you've got."

Their instructions were to go wherever they wanted but
ultimately land in Taiwan. Kenyon felt they would be unable
to get any maintenance work done on the plane at the civilian

base in Brunei so changed course for the USAF base in U-Tapao. "So after about five and a half hours flying time out of Saigon we pulled into U-Tapao and tried to drop the gear, which in a C-47 should come down even without hydraulics. But we didn't get the safe indication; the red lights stayed on. So we had an unsafe indication on the gear and couldn't get the flaps down, and as I pulled the throttle back for landing the warning horn was blowing.

"The indication which we had in the cockpit was that one of the main wheels was not down and locked, but there was no way to tell which one. You look out of the cockpit window and you can see a little bit of the tire but you can't tell from that if it's safe or unsafe. Both myself and the copilot could see tires, and we both felt that the wheels were actually down and locked and that the indicator was somehow malfunctioning, but we couldn't be sure."

Kenyon called the tower and told them that they were going to be making an emergency landing. Ominously, a crashed C-47 which had run off the edge of the runway going south lay a few hundred feet to the left. If the wheel on the left-hand side of Kenyon's plane was not locked into position and the gear collapsed on landing, the aircraft would career off to the left and smack into the crashed C-47. In order to avoid that particular danger Kenyon landed alongside the crashed plane, some three thousand feet down the ten-thousand-foot runway.

But the gear proved to be down, and they landed safely, with the red lights still burning and the warning horn blowing. The next operation was stopping the airplane. They were burning up the remaining seven thousand feet of runway fast; there was not enough wind to stop them, and at the south end was the Gulf of Siam.

In order to stop an airplane the pilot can use the brakes on the wheels individually or the engines. With wheel brakes it is possible to make a controlled turn, but with the engines alone the pilot has to trust to luck. Kenyon had to trust to luck.

They gunned the engines and began to turn. "If we'd quit there we would have rolled on and landed up a pile of junk in the hangar, so we continued to turn, and pretty soon we had completed 180 degrees and there was a parallel taxiway going north. It was at this time that we discovered that we couldn't lock the tail wheel."

The tail wheel on a C-47 swivels freely until it is put into a lock position, when it can move only a little. It is difficult enough to steer the plane with full brakes when the tail wheel is not locked, but virtually impossible without them. The C-47 began to make a crazy series of S turns.

"We increased power on one engine and it would overturn to the right; increased power on the other to compensate and it would overturn to the left. I sat there blasting one throttle after the other, doing S turns and gradually going faster and faster down the taxiway. We both saw this wasn't going to do it.

"We finally decided to cut the engines and let the plane stop where it was going to stop. By this time the runway was to our right across a large grass area, which probably would have stopped us before we reached the runway, but there were B-52s taking off and going in the opposite direction. So if the grass didn't stop us, a B-52 was going to run right over us. To the left there was a narrow grass shoulder and a ditch with about five or six inches of water in it. And that was not too desirable either.

"So we figured, what the hell—cut the throttles and take your chances. We pulled the power mixtures back, turned the switches off, and a little gust of wind hit us, just enough to turn us left. We went down into the ditch and stood up on our nose, and for a moment I thought the airplane was going to go over backwards." Kenyon and his co-pilot were standing on the instrument panel looking straight down at the grass. The plane stayed in that position, rocking gently for a long moment, and then crashed back down. They had arrived.

The tower had given them very little help and had no fire equipment or ambulance standing by in case the crazy meanderings of the C-47 ended up in disaster. Once the plane settled the deputy base commander, a full colonel in the USAF, made his way over. Kenyon and his copilot had climbed out of the aircraft and were standing on a patch of mud, looking at the steaming remains of the C-47. The colonel joined them. "Sure messed up your airplane, didn't you?" he said after a moment's inspection.

"Colonel, that's not my airplane—that's your airplane. That's a bail airplane that belongs to the Air Force and I'm giving it back to you. I don't even need a receipt. I'm just going to walk away."

C-47 #083, like all the C-47s and many other planes used by AA, were bail aircraft, which meant that they had been leased from the Air Force for a nominal fee like a dollar a year. AA operated and maintained them, but the Air Force still owned them, and if they crashed they were written off. It is a profitable way to run an airline. C-47 #083 had been in AA service for almost twenty-five years, but there in U-Tapao the Air Force had finally been given back their airplane.

Back in Saigon the chopper pilots skipped from the top of one building to another, picking up those who were to be taken out of the country. Their day had started uncertainly. After waiting hours on the top of the USAID building to be taken to Tan Son Nhut, they were subjected to further delays, which led to arguments between pilots and Operations. As things grew increasingly precarious at the airport, the pilots were impatient to get on with the job.

"Cool it," the operations manager told them. "The ambassador hasn't given the word to go yet."

"Hey, let's get our people out," Lannin argued. "Bus them out, for Christ's sake—but let's go."

Incredibly, even at this late stage in events, the ambassador still felt a fixed-wing airlift using military C-130s would be possible and that it would not be necessary to revert to the helo-lift of Option IV.

Finally AA chopper pilots were allowed out to their helicopters to begin the evacuation. Wayne Lannin and Izzie Freedman were about to board their Huey when a jeepful of Vietnamese drove over to them. One explained that they were pilots and were going to fly the helicopter.

"You're not flying my helicopter," Lannin told them. He let the Vietnamese see the submachine gun he was carrying but was careful not to point it at them. "Frank," Lannin yelled to the mechanic, "they're trying to steal the helicopter." After that, armed guards were posted out by the machines.

Lannin went to climb into the chopper when incoming began to hit the airport and a round exploded within what seemed to be ten feet. Freedman was running toward his colleague but stopped short as soon as the shells and rockets began to land. He jumped into the first helicopter he came to, and the men took off together.

After the rockets hit the AA ramp, its flight control center was moved to the comparative safety of the DAO compound. The problem there was a lack of facilities for refueling, so pilots were forced to fly out to the fleet for gas. At first this seemed a very inefficient process, until the choppers began to make the trip out with a full load instead of dropping them at the DAO or the embassy. This meant that AA began to fly evacuees out of the city long before the military.

It was not until twelve-thirty P.M. that the first of the Marine helicopters left the fleet on the forty-minute flight into Saigon. Thirty-six heavy-duty "Sea Knight" choppers accompanied by Cobra gunships were in the first wave, although the military pickups were postponed until two o'clock.

Lannin and Freedman had already been flying for a couple of hours, landing on makeshift rooftop pads and hauling people off, when they were suddenly ordered to shut down. They were given no reason but told to find a pad, land the chopper, and shut it off.

Lannin had just landed when he was approached by an American army colonel and asked to take some people and cargo out to one of the ships of the Seventh Fleet. He was given permission by operations to go ahead. "My radio wasn't working, so I had a little bit of a look for the ship the colonel wanted and eventually found it. It was being circled by about five Vietnamese helicopters. I didn't have the gas to waste, so I just went on in and landed on the back of the ship. We let off the passengers and the cargo and I asked them to fix the radio, and they refused, so I asked for gas and they began to refuel the bird. All of a sudden the front of the ship was hit by a terrific explosion. The Vietnamese were ditching their helicopters into the water, and one of them had flown into the side of the ship and disintegrated."

The tail rotor of the exploding chopper sailed five hundred feet through the air like a knife and severed the engine oil line on Lannin's craft, knocking the engine out. He jumped out with his bags and then returned to the helicopter to take out more equipment. The blades were still turning when a Vietnamese chopper loaded with about twenty passengers attempted to land right next to him. There was not enough space and Lannin ran for his life. The blades of the two aircraft locked together, and the Vietnamese chopper was almost thrown off the back of the ship. Passengers and crew were hazardously loaded off and both choppers slung into the drink.

Tom Grady, who flew a Huey 204 throughout the last day, said that conditions improved as the day wore on. His first flight was made low into the downtown section of the city to the riverfront area. "The reason we flew so low was that we saw two airplanes get shot down as we took off and the friendlies were shooting at us all the way. It was what we had grown to expect from them, but then we never put much faith in the South Vietnamese anyway. In those last weeks there was nowhere to relax, and we were shot at in the air and on the ground by our own people."

Despite the elaborately laid plans of the DAO, AA pilots soon fell back to relying on one another for intelligence on how many evacuees were at the various rooftop pads. "It was strictly pilots going into the pads on their own," Lannin said. "You'd land, get as many aboard as you could, come off leaving a dozen or so behind. Then you'd radio another chopper and say, 'I've got twelve people left on this roof.' Despite all the plans, for the most part of the operation it was strictly what it always was, the pilots talking among themselves."

Tom Grady was also ordered to shut down at about eleven-thirty in the morning. He found a roof and landed the Huey and stayed there for about half an hour. "Then I thought—enough of this." He loaded it with a few people, including a friend's girl, and flew them out to the Seventh Fleet. He continued to fly until dark, when he made his last trip out and landed his machine on a small carrier.

AA had three choppers on the top of the USAID building, where the crowd was getting scared. Artillery was still hitting Tan Son Nhut a mile and a half away. Down in the street a crowd of thousands, armed and in a desperate mood, tried to storm the building.

The CIA Station Chief in Saigon, Thomas Polgar, was particularly concerned in evacuating a group of thirty Vietnamese, made up of friends and associates, he had promised to help. He had instructed the group, which included politicians,

policemen, and friends to gather at his home at eleven o'clock
that morning. Polgar had intended to go over personally and
arrange for their safe evacuation but at the critical time found
himself trapped in the embassy.

Polgar was a man who had made real contact with the
Vietnamese and felt desperate about deserting those to whom
he had given his word he would help. Indiscriminate sniping
in the area meant that it would be impossible to lift them off
from where they were, but a colleague suggested moving
them to a rooftop pad nearby. The emotionally distraught
station chief turned to the ranking Air America officer at the
embassy, who went under the alias of T. D. Latz, to organize
the lift-off.

Latz was a former U-2 pilot who walked with a limp and
was blind in one eye, but his courage was unimpaired. Polgar
called the pilot over the radio and within twenty minutes he
landed on the embassy roof. He entered the station chief's
anteroom, muttering about fuel gauges and lost air time.

"Look, I want you to go over to 6 Chien Si Circle and pick
up thirty of my people," Polgar said. "Okay?" he asked, clutching the pilot's hand.

The pilot knew that the rooftop pad mentioned was perilous
because of its size and its vulnerability to ground fire. "Okay,
Mr. Polgar," Latz replied. "But I'll have to take me a sidearm
for security."

Latz climbed into his chopper, flew over to the site, and
landed on the roof, but the thirty Vietnamese could not get
near because of a mob milling around the street threatening
to storm the building if the gate was opened. Latz hung
around for an hour, but the evacuees remained trapped
among the street crowds and he was eventually forced to
return to the embassy without them.

"No way I could get those thirty Viets out of Chien Si," the
pilot apologized to the CIA chief. "Nung guards locked the
front gate, wouldn't open it even when I waved this thing at
them." Latz indicated the machine gun he carried. "Can't
blame them. Must've been five hundred Viets in the street
outside, banging to get in. We'd have been trampled before
we pulled off the roof."

A CIA man asked if there had been any ground fire.
"Strays," Latz replied. "But most of the Viets are so damned

anxious to get out of this city they're not doing us the damage they could."

Polgar, reduced by emotional strain to taking large draughts from a bottle of cognac, outlined a new pickup plan. The thirty Vietnamese were to be directed to a small patio on another rooftop. "It's not big enough for a two point landing," a CIA man explained, "but if you could get one chopper skid on the edge of it, you might be able to hover long enough to take on Ut [Polgar's chauffeur] and his group."

Latz returned to his chopper and flew out to the new rendezvous. Later he returned to the embassy, nursing a bleeding right hand. "Goddamn Viets," he growled. "Rushed me on the roof over there. I had to slug one or two to get them to line up, nice like. Hell of a lot of 'em, though. Some trips, I couldn't even squeeze myself on the chopper. Had to ride the skids."

During this operation Latz and his helicopter were photographed by a newsman. The result was printed throughout the world and became one of the memorable images of the last, hectic day of American involvement in Vietnam. But in the confusion Latz was not sure whether he had picked up Polgar's group.

"The translators haven't been heard from," a CIA agent said. "Maybe we ought to try another rooftop pickup."

Polgar was beyond any response at all.

"No way I can go out again," Latz said. "Ain't easy landing a chopper on an unfamiliar pad even in broad daylight. After nightfall it's suicide."

The AA choppers were dangerously low on fuel, and the fall of darkness made operations an impractical gamble. Thousands of "sensitive" Vietnamese were to be left behind at the mercy of the enemy, who finally captured the embassy, complete with dossiers on every agent and friendly the Americans had ever dealt with.

Among the last to be pulled out were the Americans organizing the evacuation from the rooftop pads. The final moments were a close-run thing for Walt Martindale, working on the top of an apartment building near Tan Son Nhut. As an AA Huey made one of the last landings out of the dark, hundreds of desperate Vietnamese stormed the gate and made toward the entrance of the building. Two Vietnamese army lieutenants offered to hold the crowd at bay with their guns if Martindale guaranteed their escape.

Vietnamese were crowding up the stairs as the chopper landed. "Come on! Come on!" the pilot yelled to Martindale, but he shook his head. He called to the Vietnamese troops holding the crowd back at gunpoint to organize another load. Ten Vietnamese with children were allowed forward to the Huey.

"We want you! Not more Vietnamese," the pilot yelled at Martindale. He ignored the airman and began to organize yet another load. The chopper lifted off without him, loaded to twice its capacity.

As it flew into the distance, the human wave of Vietnamese pushed the troops back and Martindale was forced dangerously near the edge of the pad. He was struck on the side of the head by an old woman and all but knocked out. Another AA chopper dropped out of the night into the chaos. A flight mechanic held the panicking Vietnamese at bay with an M16 while the pilot yelled, "Come on! Come on!" Martindale and the two troopers walked over to the chopper and were pulled aboard. The Huey lifted off as the deserted Vietnamese screamed for help and shouted abuse. Until that moment Martindale had remained controlled and dignified. Now he wept uncontrollably.

Before making their way out to the Seventh Fleet in the South China Sea the pilot, worried about the lack of fuel, set down at burning Tan Son Nhut in an attempt to refuel. There was another reason for stopping off: AA management had neglected to remove $50,000 in cash which was supposed to be in the office safe. There was no one about when the chopper set down, and while the copilot began to refuel, the Filipino mechanic ran to the office and attempted to open the safe. A group of Vietnamese troops suddenly appeared on the far side of the runway and began to take pot shots at the landed chopper. The passengers climbed back on board, without the money, lifted off, and began the last journey of the day out to the Fleet (just what happened to that $50,000 is one of AA's unsolved mysteries. One strongly favored theory is that the money had already been removed from the safe by a thoughtful employee long before this last attempt was made).

AA finally shut down its rooftop extraction operations in

downtown Saigon at six-thirty P.M. Pilots were told to make their own way out to the fleet. One took out a chopper filled with liquor, but there was no room for it on the ship. The captain watched it land, screaming, "Off, off, off!" and the machine, together with its precious cargo, was dumped over the side. Most of the helicopters met the same fate. Pilots were landing them on the water and then jumping for it, a haphazard and hazardous method. "As soon as they hit the water, the rotors went crazy and the guys were getting pretty shook up," Bob Murray said. One Vietnamese pilot hovered fifty feet above the water and jumped out of the side.

Once aboard the various ships of the Seventh Fleet, the pilots of AA, whose last mission in Vietnam had been one of the most courageous of the war, found themselves badly treated. "We got hassled by the Marines on the ship and treated in a very abusive manner, like criminals," Wayne Lannin said. "They probably heard the stories—the highly paid mercenaries who flew dope. They gave us a body search and impounded our personal weapons. We never got them back. One guy lost five hundred dollars, and his passport was taken by a Marine security guard. We all lost more in that night with the Seventh Fleet than we did with AA in the whole of our years of operation in Vietnam."

At eight the following morning evacuees were seated in a room that was well over 100 degrees and had no air conditioning. Embassy personnel were quickly dealt with, but the AA pilots were still there at six that night. Marine guards were on the door, and anyone who tried to leave the room was physically restrained. "I hated to leave Vietnam that way," Lannin said. "I felt the lowest I've ever felt in my life. It made me feel extremely bitter."

In a war shamed by stories of massacres, mass bombings, and brutality by the military, these brave civilian pilots of AA who stayed until the end deserved better. Option IV, the heli-airlift, was a courageous operation, dedicated to saving lives, not taking them. It was the largest evacuation by helicopter in U.S. history, and the rescue force of seventy choppers and 865 Marines flew over 630 "sorties" during those last eighteen hours and evacuated 1,373 Americans, 5,595 South Vietnamese, and 85 third-country nationals. Of these, nearly 2,100 including 978 Americans, were helilifted out of the embassy courtyard alone. AA pilots hauled more than 1,000 passengers to the embassy, DAO, or the fleet. Unlike the military or the embassy personnel in Saigon, at the end they did not have to be there. In the long, checkered, and often murky history of AA, the evacuation of Saigon is an accomplishment of daring and courage on the heroic scale.

TWELVE

PRIVATIZATION

The CIA has changed its policy about airplanes. The days of wholly-owned proprietaries are over. They proved in the end to be unwieldy, vulnerable to exposés, and no longer necessary. "Eventually the 'Customer' decided it really couldn't keep owning the aircraft," William Colby, ex-head of the CIA, explained. "That the kind of pressures we got into in the early 1970s made it desirable to end that ownership. But I can tell you something—that when we sold it we made one hell of a profit—which we turned into the United States Treasury in the best form that you would recognize: 'Miscellaneous Receipts.'"

This is not to suggest that the CIA has cut off its air arm, but without the war in Indochina and only a limited role in Africa—albeit burgeoning activity in Central America—it has shifted its tactics to avoid the long-term costs of large underworked proprietaries.

Former CIA General Counsel Lawrence Houston, who was involved in setting up the Agency's first set of proprietaries, now believes they should be used only as a last resort. The CIA learned its lessons the hard way about proprietaries, mostly from AA in the Far East. "Others had their own special problems, but I think the Air America complex had pretty most everything," Houston said.

The worst problem was the size of the complex, which made inevitable that cover could not be maintained indefinitely. It is mainly for this reason that the agency is unlikely to create other proprietaries, although it has declared its intention to maintain safe ones. The CIA Chief of the Cover and Commercial Staff told the Senate Committee on Intelligence Activities: "We need a variety of cooperating personnel and organizations in the private sector. Proprietaries... are part of this arsenal of tools that the Agency must have in order to fulfill its job.

"On the basis of our experience with proprietaries we have come to the conclusion that wherever possible we try to use other means of providing cover and hiding the CIA hand. But where there is no other way, or where it is the best way in order to achieve the operational objective, we have used proprietaries in the past and we propose to continue to use proprietaries. So we are not getting out of the proprietary business as such. But it is true that the proprietaries that we are using at the present time, and what I can foresee for the immediate future, are going to be of a smallish variety."

When asked by the Senate Committee whether the CIA would ever again seek to establish a large proprietary conglomerate such as the AA complex, the Chief said that the air arm had grown in the pursuit of an existing operational requirement. "If such an operational requirement should again arise, I would assume that the Agency would consider setting up a large-scale air proprietary with one proviso— that we have a chance at keeping it secret that it is CIA."

But Houston does not believe that there is any chance at all of keeping the existence of such an airline secret. "I don't believe it's possible. In the aviation industry, everybody knows what everybody is doing and something new coming along is immediately the focus of thousands of eyes and prying questions. And that, combined with the intricacies of a corporate administration these days, and the checks and balances, I think make a large aviation proprietary probably impossible.

"They are cumbersome," he told the Senate Committee. "To be properly run they take money, many man hours of many, many different parts of the Agency. So they are expensive in man hours. There are built-in difficulties in running what appears to be a normal business for operational purposes. There's really a built-in dichotomy there that leads to a continual conflict with policies. And due to the number of people involved, there is a security problem on the old grounds that security doesn't go by the mathematical increase in the number of people. It goes geometrically as the number of people, the security risk."

Without the vast and varied fleet of aircraft which the

proprietaries provided all over the world on a round-the-clock, seven-days-a-week, all-year-round basis, the CIA had to make other arrangements. It is the nature of clandestine airlines that they expand or disappear as the need for them ebbs and flows, but the Agency will always need airplanes at some time in some place. The war in Vietnam demanded an enormous capability, while small operations might call for only a couple of ancient transports. But whatever the need, the Agency clearly is obliged to find a way to satisfy it.

The question the Agency faced in the mid-seventies was, what would it do when an operational need for clandestine air support arose? Could some substitute be found which would also meet the requirements of secure, well-maintained local aircraft?

After Vietnam, the CIA entered a new and different era of air support, rejecting its long-held doctrine of a "standby" capability—which meant investing large amounts of capital to maintain operating resources and permanent assets ready for use in any contingency. The Chief of Covert and Commercial Staff suggested the use of third-country assets, but although this method can sometimes be used, it is beset by problems of control, deniability and political considerations. The solution seemed to be privatization.

The Agency had learned in Laos that private contractors—particularly Continental Air Services—responded remarkably well to their needs, while attracting much less attention than the clandestine proprietaries. The CIA could look to friendly air companies, with no direct connection—known in the parlance of the business as "cut-outs"—for well-rewarded favors. The Agency set about disposing of its air assets, at what seemed to be knock-down prices, to contractors who could be relied upon in the future.

The CIA sold Southern Air Transport on December 31, 1973, to Stanley G. Williams, the man who had fronted for the Agency's ownership for thirteen years. Williams paid only $2.1 million for the company, although the stockholders' equity was $4.2 million. He also agreed to pay back $3 million which the CIA had loaned the company, but apart from that debt, SAT had only $868,490.09 in liabilities compared to $8.1 million in assets.

"It was a long, hard, arm's-length transaction," Williams said, who originally offered to buy the company, free of any debt to the Agency, for $4.5 million. "I tried my best to get the very best purchase I could do. Wouldn't you? Isn't that the best way to do business?"

In fact, he did not get as good a deal as he had wanted or as the CIA had planned to give him. The original plan was for Williams to buy the company outright and continue to operate it as a globe-spanning common courier. But when the airline's competitors complained that it had grown through illegal government subsidies, the company surrendered its status as a certificated airline. This took it out from under the jurisdiction of the CAB and allowed the CIA to sell it however it pleased. It also reduced the value of the firm somewhat, although it is still able to fly anywhere in the world on a contract basis. Its giant L-100 Hercules cargo planes have since been leased to Alaska International Airlines in Alaska, and Texaco in Nigeria, Africa, while its DC-6 has been leased to a company in Detroit. But Southern Air Transport managed to go about its business in relative obscurity, until its connection to contra airdrops was disclosed.

Intermountain has been similarly disposed of by the Agency. The company's assets—much of which had already been sold—were acquired by Evergreen Helicopters of McMinnville, Oregon, in March 1975. "Intermountain was picked up for a pretty good price because it was going bankrupt," said John Straubel, a spokesman for the company.

The Intermountain Marana base has become the Evergreen Air Center. The company paid an undisclosed sum of money to take over the lease on the facility, owned by Pinal County, Arizona, and a total of $2.8 million for twelve aircraft: these included one Electra, four Twin Otter STOL aircraft, and four Bell Jet Ranger helicopters.

Evergreen's president at the time, Delford Smith, said that he was unaware of Intermountain's CIA connection until that company's chief negotiator told him about it. He was shocked but went ahead with the deal, he said, because he was not buying a company but some flying machines, and only picking up the lease on a maintenance base and the services of flight areas and mechanics.

There are no ties with the CIA today, Smith said. His decision to buy Intermountain was made on a purely commercial basis because it complemented his company's need for a year-round good-weather maintenance base and aircraft he could use. It also provided a jumping-off point for its expanding oil operations in Bolivia, pre-Sandinista Nicaragua, and Peru. The two companies had been flying forestry and fire-fighting operations side by side for ten years, and throughout that period Smith would have us believe he never suspected CIA involvement, despite the fact that a number of exposés had been published.

The company expanded rapidly to own almost one hundred aircraft operating on four continents. It has a number of bases in the States, including one at Missoula, Montana, where General Vang Pao, on leaving Laos, went to farm (not poppies) under CIA protection. Among Evergreen's pilots at Missoula was Ernest Brace, who when flying for Continental Air Services in Laos became the first man to be captured by the Pathet Lao when he was shot down. He served seven years in captivity.

Most of the original Intermountain personnel was kept on, including Garfield Thorsrud, its former president, known to employees as Gar. (Cuban pilots flying CIA resupply missions to rebels just before the Bay of Pigs invasion were given the telephone number of a man known simply as "Mr. G." If forced down outside Cuba, they were to telephone Mr. G. immediately. Later, during the actual invasion, the CIA's top air operations adviser was a man identified as "Gar.") Thorsrud left Evergreen in 1975 to start his own airline.

Among Evergreen's purchases was Johnson Flying Services, one of the U.S. supplementary charter airlines. A senior intelligence official in Washington advised investigative journalist Robert Fink that the company was to be used for transferring AA's salvageable assets back to the United States. Fink was also informed by a former associate of Delford Smith that Evergreen's president had been approached by AID in 1974 to take over AA's operations in Phnom Penn, but he refused because of the short-term duration of the contract. Smith says that neither allegation is true. His sole relationship with AA was that he had bought one of their airplanes, while turning down many more he considered too expensive. He also says that he was never approached by AID on AA's behalf and that his companies will not perform any government contracts that could be considered as CIA related. Johnson Flying Services evolved into Evergreen International with its own substantial jet fleet.

Air Asia, the Agency's enormous repair and maintenance facility on Taiwan, the largest in the Pacific, was also sold in 1975. A booklet put out by Air Asia to facilitate the sale gives an indication of just how big the company had become. The main plant incorporated over 360,000 square feet of paved ramp and 150,000 square feet of hangars. Adjoining the ramp area was a runway which could accommodate any existing type of military or commercial jet.

Directly across from the airfield perimeter road was the secondary plant comprising a maintenance support area encompassing more than 216,000 square feet of fully equipment and staffed shop facilities, jet and reciprocating engine test stands, 64,000 square feet of modern warehousing space, 67,000 square feet of open storage area and 39,000 square feet for gas and chemical storage. In addition there was a wide variety of miscellaneous support systems, including extensive motor vehicle shops servicing over 180 company vehicles, power units, water treatment plants, emergency diesel power plants and other general maintenance facilities. Air Asia's aircraft maintenance division was made up of five departments, a separate cleaning and handling section manned by complete technical and administrative staffs of 2,000 experienced personnel. The company had a capability of working on thirty different types of aircraft, from helicopters to Boeing 727 tri-jets, and could completely rebuild accident-damaged aircraft.

It also carried out Inspection and Repair As Necessary (IRAN) of military jet fighters and transport aircraft to such an extent that the USAF relied on them. Any modification, interior conversion, or rewiring could be carried out within the plant. Its machine shop was equipped with some of the finest and most modern metal-working machines and maintained an incredible stock of parts supplied by its procurement office, Air Sea Forwarders, in North Hollywood, California, and buyers in every principal city in the Far East.

The company was eventually bought by E-Systems Inc., a Dallas-based electronics company. "We bought it right," John W. Dixon, the company's president and chairman of the board, told stockholders at a briefing. "Paid cash, but won't tell you how much." The figure $1.9 million plus assumption of liabilities was later reported.

E-Systems was originally LTV Electrosystems, a spin-off

of the giant Ling-Temco-Vought conglomerate. In 1970 William F. Raborn, a retired Navy vice-admiral and director of the CIA for fourteen months in 1965 and 1966, became a member of the board of directors and a consultant of the company. The company was sold by LTV in 1972 and became E-Systems. Admiral Raborn stayed on.

As a company E-Systems is primarily engaged in the design, development, production, and servicing of electronic systems and products for the Department of Defense, NASA, and other government agencies that are used to carry out missions of reconnaissance, surveillance, and intelligence. Its largest customer is the U.S. government, and just after it bought Air Asia, its first quarterly report for 1975 stated that the company booked over $31 million in defense business. "Well over a third of this was in the intelligence, reconnaissance, and surveillance area," the report said.

At the time of the Air Asia purchase, E-Systems went out of its way to deny any CIA connection. Admiral Raborn, the ex-CIA chief, had not participated in any negotiations or discussions regarding the purchase, the company said, "except in his capacity as a director when the acquisition was considered by the board." The company had no contracts with the CIA, and most of its classified contracts in the intelligence, reconnaissance, and surveillance field were with the U.S. Air Force. On January 16, 1976, the company was awarded a $16.6 million contract to install and maintain the sensoring devices that monitor the Sinai buffer zone between Egyptian and Israeli forces. But president Dixon insists, "We have never done any business with the CIA."

The gradual winding-down of the U.S. presence in Indochina until its final collapse was mirrored by a cutting back of AA's total capability. By 1975 the parent Pacific Corporation had been trimmed by 90 percent and the all-time high of 11,200 employees directly accountable to it in 1970 was down to little more than, 1,100. AA had been so strongly identified with the CIA that it was decided that the best method of disposing of it was liquidation.

The CIA spent a long time liquidating the company. Early in 1973, for instance, when the U.S. war apparatus was being phased out, AA was actually hiring more pilots to fly helicopters to fulfill the contract it had landed with the International Commission of Control and Supervision.

But elsewhere in Southeast Asia the January, 1973, cease-fire settlement meant that AA was redundant. What followed has been described as the biggest rummage sale of spy equipment in history. State Department negotiators spent six months trying to figure out who owned what at the Udorn air base in Thailand. Different procedures had to be followed for selling or transferring equipment owned by the CIA, the Air Force, or a private company. The negotiators found a way to retain jobs for the 1,700 Thai nationals the CIA employed at the base when Thai-Am, a company jointly held by the Thai government and an American firm, agreed to keep them on to work on Cambodian and Laotian air force planes repaired at the base. But was Thai-Am just another CIA front? The State Department had its doubts, ran a check, and decided that it was not.

But there was certainly a cloak-and-dagger atmosphere about some of the sales negotiations. In February 1975 there were clandestine meetings in Hong Kong between AA officials and senior representatives of South American republics lasting for ten days. Top-secret deals were made involving millions of dollars, involving the sale of a large number of transport and semimilitary aircraft.

The negotiators made the most of the exotic setting for the meetings, which included a series of lengthy luncheons at the best hotels and dinners aboard Hong Kong's luxurious floating restaurants. Perhaps the most dramatic meeting of all, when a Central American republic agreed to buy three military transports, was held aboard a high-powered yacht anchored off a remote island beach. When the deal was concluded, there were celebratory cocktails and a freshly prepared grouper was served which the cook claimed to have caught while the negotiations were taking place.

By mid 1975 aviation journals in the States were carrying ads seeking reemployment for AA pilots, flight crews, and ground crews with anything from three to twenty years' service. "Air America Inc. is curtailing activities in overseas locations," the ads stated. Anybody with a job to offer was asked to call or write to James E. Meals at AA's Washington office.

Other AA planes were ferried back to the United States, where they were mothballed at an airfield in Roswell, northern New Mexico. One of the Volpars was lost on the journey in 1976 when it ditched into the sea somewhere off the Aleutian Islands on its way to Alaska from Japan. A life raft was found containing the pilot's suitcase, but the man himself was never found.

The company with the contract to sell the remaining AA aircraft was an extraordinary broker in Washington, D.C., called Omni Aircraft Sales. In 1979 the company was totally owned by an unusual entrepreneur by the name of Lee Hillmer, a man in his mid-thirties who started life selling used cars. Omni was run very much as an intelligence operation in which research was the key to business success. A retired military colonel bossed a staff that used the phone to find intelligence on what planes were available, where, and at what price.

The CIA told the Senate Committee on Intelligence Operations that AA would be phased out by June 30, 1976, ending its airlift capability and returning an estimated $20 million to the U.S. Treasury. The Agency also said that it did not expect to set up new air proprietaries but kept open the option to do so.

Yet, AA's office in Washington was still open many years after its air operations ceased, manned by a skeleton staff, headed by president Clyde S. Carter. "My job is pretty damned specific," he explained. "I am engaged to close up a Delaware corporation and that's my activity. I'm doing exactly here what I'd be doing if I was closing up IBM, Pan American, or General Motors or anything else. I'm dealing with the practical corporate problems in putting this corporation out of business.

"Now we're involved with settling injury insurance cases, stuff like that. This is pretty humdrum, menial crap that I'm doing. It might take some experience and legal ability to do it, but it's real mundane drudgery. I'm getting kinda tired of it as a matter of fact."

Menial crap aside, there were to be a number of headaches facing the Agency, as it strove to reorganize its air arm, which were not at all humdrum. The consequences of almost three decades of direct ownership in the aviation business would be felt for years. Clandestine activities which included war, operating under profitable business cover, had made it possible for Air America to land lucrative government contracts in direct competition with the private sector. Some companies had been forced out of business as a result, unable to compete, while others became the victims of cruder tactics.

The most dramatic case resulting from this dichotomy surfaced in the mid-seventies in a multimillion-dollar legal suit filed against AA and the CIA by the General Aircraft Corporation, the company which had manufactured the Helio-Courier.

GAC alleged that the aircraft operations of Helio were effectively destroyed by the acts of the CIA and its proprietaries, which were so manifestly illegal and corrupt that Helio was tainted to such an extent that it was effectively precluded from selling and marketing operations everywhere in the world. Named as defendants alongside Air America were former counsel Lawrence R. Houston, George Doole, Jr., Air Asia, and the non-CIA firms Bird & Sons Inc, Continental Air Services, and Fairchild Industries. The CIA refused to comment on the allegations. Together with the Justice Department, the Agency fought GAC's requests for information on a number of grounds, including national security.

"The facts alleged will demonstrate that the Agency, its proprietaries and individuals acted willfully and knowingly to misuse the company's name, misrepresent the company and otherwise appropriate the company's assets and goodwill to their own benefit for purposes of carrying on acts illegal under U.S. and foreign laws and gathering revenues for the individual profit of those involved and to avoid the laws of the U.S.," the company claimed.

The Air Force bought 130 Couriers for use in Vietnam, and other aircraft from the company, on top of the CIA's substantial fleet. The company acknowledged that it provided "irregular" assistance to the CIA, such as transporting agents, but had no connections with the Agency. "Nevertheless it now appears that agents of the CIA obtained by forgery, misrepresentation, and other devices, credentials indicating they were sales employees of Helio, knowing well that such was not the case."

In 1960 and 1962 Helio had made an intensive effort to sell its systems and aircraft in East Africa, the Congo, and the Philippines. Negotiations were suddenly terminated, and in the Congo, where Helio's cover was used to carry out "illegal and immoral activities" which resulted in the death of government officials and the fall of the government, genuine

Helio personnel were declared personae non gratae.

"A similar pattern of facts, in each case resulting in Helio's personnel being excluded from the country, was repeated in Thailand, Vietnam, Laos, Nepal, Cambodia and Micronesia," the claim alleges. "The exclusion from its logical and historical markets had required Helio to contract very substantially its operations in toto and discontinue its aircraft manufacturing operations entirely. Such exclusion has, in sum, nearly destroyed the company's aircraft operations." Decent profits had become substantial losses.

Although many of the CIA's activities were conducted in the 1960s the "stigma" of the Agency link to the name prevented Helio from participating in a competition for turbine-powered STOL aircraft in Thailand in 1972 and 1975. "The CIA and its proprietaries, acting through other United States government officials, encouraged the foreign government to reject Helio aircraft and refuse to deal with its personnel."

When the company refused to turn over its worldwide selling operations to the Agency in 1962, it was warned by AA chief George Doole that it would "never sell another plane in Asia." Looking back through its records the company realized that it had sold Air America an incredible number of spare parts and that the CIA must be manufacturing its own aircraft to conceal the actual number the Agency had in use.

Helio was to become the victim of a vendetta carried out by George Doole. GAC's trade secrets had been illegally stolen from them to enable Air Asia to produce Helios. At first the company tried to get this data by complaining about faulty parts and requesting information for the making of so-called necessary parts. When this was refused, Air Asia set up an elaborate scheme with King-Hurley, a CIA propriety, to surreptitiously obtain microfilm of the data. When this scheme was thwarted, Air Asia resorted to the services of a secret agent, Nathan C. Fitts, who was planted in GAC's Washington, D.C., office.

Eventually the data was obtained by the CIA in the form of reports, drawings, plans, microfilm and written material, all containing information about the design, production, and assembly of Helio planes and parts. By the end of 1962 Air Asia was able to build its own Helios; GAC was unable to sell them any more planes and eventually went out of business. Also at this time Air America refused to buy the com-

pany's new plane, the Helio Stallion, which had been
developed at great cost, and began to buy the Pilatus Porter
instead.

Herbert Fenster, an attorney with Sellers, Conner and Cu-
neo who originally acted for GAC, said that the evidence
would have sensational disclosures if the CIA refused to settle. "Do you want some key words—corruption, murder,
blackmail."

Another disclosure which Fenster did not mention, and
which caused him to resign from the case, was that his company also happened to represent E-Systems, which had
bought Air Asia—a defendant. The case was given to Theodore E. Dinsmoor of Gaston, Snow and Ely Barlette of Boston,
who marshalled a formidable amount of information and prepared for a lengthy and drawn-out battle. The CIA denied
the claim, but eventually settled out of court for an undisclosed sum.

Then in 1981 Air-Sea Forwarders Inc, an international
freight forwarding company based in Los Angeles, also took
the CIA to court—in a suit against Air Asia and E-Systems.
Air-Sea Forwarders claimed that they had provided business
"cover" for clandestine shipments all over the world since
1956. The company president, Erwin Rautenberg, said he had
made a secret, oral agreement with the Agency that in return
for business "cover" he would be the exclusive forwarding
agent for Air America and Air Asia in Taiwan. The relationship could only be terminated in the event of "good
cause."

Things ran smoothly for twenty-five years. At first Rautenberg was unaware that his company was being used by
the CIA, and thought he was involved in normal commercial
contracts. He sent aircraft parts, seat covers and napkins to
General Chennault's airline Civil Air Transport. But as time
went by, and after a few trips to the Far East, the true nature
of the operation became obvious. Aircraft parts later became
weapons accompanied by phony customs' declarations, and
the destination was not always that stated on the manifold.

The CIA then entered into an oral agreement with Rautenberg. "They didn't tell me very much, arguing that I didn't
need to know," Rautenberg explained. "They do not always
answer all your questions. They do not volunteer information." But he was happy enough with the arrangement, feel-

ing he was serving the U.S. government as well as making money. As a German Jew, he had fled Germany in 1937 to escape Adolf Hitler, and gone to live in Argentina where he indulged in some amateur intelligence work for the allies down in Patagonia. He arrived in the U.S.A. in 1946, grateful for the asylum the country offered him, and saw his work for the CIA as a patriotic act.

At first the people he dealt with were an exceptionally well-educated and dedicated group, but as the Vietnam war dragged on the caliber changed for the worse. "The basic concept was sound, but it degenerated into a bunch of bandits. There was all kinds of smuggling going on—mostly currency. People thought they had the right to break the law as a privilege for dangerous work. It was not official policy as such, but the policy was to look the other way which encouraged these individuals. People made their own laws. Everything became so inefficient and wasteful."

Even after the CIA sold Air Asia to E-Systems in 1975, Rautenberg was assured that the terms of the agreement were still in effect. But then in 1981 the oral agreement was broken and Air-Sea Forwarders were dropped. "I received a crude termination letter signed by an underling saying they were moving their operation to another airport."

At first Rautenberg was alarmed that, without CIA cover and legal aid, he would become personally responsible for various liabilities and end up in jail. "If it ever came out I would hang. I would be stuck with the legal consequences of all the accommodations which were made over the years. They were always bending the law—tax, customs, the Teamsters' Union." The first suit he filed was merely legal self defense, which did not broach the secrecy of the CIA agreement. The hope was that the Agency would settle for a small amount of money and take on the responsibility for any liabilities that might crop up.

Instead, the CIA fought the case tooth and nail. Rautenberg felt betrayed after almost a lifetime of loyal service. Despite the advice of some skeptics, who told him not to confront the CIA and the government, he turned his case into a crusade. Legal costs have been fantastic. "I hate to tell you the figure," he said.

The CIA have handled the case badly, putting themselves into the harsh light of publicity, attempting to gag newsmen, lawyers and judges in a series of dubious maneuvers. Various Agency lawyers seemed almost totally ignorant of the history of the CIA's involvement with air proprietaries. (When Rautenberg showed up at one meeting with a copy of this book, the CIA's lawyers leafed through it in horrified fascination. "They had no idea such a detailed record of the air proprietaries' activities had been published," he said.) But in mid 1986 the jury of a Los Angeles federal court awarded Air-Sea Forwarders $6.2 million in punitive damages and $216,000 in compensatory damages. The case was immediately appealed by the CIA while Rautenberg was placed under a security muzzle of extraordinary severity. "I will prevail," he said.

Disposing of the directly owned proprietaries resolved one set of problems, but the move to privatization and "cut-out" corporations created others. As early as 1964 the CIA had put its air operations on two tracks, when there was a fear that press exposure of Air America as an Agency airline would lead to its expulsion from Laos. Robert F. Six, the president of Continental Airlines, was approached by Ray Clines, then a deputy director of the CIA—and the man who had taken the U-2 pictures of Soviet missiles on Cuba to President Kennedy. Over cocktails in the Ritz-Carlton in Washington, D.C., Clines explained that the Agency would like Six to start a small airline in Southeast Asia. "From scratch, out of the mud so to speak," Six said.

Six was open to the idea, and the next day he was taken to the Agency H.Q. at Langley and given lunch—a lavish affair served on exquisite china plates incongruously embossed with the CIA crest—and the deal was on. Continental Air Services was incorporated in Nevada as a wholly-owned subsidiary of Continental Airlines. Apart from providing a parallel service to Air America, this private company also took on the highly unusual contract to provide airplanes and pilots to fly Air Commandos, acting as forward air controllers, over the combat zone during the secret war in Laos.

Six said he did not know why he was chosen. "I never asked," he said laughing, "and they never told me. They're not too free with information at times. Right?" But it is significant that Six was personally represented by William Casey—in private legal practice at that time, but later to become director of the CIA. "The airline made a hell of a lot of money," Six said. "Hell, yes. Christ, we had some great contracts."

Continental Air Services, controlled by competent and honest businessmen, had proved to be an extremely successful model and perhaps lulled the Agency into a false sense of security. Another type of privatized operation was to cause untold embarrassment and harm to the Agency. Instead of bringing in respected businessmen who could be trusted from outside, the Agency put clandestine agents of its own into business—a very different proposition. Although the new generation of commercial companies has been more difficult to link directly to the Agency, and therefore runs less risk of exposure, the lack of complete control has made the CIA vulnerable to the people who run them. Profiteers and crooks—Rautenberg's "bunch of bandits"—would become as great a menace to the CIA as Communist infiltrators or traitors.

One operation, involving Air America, Continental Air Services and CIA personnel, exploded into an international scandal which continues today. This was the Nugan Hand Bank of Australia, founded in 1973 by Michael Hand—who had served in Laos as a CIA paramilitary officer—and Frank Nugan—an Australian super-salesman with a dubious law degree and little or no banking expertise. In the early years of the bank's activities Hand made numerous trips to the war zone to talk former colleagues from the secret world into investing. Among the original shareholders, four listed their addresses as c/o Air America, APO, San Francisco, and one c/o Continental Air Services. High-ranking American generals and admirals were hired by the bank, and William Colby, ex-director of the CIA who had retired and gone into private legal practice, was retained as the company's attorney.

The bank seemed to expand and grow for seven years, until in January 1980 the dead body of Frank Nugan was found slumped in his Mercedes outside of Sydney. He had shot himself with a .30 caliber rifle. The suicide triggered the bank's collapse, and six months later Michael Hand disappeared into thin air.

The collapse brought in its wake charges that the bank had not only bilked investors out of $50 million, but also that it had laundered money earned from illegal weapons and drug

transactions. Those linked to the failed bank read like the
Who's Who of the clandestine world: Michael Hand, it tran-
spired, had originally gone to Australia on the advice of ex-
Air America pilot Kermit "Bud" King; the Taiwan branch
was run by ex-CAT and Air America flying services manager,
Dale Holmgren; personnel at the Thai branch at Chiang Mai,
drug capital of the Golden Triangle, included two Thais who
were ex-Air America, as well as William Young, the CIA
agent active with the hill tribes in Laos; also involved with
the bank in Thailand was Robert "Red" Jantzen, ex-CIA station chief in Bangkok. Other names linked to the bank were
Ted Shackley, onetime station chief in Laos, his deputy Tom
Clines, Air Force General Richard Secord, head of logistics
to the secret war in Laos, and ex-CIA agent Ed Wilson.

A 1983 study by the Commonwealth-New South Wales
Joint Task Force on Drug Trafficking reported that in 1976
Hand shipped ten million rounds of ammunition and 3,000
weapons, including rifles and machine-guns, to U.S. intelli-
gence-supported forces in Angola. In the same year the bank
was also involved in a transaction to move a U.S. Navy spy
vessel to the Iranian Navy. Both deals were masterminded
by Ed Wilson. The Task Force report stated that during the
years the bank was in business Nugan Hand engaged in a
wide range of both legitimate and illegal activities conducted
from offices and mail drops in thirteen centers in two hem-
ispheres, including the United States, the Cayman Islands,
Hong Kong, Taiwan, the Philippines and Thailand. Although
parts of the report remain classified, it stated that there was
evidence that, "Hand retained his U.S. intelligence ties
through the 1970s and probably the 1980s."

Two other Australian investigations confirmed these findings, although the most recent, a study by the Royal Commission, disputes some of the Joint Task Force conclusions.
Despite all of the investigations there are still more questions
than answers, and so far there have been no criminal charges
brought against anyone. While the bank was probably used
by the CIA, the major outrages were committed by outright
criminals for personal gain. The dangers of crooks working
behind secret intelligence cover are incalculable.

The most extraordinary example of this—and the most
damaging to both the CIA's image (hardly gleaming by the
mid-seventies)—turned out to be Ed Wilson, described by a

retired senior Agency official as, "Our bad one." Starting as a low-level agent, Wilson made a fortune from the manipulation of his CIA contacts, and eventually turned into a terrorist harboring plans to provide Qaddafi of Libya with a nuclear weapon.

He joined the CIA in 1955 and was assigned to the Office of Security as part of a new sixty-man detachment to guard the CIA's U-2 high-altitude spy planes. Later he was sent to Turkey where four U-2s were stationed, and among the pilots he watched over was Gary Francis Powers, who would be shot down by the Soviets.

In September 1960 he was recalled to CIA H.Q. at Langley and put under deep commercial cover. His status at the Agency was changed to that of a contract employee, which provided "plausible deniability" if any other agency should make enquiries about him. His "control," and link to Langley, was Tom Clines—the deputy of Ted Shackley. The three men were destined to become good friends.

In his new job Wilson set up Maritime Consulting Associates, a sort of Air America of the waves, which shipped all manner of clandestine cargoes. The ships of MCA often had their registration numbers painted over, sailed with no flags, and the crews spoke no English. The cargoes these ships carried were mixed: crowd-control equipment to Chile, Brazil and Venezuela; electronics to Iran; advanced communications to Morocco; arms to Angola, the Dominican Republic, Indonesia, Taiwan and the Philippines; flotillas of boats were bought for use in continuing raids against Cuba, and in the Congo; all sorts of stuff for the secret war in Laos. (It was probably in Laos that Wilson first met the man responsible for the war's logistics, a young Air Force major called Richard V. Secord. Ted Shackley, meanwhile, had become Station Chief in the country, while Tom Clines was his deputy.)

Wilson did a competent job, and the Agency smiled upon his expanding network of proprietaries. He, too, prospered—although not on the level he wished. Then, in 1971, he became the victim of a change in CIA policy which closed down many of the proprietaries precisely because they were difficult to control. (During an investigation by the Office of Management and Budget it was discovered that Wilson had tried to borrow money for a private venture using a CIA proprietary as collateral. Wilson left with a year's pay as severance, but does not seem to have been punished in any way or even to have earned a black mark.)

Within two months of quitting the CIA he joined Task Force 157, a top-secret and specialized unit of the Office of Naval Intelligence. TF 157 welcomed Wilson's expertise in proprietaries, and he did business which put millions of dollars through a variety of shell corporations—and began to complain of only being rewarded with a "piss-ant" government salary in return. As he grew increasingly greedy, he also harbored a lunatic ambition to create and head a new intelligence outfit that would eventually take over from the CIA.

He was careful to mention his Agency connections, and often dropped the name of Shackley, a rising star. Richard Secord, meanwhile, had become a colonel heading the Air Force Military Advisory Group in Iran, and was later to supervise the entire military sales program to that country worth more than $60 billion. All of these contacts gave Wilson—a crude man in person whom one acquaintance said "did not know Budweiser from Beaujolais"—international credibility. This credibility was further enhanced when he hired an assortment of retired admirals and generals, and gave them desks and telephones at the company offices in Washington, D.C., encouraging them to drum up business on a freelance basis. Wilson prospered, joined exclusive Washington clubs, bought a 2,000 acre country estate in Virginia hunt country (Shackley's daughter boarded her horse on the farm), and a private plane (to which Secord was given generous access).

In 1976 Rear-Admiral Bobby Ray Inman, Director of the Office of Naval Intelligence, ordered an investigation into the use of proprietaries. He was worried his office might be unwittingly committing abuses, and harbored the private belief that they did not produce enough intelligence to warrant their risky operation. An encounter with Wilson, who virtually offered the admiral a bribe, led to the rapid termination of all contracts with his companies. As of April, 1976, despite the lobbying of senators on the Armed Services Committee, Wilson's direct involvement with the U.S. intelligence community ceased.

He now joined the ranks of a dangerous and embittered breed—the agent who feels slighted and harbors a grudge, and turns against his previous patrons. (They come in various forms. Among the more vociferous critics of the CIA are those men who claim to quit for reasons of conscience, but who on closer examination are often found to be disappointed because of lack of promotion or some backwater posting. Wilson was just a self-aggrandizing, amoral crook.)

One ex-general who went to Wilson for a job, and asked who they would be dealing with, was told, "Anyone with a buck." The general turned down the appointment, but others were not so fastidious. Another disgruntled ex-CIA man, Frank Terpil, offered introductions into the military hierarchy of Libya. Terpil was a petty thief and currency black marketeer whose services to the Agency had been terminated when he was discovered absent from his post. His grotesque boast was that he had been an assassin and had once disembowelled a leftist Thai politician for the Agency—in fact he was a low-level contract employee in the Technical Services Division of the CIA who worked as a communications technician. Like Wilson, he intended to parlay the experiences of a dubious secret past into a profitable future.

Libya offered rich pickings for the unscrupulous. Its dictator Muamar Qaddafi, had bought $12 billion worth of arms from the Soviet Union in 1976 alone. The Russians, however, refused to sell him electronic equipment. He also wanted western weapons for use in terrorist activity, and C-4 plastique explosive for terrorist bombs. Wilson would fill the gap and the various contracts granted to him in electronics, training and weaponry eventually amounted to $18 million.

Wilson smuggled badly-needed C-130 parts into Libya and supplied "trainers" for the Libyan Air Force, and inveigled himself into a position where he became the dominant force in the country's aviation business. The Libyans needed men to run its considerable Chinook helicopter program, and in late 1979 Wilson hired an old Air America hand, Robert "China Blue" Hitchman. "Man, oh, man, could he fly helicopters," a colleague said admiringly. "Hitchman was a guy who could put it down on the deck, just a tick off the treetops, and follow the contours of the hills like he was taking a Sunday drive." Another colleague added that China Blue was the "hottest goddamn helicopter pilot you can imagine...a son of a bitch who could look death in the face and reach out and chuck it under the chin—absolute ice water."

Hitchman was recruited as a training officer and mainte-

nance supervisor, overseeing Libyan nationals as pilots. He
was not impressed. "These rag-heads have twenty Chinooks
now. The rate they're going, they'll be out of aircraft in a
month. They can't fix 'em, they can't fly 'em—hell, this is
some kind of Camel Air Force." The breaking point for Hitchman came when a Libyan pilot froze at the controls on a
training mission and the American had to take over. He
threatened to quit unless the Libyans stayed out of the way.
"They can come out and stand around the planes and do
whatever they want to do, just so long as they keep their
hands off the goddamned aircraft."

This meant that Americans would be needed to replace
Libyan pilots to fly in the combat and supply missions in the
undeclared war with Chad. Hitchman recruited a dozen Vietnam veterans and ex-Air America hands through an outfit
called Western Recruitment Inc., a Swiss-based Liberian Corporation that was no more than a post office box in Geneva.
The combat flights into Chad were like old times, and one
chopper pilot returned with twenty-nine bullet holes in the
fuselage of his aircraft.

Wilson also ran a separate clandestine C-130 operation,
and a small private airline officially incorporated in Panama—Wendy Airlines (unofficially known as Air Wilson, it
consisted of a Convair, a Piper Cherokee and a Beechcraft
Baron). Two Americans who flew the Beechcraft into Chad
crashed and were taken captive, and the Libyans had to buy
them back from the Chadian military. (Two French mercenaries who flew a DC-3 into Chad for Wilson were less fortunate when they were captured. They were executed.)

The Libyans also asked Wilson and Terpil to recruit western assassins to murder enemies of the Libyan regime living
abroad. Wilson turned to a group of anti-Castro Cubans—
whom he had originally met through Tom Clines—offering
them a million dollars plus expenses. The men turned the
proposition down when they heard Libya—hand in glove with
the hated Communist Russians—was involved, and reported
the incident to the CIA. Nothing was done at first, but further
complaints to the FBI led to the launching of a halfhearted
investigation by the Justice Department, and then a relentless one by the U.S. Attorney's office.

Wilson used his contacts in the U.S. to buy guns which
were later used in terrorist assassinations. One of these Wil-

son-sponsored murders led to the U.S. breaking diplomatic relations with Libya. He also ran an explosives' training program for Libyan military intelligence (although they failed to produce a single workable bomb in over a year, but did kill three "students"). More importantly, he procured twenty-two tons of C-4 *plastique* explosive.

Wilson even attempted to provide Libya with a nuclear capability, a scheme from which he expected to earn hundreds of millions of dollars. Fortunately for the world it came to nothing. Fearful that he had outlived his usefulness to the Libyans, Wilson made approaches to other countries and even the PLO. His aides attempted to sell the idea of a security service, run on the basis of the U.S. Secret Service, to the Sudanese, and instigated a plot to overthrow President Nimeiri. But the pressure of the investigation seems to have weighed heavily on Wilson, who regularly drank a quart a day of "flash," the lethal, locally-made bootleg potato liquor of Tripoli.

Retired CIA men, disgusted by Wilson's antics, formed an ad hoc committee to discuss ways of capturing him (while Mossad, the Israeli secret service, nursed plans to have him killed). But it was an elaborate plot hatched by the U.S. Attorney's office which finally led to his arrest, luring him from Libya with a story that the National Security Council would provide immunity from prosecution.

In jail in the U.S. awaiting trial, Wilson plotted schemes to smuggle narcotics, and attempted to recruit fellow convicts to murder hostile witnesses and even prosecutors from the Attorney General's office. His final mad act was to try and arrange for the murder of his wife of twenty-seven years who was seeking a divorce settlement (he was found to be worth $20 million at the time of his arrest). Wilson was finally sentenced to 52 years in prison.

His associate Terpil was arrested after a stint as the security adviser to Ugandan dictator Idi Amin (a $3.2 million contract which Terpil boasted allowed ample opportunity for brutal murder). Back in New York he was released on $15,000 bail which, not surprisingly, he jumped. Sentenced in *absentia* to 53 years in jail, Terpil is currently rumored to have joined the PLO and to be living somewhere in the Middle East.

The earlier investigations into Wilson were to finish the

government careers of his highly-placed associates. Ted Shackley—who had risen within the Agency to become associate deputy director in the Directorate of Operations, second in command of the CIA's worldwide "dirty tricks"—and Tom Clines were forced into early retirement under an ethical cloud. Undeterred, Clines borrowed $500,000 from Wilson so he could go into the arms business. Shackley went to work for Clines but soon branched out on his own. Clines prospered, until an investigation was made into the company he set up— Egyptian American Transport Services Inc. (EATSCO). A 1983 Pentagon audit of the company, which had shipped more than a billion dollars' worth of arms to Egypt, uncovered evidence of massive corruption. The Defense Department had been cheated out of $8 million. Although Clines had taken $2½ million out of EATSCO, he paid only a corporate fine in an elaborate plea bargain.

Wilson's association with Maj-Gen. Richard Secord abruptly ended a rapidly escalating government career and blocked his promotion to three-star general (Secord had risen in the Pentagon to head the Air Force's military assistance and aid program to more than 40 countries). The Defense Department investigated charges that Secord had helped Wilson sell military equipment to Iran in the early 1970s. Although it was discovered that Wilson had stepped in to bail Secord out of a bad investment when Clines had sold him a house, no basis for criminal charges was found. But the damage was done, and Secord took early retirement from the Air Force.

The same month that Secord retired, he was hired by Stanford Technology, a Silicon Valley company run by Albert Hakim, an Iranian of Palestinian origin who eventually became an American citizen. Hakim had sold a surveillance system to Savak, the Shah's secret police, and had once had many business dealings with Iran where he often came across Secord. Together Hakim and Secord founded a subsidiary called the Stanford Technology Trading Group International, based in a suburb of Washington, D.C., to allow Secord to lobby his old government contacts. Ted Shackley was retained as a consultant.

Hakim had a history of hiring ex-spooks with clandestine contacts. Another subsidiary of Stanford Technology Inc.— Intercontinental Technology, set up in the mid-seventies—

was run by Frank Terpil. Terpil had introduced Ed Wilson to Hakim, and the two men had business dealings. (Later from prison Wilson would describe the Iranian as a man who would "steal a hot stove.")

At first, despite Secord's connections, business did not go well. Large arms contracts with Saudi Arabia fell through and the ex-general seemed ill-equipped as a businessman. And then the U.S. Congress cut off aid to the Contras.

A private-aid network was set up to fill the gap left by the government funding, masterminded by CIA director William Casey and run by Lt Col Oliver North from the basement of the White House. North had met Secord when the general was at the Pentagon, and the two men had successfully teamed up to lobby Congress for approval of the sale of sophisticated AWAC electronic surveillance planes to Saudi Arabia. He thought highly of Secord, and must have felt that the move into the public sector of such a competent officer, with a lifetime's experience in covert operations, was a godsend.

The relationship blossomed until Secord became indispensable. North reported admiringly to his boss at the National Security Council, Admiral John Poindexter: "Why Dick can do something in five minutes that the CIA cannot do in two days is beyond me—but he does." Secord proved himself time and again. "A man of many talents ol' Secord is," North concluded.

Among the talents was the know-how to recruit pilots and crews for a clandestine air-supply operation into Nicaragua, and arranging for the leasing of airplanes through "cutouts"—intermediaries between the lessee and the ex-CIA companies like Southern Air Transport. Among those used for the recruiting was Tom Clines. There was an obvious pool of pilots to pick from—old Air America hands. These could be contacted easily enough through organizations like the Air America Club—which holds annual reunions and publishes a newsletter—and a highly unorthodox American Legion post: Soldiers of Fortune World Wide, Generals Ward and Chennault Post No.1, China, Inc. (Operating in Exile Since 1948)—known as China Post One.

The Contra air force that existed before Secord's operation was a motley collection of half-a-dozen obsolete prop planes: there were four 0-2 Forward Air Control planes from the Air

National Guard, two Twin Beeches, two twin-engine Cessnas and a beautiful silver spook DC-3 with no markings or data plate. The pilots available to fly these craft were similarly mixed. The American sent down to put some structure into this force was none other than Ed Dearborn—CIA veteran of the Congo where he ran an air force of Cuban mercenaries, and ex-chief pilot of Continental Air Services in Laos.

Dearborn had received a call from Robert K. Brown, editor of *Soldier of Fortune* magazine, asking him to meet with Contra, Mario Calero—Adolfo's brother. "I arranged to meet Mario in New Orleans. He told me the Contra air operations were in complete disarray and that they had an airplane down there they had bought for airdrops but which nobody knew how to fly."

Dearborn traveled down to the secret Contra air base at Aguacate in Honduras, just across the border from Nicaragua, in February, 1985. He took with him Air America veterans O'Larkin "Rocky" Nesom and Morrie Kenstler. "We took a look at the planes and the airdrop facilities. There was nothing there, it was really bad. They had a PV II—a World War II anti-submarine plane—they had bought for airdrops because it was fast. They had $125,000 invested in it and they had been screwed. It was a dog, a piece of shit. Nobody was checking out the pilots. We stayed four days and returned to New Orleans where we told Mario, 'There isn't a damned thing we can do—we'd be wasting your money.'"

Mario Calero was extremely upset, and told Dearborn of the terrible plight of the Contra guerrillas in the field: no food, ammunition or even boots. Without air support they were doomed. Dearborn returned to Honduras and checked out four pilots in the DC-3 and airdrops began. He then sat down and wrote a twenty-page battle plan incorporating Helio-Couriers, helicopters and C-47s—the same basic structure used so effectively by Air America and Continental Air Services in Laos.

Dearborn flew back and forth to the U.S., scrounging aircraft which he then smuggled back to Honduras: a helicopter, a Helio-Courier, and a small Cessna 0-1. In the meantime he met General John Singlaub, whose World Anti-Communist League was raising money for the Contras. Singlaub made Dearborn his Air Operations Adviser. "I didn't ask for the job but became his unpaid skilled labor. I get expenses and that's it." (Dearborn supports himself as a commercial pilot and by running a travel agency at John Wayne Airport in Orange County, California.)

The half dozen planes kept the Contra force alive in the field, while Secord set about building up a separate operation which would fly out of Ilopango air base in El Salvador. Two C-123s and two Caribous, using five crews of pilots and kickers, began to make drops over Nicaragua.

At the same time the volatile mixture of North's zeal, Secord's clandestine experience and Hakim's middle-eastern business methods, came together to form a dangerous covert foreign policy—Ollie's "Neat idea." The plan was to merge a number of disparate policy goals into a single operation benefiting all: secret weapons shipments would be sold to Iran at a great mark-up, American hostages would be released as a result, and the profit would be funneled to the Contras. It was the sort of plan which might have elicited a low whistle of respect from the jailed Ed Wilson (who would later claim credit from behind bars for initiating Secord into the art of turning government experience into private profit).

In 1986 Secord boarded a Southern Air Transport plane and flew to Iran, together with the recently retired National Security Adviser—Robert C. McFarlane—a cake in the shape of a key, a Bible autographed by President Reagan, and the first of many cargoes of arms. Fat profits were duly made—although only a fraction ever reached the Contras—and hostages were duly released. Albert Hakim began negotiations with the Iranians on behalf of the United States of America.

The whole scheme was brought down to earth with a shoulder-fired, heat-seeking missile, when the Sandinistas downed one of the C-123s making a secret supply drop over Nicaragua.

In October 1986, television viewers around the world watched as the handcuffed and dejected figure of Eugene Hasenfus was led by his Sandinista captors through the jungle of Nicaragua on the end of a rope. Hasenfus, the world soon discovered, had been the kicker on the plane, while the pilot, William Cooper, and the co-pilot, Wallace "Buzz" Sawyer, had died in the crash. All three men were veterans of Air America, and had flown together in Laos.

The super-secret, privately-funded supply network soon came to seem like a sloppily run operation. Phone calls had been placed from the crew's safe house in El Salvador directly to Secord at Stanford Trading in Washington, and also to Lt. Col. Oliver North at the White House. These calls had been monitored by Cuban intelligence, who leaked telephone records to the American press. Among the documents found on board the crashed plane was the Air America Operators' Manual, and a roster with the names and addresses of every ex-member of the CIA who had joined the Air America Club (including that of the author, who receives the newsletter). The Sandinistas exhibited it all to the press.

The imprisoned Hasenfus proved to be very chatty with his captors. Although it was obvious he did not know much, he quickly told everything he knew. The chief of the supply operation in El Salvador was named as Max Gomez, the *nom de guerre* of Felix Ismael Rodriguez Mendigutia. A "retired" CIA agent, Felix Rodriguez had taken part in the Bay of Pigs invasion of Cuba, and had since landed on the island at least six times, and had fought in America's secret operations in the Congo, Vietnam and El Salvador. It was his boast that in 1967 he headed the operation of Bolivian troops to capture and kill Che Guevara, the Marxist revolutionary.

As Hasenfus languished in jail, the U.S. government denied all involvement in the air drop. It was suggested that the whole thing was planned, financed and executed by a group of freedom-loving patriots (echoing the denials of President Eisenhower in the fifties when CAT pilot Allen Pope was shot down: "Every rebellion that I have ever heard of has its soldiers of fortune"; while the U.S. ambassador to Indonesia at the time attempted to explain Pope away as, "A private American citizen involved as a paid soldier fortune"). The author was invited to give his views on nationwide television in the U.S.A. and opined that if William Casey, director of the CIA, said it was nothing to do with the Agency, then Casey had his fingers crossed behind his back. The Nicaraguan airlift was a CIA classic: the choice of the pilots; the "cut-out" companies from which the airplanes were leased; the contingent of ex-spooks and Special Forces types on hand as advisers. I also pointed out that private citizens would find it extremely difficult to ship large amounts of weapons through Miami airport and at least two other foreign countries without some sort of government complicity. I added that this was nothing new, but pretty much business as usual gone wrong. (On subsequent talk shows angry citizens called in to accuse the author of being as good as a KGB agent—if the audience happened to be conservative—or of writing white propaganda for the CIA—if the audience was leftist.)

The Sandinistas milked Hasenfus for maximum publicity and propaganda, before releasing him to return to the U.S. Over the following months TV film footage of his capture ran in a seemingly endless loop. For the author, and those who know the history of Air America, the sight of the downed American in the jungle brought with it a disturbing sense of déjà vu. Out of context, the disheveled form of Eugene Hasenfus might have been any Air America crewman at any time in the past three decades, in any number of countries. It brought back memories of the men shot down over China, or over the jungles of the Congo, Laos or Vietnam. The sixty-second loop of film stands as a visual symbol of countless covert air operations staged by the CIA, past, present and future, endlessly repeated—except this time the whole world was watching.

THIRTEEN

AIR AMERICA
IN MEMORIAM

For most of the pilots who flew for the CIA the great adventure of their lives is over. Many of the young helicopter jocks have found jobs bush flying in Alaska, servicing oil rigs off the coasts of Indonesia and the Arabian Gulf, fire-fighting and crop dusting in the States. Bell Helicopters hired a number of AA personnel to train Iranian military, offering lucrative long-term contracts in Iran with special housing, American movies, and bowling alleys—abruptly terminated by the downfall of the Shah.

But although crop dusting and fire fighting are considered among the most hazardous professions there are in civilian life, and landing on offshore oil rigs and flying in the ice deserts of Alaska is the most challenging aviation in the world at present, it is all tame stuff compared to the missions flown for the CIA.

"People who are used to living for excitement, like flying in a war, have got nothing to live for when the war is over," Mike Barksdale, currently crop dusting in California, said. "Those of us who were together in the Marines used to get together and tell the same old war stories over and over because the last thing that happened to us was Vietnam. The Marine squadron I was in had a reunion in Ohio last year and we were still all talking about the war. The same old shit. And there's nothing wrong about that unless you've got nothing else."

Old AA hands share a nostalgia, a *tristesse*, for their years of high adventure in Indochina. At a party I attended in Florida, a group of them gathered together. The heavy gold

310

AA jewelry was on display, and one had brought the offical AA film to show; it was greeted by much raucous comment, but the boys were living through old times once again.

Bob Murray, who lives on Key Biscayne, tends to mix only with pilots. "Pilots are the only kind of people that I like. They do the same kind of thing, have the same kind of background, and think the same kind of way." Murray has replaced the thrill of AA by flying old jet fighters down to Honduras for the air force there, a risky operation. "These airplanes have been in crates in Yugoslavia for three years. They can blow up on you; they can come unglued at any time. It's very well paid because of the risk factor, one thousand dollars for less than two days' work. Better than AA." It is odd, Murray said, where you come across old AA aircraft. "I was sitting on the bluff down in (in pre-Sardinista) Nicaragua when I saw a G-46 that was with the state airline. I thought, this looks as good as our airplanes did; I can't believe it. Then I found out it was one of our old airplanes—G-46 number 94. They had bought it from Omni in New Mexico."

Many of the older pilots have accepted that they will not fly again. "I would do it again in a minute, but at fifty-seven I'm not a very employable pilot anymore," Bob Dawson said. "I have to keep doing things, stay busy and active. I party a lot." Before he bought his condominium in Sarasota, Florida, he hired an airplane and flew up and down the coast, marking on the map those places that looked good. It was his last flight at the controls.

"Every pilot knows that sooner or later he is going to have to give it up," Art Kenyon said. "I used to sit up there watching the clouds go by and thought that it would be sad when it was gone, but I haven't missed flying all that much. But if AA was still in operation and working in Saigon, I'd probably still be there. As it is I'm content to take my boat out and do a little fishing with my wife."

Ron Zappardino is now running a successful bar and restaurant business in San Diego and strongly believes that the past must not be lived as the present. "It's something I did and I enjoyed it. I loved it and it's gone, it's over. It's a pleasant, pleasant memory, but there's nothing there I'd like to have again except for the money. But it saddens me to think that there were guys out there risking their lives every day and they came back to the States and they're scared to death of their new boss."

But, like everybody else, it took Zappardino time to adjust to the ordinary world. One day as he was lying on the beach with another ex-AA pilot, a jet screamed over very low. "Hey, Ron, I'm proud of you," Zappardino's companion said. "You didn't look up—you're finally over it."

When I first started to research this book and traveled across the States talking to ex-AA pilots, I made my way down to see Walter Rosenfield. "Rosie," a onetime U-2 pilot and AA veteran, was the first CIA pilot I had met on that morning during the monsoon in Bangkok. He later became involved in a small commercial-airport venture in Douglas and lived in the monumental Gadsden Hotel, a vast, rambling place with great marble pillars in the foyer, and gold leaf on the ceiling.

Apart from AA business I was also interested to know the fate of his two gibbons, Elizabeth Taylor Rosenfield and Lyndon Johnson. Lyndon, I learned, had broken free and sadly been electrocuted on a high-voltage cable, but Elizabeth Taylor is alive and well and living in Phoenix Zoo.

I spent several days with Rosie, quartered down the corridor from him in the Gadsden, and he was charming and helpful. He gave me contacts among his former colleagues, arranged introductions, and told me much about the daily routine of AA but gave away no secrets. "I never had much to do with that CIA stuff," he said unconvincingly, and I knew better than to press him.

During the few days I was with Rosie, we crossed the border into Mexico to have dinner, listened to a *mariachis* band serenading a wedding group, and drank too much tequila. We drove out to his ranch, a beautiful place leased to a friend which had a view across the mountains of faraway Tombstone. We drove into that gunslingers' town, now a sleepy tourist attraction, and drank a pitcher of beer in the Crystal Palace Saloon.

On the drive back into Douglas, Rosie played me a tape made of a young twenty-five-year-old special forces officer directing an air strike against attacking North Vietnamese troops. He was the only American in a base being defended by South Vietnamese against a human-wave attack. It was night and the North Vietnamese charged relentlessly against the wire, clambering over their dead colleagues as they were cut down by machine-gun fire and bombed from above. The South Vietnamese were hopelessly outnumbered, and the young American was directing the planes and gunships of the USAF in an attempt to stave off the attack.

The recording was difficult to follow for anyone unused to the static and crackle of such radio contact, but the desperation in the young soldier's voice cut straight through. He yelled frantically into his radio set as machine guns and artillery rattled and boomed behind him. At one point someone accidentally cut into his conversation. "Get the fuck off this frequency!" he yelled. Rosie and I smiled. It was the only time we did so during the forty taut minutes of the recording.

The gunfire grew louder and louder, the special forces officer's instructions were more and more frantic, and then suddenly his voice was cut off. But the radio link remained open wire and only gunfire could be heard. The enemy were over the wire and had taken the position.

Rosie told me he had flown in the following morning. The camp consisted of a fortified barbed-wire perimeter with a larger wooden observation tower in the middle of it flanked by an airstrip. "When I got there, it was just a camp full of dead bodies," he said. The enemy had lost hundreds of men in the attack and there bodies hung over the wire and were piled three deep. They had attacked, paid dearly for their victory, killed every one of the defenders, and withdrawn before daylight. The young American's body was found and flown out.

When the tape finished, Rosie and I drove on into Douglas in silence and did not look at one another. As we pulled into the car park near the hotel, Rosie spoke for the first time. "I need a drink."

Inside the bar we sat over a couple of stiff shots of bourbon. "I don't know why I play that tape—it always has the same effect on me," Rosie said. "I don't know, but that guy was just a kid and he lost his life. For what? Nothing." Rosie shook his head. "All for nothing."

That phrase also stands as the final verdict on Air America. Here was this vast complex of airlines which had flown guerrillas into Tibet, supported rebels in Indonesia and Cuba, supplied a secret army in Laos, and obeyed the paramilitary, covert will of the CIA throughout the world. And for what?

Superbly managed as it was, manned by the most experienced and highly trained pilots available, the sum total of its quarter of a century of clandestine flying amounts to very little. The men who flew the planes deserve better, but for all their skill and courage, AA is doomed to share the sad epitaph of the young soldier: "All for Nothing."

AA committed its men to a long line of losing battles. They were chased from the mainland of China, shot out of the sky while supporting the French at the besieged garrison of Dien Bien Phu, abandoned in their futile support of rebel forces in Indonesia, and among the last to leave when Laos, Cambodia, and Vietnam collapsed. They were to receive no medals for these thankless tasks, which were often too delicate, or simply too dangerous, for the military to undertake. Instead, tarred with the tainted brush of the CIA, their very existence has been denied by the government, while their fellow countrymen largely dismiss them as rednecks following a mercenary calling.

For the most part the pilots of Air America have been a very special sort of mercenary—patriots pursuing the country's covert policy for pay. The airline attracted its share of crooks over the years, men who have since smuggled drugs for personal profit or even flown as mercenaries for governments hostile to the U.S. But this group accounts for only a very small percentage, bitterly resented by their colleagues.

The history of Air America brings up all of the familiar questions about accountability, the desirability and efficacy of clandestine organizations operating within a free society, and the way in which covert operations should be conducted. It is a debate which has intensified over the years, and one which cannot be easily or speedily resolved. Every president has resorted to covert operations of one sort or another, and one thing is certain: there will be covert operations in the future, and some of them will need air support. Whatever mechanism is created to supply it, the men who crew the planes will be of the same type as those who flew for Air America. "We still have people that are willing to do this kind of mission," William Colby, ex-director of the CIA said. "You can have your own views to the direction they've been given, or whether they should have been sent, but there have been some unmarked planes flying in Central America with two efficient pilots and a kicker or two to shove out the weapons to whoever the Customer asked them to. So the capabilities are still there, and I think they always will be in this country."

Until very recently Air America's dead went unhonored. Their names are not inscribed on the Vietnam Memorial in Washington, D.C. although a total of 242 people serving with either CAT, Air Asia, Air America or Southern Air Transport—not including another twenty or so with Continental Air Services—were killed over three decades of clandestine operations between 1947 and 1975. But it was not until May 1987, that a memorial in bronze inscribed with their names was finally unveiled.

It was paid for by family and friends and stands in McDermott Library of the University of Texas at Dallas. The bronze consists of panels in relief of China, Dien Bien Phu, Korea, Laos and Saigon. A large number of podgy, Polyester-clad, middle-aged men and their wives turned up for a memorial week-end in Dallas to pay their respects to fallen comrades. It was an occasion of self-congratulation, when not many hard questions were addressed, but then the Air America people have always been men of action rather than introspection.

President Ronald Reagan sent a message saluting them. "Unsung and unregarded, each of you confronted danger and endured terrible hardships, and each of you rose to the challenge; you never faltered. Although free people everywhere owe you more than we can hope to repay, our greatest debt is to your companions who gave their last full measure of devotion."

Ex-director Colby flew in to pay the Agency's respects in the form of an address he called "Courage in Civilian Clothes." "Here we have a group that doesn't expect a parade, doesn't expect public praise. They do, however, expect us to honor our own." The Agency, which had denied involvement for so long, was acknowledging its debt at last. However faulty the policies might sometimes have been, the men deserved as much. It is fitting that the most accurate epitaph for Air America should come from the CIA, delivered by William Colby, the director who saw the airline in operation during the height of the Vietnam war. It is a simple, unemotional tribute to professionalism: "The Customer was well served."

ACKNOWLEDGMENTS

I am indebted most of all to the many pilots who flew for Air America and agreed to talk to me. These interviews were conducted all over the States in a great variety of circumstances. Sometimes there were days of hospitality and goodwill, sometimes an interview would be snatched over a cup of coffee or the telephone. I developed a great respect for the pilots as a group and was surprised by how much I liked them as individuals. There were, of course, a number who refused to see me, and while they were firm they were never hostile. Most of the Air America pilots I spoke with were decent, courageous and honest, and while most of them told me no secrets they also told me no lies. Deceit, prevarication and falsehood came from other bureaucratic areas of the Air America operation.

I have used names, when applicable, in the text, except in those cases where I was specifically asked not to. It would embarrass and probably anger some of the pilots to be mentioned individually, and it is quite possible that they will disagree with much of what I have written. However, I feel I must take the risk of especially thanking Walter Rosenfield, Barbara Ritter and Art Kenyon for their personal kindness to me.

I would also like to thank David Hill of Press Corps International (London) for his efforts to drum up initial support and help throughout, Keith Colquhoun of *The Observer* (London) and Hans Wilbrink of *Nieuwe Revue* (Amsterdam) for their responses, and the librarians of *The New York Times* and *The Washington Post*.

The following people allowed me to benefit from their personal experiences in Indochina, or with the CIA, through personal interviews and generous help: John Robatan of *Newsweek*; Richard Pyle and Mike Putzel of the *Associated Press*, Washington, DC; William R. Corson, author of *The Betrayal* and *The Armies of Ignorance*; Fletcher L. Prouty, author of *The Secret Team*; Al McCoy, author of *The Politics of Heroin in Southeast Asia*; John Marks, co-author of *The CIA and the Cult of Intelligence*; Frank Snepp, author of *Decent Interval*; Robert Fink, author of *The Cloudy Skies*.

I would also like to thank the following writers whom I have drawn on for background material: Andre del Amo, for his interview with Emmet Kay in Hawaii; David Wise and Thomas B. Ross, *The Invisible Government*; David Wise, *The Politics of Lying*; Fred Branfman, contributing author to *The CIA File*; Don A. Schanche, *Mister Pop*; Theodore E. Dinsmoor, *GAC's Complaints Against the CIA*.

Special personal thanks to Valerie Eldridge, not only for typing the manuscript, often from the most appalling scrawl, but also for being so enthusiastic about it.

NOTE TO THE READER

The bulk of information throughout the book has been gleaned from personal interviews with pilots, copilots, kickers, ground personnel, administrative workers, CIA men, journalists, and people on the fringe of the strange world of the Agency's air proprietaries. Pilots' stories have been checked against one another whenever possible and all controversial material has been confirmed by at least two separate sources. Facts from news reports carried in either *The New York Times* or *The Washington Post*, or both, have also been incorporated in the text. Background information on various sections of the book have been culled from the following sources in the order they occur in the text:

INTRODUCTION, JOINING THE LEGION, FLYING TIGERS, INSIDE THE COMPANY

The CIA and the Cult of Intelligence, Victor Marchetti and John Marks.

The Secret Team, Fletcher L. Prouty.

"Foreign and Military Intelligence" (Senate's Final Report).

Flying Tiger—Chennault of China, Robert Lee Scott, Jr.

"The Flying Tigers Carry On," Corey Ford, *The Saturday Evening Post*, Feb. 12, 1955.

Stilwell and the American Experience in China (1911–1945), Barbara W. Tuchman.

"The CIA's Corporate Shell Game," John Marks, *Washington Post*, July 11, 1976.

The Invisible Government, David Wise and Thomas B. Ross.

The Pentagon Papers.

The Cloudy Skies, Robert Fink, unpublished draft manuscript. Archives of the Center of National Securities Stud-
ies, Washington, D.C.

SECRET MISSIONS
"Foreign and Military Intelligence" (Senate's Final Report).
The Politics of Heroin, Al McCoy.
"Kuomintang Aggression Against Burma," Burmese Minis-
try of Information.
The Invisible Government, David Wise and Thomas B. Ross.
The Politics of Lying, David Wise.
The CIA's Secret Operations, Harry Rositzke.
The Secret Team, Fletcher L. Prouty.
My Land and My people, Dalai Lama of Tibet.

LAOS, VIETNAM, CAMBODIA, AT HOME, OPIUM, LAST DAYS
"American Military Airlift During the Laotian Civil War"
1958–63, Robert L. Kerby, *Aerospace Historian*, vol. 24, vol.
no. 1.
Mister Pop, Don A. Schanche.
An Eye for the Dragon, Dennis Bloodworth.
Air America Log (company magazine), 1967–72.
The President's Secret Army (from the CIA File), Fred Branf-
man.
The Politics of Heroin, Al McCoy.
"The World Opium Situation," U.S. Bureau of Narcotics and
Dangerous Drugs, New York, 1976.
Interview with Emmet Kay in Hawaii, Andre del Amo.
The CIA's Corporate Shell Game, John Marks.
55 Days, Alan Dawson.
Decent Interval, Frank Snepp.

PRIVATIZATION
"Foreign and Military Intelligence" (Book I, Final Report of
Select Committee to study Government operations with
respect to Intelligence Activities, United States Senate,
April 26, 1976).
The Cloudy Skies, Robert Fink.
"Yes! We Have No Maranas," Ronald Ridenhour, *New Times*,
July 12, 1974.

"Complaints for General Aircraft Corporation Against Central Intelligence and Its Air Proprietaries," legal complaints lodged with court by Theodore E. Dinsmoor of Gaston Snow & Ely Bartlett, One Federal Street, Boston, Massachusetts.

BIBLIOGRAPHY

Bloodworth, Dennis. *An Eye for the Dragon.* New York: Farrar, Straus and Giroux, 1970.

Branfman, Fred. "The President's Army," from *The CIA File*, edited by Robert L. Borosage and John Marks. New York: Grossman, 1976.

Dalai Lama of Tibet. *My Land and My People.* New York: McGraw-Hill, 1972.

Dawson, Alan. *55 Days—The Fall of South Vietnam.* New Jersey: Prentice-Hall, 1977.

Fall, Bernard B. *Hell in a Very Small Place.* Philadelphia: J. B. Lippincott, 1967.

———. "Foreign and Military Intelligence" (Book 1) Final Report of the Select Committee to Study Governmental Operations with respect to Intelligence Activities. United States Senate. Washington, D.C., 1976.

———. Government of the Union of Burma, the Ministry of Information. "Kuomintang Aggression Against Burma." Rangoon, 1953.

Lansdale, Edward. *In the Midst of Wars.* New York: Harper & Row, 1972.

Marchetti, Victor and Marks, John D. *The CIA and the Cult of Intelligence.* New York: Alfred A. Knopf, 1974.

McCoy, Alfred W. (with Cathleen B. Read and Leonard P. Adams II). *The Politics of Heroin in Southeast Asia.* New York: Harper & Row, 1972.

Prouty, L. Fletcher. *The Secret Team.* New Jersey: Prentice-Hall, 1973.

Rositzke, Harry. *The CIA's Secret Operations.* New York: Reader's Digest Press, 1977.

Schanche, Don A. *Mister Pop.* New York: David McKay, 1970.

Scott, Robert Lee, Jr. *Flying Tiger: Chennault of China.* New York: Doubleday, 1959.

Snepp, Frank. *Decent Interval.* New York: Random House, 1977.

Taylor, John W. R. (editor). *Jane's Book of Commercial Transport Aircraft.* New York: Macmillan, 1973.

_____. *The Pentagon Papers.* Senator Gravel Edition (4 vols). Boston: The Beacon Press, 1971.

Tuchman, Barbara W. *Stilwell and the American Experience in China* (1911–45). New York: Macmillan, 1971.

Wise, David. *The Politics of Lying.* New York: Random House, 1973.

Wise, David and Ross, Thomas. B. *The Invisible Government.* New York: Random House, 1964.

Index